SICK AND DIRTY

SICK AND DIRTY

HOLLYWOOD'S GAY GOLDEN AGE and the MAKING of MODERN QUEERNESS

MICHAEL KORESKY

BLOOMSBURY PUBLISHING

NEW YORK · LONDON · OXFORD · NEW DELHI · SYDNEY

BLOOMSBURY PUBLISHING
Bloomsbury Publishing Inc.
1359 Broadway, New York, NY 10018, USA
50 Bedford Square, London, WC1B 3DP, UK
Bloomsbury Publishing Ireland Limited,
29 Earlsfort Terrace, Dublin 2, D02 AY28, Ireland

BLOOMSBURY, BLOOMSBURY PUBLISHING, and the Diana logo are trademarks
of Bloomsbury Publishing Plc

First published in the United States 2025
Copyright © Michael Koresky, 2025

ISBN: HB: 978-1-63973-254-8; eBook: 978-1-63973-255-5

Library of Congress Cataloging-in-Publication Data is available

2 4 6 8 10 9 7 5 3 1

Typeset by Westchester Publishing Services
Printed in the United States by Lakeside Book Company, Harrisonburg, VA

To find out more about our authors and books visit www.bloomsbury.com
and sign up for our newsletters.

Bloomsbury books may be purchased for business or promotional use. For information on
bulk purchases please contact Macmillan Corporate and Premium Sales Department at
specialmarkets@macmillan.com.
For product safety–related questions contact productsafety@bloomsbury.com.

For Terence Davies, whose private dreams became cinematic revelations.

"They're writing songs of love. But not for me."

—IRA GERSHWIN

CONTENTS

Tell Us How You Really Feel

It begins at the end, with a death.

In fall of 2021, I taught a course called Queerness in American Cinema in the Undergraduate Film & Television department at NYU's Tisch School of the Arts. It was the end of October, halfway through the semester, and for that week's screening I had selected 1961's *The Children's Hour* to watch in its entirety with the class.

Though long cited as a landmark for anyone studying the history of gay and lesbian film, *The Children's Hour* was a last-minute addition to my syllabus. I wasn't convinced of the prudence or efficacy of showing this movie to twenty-first-century eighteen-to-twenty-one-year-olds. It could play to them as both upsetting and horribly dated, perhaps too melodramatic in its plot machinations (triggering mockery from the students) and offensive in its tragic final moments (courting outright rejection from them).

Nevertheless, I forged ahead with the screening, a touch queasy but more than a little curious. None of the thirty-five students had previously seen the film, I learned. How would they react?

My syllabus was linear, a chronological survey through the last eighty or so years of film. The first half of the semester stayed largely nestled within the era of classical Hollywood cinema—a period of roughly thirty years, from the late twenties to the early sixties—when, due to the heavy, era-defining restrictions of the Motion Picture Production Code, it was permissible for filmmakers only to imply or metaphorically evoke the existence of lesbian and gay life on-screen. In the second half, we moved into films in which queer characters were "represented"—a loaded term, but in this case used quite literally, as it was only after an October 1961 amendment to the Code that films could feature lesbian and gay characters at all, never mind that for many years most of those representations would be embodied in ways many of us today would decry as "negative."

In *The Children's Hour*, Shirley MacLaine and Audrey Hepburn play Martha Dobie and Karen Wright, best friends whose teaching careers are jeopardized when a student accuses them of lesbianism. The film, released in late 1961, could not have seen the light of a projector before that year's Code amendment.

New freedoms, as they often do, came with fresh limitations and rules, however unspoken. Made many years before the term "pride" would be synonymous with the gay rights movement, *The Children's Hour* had no interest in happy endings. As had been the case in the source material, a 1934 play by the imperious theater legend Lillian Hellman, the false accusation leads to self-realization and also tragedy: Martha and Karen were not lovers, but Martha *has* been secretly harboring romantic desire for Karen, as she reveals to Karen in a climactic monologue beside a crackling fireplace. MacLaine performs the speech as though it's being wrenched out of her with a dentist's pliers, culminating in the tear-stained admission, "I feel so damn sick and dirty I can't stand it anymore!" Later, Martha nobly disappears into an upstairs bedroom of the former schoolhouse she shares with Karen. Her horrible fate is soon revealed, as panicking Karen busts open the door to find Martha's body hanging limply from the ceiling.

History trains us to watch movies in a certain way, with ingrained expectations, so one cannot conceive of a film from this era—or many subsequent ones—that would allow a character with Martha's "sex aberration" to go boldly off into the sunset, or to find her happiness in greener pastures. Those endings are for cowboys or private dicks, whose lonesomeness is a mark of character and strength rather than an indicator of irreparable social marginalization. Martha lives alone in her own mind, and thus she dies alone, the tragic lesbian, just one of the many outcast queer archetypes who have long been part of the American cinematic heritage. My students might not have seen *The Children's Hour*, but they would *know* Martha: her persistence as a type, her hovering presence, a lingering historical ghost.

My expectations for the mood of the screening were wrong. There was some tittering throughout the classroom as the story unfolded, much of it understandably directed at Mary Tilford, the accusing child; as played by little Karen Balkin, she deserves all the boos and hisses one might hurl at a silent movie villain. As the narrative reached its tense apogee, with Martha and Karen desperately combating the false accusations that promise to ruin their lives, there were sympathetic harrumphs—the plot still functions with clockwork precision, putting you in the complicated, uncomfortable position of wanting, even in the third decade of the twenty-first century, an accusation of homosexuality to be revealed as false. To be exposed as a damn dirty lie!

Yet by the end, we were left silent. The reveal of Martha's dead body elicited no groans. The students hadn't rejected the film. They were hushed and attentive, as though bearing witness. The death of Martha Dobie was here, and it was awful. There was no turning back. Here, finally, was the class's first admittedly gay character, and she was snuffed out.

I tried to offer a few words of care, though I found myself choked up. This surprised me—to be moved anew by a film that I, like so many queer scholars and critics and movie lovers, had a long, complicated, even superior attitude about. Most of the students shuffled out wordlessly, but a few came down to the front of the sloped lecture room; some had tears in their eyes, others were ashen. "I know" was one of the small responses I had to offer, promising we'd talk more about it at next week's class.

I learned then that the students' response to the film was partly a testament to the performances—the brittle stoicism of Hepburn and especially the emotionally volcanic work by MacLaine. Director William Wyler's career in Hollywood, which at that point stretched back nearly forty years to the silent era, was rife with movies of emotional delicacy and technical precision, films so perfectly composed that the spell they cast is rarely ever broken. According to the class, *The Children's Hour*, however contentious it remains, however much a "bad object" it has long been for queer scholars and academics, still *works*—as a movie that plays on the viewer's senses and sympathies.

I think the tears that day also speak to something else: something more profound, primal, and perhaps even more difficult to reckon with than the sad death of Martha Dobie.

· · ·

The phrase "post-gay" gained a bit of cultural relevancy in the early years of this millennium, a feeling that had been cemented for many during the Obama administration. The term once held utopian promise but already seems antiquated. It appeared in print at least as far back as 1994, when a British author and journalist coined "post-gay" in response to the increasing assimilation of gays into mainstream culture. A few years later, a 1998 *New York Times* article profiling *Out* magazine's new editor, James Collard, explained his "'post-gay' philosophy," which "champions the idea that gay culture and mainstream culture cross-pollinate." In a 2011 article for *Social Problems*, Professor Amin Ghaziani of the University of British Columbia expanded on these definitions while also acknowledging their limitations, arguing that the "post-gay era may be marked by the acceptance of a segment of gays and lesbians who are gender conforming, middle class, upwardly mobile—in other words, those best able to take advantage of the benefits of assimilation and the valorization of a particular type of diversity." As the term increasingly gained acceptance—or, for some, notoriety—it became evident that "post-gay" reflected only those with the privilege to able to look past their own marginalization.

By the time the term popped up in a June 2019 article in *The Atlantic* about the state of gay America on the fiftieth anniversary of the Stonewall uprising, "post-gay" had taken on its most literal political meaning. The article, emblazoned with the definitive headline THE STRUGGLE FOR GAY RIGHTS IS OVER, represented continued queer activism as little more than a litany of petty grievances by niche groups. "America is rapidly becoming a post-gay country," wrote the conservative gay reporter James Kirchick. "Post-gay" is here waved as a new kind of flag, one meant to elicit admiration for those who fought for the essential rights and freedoms of contemporary queer people throughout the twentieth century. The battles are won, and it's time to move on, away from the trauma, the victimhood, the sad old stereotypes that once burdened us and kept us silenced. Away, away, from Martha Dobie.

Yet if shared and personal traumas, the pain of social and familial marginalization, and the fight for basic equalities are supposedly things of the unenlightened past in this "post-gay world," why does the death of Martha Dobie, this character from a sixty-four-year-old movie, still feel so raw? And why does that death matter to those who still witness it?

There's something pure, empathic, even synaptic in what passes between a contemporary queer viewer and Martha. Regardless of what motivates the viewer's feelings for her—whether we find ourselves connected to or repulsed by her irremediable alienation—her outrage and oppression transcend historical parameters. Sometimes movies unshackle themselves from the entrapment of time, especially when they reflect buried truths. *The Children's Hour* maintains its immediacy because we do not live in a "post-gay" society; however you want to define that term, its insistent wielding only emphasizes how completely patriarchal, heteronormative culture permeates every facet of our lives. Martha Dobie's lacerating self-hatred still stings, a reminder that we're negotiating traumas large and small around identity and belonging on a daily basis.

In his 2019 book *Out of the Shadows*, the psychotherapist Walt Odets narrates a series of case studies, spanning multiple decades, to document the continued centrality of trauma, anxiety, fear, and self-loathing in the lives of gay men, the scars of generations of parental rejection, community marginalization, the AIDS epidemic, and the constant, tiresome fight for political and social personhood. One of the main issues affecting the queer community, Odets writes, is "the still-ongoing childhood and adolescent trauma that gay people are subjected to, and the often-lifelong emotional legacy it bestows." This is key to understanding why *The Children's Hour* drew tears from my students. It's also why movies like *Boys Don't Cry*, or *The Hours*, or *Brokeback Mountain*—all of which have been roundly, occasionally rightly, criticized for propagating and exploiting notions of the tragic queer outcast—retain their affective power.

"Homosexuality is experienced as a stigmatizing mark as well as a form of romantic exceptionalism," writes the queer theorist Heather Love. This exceptionalism "appears at the structural level in the gap between mass-mediated images of attractive, well-to-do gays and lesbians and the reality of ongoing violence and inequality." Here is the often head-whipping experience of being queer in our contemporary world: we constantly negotiate between modes of pride and shame. A steady diet of flag waving and rainbow-colored June programming ("The ten best LGTBQ+ shows currently streaming!") encourages us to believe these modes cannot exist side by side, and it even infiltrates our thinking about the media we consume—those movies and shows that are good for us *or* not, that shed a positive *or* negative light on our history and being. As Love writes, "Many contemporary critics dismiss negative or dark representations entirely, arguing that the depiction of same-sex love as impossible, tragic, and doomed to failure is purely ideological."

But to erase a text like *The Children's Hour* is to assume that something truer has surfaced to take its place. In her book *Double Negative*, the author and historian Racquel Gates argues for the validity of analyzing and even reclaiming films and TV shows that have come to be considered "negative" representations of Black popular culture: "If our strategy is simply to replace alleged negative images with positive ones, then we are merely adding more definitions of what it means to be black into circulation, without necessarily contesting the racist assumptions under which the negative ones were formed in the first place." The difficult feelings that Wyler's film of Hellman's play dredges up are not invalidated by our presumed enlightenment. What if, on the contrary, accepting and even embracing "negative," unwanted, or retrograde images in our entertainment could deepen our understanding of the present?

. . .

In recent years, the sense of safety and complacency that encouraged so many hopeful gays and lesbians even to consider the word "post-gay" has steadily disintegrated. A 2019 Pew Research Center poll concluded that 72 percent of Americans said homosexuality should be, in the poll's phrasing, "accepted by society." However, the forces of conservatism are cyclical, so of course, following the rise of mainstream acceptance of gay people in America, there has been a steady reactionary increase in our demonization.

In 2022 and 2023 alone, the litany of anti-queer hate crime and legislation was so unceasing as to feel sadly ordinary. The passing of the Florida Parental Rights in Education Act, also known as the "Don't Say Gay or Trans" bill, made it illegal to discuss the existence of homosexuality with children from kindergarten to third grade. Armed protesters stormed "drag queen story hours" at children's libraries from Portland to New York City. The fatal shootings in a Colorado gay nightclub were followed by widely shared television footage of the killer's father saying of his son when he heard the news, "Phew, he's not gay." Soon after former Democratic congresswoman Nancy Pelosi's husband was the victim of a hammer attack in a horrific home invasion, unfounded homophobic theories began to circulate that it was done by a spurned gay lover (a reminder that, as in *The Children's Hour*, gay rumormongering still grips the imagination as negative). Anti-LGBTQ+ backlashes and boycotts swirled around the Target department store chain for promoting Gay Pride Month and Bud Light for an ad campaign featuring the transgender TikTok personality Dylan Mulvaney. Amid all this, violent deaths were constant reminders of the dangers of such culturally and politically entrenched homophobia. Bre'Asia Bankz, Savannah Ryan Williams, Jean Butchart, and Kejuan Richardson, all murdered by gunshot, are but drops in the well of killings of transgender and nonbinary Americans, who are four times more likely to be on the receiving end of violence than cisgendered people. A sixtysomething mom named Laura Ann Carleton was shot to death for hanging a rainbow Pride flag outside her business in Southern California. O'Shae Sibley, a twenty-eight-year-old gay man, was stabbed to death at a Brooklyn gas station.

In February 2023, the *New York Times* reported new data from the Centers for Disease Control and Prevention on "high levels of violence, depression, and suicidal thoughts among lesbian, gay, and bisexual youth." Nearly 70 percent of queer teenagers reported feelings of sadness; though doubtless exacerbated by issues of isolation and depression resulting from the COVID-19 pandemic, the numbers point toward a continuing crisis. Data elsewhere indicate that transgender youth are at the highest risk. The suicide prevention organization called the Trevor Project reported in December 2022 that more than 50 percent of transgender and nonbinary youth in the United States had seriously considered suicide over the past twelve months.

The individual trauma felt by LGBTQ+ youth and the politically motivated brutality that permeates our news cycles are impossible to separate from the mainstream enfranchisement of extreme right movements like the Proud Boys and the increasingly hard-line conservative rhetoric of the Christian Right and celebrities like the former Fox News host Tucker Carlson. The result is an atmosphere of high anxiety that feels anything but safely "post-gay." At the start of June 2023, the Human Rights Campaign declared a "state of emergency" for LGBTQ+ people in the United States in light of the number of homophobic and transphobic bills being passed in various states. The demonization of trans people in this country became an unavoidable reality by November 2024 when Donald Trump's winning presidential campaign featured flagrantly antitransgender national ads in order to discredit opponent Kamala Harris for her allegedly overly liberal views on the matter. On his first day in office, Trump signed Executive Order 14168, requiring federal departments to recognize gender as a male-female binary, an edict with blurry practicable effects but enormous symbolic meaning. Two weeks later, the T and Q were quietly scrubbed from after the letters LGB on several government agency websites. Against this onslaught, one can imagine how the tragedy of *The Children's Hour*—which has been deemed rote, stale, problematic, and even harmful—can pierce through decades and capture the embattled heart of a young viewer. Carrying the promise of pride doesn't mean we are immune to shame. In fact, they're inextricable; living with the negative stigmas that a homophobic society forces upon us can help to elucidate and ennoble the positive aspects of our best selves. It's only fair and honest to acknowledge the constant external *and* internal battles one wages within a society that has historically been, and still is, profoundly antagonistic to us.

. . .

The generative discussions about *The Children's Hour* and other screenings throughout that semester inspired me to contemplate these films anew—and led me to believe there's a new history to tell. The one that we have long heard, especially since the 1981 publication of Vito Russo's groundbreaking *The Celluloid Closet*, is a tale of marginalization, invisibility, and debasement. Russo's book, a furious, deeply researched tidal wave of film criticism that uncovered decades of gay and lesbian characters, themes, and subtext in cinema, most of it negative and framed as damaging to the psyches of generations of young queer people, was written on the cusp of the AIDS crisis and followed a decade in which the gay rights movement became more visible to broader swaths of the American public. A fire-tipped arrow shot right through the heart of the official narrative of our national film history, *The Celluloid Closet* diagnosed a culture infested with homophobia, antifeminism, and an obsession with masculinity, written with naked anger and the unmistakable desire to create awareness. It brought cinema's skeletons out of that closet once and for all. And thanks to Rob Epstein and Jeffrey Friedman's celebrated 1996 documentary adaptation, it continues to resonate, its title becoming shorthand for the history—or the lack—of gay representation in our national cinema.

Russo, who grew up in East Harlem in the 1950s, was obsessed with movies from an early age. Called a "faggot" and a "queer" as a kid, he knew he was different from the other boys, and when he began to notice gay characters on-screen, he sensed that something was very wrong—unfair, reductive, dehumanizing—in the way they were being depicted. His coming-of-age as a political-minded adult coincided with his realization that the movies had long been working to expunge his humanity. Russo learned about film aesthetics and history as a graduate student at NYU's Tisch School of the Arts; by 1971, he had a job in the Museum of Modern Art's film circulation department, where he had access to the museum's film archives—a great boon in the pre-VHS years. He began rigorously seeking out representations of gay characters, which he found went all the way back to the silent era. He started to share his findings in 1973, when he embarked on college tours as the host of a program he called "The Celluloid Closet." In these lectures, accompanied by film clips, he used cinema history to articulate the self-loathing he knew so many gays and lesbians felt. Reflecting the latent desperation for positive queer images, appreciative audiences came out in droves.

Russo's book would represent a summation of these years of research, touring, and journalism. His eloquent writing about gay viewers' identification with films that nevertheless denied their place in society is essential to our continued cultural discussion about queer belonging and political enfranchisement in movies. As Russo asserted, "It is common to wax nostalgic over one's lost cinema past, however stereotypical; the practice is perhaps even more common among members of a minority group that has been invisible in real life. Inclusion in the myth, even token representation in the American dream being played out on-screen, was of paramount importance, for it was confirmation that one existed."

The political current that propels Russo's book is inextricable from his activism: Russo was a founding member of both the Gay and Lesbian Alliance Against Defamation (GLAAD) in 1985 and the game-changing grassroots AIDS advocacy organization ACT UP in 1987. When Russo died of complications from AIDS in 1990, he left behind an unparalleled legacy. The filmmaker and author Andrea Weiss, who knew Russo and whose own book, *Vampires and Violets: Lesbians in Film*, was released in 1992, told me she considers *The Celluloid Closet* not just "a pioneering book, but an encyclopedia of the subject," adding, "It reflected a life's work." The filmmaker and film conservationist Jenni Olson, who considered Russo a mentor, first read the book in 1986. "It saved my life," she says. "It's how I came out. Which is funny, because I was obviously so gay. I read *The Celluloid Closet* and was like, 'Oh my god, this is the vehicle for how I can come out. There are people like me, and I can actually feel good about who I am.'"

Russo wrote *The Celluloid Closet* at a time when the United States was coming off a decade of relative social progressiveness. A year after its publication, there would be a wave of serious-minded mainstream films from major directors featuring gay, lesbian, and transgender characters: 1982 alone saw the releases of *Victor/Victoria*, *The World According to Garp*, *Making Love*, *Personal Best*, *Deathtrap*, and *Come Back to the Five and Dime, Jimmy Dean, Jimmy Dean*. The trend was so unmistakable that even Siskel and Ebert, mainstream America's most trusted film critics, devoted a full half-hour episode of their syndicated series to it. Gene Siskel opened the show by citing Russo's book and declaring, "The treatment of homosexual characters has been pathetic in Hollywood." At the end of the episode, the critics wonder whether this flood of movies that dared to explore questions of queer identity and desire was a momentary thing, a bubble about to burst, much like the American studios' brief flirtation in the early 1970s with films for Black audiences. Predicted Siskel, "I fear this is just a trend." Sure enough, with the AIDS crisis looming (337 reported cases by the end of 1981, more than twenty thousand around the world by 1985), the culture of homophobia came roaring back. Gay characters would mostly disappear from mainstream screens again for the next two decades.

Any devotee of queer cinema owes an enormous debt to Vito Russo. At the same time, there is a need to move forward, to acknowledge *The Celluloid Closet* as a watershed but not the final word on the subject of gay American cinema. The book was essential in highlighting how stereotypes of queer people are often movie-made, and that for decades the movies had a dehumanizing effect on us; to prove this, time and again Russo writes with righteous anger. Thus the occasional beauty and meaningful nuances of the films are sometimes left as smoldering ash in the wake of his fiery pen. Many of these movies still capture the imaginations, emotions, and live-wire nerve centers of viewers today, inspiring critics, writers, musicians, and casual movie lovers. These are not simply the closet-case products of an unenlightened age.

. . .

Almost a decade after the first edition of *The Celluloid Closet*, the critical theorist and queer studies professor Eve Kosofsky Sedgwick published *Epistemology of the Closet* (1990), a volume as influential in its own way as Russo's book, as polemical and certainly as foundational. To reduce Sedgwick's expansive and trickily conceptual gambits by handpicking specific ideas might be as foolhardy as plucking individual whiskers from a sleeping tiger. I will, however, venture to say that *Epistemology of the Closet* memorably assesses our collective and individual relationships to the idea of the "closet," arguing that it creates a social reality based on the assumption of a hetero majority and a homo minority, and that to deny the centrality of queerness is to deny basic truths about how we live, interact, even speak. After all, the binarism of sexuality and gender with which our culture is obsessed is predicated on the idea of heterosexuality, which didn't even exist as a term until "homosexuality" was invented in the late nineteenth century.

One clear result of this binarism—and it's one we're all hopelessly used to—is that the concerns of queerness are presumed to matter or appeal only to that perceived small segment of the population. In late-twentieth-century popular culture, that meant niche entities like gay bookstores, TLA video rental catalogs, film festivals like NewFest or OutFest, or the occasional PBS documentary series about gay communities, such as *In the Life*. In twenty-first-century parlance, we might think of "Pride" trays on streaming channels (usually more visible in June). Such continued cubbyholing of queer content, the insistence on its separation, only reinforces the fallacy that transgender, gay, lesbian, and bisexual lives deserve little more than some kind of "honorable mention" within the larger, presumably "straight" culture. Even our basic communication is affected by the persistence of "closet" mentality: if we don't choose to "come out" or proclaim ourselves as gay, or lesbian, or transgender, or bisexual, then does society assume—or *insist*—that we are "straight"? In a Western civilization so long reliant on biased thought and knowledge, the act of silence itself becomes its own type of performance. After all, what we "know" today about the sexuality of movie stars like Rock Hudson and Marlene Dietrich or filmmakers like George Cukor and Dorothy Arzner doesn't necessarily change the films they made in the rearview mirror, but our historical knowledge makes them meatier, objects of fascination and ecstatic, shifting desire.

Sedgwick's project of sussing out the centrality of the closet, and of queerness, to twentieth-century thought seems at least as important to understanding the weird history of queer Hollywood cinema as Russo's inexhaustible sleuthing for homophobia. What a film doesn't say is as important to its meaning as what it does. Movies are an inherently collaborative medium, allowing for a multiplicity of expression from a variety of people, from the actors in front of the camera (talk about a history of concealment and divulgence!) to the cinematographers, screenwriters, composers, editors, art directors, costume designers, producers, studio heads, and, yes, censors. There's so much in a film, and so many lives with so many facets behind each one, that to reduce them to negative/positive, wrong/right, or naïve/enlightened is to fall into another form of fruitless binary thinking.

It might seem perverse to insist on the continued challenges and struggles of today while in the same breath acknowledging the coded, more censorious past as a time of nuance, even occasional triumph. In no way do I intend to nostalgically celebrate such a hidebound history. I do intend two things. First, to make a realistic reevaluation of a period marked by artists and viewers who either explicitly or tacitly acknowledged their own gay or lesbian identities and thus imbued popular art, whether as creators or watchers, with their queer sensibility. Second, to reconcile this reevaluation with an unabashed appreciation of a span of time in which great popular art was produced not merely in spite of the restrictions put on it but also because of them. From this, I can only hope, the reader will come to appreciate anew films that still dazzle, delight, and shock us seventy, eighty, ninety years on, and to acknowledge how their queer affects are a result of pleasure and frustration working in tandem. After all, the reason to write criticism in the first place should be an attempt to understand why art makes us feel the way it does.

.   .   .

The period we are talking about is commonly referred to as the Golden Age of Hollywood, an unofficial title that has different meanings for different people, and an appealing one, even if reductive and rose-tinted. One cannot begin to discuss this era of filmmaking without talking about the craft. From the early 1930s to the early 1960s, the industry was in top form, its true classical era. It had been able to marshal technical and aesthetic advancements in camerawork, sound recording, and performance style to generate movies of unparalleled splendor and intelligence. The industry certainly suffered its moments in the trenches—from the lingering effects of the Great Depression to the Supreme Court's 1948 Paramount Decrees, which busted up the monopolies the studios had on theatrical distribution, to the rise of television in the fifties as the American public's favored pastime. Nevertheless, this sustained historical period still holds sway over the imaginations of new generations of movie lovers, many of its stars and practitioners remaining icons, ever-present phantoms that have lingered long after corporeal death.

The tough truth of this starry-eyed history is that the same conditions that made these movies such rapturous, widely embraced cultural commodities are also those that bind and constrain them. The Motion Picture Production Code was a strictly enforced list of what was unacceptable to represent or depict on-screen, and movies didn't so much exist in its shadow as they were made in its image. Also known as the Hays Code (after its initial implementer, the former U.S. postmaster general Will Harrison Hays), it was written in 1930 in response to growing conservative consternation following a number of behind-the-scenes industry scandals and a perception of a general moral looseness on-screen, fears that had been brewing amid the increasing popularity of silent cinema of the 1920s. Yet it wouldn't be until 1934, and the appointment of the hard-liner Joseph I. Breen to the head of the Production Code Administration, that the Code grew teeth. Its strictures were no longer shrugged-off suggestions but rules to live by—or else. After this point, films would have to adhere to the guidelines to receive exhibition certificates; if their films didn't pass inspection, studios were vulnerable to being sued by Catholic Church officials and other powerful conservative leaders. Reeling from the Depression, movie studio heads were unwilling to take the risk. All capitulated, embarking on an era of self-censorship.

The Code's demands were many and blunt, at times comically specific, at others maddeningly vague. Its evaluation of gayness fell into the latter category: the designated no-no was "sexual perversion," a generalized catchall perhaps, but the industry didn't seem to have any doubt about its meaning. The Hays Office's objections to gay or lesbian characters or situations had already been made clear in the wording of the Code, but without the Code's enforcement, its practical application was nebulous. For instance, the word "pansy" was not allowed, but early sound films frequently featured character actors like Edward Everett Horton and Franklin Pangborn, whose stock-in-trade was the comic pansy sidekick. And before 1934, in the era today mythologized as "pre-Code," knowing jokes and sly inferences to homosexuality abounded, from backstage musicals to romantic comedies to Cecil B. DeMille costume epics of ancient Roman debauchery. In the Code years, filmmakers would either eliminate such material completely or get more creative in their methods of concealment. The result was frequently, frankly, better movies. Concurrent with advancements in technology and the studios' increasing confidence in sound cinema, the directive to blunt its edges inadvertently consigned the depiction of sexuality to innuendo and subtle eroticism. This led to a new form of corseted yet highly charged, layered, meaningful work. So many films of the Golden Age are richly subtextual objects of longing and displacement, films that constructed an entirely new language of attraction and sensuality, in which aesthetics reflect sublimated desire. Glances, color, shadows, cutting, composition, camera movement, and music communicate the intense libidinal drives that course through the characters' veins.

．　．　．

The systematized exclusionary nature of Hollywood necessarily complicates our response to it, and not merely in terms of queer eroticism. As integral to our understanding of this hallowed era of filmmaking as the attempted eradication of sex is the era's largely unmitigated racism; clauses in the Code all but mandated the white supremacy of the industry. To help comprehend why classical American cinema is so unflinchingly Caucasian, one need only read the following two sentences: "Miscegenation is forbidden" and "White-slavery shall not be treated" (the latter implying that images of actual chattel slavery are not only fair game but encouraged as an acceptable narrative engine for representing Black lives). It's worth noting that these forbidding words appear in the Code under the category of Sex, which indicates that Americans' deep-seated racist assumptions are often entwined with our fear of human eroticism. This would be reflected in the treatment of Black bodies and sexuality on-screen throughout at least the twentieth century. Black men commonly appear as either asexual buffoons or sexual threats, while Black women were traditionally either the nurturing mammy or the sexualized, tragic mulatto or Jezebel.

Make no mistake: the reactionary corporate forces that kept Hollywood fundamentally conservative throughout the Code era persist to this day, even as standards in American society shift and evolve. American studio film and television production still capitulate to the whims and desires of advertisers, whose companies remain beholden to often imaginary ideas of public acceptability. In the past decade, such issues have been relitigated under the always resurfacing, ever more politicized rubric of "culture wars." This is one reason why a company as powerful as Disney—which has all but monopolized the culture by also owning Pixar, the Star Wars franchise, 20th Century Studios, Hulu, and Marvel—is continually on the defensive, making headlines for either its condemnation of or perceived complicity in a culture that still doesn't know what to do about gay representation in mainstream entertainment.

The legacies of Code-era Hollywood—what we can and cannot see—have lasted far beyond 1968, when the Motion Picture Association of America ratings system was instituted, ostensibly ending the Code's reign. That system, initially assigning movies letter grades with a G, M, R, or X rating, was advertised as a guide for parents, but it also functioned as a new, and still dominant, form of industry regulation for an era of rising permissiveness. The sense of movies as dangerous, with the potential to damage children, remains a through line of our country's cinematic history.

This doesn't seem likely to change, especially with the third decade of the twenty-first century as evidence. The culture's increasing obsession with the protection of youth has crossed the line into political mania, in ways both nebulous (the specters of pedophilia and "grooming" have become catchphrases for baseless accusations and ever wilder conspiracy theories on the Right) and troublingly concrete. In 2022, the free speech nonprofit PEN America released a report on the alarming rise in organized efforts at book banning in American schools, listing 2,532 instances of banned books, affecting 1,648 works. It shouldn't come as a surprise that these titles include not just classic, socially liberal novels like Toni Morrison's *The Bluest Eye* and George Orwell's *1984* but also a wealth of LGBTQ+ titles such as *Beyond*

Magenta: Transgender Teens Speak Out and Alison Bechdel's *Fun Home*, as well as many young adult or children's books, such as *And Tango Makes Three*, a picture book about cuddly male penguins raising a baby at the Central Park Zoo. Accompanying this, naturally, is a rise in conflicts between teachers and parents, who, driven by political media, are more eager than ever before to control the material their children read and watch. Schools have inevitably become ground zero for the cultural debates—around race, sexuality, and gender—that have overtaken and largely defined so much of the contemporary media discourse.

In an era when teachers are increasingly embattled by the small-minded and the hypercritical, *The Children's Hour* might have renewed relevance. Martha Dobie and Karen Wright are targets of both homophobia and puritanical parental outrage. Their rumored lesbianism, a lie born of malice, is particularly abhorrent to the parents because the women are educators and thus have the power to *infect* their young charges (homosexuality as contagious). The ultimate humiliation comes when the scandalized parents all remove their children from the school. Now the abandoned Martha and Karen have little to do but stew or self-flagellate, leading to Martha's final revelations.

The reactions of the fictional parents in Lillian Hellman's story and the conservative forces that cohered into the censorious Production Code are one and the same. Both operate out of fear—or, as they would like you to believe, *concern*—for the hearts, minds, and bodies of our nation's fragile children. The self-appointed moral guardians' desire for control issues from a belief that the sexual lives of adults can corrupt the young merely by example, a fallacy that only serves to distract from the very real, tragic instances of sexual abuse of children that occur every day in the United States. The Code is inextricable from these concerns: among the piles of "evidence" of Hollywood corruption in the buildup to the Code's enforcement was a 1933 study by a watchdog group called the Motion Picture Research Council. The five-year research project, partly paid for by a private conservative philanthropic foundation called the Payne Fund, intended to prove that movies were not just entertainment but agents of contamination imperiling American youth. The exaggerated findings were cited as evidence in a bestselling polemic called *Our Movie Made Children*, in which the author Henry James Forman declares, "Here is evidence of the influence of motion pictures and their impersonations upon the character, conduct and behavior of vast numbers of our nation and especially upon the more malleable and younger people." Forman devotes an entire chapter to the testimonies of teenage "sexual delinquents" who claim to get ideas for their "bad" lifestyles from the movies.

The Code's swift transformation of Hollywood speaks to how susceptible American culture is to the phantasms of moral turpitude and corruption. This country's film industry at its most cherished—"the dream factory"—is impossible to conceive of without the limitations enforced upon it. Between 1935 and 1961, the years this book traverses, we had stars like James Stewart, Bette Davis, Barbara Stanwyck, Humphrey Bogart, Ingrid Bergman, Marlon Brando, Gene Kelly, James Dean, and Marilyn Monroe; directors like Alfred Hitchcock, William Wyler, Vincente Minnelli, Orson Welles, Nicholas Ray, George Cukor, Michael Curtiz, and Billy Wilder; screenwriters like Ben Hecht, Charles Lederer, Adolph Green and Betty Comden, and Raymond Chandler; cinematographers like Gregg Toland and Stanley Cortez; composers like Alfred Newman and Bernard Herrmann. The list of virtuoso artists and technicians is nigh endless. The period of capacious prohibition spotlighted in this book is also one of marvelous craft and creativity, an era of screen wish fulfillment—overwhelmingly white and heterosexual—that carried viewers from a period of national deprivation through the Second World War and into the economic rebound of the 1950s.

. . .

The Children's Hour is not merely an indication of Hollywood's tender, equivocating relationship to queerness within this historical span—it's a crucial text that bookends Code-era Hollywood. William Wyler's 1961 film with MacLaine and Hepburn wasn't the first screen adaptation of Lillian Hellman's play; it wasn't even the first by Wyler. In 1935, less than a year after the Code had been strictly enforced, the powerful Hollywood producer Samuel Goldwyn bought the rights to Hellman's play, which had been a contentious yet undeniable sensation on Broadway. The film would be directed by Wyler, just coming into his own in the industry, and adapted by Hellman herself, then working in Goldwyn's stable of screenwriters. Yet the Code's new policies dictated that practically everything about this lesbian-themed drama would have to be changed: the result was *These Three*, a heterosexual love triangle that eradicated the play's queer content entirely.

Wyler had become one of the most powerful, acclaimed, and Oscar-lauded directors in Hollywood when he set out to remake his own film in 1961. By this time, the power of the Code was in decline, following years of rebellious producers and directors like Otto Preminger and Joseph L. Mankiewicz chipping away at it.

Coming off his third Oscar, Wyler cast major stars as Martha and Karen, roles that most New York stage actresses had treated like career poison twenty-five years earlier. Considering the public's growing taste for provocative, sexually suggestive material throughout the fifties—much of it hailing from adaptations of Broadway hits by the likes of Tennessee Williams, William Inge, and Robert Anderson—it seemed as though the time was right for a new and faithful version of *The Children's Hour*. The public and critical response was certainly not what its makers expected or hoped for, yet its effects would be felt for decades to come. It's a film queer critics still struggle with, and so it continues to matter. Drawn to it and repelled by it in equal measure, we haven't completely come to terms with *The Children's Hour* and what it means to gay and lesbian history.

The same could be said for so many of the intrinsically queer films that were made in the decades between these two movies. This book spans twenty-five years, from *These Three* to *The Children's Hour*, delving into the production and cultural meaning of a handful of movies that were and remain essential to an understanding of gay and lesbian lives, then and now, on-screen and off. The films are disparate, covering a range of genres, including suspense thriller, musical, and melodrama. In them, queerness is perceptible as a trace, as a wink, as an identity, as a sensibility. As something to be hidden but also, crucially, something to be decoded. Yet these films, I would argue, have done something even broader: they have helped create a contemporary under-standing, even a lexicon, for the phenomenon of modern queerness. Popular culture, for better or for worse, often catalyzes the borders of our reality, and these films have given us both walls to push against (the stereotypes/archetypes of the "tragic lesbian," the "killer dandy," the "sensitive sissy") and aesthetic pleasure to luxuriate in. Some-where in that contradiction perhaps lies the split consciousness of queerness itself.

Whether through concealment or exposure, the movies considered in this book tilled the soil for the changes to come in the second half of the cinematic twentieth century and the beginning of the twenty-first. Many of these films, cloaking stealthily progressive values beneath their conservative duds, have too long been dismissed as relics of an unenlightened time. It's key to remember that queerness is central to an understanding of the movies—not some inconsequential, marginal-ized segment of Hollywood but a core part of its texture and temperament. Thanks to the number of gay and lesbian people who plied their craft in the industry, a queer consciousness permeated the fabric of American movies.

. . .

It's worth defining here what we mean by *queerness*. The word "queer" has histori-cally been a synonym not just for "odd" or "unusual" but also, per Merriam-Webster, "sick," "unwell," "questionable," or "suspicious." A derogatory term for gay people throughout much of the twentieth century, "queer" as a slur goes back at least as far as 1894, when the Marquess of Queensberry wrote a letter to his son, Lord Alfred Douglas, to express his disgust and dismay at his association with "snob queers." (Douglas's infamous crime was being a lover of Oscar Wilde, who was eventually jailed for sodomy, an experience that likely led to his death at age forty-six.)

The word was redeemed by academics, most dramatically in the eighties, as an affectionate, politicized, self-identifying catchall. Its champions meant to weap-onize a once hurtful word against those who had no right to it, as well as to unite various definitions of sexuality (trans, gay, lesbian, bisexual, and more). Yet "queer" is also a meaningful term for the ways in which it straddles several categories of cultural currency and being: it's sexual, yes, but it's also political and psychological. Queerness refers to how one relates to the world, a sensibility rooted in difference yet free-floating.

In recent years it's become commonplace to hear the word wielded with a sense of empowerment by those whose sexuality or identity exist outside heteronormative expectations and definitions. It's in this spirit that I use the term "queer" throughout this book, evoking its applied usage in both academic circles and increasingly main-stream parlance. At the same time, I offer up the terms "gay" and "lesbian" about as frequently as traditional markers of same-sex desire and identity, which are essential to understanding the films considered here. Discussions around transness, and the complex ways trans and gender identity have been represented and evoked in American cinema, are outside the scope of this book, and I would suggest that readers seek out Caden Mark Gardner and Willow Catelyn Maclay's *Corpses, Fools, and Monsters: The History and Future of Transness in Cinema* for a deep dive into this subject. Nevertheless, the centrality of nonbinary thinking—in terms of gender, sexuality, narrative, costuming, music, performance—comes up again and again as a through line, and one of the most lasting markers of queerness.

My apologies in advance to any readers who take offense at the term "queer," although I do regard as helpful its intersectional ability to encompass various cate-gories and registers. The malleability and fluidity of identity and sexuality, to my mind, can be explained only via such enigmatic terminology. The elliptical nature of the word remains immensely appealing to many, as well as emotionally confirming, and until a better one comes along, I'm happy to use it with hopeful aplomb in tribute to my predecessors who dared to reclaim it.

To apply this productively nebulous term to cinema is to acknowledge that a film can have a queer sensibility without being a "gay movie" to the naked eye. There are numerous ways to define queerness in a movie, just one of which is authorship—having been directed or written by someone who was or is now known to have been gay or lesbian. Other markers of queerness include, of course, the characters in the film being explicitly gay, lesbian, bisexual, or transgender, but this was basically impossible during the Code era, so this marker would largely apply to films made later in the twentieth century. Or the actors on the screen can be queer, or were strongly rumored to have been, as in the cases of Greta Garbo, Marlene Dietrich, or James Dean, whose personas are now difficult to untangle from gay supposition, innuendo, or biographical fragments. Or a film can be queered by its reception history: gay audiences have long claimed particular movies and stars for their own, most prominently Judy Garland, whose cinematic image and legacy are symbiotically conjoined to her perennial gay fan base even more than half a century after her death.

Queer movies reject fixed identities, open their arms wide to the marginalized, and pull back the curtain on social roles, acknowledging the constructedness of everyday life. Even and especially now, when the wider social acceptance of gayness results in gay characters occasionally appearing in Hollywood movies, queer cinema remains marginalized. A rule of thumb in elucidating heteronormativity in cinema: consider any mainstream movie you've ever seen and ask yourself this: Do you assume a character is straight until they are "proven" gay? Of course, in movies, the gulf between intentionality and inference is vast, but explicitly gay characters have for decades been so nonexistent as to barely crack even minority status.

Without overt evidence of actual gay lives on-screen, generations of movie watchers in the classical Hollywood cinema era were left to find reflections of their own queerness somewhere on or behind the screen. "It was a gay sensibility that, for example, often enabled some lesbians and gay men to see at very early ages, even before they knew the words for what they were, something on the screen that they knew related to their lives in some way, without being able to put a finger on it," wrote Russo. "It was the sense of longing that existed in such scenes, the unspoken, forbidden feelings that were always present, always denied. It said, this has something to do with your life, and it was a voice that could not be ignored, even though the pieces did not fall into place until years later."

I can attest to this observation. Born in Massachusetts in 1979, I came of age at a more permissive time than the one in which Russo was raised, but still one in which movies were clearly products of an intrinsic, longstanding homophobic culture. During these years, this homophobia was amplified both by a newly ascendant fear born of the AIDS epidemic and an increasing obsession with berserk masculinity (the era of Stallone and Schwarzenegger). Throughout the eighties, there was nothing of gay significance that would have penetrated the suburban walls that housed my burgeoning cinephilia, save a chaste, mysterious kiss between Whoopi Goldberg and Margaret Avery in Steven Spielberg's *The Color Purple*. So, along with legions of kids raised on Hollywood movies, I had to read between the lines, peer into the crevices, unlock the secrets. And being raised in the VHS era, I was able to relive my cinematic crushes again and again.

I would not come out of the closet until my early twenties, but in retrospect I see the trail of breadcrumbs leading me to my own queer sensibility. Some of these were latently sexual, like my deep fascination with the fit of Marlon Brando's T-shirt in *A Streetcar Named Desire*. Others reflected the alienation I felt from masculine culture, resulting in an almost exclusive interest in women film stars (Goldberg, Jessica Lange, Sigourney Weaver, Meryl Streep), whose complex, multifaceted femininity opened essential emotional entry points to the movies. Very rarely there were moments in which a gay character burst through the screen with heartbreaking directness, as in the movie version of the musical *A Chorus Line*, which features a monologue in which a timid dancer tells the tearful story of his father's rejection of him. But there was something stronger and more firmly rooted about my queer scaffolding that went beyond—or beneath—sexual attraction or gender identification, something closer to Russo's "sense of longing." It would be easy to point to my childhood adoration of *The Wizard of Oz* and *Meet Me in St. Louis* as an adhesive force in that growing queer sensibility, but I think it's something a little less obvious than a fondness for Judy Garland. Rather, it stems from a belief in cinema's ability to animate the intangibility of life, in the movies' desire to show the world beneath the one we can see. My own queerness makes me crave the movies for their willingness to identify with outsiders, for the unfinished, the indescribable, the nonlinear. I was unfixed, hungry, impatient to be part of a world without strict boundaries or definitions. Intrinsic to this inchoate sense of myself were movies like *Vertigo* or *Portrait of Jennie* or *Laura*, which swooned with desire, no matter the object of their affections and no matter the sexuality of their makers, or movies like *All*

About Eve or *The Magnificent Ambersons* or *Sunset Boulevard*, which looked at the world with appealing jaundice. They were movies not only to watch but to hold up to the light; they looked different depending on the angle at which I held them or which way my internal sun was casting its rays that day.

At some point in the early nineties, I sensed I wasn't alone in my communion with the desirous films of a long-lost past, and this realization coincided with the rise of an important gay movement in American cinema. I didn't yet know what the terms "camp" or "pastiche" meant, but Todd Haynes's groundbreaking omnibus film *Poison* (1991) communicated to me in a clear, direct way how the latent aesthetics of desire of an earlier era could be redefined as blatantly queer. In later films like *Far from Heaven* (2002) and *Carol* (2015), Haynes has continued to demonstrate that the grip our Hollywood past maintains on our queer present has little to do with mere nostalgia—the melodramas, musicals, and noirs of the Golden Age were seed bearers, planting within gay and lesbian viewers a feeling of erotic belonging embedded in the aesthetics. Haynes recalls the cinema education of his youth: "As I learned more and watched more films, the form and the structure of cinema would always become more and more important to me, over and above the content. How it informs us, how it mirrors the structures of a society, the way we fit into society, what we are free to do and not free to do, how we're defined by form, structure, and language." *Poison* featured purposely outmoded visual and narrative approaches: glossy Jean Cocteau– and Jean Genet–inspired prison melodramas, black-and-white "B-movie" science fiction. It would mark a turning point, auguring an unofficial yet undeniable entry into what the scholar B. Ruby Rich would dub the New Queer Cinema. Born of the low-budget film boom that made household words out of "Sundance" and "indie," the movement gained in respect and popularity as the decade went on, presenting movies in which queerness became primary text.

Nothing indicates the growing notoriety of a serious American work of art better than the censorious forces that rise to tamp it down. Even as a preteen I had heard about such gay movie landmarks as *Poison* and Marlon Riggs's *Tongues Untied*. Both became lightning rods in the culture wars of the nineties, making headlines for stoking the ire of conservative politicians who had no time for art unless it gave them something to gnash their teeth over. After its sensational premiere at Sundance, where it won the festival's prestigious Grand Jury Prize, Haynes's movie was denounced by Senator Jesse Helms and the Reverend Donald

Wildmon, head of the Christian fundamentalist group the American Family Association, who was all too eager to decry "explicit porno scenes of homosexuals involved in anal sex" that weren't even in the movie. Also in 1991, the epochal *Tongues Untied* would make waves when scheduled for broadcast on PBS's POV documentary series. Dangerous for being a film about Black gay sexuality made by a Black, gay, HIV-positive man, *Tongues Untied* became a bugbear for public hand-wringers like Wildmon and the former Reagan adviser Pat Buchanan. Like *Poison*, *Tongues Untied* was targeted for receiving partial funding through the federal government's National Endowment for the Arts, allowing politicians to exploit the anger of a public as ignorant of the arts as they were about where their taxpayer money goes anyway.

This is all worth bringing up for the way that my burgeoning awareness of "out" gay movies was complicated by concurrent strategies to suppress them. Conservative politicians in the culture wars of the 1990s surely would have preferred to live in an era still ruled by the Production Code or worse.

The incessant politicization of art in the last decade of the twentieth century set the stage for how popular entertainment with queer themes and characters would be treated in the next, by forces on the right and the left. The breakthroughs of the New Queer Cinema's independent filmmakers paved the path for a series of higher-budgeted queer productions championed in the mainstream press as much for their social-minded bravery as for their cinematic tastefulness. These include *Brokeback Mountain* and *Milk* (Oscar winners that sit squarely within the tragic-historical view of gayness) and *Transamerica*, which garnered enough attention to earn the cisgender female actor Felicity Huffman an Oscar nomination for playing a trans-gender woman. Buoyed by mainstream entertainment, LGBTQ+ assimilation into normative American culture was gaining momentum, even if we were still most often used as a sprinkle of flavoring or for political advantage.

The following decade would see the December 2010 overturning of the U.S. military's homophobic "Don't Ask, Don't Tell" policy, and the June 2015 Supreme Court decision on nationwide marriage equality in *Obergefell v. Hodges*, following years of individual states passing their own marriage equality laws. The sense of a sea change for queer lives in America was so pervasive that even the more suspicious among us could be forgiven for complacency as we headed into the irretrievable danger zone of 2016—and a subsequent era marked by such catastrophic cultural division that the term "post-gay" now seems like a quaint joke. Even putting aside the inevitable widespread cultural backlash that greets any progressive movement in the United States, assimilative political gains as symbolically meaningful as gay marriage and military service cannot and do not have the effect of erasing centuries of trauma from violence, marginalization, and disenfranchisement. Queer visibility will remain precarious in a corporatized American culture in which we're all only as useful as our status as consumers, and where representation is a catchphrase for companies large and small courting customer credibility and shareholder favor.

I am simplifying recent gay history with this broad-strokes précis to hint at the expanse separating lived experience from received narratives. To presume that mainstream twenty-first-century American culture—with its sharp dividing lines of race, class, gender, and sexuality—*understands* queer lives in a way that it did not fifty or sixty years ago feels naïve at best. This is why the cinematic history of Hollywood's Golden Age remains not just foundational but ever present, and why these films continue to throb with vitality and speak to viewers with a thrilling emotional directness. We're still wrestling with the same questions about who we are, the same secret desires, the same undercurrents. Movies at their worst tell us what to think. Movies at their best still speak in code.

. . .

The handful of movies that I write about at length in this book are wildly different in tone, atmosphere, and genre. Some of them are bowdlerized products of the Code's draconian policies; some bear the mark of easy capitulation; others were spared by Joseph Breen's red pen. Some of these films I have been watching since childhood and have long been a profound part of my emotional and intellectual makeup; others I saw first as an adult, allowing me the kind of analytical distance hard to muster for a movie that feels as if it's always been inside you. Some of these films engage with questions of queerness in as direct a manner as was possible in their time; others would seem to have nothing to do with queerness, at least on the surface. Some of these films are tours de force, exemplars of their form; others are solid, well-crafted entertainment. Yet taken together, these movies tell a single narrative: the story of a quarter century in the history of cinema crucial to understanding modern queerness, when the industry was slowly evolving, barely playing catch-up to an American society that was more rapidly moving forward.

It's not a tale of sweeping social transformation. At no point in this narrative would or could someone say, "And things would never be the same again." History doesn't quite work that way, and queer history—a long process of inches forward and steps back—certainly doesn't heed the demands of linear cause and effect. This is the story of artists and entertainers who forged ahead and created while living under a repressive set of circumstances. These are films made in factories with their own rules and processes (movie studios) that functioned as microcosms of a larger enclosed world with its own rules and processes (the United States). Change is incremental. Often the events that lay the groundwork for change are not the epochal moments but the small gestures. The movies in this book are imperfect, complex compounds in which the desire for social progress is all mixed up with the traditional, conservative values that defined the times, movies that scream and shout but stop short of telling us how they really feel.

Like so many scholars of this country's strange gay cinematic history, I've long papered over *The Children's Hour*, treating the death of Martha Dobie with a simple headshake. But even before that revelatory classroom experience, I must admit, the film stuck in my craw. It's talked about in hushed tones, dismissed almost as soon as it's invoked. When Shirley MacLaine appeared on camera in Epstein and Friedman's *Celluloid Closet* documentary to discuss *The Children's Hour*, she came across as someone paying penance for a misdeed, confirming the film as historical embarrassment. "We didn't do the picture right," she says with candor. Asked about her character's emotional breakdown and self-laceration, MacLaine imagines how Martha would react to the revelation of her sexuality today: "She would fight! She would fight for her budding preference." With a character as ferocious as Martha, perhaps MacLaine is right. But it nevertheless sounds like a lovely bit of wish fulfillment possible only in hindsight.

Martha's death provides the beginning and ending of our story—and the beginning of a new one. This book is not a tragic narrative of shame or misery. The often buoyant, enlightening visions explored in these chapters speak to an art form that captures imaginations rather than kills them. Too often we've looked back at these movies from a contemporary vantage, as though trying to make them out through an obscuring lattice of dead tree branches. Clean out the bramble of the past—and whatever superiority we may feel as modern viewers—and these movies reveal themselves as bracing and vital, allowing us to see our pasts, and therefore ourselves, more clearly.

I

The Original Sin

Lillian Hellman immediately despised Los Angeles. Upon her arrival in 1930, she found the sprawl of the city unwelcoming, the drab color palette uninviting, the sense of community nonexistent. Hellman had been hitting the pavement in New York as a wannabe short story writer and had few published works to her name. Such career struggles hadn't loosened the metropolis's fairy-tale-like grip on Hellman, however, and she hesitated looking for work out west as so many others, including her husband, had begun to do.

Hollywood in the early thirties nursed a growing infatuation with New York artists, hoping to harness the creative powers of the East Coast intelligentsia. If playwrights, novelists, and critics could be seduced to the West Coast, then hopefully they could bring their skills to bear on a burgeoning art form seeking authentication. Sound cinema was still a recent phenomenon, and the movie studios had to recalibrate everything they'd been doing for an entirely new popular mode. This technological leap brought the promise of artistic advancement: more realism in performance, experimentation in form, and fluidity in storytelling. This necessitated finding new talent—actors who could properly vocalize, directors to harness large-scale productions with multiple speaking parts, writers who could compose dialogue for characters that sounded like the way people talked. The movies were already Americans' most popular source of entertainment, but the advent of "talkies" was dramatic evidence that this medium was still in the process of being invented.

The studios began enticing writers of titanic talent like William Faulkner, Ernest Hemingway, F. Scott Fitzgerald, John O'Hara, Nathanael West, Dorothy Parker, Robert Sherwood, Ben Hecht, and Clifford Odets to work on screenplays. Yet it was rarely a good match for artists of their temperament, and with the exception of writers like Hecht, who would flourish in the studio system, many of them would bake only briefly under the California sun. Summing up the inevitable tensions between L.A. moguls and New York creatives, Hellman would describe those in charge in Hollywood as superficial moneymen without artistic instincts: "They wouldn't know an idea if they saw it on the Coast. And if by any chance they should recognize it the film people would be frightened right out of their suede shoes."

Hellman had made a habit of not fitting in from an early age. Independent-minded with a fierceness that occasionally bordered on self-destructive, Hellman was skeptical of everything but her own talent. She often referred to her family—well-off Southern Jewish entrepreneurs—with an offhanded sharpness that seemed to mark them as fodder for some future roman à clef. (Indeed, 1939's *The Little Foxes*, an acid-tongued portrait of an avaricious nouveau-riche Southern clan, would be a definitive work of Hellman's career.) Uninterested in being a Hollywood wife before she had made a name for herself, the twenty-four-year-old Hellman was lukewarm when in 1930, her husband, Arthur Kober, landed a $450-a-week screen-writing job at Paramount in Los Angeles (which she called "more money than we had ever seen") and summarily left his job as a Broadway press agent. She resisted the trip for months, telling Kober to go ahead without her. "I fooled and fiddled with excuses until the day when I did go, knowing even then, I think, that I would not stay," she would recall. Finally, she drew the blinds on their modest, "beat-up old house on Long Island" and hopped the train to join Arthur in a one-room apartment on Sunset Boulevard.

Hellman would never have to worry about just being "someone's wife," of course—her disposition and talent never would have allowed for it, and, after all, Kober, whom she would divorce just two years later, would remain her only husband. Soon enough, upon Kober's entreaties, MGM's head story editor, Sam Marx, hired her as a script reader for $50 a week. She had landed an enviable job at the studio that, only a few years into the sound era, was already considered the imperial granddaddy of them all. The gig would teach her the basics of the craft and skill necessary to visualize stories for the screen. Nevertheless, she was unstimulated by the work, depressed, and drinking too much. As described in her memoir *An Unfinished Woman*, her days at MGM were hardly the stuff of fairy dust, but there was an appealing mix of the mundane and the surreal to her new life of estrangement: "I would leave home at eight-thirty, drive to Culver City carrying a small basket with my lunch and a bottle of wine. I would, by one o'clock, have a vague headache that would disappear as I ate my picnic on the back lot of the studio and got fuzzy on the wine and the surrounding dream of old movie sets piled next to one another, early Rome at right angles to the painted roses of a girlie musical, at the left of a London street, side by side with a giant, empty whaling ship." At the end of the workday, exhausted from reading what she called "junk," she would drive back home in the dark across the "flat soggy land" of those pre-freeway years, murky country back roads that instilled an almost primal fear in Hellman.

Despite her impressions of Hollywood as haplessly, inhospitably provincial in both form and function, Hellman would come to appreciate the city on its own schmaltzy terms. She'd remain an unapologetic fan of the movies' singular combination of glamor and desperation, an impression that would become only more pronounced as the decade wore on and the American cinema increasingly peddled its illusions of wholesomeness. At that point in her career, though, she was considered too low in the Hollywood caste system to feel as though she were making any significant contribution to that magic. In this first L.A. layover, which hardly portended the successes to come, she was mostly fascinated by "the foggy edge-world of people who had come to Hollywood for reasons they had long ago forgotten. They lived in the Murphy bed, modern apartments that were already the slums off Hollywood Boulevard, or in the rickety houses that stuck out like broken tree-geraniums from the Hollywood mud hills."

Committed once again to making a name for herself in New York, Hellman would quietly escape Southern California in 1932—but not before she met someone who would change the trajectory of her life, professionally and personally. The crime novelist Dashiell Hammett, in the midst of his own Hollywood experiment, was the wiry, dapper writer of the slyly queer-tinged detective novel *The Maltese Falcon* (1930) and later *The Thin Man* (1934), both of which would be adapted into films so popular they would supersede their source material in the American consciousness. Hellman first met Hammett in November 1930, and though married, she actively pursued a romantic relationship with the author, who was known around town for his sexual rapaciousness and intellectual prowess but also his alcoholism, which would frequently manifest in public altercations. Hellman and Hammett, known to romance chroniclers as Lilly and Dash, formed a bond that would go much deeper than the carnal; he encouraged her creativity and would remain a guiding spirit for her work. Even after she had first escaped Hollywood and gone back east, the two remained inseparable, first via written correspondence and then physically when Hammett relocated to the more baldly Depression-plagued New York.

Following Hellman's divorce from Kober in 1932, she and Hammett moved in together in a rented room at the Sutton Club Hotel on East Fifty-Sixth Street, a dingy writers' refuge where they began living the romantic, precarious life of disso-lute artists. In 1933, Hammett wrote *The Thin Man*, whose socialite private detec-tives Nick and Nora Charles share a witty repartee based in no small part on that of Hellman and Hammett; the eventual film version, starring William Powell and Myrna Loy as glamorous funhouse mirror versions of the two writers, would spawn five sequels. The same year that Hammett finished *The Thin Man* and cemented his legacy in the popular imagination, Hellman began writing her first play, one that would launch her career and establish her artistic, risk-taking persona.

Hellman would credit Hammett with giving her the push she needed to embark on the writing of *The Children's Hour*; he even gave her the kernel of the idea. In 1809, an Edinburgh girls' school had been shut down after its female heads, Jane Pirie and Marianne Woods, were accused of carrying on a lesbian affair. The women responded with a defamation lawsuit, which they eventually won on appeal, but their careers and reputations had already been ruined. Hammett had read about this incident in *Bad Companions*, an anthology by William Roughead, a Scottish lawyer turned true crime writer. In the story "Closed Doors: or the Grand Drumsheugh Case," a student initiates the rumor, which then expands to engulf a small community. Removing the story from its colonialist origins, Hellman would leave out many details of the sensational case—most notably the fact that the accusing tyke, Jane Cumming (described in the story as an illegitimately born "mulatto"), had been the child of an unknown Indian woman and a white father employed by the British trade giant East India Company. The basic outline of this episode, however, would allow Hellman to show how little had changed in the intervening hundred years: as both her play and its reception would prove, even the intimation of homosexuality still had the power to scandalize, and human nature continues to demonstrate that one malicious lie can prove disastrous. The material wasn't connected to her life or experience in any way, as Hellman would insist over the years. In 1952, she told the *New York Times*'s Harry Gilroy that she chose a story she could "treat with complete impersonality. I hadn't even been to boarding school."

Hellman was attracted to the tale not because she had any emotional stake or interest in representing gay and lesbian lives on the stage, but because she felt that art should retain the power to shock and shake people up. Never one to shrink from the discussion of taboo subject matter, Hellman now could apply that same daring to her writing. Driven by a newfound passion, Hellman pounded away at her type-writer. She wrote first in her digs at the Sutton Club Hotel, and as the year stretched on, in a rented house in Florida, writing and rewriting, all the while receiving detailed, sometimes cutting notes and critiques from Hammett. Together they went through six more drafts. Hammett has long been recognized for his integral role in the play's creation, though he never sought any kind of credit; the finished work is dedicated to him "with thanks."

The seething fury and intensity of *The Children's Hour*, the cynicism and tragic depiction of people undone by callousness, intolerance, and small-mindedness, were all Hellman's. Increasingly political-minded, the unapologetically left-leaning Jewish woman from New Orleans had little time for pietists or the easily offended, and *The Children's Hour* would allow her to explore themes that were practically guaranteed to offend: American puritanism, female independence, the dangers of social conformity, sympathetic homosexuality, and unsympathetic children. Many of these themes had undeniable political undercurrents in the early 1930s, as the frightening spread of fascism throughout Europe emboldened the American Left across the United States. Hellman's own progressivism hadn't yet reached its full flowering when she wrote *The Children's Hour*, yet in the play's fearlessness one can see the seeds of her political activism.

. . .

To read *The Children's Hour* is to be immersed in impossibilities—of its characters' happiness, of maintaining integrity in a world prone to the invidious tactics of dehumanization. The play's emotional anchor is the touching and tragic bond between the New England boarding school's two headmistresses, Karen Wright (in Hellman's description, "an attractive woman of twenty-eight, casually pleasant in manner, without sacrifice of warmth or dignity") and the doomed Martha Dobie.

In the final published play, Hellman describes Martha as "a nervous, high-strung woman"; in an early draft, Hellman was more succinct: "Unconscious Lesbian. Age 32." The play's driving force is maleficent young Mary Tilford. Fueled by profound insecurity and a need to destroy everything around her in order to feel powerful, Mary is a bad apple that ends up contaminating the whole orchard.

The Children's Hour is preoccupied with the banality of corruption and the prosaic ways in which the evils of small-mindedness engulf society; bigotry (and what we would today call homophobia) reveals itself only as a by-product of that vulgar mundanity. It's fitting then that the first scene focuses on something so commonplace as the self-centered tactics of a nasty preteen. Mary arrives late to a sewing and elocution hour being overseen by a half-dozing Lily Mortar, Martha's aunt, an aging former actress who ends up being more trouble than help to her niece and whose toxic narcissism has its own negative effect on the culture of the school. Clutching a bunch of faded wildflowers, Mary—"undistinguished looking . . . neither pretty nor ugly"—tries to sneak in the back door undetected. When Mrs. Mortar begins to admonish her for her tardiness, the girl quickly and slyly turns the tables and tells the older woman she was late because she went out of her way to pick flowers for her. The flattery works, and Mrs. Mortar gives her a simple pat on the head. Yet Mary's triumph is momentary; when Karen enters the living room and sees the bouquet, already placed in a vase, she reveals to Mrs. Mortar and the class that the flowers were plucked not from a field but from the garbage can—a dead, discarded bundle. Karen's reprimanding of Mary after class incites recalcitrance and more lies, culminating in a showy display of feigned illness from the child, who clutches her heart and tumbles to the floor with a dramatic flair that could earn sympathy only from a hammy drama queen like Mrs. Mortar.

As is established in this first scene, Mary is both a natural manipulator and an unrepentant liar, a suitable vessel for Hellman's forthcoming narrative of deception, gossip, and intolerance. Deepening and complicating the vise grip that Mary has on the play is the fact that of all the characters, this villainous child is the one Hellman identified with the most—or at least claims to have best understood. "What I know about children, I only know because I myself have been a child. The imp came out of my own head," she told the *New York Post* in 1934. "I was a naughty child. All the children I knew were naughty." Having been a girl of sass more than sugar and spice, Hellman admitted to having faked a heart attack, to throwing tantrums, and to telling tall tales. The only child of New Orleans's Max Bernard

Hellman and Julia Newhouse Hellman (whose side of the family the playwright would famously mock as moneyed, status-obsessed predators in *The Little Foxes*), Lillian was mouthy, bold, disruptive; she was marked by a pronounced curiosity that verged on voyeurism and had an aversion to Southern feminine gentility even as a child. At too early an age, she became a wide-eyed frequenter of the city's French Quarter, where she was drawn to the thriving jazz scene; the forbidden district, populated by female sex workers and hungry johns, also piqued her interest in the underbelly of life. By the time she grew up and moved to New York, Hellman had prepared herself well for the precarities and perversities of urban living.

Unlike with Hellman, young Mary's cleverness, brash bearing, and proclivity for robust storytelling would not prove to be fronts for an artistic spirit in bloom. Hellman would use her gifts for creation; Mary uses hers for destruction. In the play's first act, Hellman does a tremendous job describing the contours of the world that Mary aims to ruin. Karen and Martha have a firm grip on their professional lives and have taken great pains to create an insular, fully functional world that has brought them evident emotional satisfaction, and it's clear that this satisfaction is due in no small part to their tremendous bond of friendship. Yet as the two women's first extended conversation details, cracks are beginning to show in the foundation. Martha expresses her surprise and discomfort at Karen's casual reference to her forthcoming marriage to Dr. Joe Cardin ("large, pleasant-looking, carelessly dressed," in Hellman's shrug of an introduction), and while her concerns about Karen and Joe's wedding are couched in anxieties that it will irrevocably affect their professional partnership at school, Martha's discomfort appears to go deeper, an admittance of feeling rejected and unloved. ("It's going to be hard going on alone afterwards.")

In a subsequent moment in the same scene, Aunt Lily pesters Martha about her evident jealousy of Karen and Joe's relationship and claims that such behavior has been apparent since Martha was a child. "And it's unnatural. Just as unnatural as it can be," Aunt Lily accuses, and it's the sort of coded language that would immediately cause the fine hairs on any queer soul's neck to stand on end. That it's coming from the mouth of one of the play's chief antagonists—and its most irritating one at that—immediately sets out the fascinating parameters of Hellman's sympathies. Even though Martha will "come out" at the end of the play, after the women have lost their careers over the child's lie and fought a libel suit, these early scenes telegraph her sublimated desires in such a clear and focused way that one cannot make the claim that Hellman intended any kind of "twist" ending.

The word "unnatural" is a central one in *The Children's Hour*. It's repeated by Mary when she tells her easily swayed, spoiling grandmother, Mrs. Amelia Tilford, the big lie, thus lighting a match that becomes the play's all-consuming house fire. She's performing out of self-interest and bitterness at being punished by Martha and Karen, trying to find a way to not be sent back to school while turning the tables on her perceived punishers, but Mary could not have foreseen the ripple effect caused by her act of revenge. She's frighteningly wise beyond her years, even referring to the existence of a copy of Théophile Gautier's scandalous nineteenth-century novel *Mademoiselle de Maupin*, about a love triangle in which a woman seduces another woman. Yet she's also very much a child, given to infantile fits and temper tantrums. The wealthy Mrs. Tilford, who it's implied had been a crucial donor when Martha and Karen had founded the Wright-Dobie School for Girls, initially brushes off her granddaughter's words as idle gossip. Yet Mary doubles down, creating an intricate web of stories and insinuations, roping her classmate Rosalie into her scheme, blackmailing the girl into corroborating her lies by exploiting her guilt over having stolen another girl's necklace.

Hellman saw old Mrs. Tilford—an adult, in a position of power, ostensibly able to see through the child's damaging falsehoods—as her story's true evocation of banal political evil. After Mary whispers in her grandmother's ear about these "funny things" she has seen and heard at the school, the trembling woman can no longer hide her shock. Hellman's choice to leave the words inaudible, allowing them to fester in the minds of her characters and audience, is dramatically effective while also perhaps done out of necessity at a time when lesbianism was more commonly talked around. In an early draft, Hellman had used the word, uttered with disgust by Rosalie's mother to Karen when she decides to remove her daughter from the school: "I think it's called lesbianism—I really don't know—I—Mrs. Tilford said that you and Miss Dobie had had an unpleasant relationship." Ultimately, the word would not be said in either the final play or in the two Hollywood films eventually wrestled out of it. The most explicit words in the performed play's text come in the crucial scene that ends the first act, when Martha, Karen, and Joe descend upon Mrs. Tilford's house to defend themselves against the spreading gossip, and Karen says, torturously, that Mary has made claims that she and Martha were seen "kissing each other in a way that—women don't kiss one another." (Such phrasing also doesn't appear in either film version.)

The powerful and frustrating irony of Hellman's play—that it's centered on a fabricated, damaging falsehood about two women that obscures and finally reveals an essential truth about one of them—does more than dramatize the adage that "behind every lie there's a kernel of truth." The conceit and themes of *The Children's Hour* remain compelling nearly one hundred years later, and they have been durable enough to withstand multiple revivals and film adaptations within that period because Hellman makes the gap between the truth and the lie so wide. This is, after all, a 1934 play featuring a protagonist whose hidden homosexual desire leads to her tragic suicide, written by a heterosexual woman who insisted on having no knowledge of what it is like to harbor forbidden gay feelings. There nevertheless remains a striking power in Hellman's ability to dramatize the psychology of a woman terrified of being "found out" that would seem to go beyond mere empathy with outsiders.

It's remarkable the pains to which Hellman goes to separate Martha's turmoil—essentially her experience, however subsumed and negated, as a homosexual woman—from the "plot," which is to say Mary's machinations and Mrs. Tilford's dogmatism, and the ingrained American intolerance they represent. Functionally and structurally, Hellman scrupulously removes Martha's anguish from the social evils her self-hatred signifies, which has both humane and dramatic purpose: in outline, clear to anyone paying attention, this is the tale of a perverse society rather than a perverse individual. Once Martha "confesses" her love for Karen in the final act, the basic story has already ended. The school has been closed, the women's libel lawsuit against Mrs. Tilford has failed, and Karen has canceled her engagement to Joe. (An early draft shows a notable sexual sophistication in Joe's reaction to the scandal; when questioning Karen about whether the rumors are true, he says, "All I want to know is that it wasn't any more than what would be to a man a drunken evening that didn't matter in the morning. I mean I wouldn't care if you just went home with someone . . . if it's only that.") Having no one to reconcile with, all that's left for Martha is self-confrontation, which is made possible only at the moment of complete desolation and narrative removal. The brief closing scene, in which Mrs. Tilford arrives at the house to admit that she discovered Mary had made the whole thing up and that the judge will exonerate the women, further cements the walls between the play's interior (Martha's despair) and exterior (the scandal itself): Mrs. Tilford has come too late to save Martha and thus cannot restore equilibrium and order.

Martha's confession and subsequent death provide the emotional climax of the play, while also allowing Hellman to dramatically hammer home what she always claimed to be the central point of *The Children's Hour*: that a life can be destroyed by a lie. Yet in subsequent years, this moment has taken on an entirely other, grander, and more unsettling significance in a way that Hellman likely could not have predicted: as a troublingly foundational primal scene in the history of queer representation in American popular culture. "I *have* loved you the way they said!" Martha finally breaks down. "You've got to know it. I can't keep it to myself any longer. I've got to tell you that I'm guilty."

That word hangs in the air. Guilty. It's related to shame, to fear, to the closet—the closet that keeps guilt, shame, and fear thriving and alive and sinister. As Eve Kosofsky Sedgwick wrote fifty-six years later, "The gay closet is not a feature only of the lives of gay people. But for many gay people it is still the fundamental feature of social life; and there can be few gay people, however courageous and forthright by habit, however fortunate in the support of their immediate communities, in whose lives the closet is still not a shaping presence." The cataclysmic emotions Martha experiences are inherent to the American queer experience—valid, real, and, even today, inextricable from our understanding of what being gay means in a virulently heterosexist society.

When the play was originally performed, Hellman had Martha tearfully exclaim during her confession scene: "There's a big difference between us now, Karen. You feel sad and clean; I feel *sad* and *dirty*. I can't stay with you anymore darling." In an earlier draft, the line was: "It's all clean and tragic with you, it's all *dirty* and *tragic* with me. There's a wide gulf there, a very wide one." Yet in published versions of the play, including Random House collections of Hellman's work ranging from 1942 to 1979, the word "sad" is removed and the line has been altered to "I feel all dirty and—I can't stay with you anymore darling." In subsequent productions, there were further tweaks: "Oh, I feel so god-damned *sick* and *dirty*—I can't stand it anymore." Why Hellman felt the need to remove "sad" and add the word *sick* in the final estimation (the version of the line that would end up in the 1961 film adaptation) remains unclear, though the wording is consistent with homosexuality's categorization as a pathology in 1952's first edition of the *Diagnostic and Statistical Manual of Mental Disorders*. The constant throughout all these versions is *dirty*, however, a far more subjective word, one that likely registers differently to different viewers. It's wrong, immoral, a sin, that Martha is made to feel this way by society—and we may feel it's also wrong that she is forced to say these words by a playwright—but it's also entirely legible for someone living in a perverse society designed to steamroll anyone who would dare admit and own her marginalization.

Her furious self-loathing and sad death, depicted as an offstage gunshot, have made Martha Dobie a prototype of the doomed or tragic lesbian in popular culture. It's an oft-cited cliché that stretches back to Radclyffe Hall's *The Well of Loneliness* (1928), one of the most widely read and referenced lesbian novels of the twentieth century; can be traced in Djuna Barnes's masterwork of poetic abstraction *Nightwood* (1935); and reappears in movies like *The Fox* (1967) and even twenty-first-century television shows like *Buffy the Vampire Slayer*, in which the groundbreaking character of Tara (Amber Benson), the love interest of the show's prominent lesbian, Willow (Alyson Hannigan), is violently murdered to provoke Willow's—and the viewer's—rage. (Adding insult to injury, Tara's death was famously "restaged" week after week in "previously on" recaps that only emphasized her use as a tragic plot contrivance.) Often recessive, dour, and jealous, the Tragic Lesbian is as prevalent a stereotype as the Effeminate Pansy Male or the Predatory Butch Dyke as an easily definable bucket for queer experience—which does not make her any less worthy of study or empathy.

Martha's tale wouldn't achieve serious notoriety or cultural cachet until decades later, once this thread had been identified for its historical meaning. Though based on a preexisting type—the repressed, vaguely masculine schoolmarm—Martha was a singular stage creation, written by Hellman with an unmistakable compassion, even if that compassion came partly out of dramatic necessity. Hellman insisted throughout her career that *The Children's Hour* was "not about lesbianism," but rather the grandness of the lie; lesbianism is simply symbolic of the forbidden in the play, and there's little interest in what being a lesbian really means, other than the outsider status it designates. Hellman herself never showed any particular fondness for gay people or incipient gay causes or cultures during her lifetime, and she was given to the casual homophobia of her times. After being called "butch" in a 1976 *Baltimore Sun* profile, she wrote a furious letter to the editor, saying, "It does not matter that the clear intimation that I am a Lesbian happens to be a lie. It is low down stuff…" Other stories abound, such as referring to her friend Dorothy Parker's husband, Alan Campbell, whom she loathed, as a "fairy," and, by many accounts, flinging insinuating invective at Leonard Bernstein following their tortured collaboration on his 1956 operetta *Candide*, for which she wrote the libretto. (Ever Hellman's compadre, Dashiell Hammett reportedly called the semi-out Bernstein a "homo-exhibitionist"; Bernstein, for his part, referred to her privately as "Uncle Lillian.")

Hellman, cantankerous, impossible to please, and notoriously loose with facts about her own history, especially as she aged, may or may not have been telling the truth when tirelessly insisting upon her indifference to lesbianism as a theme of her play. Later, in the 1970s, when Hellman had reinvented herself as a literary icon, there would be, at least, a clue to Hellman's acknowledgment of a latent queerness in her own personal past. In her celebrated—and controversial—story "Julia," from her bestselling 1973 memoir *Pentimento*, she recalls the devotion she felt for her dear friend of the title, describing "the love I had for her, too strong and too complicated to be defined as only the sexual yearnings of one girl for another. And yet certainly that was there. I don't know, I never cared, and it is now an aimless guessing game." That "Julia," later adapted into an Oscar-winning movie of the same name in 1977, would become a site of infamous dispute after many critics and acquaintances claimed Hellman distorted or invented most aspects of the allegedly true tale, does nothing to quell the meaning of her casual admittance in those few lines quoted above. It's also worth noting that at several points during "Julia," set in the 1930s, she reminds readers that she had been hard at work on writing *The Children's Hour* while the events took place. Hellman's notorious bending of the truth is an indelible mark of fascination, and especially so when it comes to *The Children's Hour*, a sly way of getting critics and the public to talk about the very thing (homosexuality) she insists we don't have to talk about. *The Children's Hour* has proven to have a life of its own outside the contingencies and motivations of its hidebound representational strategies around gayness.

The controversy the play engendered even before it was staged is testament to Hellman's daring. Once she finished the enormous, attenuated task of writing and rewriting it with Hammett's editorial assistance, she set out to get the play produced, finding almost immediate interest in the project from those in the New York drama community with whom she had made inroads alongside her ex-husband, Arthur Kober. Among her most fortuitous and important connections was with an up-and-coming theater producer-director named Herman Shumlin, known—as Hellman would be—for a tempestuous manner and ambition. Their fates had first crossed when Shumlin directed and produced the smash 1930 Broadway melodrama *Grand Hotel* (adapted two years later into a Best Picture Oscar winner for MGM, a property that Hellman could take the credit for having first discovered while working as a script reader). Years later, their lives—professional and personal—would become intertwined when she approached Shumlin with her own work: an odd, risky project that was sure to meet with no small amount of controversy.

Upon returning to New York from her first extended stay in Hollywood, Hellman had rekindled Shumlin's acquaintance. A lover of melodrama, Shumlin was a second-generation American Jew of Russian and Ukrainian heritage who would go on to become one of Broadway's leading directors, unafraid to tackle big, potentially incendiary subjects for mainstream New York theater audiences; his credits would include the classic courtroom drama *Inherit the Wind* (1955) and two of Hellman's most successful later plays, *The Little Foxes* and *Watch on the Rhine* (1941). Though, like Hellman, Shumlin would prove willing to ruffle feathers, *The Children's Hour* was going to take stern constitutions to mount and unveil to a potentially wary public.

In 1926, producer Gilbert Miller had brought an American adaptation of a sensational French play, *The Captive* by Édouard Bourdet, to Broadway, but it had been shut down after its themes of tortured lesbianism had provoked outcries of obscenity. The "captive" of the title is Irène, an ambassador's daughter kept spiritually imprisoned by love for another woman, who remains entirely offstage. The scandal had in part erupted as a result of condemnations published in two separate William Randolph Hearst papers, the *New York Daily Mirror* and the *New York American*, leading to virulent campaigns against the play by morality policing institutions like the New York Society for the Suppression of Vice and the Colonial Dames of America, and even an indecency trial. Though charges were ultimately dropped, the firestorm only grew, reaching the attention of the mayor's office. In February 1927, police, under orders from the New York County district attorney, interrupted the second act of the performance and plucked the actors right off the stage, arresting them and tossing them into the back of a police van. Cited as prime evidence of a pervasive immorality in the New York theater scene, *The Captive* was shut down, as were a handful of other plays, including *The Drag* (1927), a groundbreaker that dealt with such taboo subjects as gay male intimacy and misogyny and was written by future Hollywood rabble rouser Mae West. The treatment of *The*

Captive in part led to the draconian Wales Padlock Law, which certified that the New York state legislature could close the curtain on any play that it judged to dramatize "sex degeneracy or sex perversion."

The New York theater of the twenties and thirties was thus marked by both a notable acknowledgment of homosexual themes and a resultant intense puritanical scrutiny. This followed the increasing permissibility of the Prohibition era, during which a gay subculture had emerged with surprising flair, leading to new cultural anxieties and crackdowns. Writes the gay historian George Chauncey, "A host of laws and regulations were enacted or newly enforced in the 1930s that suppressed the largest of the drag balls, censored lesbian and gay images in plays and films, and prohibited restaurants, bars, and clubs from employing homosexuals or even serving them."

Against this volatile backdrop, *The Children's Hour* was fearsome material. Even though the play could be viewed as breaking the law just by virtue of its subject matter, the excitement of Hellman's words and intricate plotting immediately grabbed Shumlin. Casting would prove a problem, especially for the role of Martha, as many leading women of the day refused to play a lesbian, or at least wanted to avoid attracting controversy for a play they were convinced the police would shut down. It took five months to fully cast *The Children's Hour*, which ended up pushing the play's premiere to the end of 1934.

It was just a day before rehearsals began that Hellman and Shumlin finally cast two women who had been mostly working in regional and stock theater troupes: Katherine Emery would be Karen Wright, and Anne Revere would take the role of Martha Dobie. While Emery is largely forgotten today (though any fan of Val Lewton's exquisite 1940s B-horror movies would remember her ghostly visage as the prematurely buried Mary St. Aubyn in 1945's *Isle of the Dead*), Revere would go on to be one of the most beloved screen character actors of the 1940s, exuding a natural, no-nonsense decency in both her Oscar-winning role as Elizabeth Taylor's mother in *National Velvet* (1944) and her Oscar-nominated one as Gregory Peck's mother in *Gentleman's Agreement* (1947). Perhaps even trickier than finding a serious-minded, undeterred actor like Revere to play Martha was the casting of the play's many roles for children. Considering the adult subject matter, Shumlin insisted that the girls all be played by women who were at least eighteen—even though they were written by Hellman as twelve to fourteen years of age, befitting a tale of seething prepubescent angst butting up against repressed adult sexuality.

After a prolonged search, they settled on Florence McGee as the schemer Mary, whose almost demonic self-regard provides the play's momentum. Born to British parents in South Africa, McGee was, according to *Time* magazine's eventual review, "a reed-slim actress of 23 who can pass on any stage for 13."

Throughout months of laborious rehearsals at the ornately designed but falling-into-disrepair Maxine Elliott's Theatre on Thirty-Ninth Street, the playwright, producer, cast, and crew all felt acute anxiety. Being shut down was a very real possibility—many felt a probability. Sitting in on a rehearsal, Lee Shubert, one of the owners of Maxine Elliott's, said out loud what everyone was trying to repress: "This play could land us all in jail."

Such fears were exacerbated by escalating tensions between Shumlin and Hellman, who threw herself into even the smallest aspects of the play's production, providing granular critiques about everything, chafing against Shumlin's firm, boss-like behavior and self-conviction as artistic visionary. When it became clear that Hellman wasn't going to back down, and that she saw her work as *her work* and needed to have her complaints and corrections heard, Shumlin wisely began to regard her as a collaborator rather than an adversary. He agreed to incorporate her thoughts, listen to her concerns, and make sure she was always a part of the process—despite the fact that he worked with an almost equally obsessive attention to detail. The two would end up collaborating on and off in the coming decades, both of them demanding perfectionists who somehow allowed their similarities to unite them rather than drive a wedge between them.

One can glean a sense of the intense, bottled emotion of the production of *The Children's Hour* that opened on Broadway on November 20, 1934, from a photograph of Revere and Emery onstage. While most of the existing images of the play have that fusty, mannered, drawing-room quality one might expect from mechanized publicity stills of a suffocating, interiorized thirties melodrama, in this black-and-white shot we see the two women standing before a fireplace; Emery's hands are clasped as though in prayer, while Revere grabs the other woman's wrists. They are looking into each other's eyes with a vivid, rocking intensity—there is no fire in the sad, unlit hearth behind Emery, but the spare room seems ablaze anyway, if only from their passionate expressions. Revere and Emery appear to be the same height, and both are wearing ankle-length skirts and matching black belts, although Revere's entirely black outfit—as opposed to Emery's lighter-colored sweater—lends Martha a more ominous, funereal bearing. In most other photographs,

Martha and Karen are surrounded by others, angrily arguing with Mary, or Mrs. Tilford, or Aunt Lily; here it is just the two of them, and they look at each other as though there's no one else in the world. This must be the scene in which Martha tells the wrenching truth about her attraction for Karen and comes to an epiphany about herself, the scene in which she says "I do love you," in which she says she feels "sad and dirty," in which she says "Maybe I wanted you all along."

These are difficult emotions for any playwright—or actor, or director—of any era to express, let alone in 1934 when expressing them meant the very real possibility of stigmatizing censorship. One cannot overestimate how much the vividness and sensitivity of their presentation—by Hellman, by Shumlin, by Revere—allowed for *The Children's Hour* to become the sensation that it did, not just critically but also with audiences. The play was an unexpected, unprecedented smash, running for 691 performances and garnering ecstatic reviews. In the *Daily Mirror*, Walter Winchell exclaimed, "It spellbound the first audience last night with its incessant tenseness . . . *The Children's Hour* will probably attract playgoers for a long run." The *Daily News* critic Burns Mantle called it "the biggest drama of the year and the boldest," and his review was punctuated by a large photo of Florence McGee with the caption "Diabolically perfect." McGee turned out to be the production's headline grabber, with articles lauding her Mary as the kid you love to hate. Entire columns were devoted to her in the *Herald Tribune* ("not in years has the stage been visited by a villainess of such dark and troubled dye as this juvenile archfiend") and the *Sunday News*, which featured a photo-laden full-page testament to "The Hell Child."

In the first sentence of his front page arts section review in the *New York Times*, Brooks Atkinson called *The Children's Hour* a "stinging tragedy . . . vigorously planned and written and so trenchantly acted." He goes on to praise Mary as "the sensation of this play, and Miss McGee's acting is one of those triumphs that take a playgoer's breath away." Overall, the review is a love letter, going into detail about the injustice at the center of the plot, of the horror of being accused of something untrue: "Miss Hellman has based her drama on the fact of their innocence," he writes, and "she has shown how circumstances arouse public opinion against Karen and Martha and brand them as social exiles."

However, despite this sensitive reading of the play and generalized use of the term "social exiles," the critic never mentions the final admission of Martha's lesbianism. In a strange, casual dismissal of the play's devastating final act, he writes, in a single throwaway line in his last paragraph: "There is a rule-of-thumb confession and a routine suicide." Atkinson's intimation that Martha's suicide was a gut-punch device for dramatic expediency, rather than offering something genuine about the character and enabling something theatrically transgressive, is revealing—and is ironic considering that decades later, *The Children's Hour* would be remembered predominantly for Martha's suicide, and that the suicide would be considered "routine" for reasons quite different than dramatic expediency.

The review makes one wonder how many theatergoers loved the play in spite of its themes and final revelations rather than allowing themselves to even cursorily wrestle with their implications. That said, one cannot discount the marginalized lesbian audiences of the day who contributed to the box office returns of movies starring Greta Garbo, Marlene Dietrich, and Katharine Hepburn. Mementoes from Hellman's own personal files reveal fascinating, even touching evidence about the diverse responses from audiences in the 1930s, reminders that queer or queer-sympathetic viewers were integral members of the theatergoing public. A hand-written letter from November 24, 1934, addressed to Hellman from a woman going by the name of Mary Frank implies that the film's themes—and words—held personal power, positive and negative. Though she writes that the play made "a profound and lasting impression on me," she was also troubled by certain aspects of it:

> There was but one thing in the whole production that jarred, and that is when Martha in telling Karen the difference between herself and Karen said, "You are sad and clean. I am sad and dirty." I can't rid myself of the impression that the offensive word "dirty" left. It sounds so physical—as if the girl had not taken a bath for some time. After that, Martha's suicide is an anticlimax. She is already dead. Several of my friends have felt the same way about the use of the word "dirty," believing that it does not convey what you mean to express. One could not question your wizardry with words after seeing your play, and it seems to me that you certainly could substitute a less filthy and physical medium to express the torment of a distraught and perhaps spiritually unclean Martha.

Hellman received a beseeching, bold, and even more poignant letter in late 1935, after the show had been running for more than a year, from a woman named Emma:

Writing this letter in the public library on an impulse. I hope you receive it safely . . . I have contacted a group of young people who are fine, worthy, and deserve to be helped in their young effort to live their own lives. You know the struggle one has in trying to submit mans. [manuscripts] to an editor on this theme of homosexuality. So, this group and myself have decided to publish a magazine of our own. We have pooled our pennies, lived on the barest food, and was [*sic*] able to rent a mimeograph machine and typewriter for a month. Our month is up Dec. 8, 1935. We obtained enough paper to put together this mag of 18 pages, which we have named "Trend." We aspire to reach tolerant, broad-minded, intelligent people, who will buy because we have something to give them: great beauty, keen insight, creative power, and intellect.

These letters, hidden among Hellman's papers in her archive, are revelatory. They provide moving, anecdotal evidence of vibrant, hidden groups and societies of sensitive gay New York intellectuals, manifestations of George Chauncey's reminder that "From the late nineteenth century on, a handful of gay New Yorkers wrote polemical articles and books, sent letters to hostile newspapers and published their own, and urged jurists and doctors to change their views." One can only dream of extant copies of *Trend*—decades before such transformative underground gay publications as the *Mattachine Review* and *The Ladder* would be published. Also revealing is the fact that Hellman kept these papers—along with the countless fan letters she must surely have received—among her personal possessions. Such letters indicate that *The Children's Hour*'s status as a cultural object varied dramatically depending on who was watching and experiencing it, and that Hellman was aware of the passions it ignited. The incredible success of the play, and the instant fame it brought Hellman, prove that most New Yorkers could at least look past their own discomfort with the forbidden subject matter—after all, audiences uninterested in a play about lesbianism (which Hellman would always say *The Children's Hour* was not) could redirect their sympathies to its themes of destructive lies and intolerance. *The Children's Hour* was so beloved in New York's sophisticated circles that one of its greatest scandals came when it *didn't* win the Pulitzer Prize for Drama in 1934, which many felt the sensational play had been a shoo-in for; the loss is credited with precipitating the creation of a new prize the following year: the New York Drama Critics Circle Award.

Even though *The Children's Hour* found receptive and appreciative audiences on Broadway, its success didn't translate to other cities. The play had become such a target for panicked conservatives that it was banned from being produced in London, Chicago, or Boston. The latter's mayor, Frederick Mansfield, went so far as to issue a decree that this "portrayal of a moral pervert or a sex degenerate" would never be produced in Boston. Mansfield, the primary defendant of the ensuing court case, of course did not see the play himself, taking the word of his city censor that "the theme centers about homosexuality and nothing could be done with the play to relieve it of this." The ban was upheld for more than thirty years, despite a public censorship battle Shumlin and the American Civil Liberties Union waged on the decision in 1936, when the director sued the City of Boston for $250,000 in damages. Shumlin lost, but the case is considered a landmark. In 2015, the ACLU published an article about the history of the case, stating, "*The Children's Hour* helped establish the ACLU's reputation for defending art and literature from censorship and marked the ACLU's first involvement in LGBT issues," indicating that at least in terms of artistic expression, the play has come to be seen by some as a political game changer. Though in her lifetime she denied its importance as a work about marginalized gay identity, Hellman, a tireless social crusader for other causes throughout her career, would likely have approved.

The Boston censor was right about one thing—that "nothing could be done with the play to relieve it" of its homosexual themes. Only a fool would change *The Children's Hour* and risk denuding it of its essence. But as Hellman herself might snicker, Hollywood was a town of fools.

"You can say what you like in the theater within any reasonable bounds," Hellman said in 1936. "You have a liberty of speech and editorial expression you can't find in any other dramatic medium. And you can present an idea for the consideration of intelligent audiences, which, of course, is completely outside the gaudiest opium dreams of possibility in Hollywood."

.   .   .

By the time she gave this interview, Hellman had returned to Hollywood, this time a runaway success in New York. The comparatively vast creative freedom of the theater scene back east would only reinforce Hellman's view of Los Angeles as provincial. This opinion would be more acute than it had been just a few years earlier during her first, failed Hollywood sojourn. Hellman would now discover—and be part of—a changed industry. There had been widespread permissiveness in the movies during the early thirties, but things had altered drastically. The studios had capitulated to years of intensifying pressure: a newly entrenched Production Code meant Hollywood would never be the same, bowing to an unprecedented and effective form of censorship. A fearless creation like Martha Dobie would be impossible in the movies, now and for the foreseeable future. However, this didn't stop Hellman and her fellow gaudy opium dreamers from trying to capture for a mass audience the dramatic essence of a play about the unspoken and the unspeakable.

2

The Children

American movie history overflows with stories of drastic alterations, of perversions of intent, of will-o'-the-wisp versions so estranged from their source material that they come across as evocations rather than adaptations. This was especially true in 1930s Hollywood, when sound cinema was still finding its voice, its audience, and its standing amid a society wringing hands over the extent of its power.

After her failed Hollywood outing at the beginning of the decade, Lillian Hellman had come back with a Broadway smash under her belt, and there's nothing that town likes more than a hit. She said in 1935, "The most interesting part of my trip to Hollywood is that that I'm going back to take a job at just thirty times what the movies paid me the last time I worked for them." By January 1936 she had signed a three-year contract with the producer Samuel Goldwyn for the impressive salary of $2,500 a week, stipulating that she had to produce two scripts a year. For her second big project, she was tasked with adapting a wildly successful Broadway play—her own. Translating her stage hit to the screen promised to be a rewarding challenge. There was a significant catch: She would have to change everything about it. Even the title.

It would have been pure disillusionment for a starry-eyed dreamer. It was a good thing that Hellman, now twenty-nine, was already disabused of illusion.

A pragmatist whose time in Hollywood was always more about curiosity than indulging in fantasy, Hellman remained fascinated to see how the factory made the sausage, and how she might squeeze some of it herself.

Hellman's undertaking was laborious, to make something unrecognizable out of her own work that at the same time recreated the exciting, lacerating drama it provoked. The story of two schoolteachers accused by a malicious, vengeful student of carrying on a lesbian affair would seem to be impossible even in outline: any inference of such a relationship was strictly verboten under the newly enforced Motion Picture Production Code. Then there was the climactic revelation of Martha's romantic feelings for Karen, the tear-soaked admittance that led to that tragic denouement. That ending—and the entire premise—would have to go.

The first question would rightly be: why? Why would a studio bother spending money on the rights to a property already dogged by scandal? Anyone with even a basic understanding of the movie industry of the 1930s, let alone a Hollywood mogul, would know the difficulty of adapting it to the screen with any semblance of fidelity. And the amount spent was substantial. The producer Samuel Goldwyn, a veteran Hollywood figure known for both his pugnacity and a glorified, almost self-parodic obtuseness, paid $50,000 ($1.5 million when translated for inflation) for the film rights to Hellman's play. It was the considerable name recognition of *The Children's Hour*, as well as Hellman's persuasion, that encouraged Goldwyn to purchase it—ironic since its title would be altered to *avoid* name recognition. Goldwyn's professional relationship with Hellman was the other major factor in his decision to jump at the property: the two had just finished working on the prestigious 1935 melodrama *The Dark Angel*, a box office hit that had earned two Oscar nominations. Hellman shared with Goldwyn a fighting spirit, a Jewish background, and an allergy to wish-wash. She was quickly rising to the top of the ranks to become Goldwyn's favorite.

A titanic personality who stood out even amid Hollywood's sea of outsized egos, Goldwyn (born Szmuel Gelbfisz in Warsaw's Jewish ghetto in 1882, renamed Samuel Goldfish when he emigrated to America in 1899) had been a major industry player ever since he formed his self-named studio in 1916. He had a reputation for being more devoted to writers than to stars, giving Samuel Goldwyn Pictures Corporation a literary air rather than one of modish frivolity—an anomaly and an increasing liability in an industry that would be ever more devoted to the box office bottom line. In 1919, Goldwyn had even created a production unit called Eminent

Authors, Inc., which allowed famous writers to adapt their own works to the screen for a good salary and guaranteed top billing. The pursuit failed, but Goldwyn's focus on writers marks a fascinating footnote that contrasts sharply with the famously sour, combative relationship with screenwriters that Hollywood producers would mythically boast throughout the coming decades. Goldwyn continued to crave the skills of savvy, street-smart writers like Hellman, the kind of intellect who might elevate an industry many cultured people still looked down their nose at.

Hellman had been unimpressed with Hollywood upon her first trip to Los Angeles, when she felt like a hanger-on to both her husband Arthur Kober and her lover Dashiell Hammett. She didn't resent being in California this second time around: while she remained suspicious of the town's simultaneous fear and envy of East Coast intellectualism, success can change a person. Though some established authors and playwrights from the east considered a Hollywood paycheck a form of selling out, it was work that she'd come to admire. "Writers would talk about themselves as whoring in Hollywood," she later said. "No, it never occurred to me that such a thing could be true. I was genuinely interested in movies. I genuinely did my best. I didn't come from the generation that felt any such degradation."

Hellman's true feelings about the difference between theater and cinema, though, might be best revealed in a seeming throwaway line in the first scene of *The Children's Hour*. "Cinema is a shallow art. It has no . . . no . . . fourth dimension." These words are spoken by Aunt Lily, the self-made theater grand dame. Though she is an entirely unlikable character, and in many ways the play's unsung villain, a woman whose flighty selfishness leads to Martha and Karen's downfall, Lily seems to be speaking for Lillian Hellman here. The movies were for stargazing; the theater, for Hellman, was truth, reality, a way to communicate important ideas to receptive audiences who were looking to be jolted awake rather than pampered into dreamland.

Hellman's eight-year post at Goldwyn would prove richly, surprisingly satisfying for this newly respected luminary of the East Coast intellectual set. She got Hollywood down—the rhythms and cadences of screenwriting but also the status-seeking of a town she once deemed silly. Hellman easily fit in as "one of the boys" at the studio, and her extracurricular hours were devoted to expanding her already vast and impressive social circle, only this time she wasn't just meeting them through Kober or Hammett. And after *The Dark Angel*, she had become a necessary right arm to the volatile Goldwyn. That experience, for all its success, had also been

Hellman's first exposure to the strictures of the Motion Picture Production Code, which had recently and quite drastically transformed the movie business, and which made the playwright's recent run-ins with the morality police back in the New York theater world seem loosey-goosey by comparison.

. . .

It's noteworthy, even a little humorous, that Hellman, an outspoken arbiter of independent thought who had little time for the closed-minded, was becoming a part of Hollywood at the very moment that the industry had begun officially submitting to a puritanical code of ethics. The newfound state of Hollywood as a willing participant in its own strict regulations was a great irony as well, one of epochal proportions: a town built by Jewish entrepreneurs, almost all of them first- or second-generation immigrants from Eastern Europe, was suddenly at the mercy of a profound, censorious Catholicism.

To fully understand where the film industry's newly formalized moral rigidity had come from—and why it would last for the next thirty years, forever altering how Golden Age of Hollywood movies would be made and perceived, and how multitudes of Americans would see not just movies but also the off-screen world around them—one must travel back to the early 1920s. This is when Hollywood was living through the growing pains of becoming the culture-leveling entity we think we know and understand from countless hagiographic history books, talking head interviews, and misty-lensed documentary clip reels: a factory slowly building into an entertainment empire, run by both bottom-line-obsessed moneymen and a growing contingent of artistically motivated craftsmen. This is the birth of the split personality that would forever define American cinema, an industry that always made art and commerce strange bedfellows, triggering debates that rage to this day about the meaning (or the possibility) of film art.

In the early twentieth century, however, Hollywood already had a much less philosophical identity crisis on its hands. By the twenties, there had been a consumerist uptick in the United States, and with the First World War in the rearview mirror, affluent and middle-class Americans were spending their hard-earned dollars on radios, cars, and newfangled kitchen appliances that promised to make their lives easier and more enjoyable. In Los Angeles, the boom translated to an influx of new workers who had moved west, seduced by the lure of movies as much as the location's oil fields and automobile manufacturers, and the city saw its population double between 1920 and 1925. Hollywood would eventually become a city within that city, made up of a series of villages (studios) founded by Jews of Eastern European birth or descent like Carl Laemmle, William Fox, Adolph Zukor, Jesse Lasky, Louis B. Mayer, and Jack and Harry Warner, émigrés or their first-generation offspring whose desire to fully assimilate into the gentile mainstream resulted in the mass entertainment of, respectively, Universal Pictures, the Fox Film Corporation (later Twentieth Century-Fox), Famous Players–Lasky Film Company (later Paramount Pictures), Metro-Goldwyn-Mayer, and Warner Bros. However, by the early twenties, the wholesome images they put on screens were frequently undercut by stories of real-life scandals and off-set licentiousness. Thanks to an incessant stream of sensational newspaper articles and a nonstop rumor mill, the public had the idea of Hollywood as a lair of iniquity and debasement. The movies would soon be a target for moralizers already suspicious of a medium that was proving to exert significant power over audiences hungry for cheap attractions.

When discussing the evils and misdeeds of Hollywood stars of this era, the sad case of Roscoe "Fatty" Arbuckle and Virginia Rappe is frequently referred to as the original sin. A hotel worker turned vaudevillian, the rotund yet balletically graceful comedy star had become such a popular comedic figure of the silent film industry that in 1921 Paramount offered him an unheard-of $3 million, three-year contract. Over Labor Day weekend of that year, Arbuckle threw a lavish party at the St. Francis Hotel to celebrate his new contract; this turned into a multiple-day binge fueled by bootleg booze. The twenty-six-year-old Rappe, an aspiring actress who was among the guests invited to Arbuckle's twelfth-floor suite, was heard screaming in pain from his bedroom. Examined and sent home by a hotel doctor, Rappe died three days later in the hospital of complications from a punctured bladder. A friend and companion told authorities Arbuckle had raped her, leading to her fatal injuries. Arbuckle denied the charges, yet the case captured the public's imagination, and he quickly became a symbol of Hollywood's wanton villainy. The highly covered trial lasted from November 1921 to April 1922; following two hung juries, a third trial found Arbuckle not guilty and he was set free. The damage to the comedian's reputation ended his career, though, and the overall perception of the industry took a hit as well. *Variety*'s headline about the case in September 1921 indicated the widespread belief that this wasn't merely a "Fatty" problem: WORLDWIDE CONDEMNATION OF PICTURES AS AFTERMATH OF ARBUCKLE AFFAIR, MUST RID FILMS OF DOPESTERS, DEGENERATES, AND PARASITES—CLEANLINESS IN

PRODUCING AND ACTING RANKS WILL BE REFLECTED ON SCREENS—
CHURCHES AGITATING AGAINST PICTURES.

The article's positioning of the scandal as the final straw of a perceived wider social problem was a sign of things to come: Hollywood's most vehement detractors began denouncing the town as a veritable Sodom and Gomorrah. The tragic stories were piling up with sensational swiftness. There were the high-profile suicides of Selznick Pictures's twenty-five-year-old movie star Olive Thomas and the twenty-two-year-old Famous Players–Lasky screenwriter Zelda Crosby. In 1922, the papers pored over the details of filmmaker William Desmond Taylor's shooting murder—still a cold case, though at the time Mabel Normand, an actress, filmmaker, and frequent Charlie Chaplin co-star, was implicated in the scandal. Two years later, another Normand scandal erupted when her chauffeur used her pistol to shoot and wound the oil tycoon Courtland Dines. In 1923, the handsome thirty-one-year-old movie star Wallace Reid died from morphine and alcohol addiction. Some studios responded to this litany of disgraces by making public shows of righteousness, as when Universal added a "morality clause" to its contracts with all new and established stars. Of course, there was no way to enforce these clauses aside from a hand slap or a tsk-tsk; the "Babylon" of Hollywood was its own, enclosed world, and to an increasing number of self-created good-soul Catholics aghast at what they saw, a godless one headed for a reckoning.

The accumulation of these events lit the fuse that would eventually lead to the explosive censoring of the American movie industry, though it was a slow and sometimes painful process. Soon after the end of the Arbuckle affair, 1922 saw the formation of the Motion Picture Producers and Distributors of America, established by Will Hays, a lawyer from Indiana who had risen to become the former postmaster general under President Harding. The MPPDA operated under the assumption of cooperative self-regulation from the studios, "to foster the common interests of those engaged in the motion picture industry by establishing and maintaining the highest possible moral and artistic standards of motion picture production." Four years would pass before the group started putting pen to paper: in 1926, Hays established the Studio Relations Committee, a group absorbed into the MPPDA, and with his associates made a list of "Do's and Don'ts" (the latter encompassing eleven things that could not be shown on-screen, including miscegenation, white slavery, and "sexual perversion") and "Be Carefuls" (twenty-six "dangerous" subjects, which included murder, rape, arson, and excessive kissing). This inventory of forbidden content was devised as a series of strong suggestions, yet these would ultimately be the building blocks for the enforced changes that altered the industry in the mid-1930s.

While Hollywood was doing its best to evade or outright ignore the mostly wishy-washy efforts of the MPPDA to regulate throughout the 1920s, a figure was rising in the Midwest who would change all that. Joseph Ignatius Breen's name might not be as well known as the famed producers, directors, and stars whose names grace film credit lists, but he would be one of the most powerful and feared men in Hollywood history. Born in Philadelphia in October 1888, Breen shuttled between jobs in public relations, newspaper journalism, and the U.S. consular service, yet the connecting thread was always his deep, proud, stern Irish Catholicism. His relationship to powerful members of the Catholic community had begun in his Jesuit alma mater, St. Joseph's College, and continued through his work facilitating access of European Catholics to America for the Bureau of Immigration, his publicity campaigning for books such as *Catholic Builders of the Nation: A Symposium on the Catholic Contribution to the Civilization of the United States*, and his editorship and writing at the monthly *National Catholic Welfare Council Bulletin*—a pulpit from which he denounced anti-Catholic bigotry and Soviet Communism in equal measure.

His associations with these various Catholic institutions landed him a gig in 1925 that would prove a turning point in his career: publicity director for the 28th International Eucharistic Congress. This massive, worldwide gathering of Roman Catholics would take place the following June in Chicago—the nation's most Catholic city—and Pope Pius XI was set to make a rare appearance. Not only would Breen oversee the mind-boggling commercial and PR logistics of this event—while also working as the PR man for the city's archbishop—he would end up running the exhibition and publicity campaign for a documentary feature about the event made by the Fox Film Corporation, with copyrights and profits donated to the Catholic Church. After its gala premiere in November 1926, at Jolson's Fifty-Ninth Street Theatre in New York, with a full orchestra performing the musical score before a sold-out crowd of 1,770 people, the ninety-six-minute movie went on the road, performing especially well in cities with Catholic populations.

Breen's success was noted by the Catholic clergymen, clerics, politicians, and businessmen with whom he had become tight, but also, crucially, by certain men from Hollywood. Will Hays, like Breen a Catholic, had come to the premiere as a prescreening guest speaker, extoling the film's ability to convey the awe, beauty, and importance of religion and faith. Through these circumstances, Breen was formally introduced to Hays, and another devout Irish Catholic who would become an integral figure in the history of cinematic regulation: Martin J. Quigley, the editor and publisher of *Exhibitors Herald* (later known as *Motion Picture Herald*), as well as the man who had brokered the deal between Fox and the Church to produce the Eucharistic Congress documentary. Breen's Catholic bona fides were essential to his steady climb up the ladder in this microcosm of American religious (and business) life, but just as important was his ability to get results. Breen was the type of guy you'd want on your side in a meeting: a hearty schmoozer and a savvy diplomat, with a boisterous, barrel-chested personality.

In July 1929, Breen attended a meeting at Loyola University that would change his life. At a special administrative council of Catholic laymen, a Jesuit pastor from Chicago's South Side named Rev. FitzGeorge Dinneen was in a rage about a movie he had just seen, *The Trial of Mary Dugan*, starring the future Oscar winner Norma Shearer as a showgirl accused of fatally stabbing her wealthy lover. Dinneen deemed it a work of filth that never should have passed the Chicago Board of Censors and been allowed to contaminate the locals, especially unwitting churchgoers. Quigley, also attending the meeting, nodded in agreement at the film's outrageousness yet suggested that boycotts, angry letters, and suing Hollywood studios would achieve nothing. The industry had to be taught to properly self-regulate, and while Hays's MPPDA rules, already three years old, symbolized a start, a stricter set of guidelines was needed. The collection of concerned Catholics kept expanding. They next employed the assistance of a Jesuit priest from St. Louis named Daniel A. Lord. A musician and movie lover, Lord had served as the Catholic on-set adviser for Cecil B. De Mille's religious Hollywood epic *The King of Kings* (1927). From this conversation among a group of Catholic laymen in Chicago, only one of whom had ever set foot in Hollywood, the Code was effectively born.

The advent of sound cinema with 1927's *The Jazz Singer* had made the industry both excited and jittery. By 1930, audiences were desperate for musical extravaganzas like *The Broadway Melody* (1929) and gripping "talkie" dramas like *The Letter* (1929). But Hollywood was biting its fingernails waiting for the effects of September 1929's catastrophic stock market crash to hit, and expensive new equipment wasn't making the transition to sound any easier. Hays, seeking a new way for the MPPDA to establish its legitimacy, was intrigued by the new document written by Quigley and Lord, with assistance from Breen. After a few meetings, the group formally ratified it on March 31.

The Code writers may have had no federal jurisdiction and therefore no real authority over them, but the self-regulating producers and studio heads initially chose to mostly concede and cooperate with the new Code parameters and suggestions. By 1931—during Lillian Hellman's failed first Hollywood trip—the reverberations of the 1929 crash, which dramatically put an end to the roaring twenties, were starting to be felt in Hollywood. The movie industry was about to go through its own temporary Great Depression. Despite a wealth of fresh stars and directors cadged from the New York stage, and a trove of expensive new cameras and sound recording equipment, box office was plummeting, dropping to a third of its former weekly moviegoers. Some studios had to severely cut corners, such as Paramount, which filed for bankruptcy in 1933 and shut down its storied East Coast headquarters in Astoria, Queens. One response from many of the studios was to begin flouting the rules laid out in the Production Code. This era revealed the Code's seemingly eager adoption by Hollywood as little more than a kiss-off gesture intended to mollify the angry Catholics out east. Even with the new Code, Hays's Studio Relations Committee was barely making a dent: though studios submitted films for approval, studios were allowed to appeal if they didn't pass, usually successful in arguing their cases to the appeals board, which were mostly made up of producer colleagues entirely sympathetic to the burdens of costly reshoots and re-edits.

With the Code basically ineffective, and studios responding to a disturbing downturn in ticket sales by trying to attract audiences with sensational subject matter, a storied, brief passage in Hollywood history began, now commonly referred to as the "pre-Code" era. This was a delectable sliver of time when the movies—which had just found their literal voice—were able and willing to offer up unhealthy doses of sexual suggestiveness, uncouth behavior, gangland violence, and adulterous melodramas, often without significant consequences for their characters. These were the years of the unapologetically horny comedies of Mae West, like *She Done Him Wrong* and *I'm No Angel*; grim relationship dramas like *Merrily We Go to Hell* and *Blonde Venus*; kinky comic confections like Ernst Lubitsch's *The Love Parade* and *Design for Living*; and gleefully sadistic mobster dramas like *Scarface* and *The Public Enemy*. Standards of the day dictated that homosexuality was still a verboten topic, yet at this point, there were outwardly queer characters and situations that would pop up on-screen in not particularly condemnatory ways. For the most part, these movies essentially played it safe and chaste, yet watched today, their tenor is distinct, even shockingly so, from the adulterated forms that came later.

The Catholic church's moral arbiters were newly incensed at what seemed like flagrant rule-flouting. No one was more outraged—or personally disappointed—than Breen. Hays first brought Breen to Hollywood on July 14, 1931, officially hiring the go-getter as his trusty assistant. Functioning as a cordial go-between for the Hays office and the motion picture studios, Breen confirmed his talent for mediating. Breen was disgusted, even shocked, by his first years in Los Angeles, witnessing the den of sin up close. It was an environment that brought out his latent anti-Semitism; soon after relocating, he wrote memos describing his new Jewish colleagues as "dirty lice" and "the scum of the scum of the earth." Despite his hand-wringing over how low Hollywood could go, Breen was personally riding high: by 1933, the country may have been in an economic free fall, with a quarter of its population unemployed, but Breen and his family lived more than comfortably in their Beverly Hills home and had a beach house in Malibu. Despite his already strong standing in the community, few in Hollywood could predict how much power Breen would soon have over them.

Back east, the Catholic campaign was revived in full force, and Breen was surreptitiously involved. Lord, Quigley, and their brethren were humiliated by their Code's lack of effectiveness. Lord wrote a pamphlet called *The Motion Pictures Betray America*, writing that Hollywood had enacted "the most terrible betrayal of public trust in the history of our country," and Breen had helped spruce up a speech given by Archbishop Amleto Giovanni Cicognani, a representative for the Pope, at a national Catholic conference in New York, in which he made the astonishing statement, "Catholics are called by God, the Pope, the bishops and priests to a united front and vigorous campaign for the purification of the cinema, which has become a deadly menace to morals." Meanwhile, Henry James Forman's 1933 bestseller *Our Movie Made Children* had proselytized on the deleterious effects movies were having on children, fomenting outrage even outside religious circles, putting fear into the hearts of parents everywhere. The true crusade had begun. In 1934, Catholics took the bold step of forming a new organization called the National Legion of Decency, which vowed to boycott any pictures it found offensive. Today, this might sound like an empty or casual threat, yet with millions of church members (an article in *Variety* estimated it at twenty million) being asked to sign pledges of support, this would be destructive for an industry that couldn't afford box office failure.

On February 5, 1934, Breen was appointed head of the Studio Relations Committee, which would now be tasked with Code enforcement. But the real changes occurred on June 13, when the MPPDA board of directors passed a resolution replacing the Studio Relations Committee with the Production Code Administration, and on July 15, when Breen officially took on the role of PCA head. The "pre-Code" era was officially over: all studios or independent producers who wanted to see their films distributed in theaters would have to get a Certificate of Approval stamp; a violation of the rules would incur a massive $25,000 fine. Making it more effective, censoring would happen at the script stage, cutting down the possibility for costly last-minute changes and establishing the PCA's control early in the process. With Breen in charge, the Catholics back east eased up, and a new era was born.

Breen's intrinsic disgust of Hollywood would make him the perfect enforcer for its code of conduct. In letters, he openly excoriated the town, writing that "sexual perversion is rampant" and calling the studio moguls "lousy Jews." Fueled by an unerring sense of righteousness, and sure that he was a crucial creative collaborator in the process of making movies, Breen took his job seriously, and the industry now had no choice but to take him seriously in turn. It would require a little persuading of the public as well as the press: Breen's appointment was initially met with skepticism in the trade papers, and there were reports that the image of the Code seal before a movie was drawing the occasional derisive hiss from audience members. But with cooperation from distributors and theater exhibitors, the PCA was a raging success, and it ultimately would review every movie in Hollywood for decades to come. In a 1934 Universal Newsreel made to introduce Breen to the world as a friendly, avuncular figure rather than the forbidding hatchet man who had been written up in the press, he can be seen sitting at the head of a boardroom table, surrounded by a gaggle of other suited white men. Defensively denying that his job amounts to censorship, he states directly to the camera that the American movies will heretofore be "the vital and wholesome entertainment we all want these to be."

By the end of 1934, box office revenue went sky high. Breen and his fellow Code enforcers were all too happy to take the credit, whether they had earned it or not. By the middle of the decade, Mae West was a faint memory, the last ember of a dirty-minded culture, and Shirley Temple was the biggest movie star in the United States. Decades later, it would become clear that Breen was as influential a figure as the movie industry ever produced. Read his 1965 *Variety* obituary: "More than any single individual, he shaped the moral stature of the American motion picture."

. . .

Because there is such a clear, nearly mythical dividing line between before and after its input, the Motion Picture Production Code is frequently discussed in terms of harm and closed-minded censorship. To call the code a document of right-wing propaganda, however, is to oversimplify what was intended by many of its original drafters to be a guide for progressive social reform. Many of the strictures of the Code remain today unquestionable, like calling for the protection of children and the scrupulous visual treatment of women's bodies. The document itself is verified at the outset as a collaboration "with educators, dramatists, church authorities and leaders in the field of child education and social welfare work," an attempt to enhance its forward-thinking egalitarianism and cooperative idealism. Yet while certain Code stipulations would still be agreed upon by most every living person (the directive that "children's sex organs are never to be exposed," and the marking of "actual hangings or electrocutions" and "cruelty to children and animals" as Repellent Subjects), the Code as written mostly expresses a governing body's highly subjective interpretation of morality, which becomes especially knotty when applied to the world of art and illusion.

It's clear from the outset that the Code's writers believed in their own lofty ambitions: "Mankind has always regarded the importance of entertainment and its value in rebuilding the bodies or souls of human beings." As it continues, the Code promises as one of its core principles that "No picture shall be produced which will lower the moral standards of those who see it. Hence the sympathy of the audience should never be thrown to the side of crime, wrongdoing, evil, or sin." Such savvily constructed sentences might sound reasonable until one begins to question the vast chasm between what any two given human beings might deem morally reprehensible. After all, the Nazi party, which had begun its rise to power in Germany after Hitler's election to chancellor just one year earlier and which would consolidate its national power in August 1934, set out its own harsh guidelines about acceptable versus deviant subject matter in books, films, and other entertainment. (Artists and writers deemed morally degenerate included Erich Maria Remarque, Franz Kafka, and Albert Einstein.)

To read the entire Code is to descend into a spiral of dubious edicts and assertions cloaked in sensible language. For example, "The technique of murder must be presented in a way that will not inspire imitation." A no-brainer, perhaps, though who is this supposed imitator getting his ideas from the movies? (These sorts of debates about violence have remained in the culture ever since, resurrected around television, movies, and video games whenever politicians or religious figures need a scapegoat for larger, seemingly unfixable social ills.) Then there is the section stating that seduction or rape is "never the proper subject for comedy." The conflating of seduction and rape as essentially the same raises more questions about representation and terminology than the stipulation itself could ever possibly handle.

Among the most lasting of the vaguely described demands would be the Code's code for homosexuality: "Sex perversion or any inference to it is forbidden." That one line, casually tossed in halfway down the list, is nothing less than a blueprint for the historical disappearance of outward queerness from American cinema. Not only would the representation of gays, lesbians, bisexuals, and any other non-gender-conforming people be strictly forbidden, they couldn't even be referred to. Breen would spend the next two decades ruthlessly ferreting out any "inferences" of the kind. Under the Code, American filmmaking would never be the same, manufacturing a sanitized, desexualized image of wholesomeness that, for decades, would require sly maneuvering on the part of its screenwriters, directors, and performers to communicate their adult themes to savvy audiences ready and willing to read between the lines.

The rationale for the fear and loathing of homosexuals by the now Catholic-controlled industry reflected the same standards and ingrained, sociologically biased belief systems as in the country at large: that gays and lesbians represent a threat to the heteronormative social order. This can be gleaned quite clearly in the Code's stance on the representation of marriage, which is perhaps even more telling of the Code's priorities when it comes to sexual traditionalism than the line about "perversion." Under the heading of Sex, the top line reads, "The sanctity of the institution of marriage and the home shall be upheld. Pictures shall not infer that low forms of sex relationship are the accepted or common thing."

So, while, according to Breen, "Sadism, homosexuality, incest, etc., should not even be hinted at in the motion pictures," it was more imperative to point out to filmmakers and moviegoers that the depiction of adultery, a common plot point of heterosexual melodrama, had to function within strictly defined moral boundaries. "The girls and boys of today are the fathers and mothers of tomorrow," said Breen, and hence must be taught "the seriousness and sanctity of the marriage state which is the very foundation of our society—and Church." One need not be a queer theorist to understand that the framing of marriage—i.e., the heterosexual relations of a man and a woman—as the bedrock of a forward-progressing society is by any rational analysis the basis for queer social marginalization. Traditionally demonized for not conforming to the norms as laid out by heterosexual procreative society—marriage, followed by reproduction—and therefore existing outside the "normal" social framework, queer people have long been scapegoated (as have independent, unmarried, or childless women) for social ills. As the historian John D'Emilio writes, "The elevation of the family to ideological preeminence guarantees that a capitalist society will reproduce not just children, but heterosexism and homophobia . . . Gay men and lesbians exist on social terrain beyond the boundaries of the heterosexual nuclear family." Some eighty years before assimilationist gays and a breakthrough Supreme Court ruling altered national perceptions of what that family could look like, the Code was engraving its only acceptable image onto the closest thing Hollywood had to a stone tablet.

Ever the PR man, Breen was ace at supplementing the Code's commandments with his own personal quirks of what made for reasonable screen fodder. His most infamous and, in later years, ridiculed declarations included that men and women (even the married kind) must be shown sleeping in single beds separated by a proper number of inches rather than sharing a queen- or a king-size mattress, and that bathrooms must not have visible toilets, chamber pots, or any other object that might hint at the human functions of urination or defecation. (This stipulation led to the PCA's risible demand that Vittorio De Sica's beloved postwar Italian import *The Bicycle Thief* [1947] excise a scene showing a child peeing on the street, shot tamely from behind.) Breen also heartily enforced the Code's mandate that human flesh should not be exposed in such a way as to entice the viewer, especially women's bodies. "Because of the natural and spontaneous reaction of normal human beings to sexual stimuli," he worried, "the portrayal of definite manifestations of sex is harmful to individual morality, subversive to the interests of society, and a peril to the human race."

One might say that the Code and thus the movies themselves were forced to conform to one man's delicate, Catholic constitution. Sex—whether premarital, nonmonogamous, or (most unthinkable) homosexual—was not merely immoral, it was terrifying in its potential to stir up natural feelings in the viewer. Any intimation of the corporeal or the sensual was an unwelcome intrusion that might make vulnerable viewers remember that they had genitals. The fear of sexuality would become a constant underlying theme in Hollywood cinema throughout the coming decades, and it would be pushed against, deviously toyed with, mocked, or exploited by directors, producers, and stars who knew exactly what they were doing. An ironic result was that this era of Hollywood would prove to be one of surpassing sensuality—of desirous men and women whose attractions and motivations would be clear to anyone actually keeping their eyes on the screen.

. . .

In his first months on the job, Breen began meddling in projects that had begun production. These included vehicles for two of the pre-Code era's most unapologetically sexual female stars: a characteristically bawdy Mae West comedy directed by Leo McCarey titled *It's No Sin*, and an MGM Jean Harlow picture, co-written by Anita Loos, *Born to Be Kissed*. Under Breen's watch, both were subject to extensive rewrites to redeem their main characters as "good girls," their titles changed to the less suggestive *Belle of the Nineties* and *The Girl from Missouri*, respectively. Breen's office also demanded new cuts to films already in the can, such as Ernst Lubitsch's Ruritanian musical comedy *The Merry Widow*, whose sexually suggestive naughtiness—definitive of early 1930s Hollywood romance—was anathema to Breen, its various offenses including a close-up of an inscribed garter belt and a man undressing a woman to the point that her . . . shoulders are revealed.

The PCA's indignities extended to rereleases of established hits, slicing out offending passages from *A Farewell to Arms*, the Marx Brothers' *Animal Crackers*, and the gangster picture *The Public Enemy*. A pair of songs were cut from Rouben Mamoulian's musical comedy *Love Me Tonight*. Cecil B. DeMille's ancient Roman bacchanalia *The Sign of the Cross*, featuring Charles Laughton as a naughty, sexually ambiguous Emperor Nero, would reemerge bowdlerized. Even the classy *Cavalcade*, 1933's Best Picture, based on a play by the gay Noël Coward, wasn't safe from the scissors: a passing shot of two women taking each other's hands in a chic private nightclub was removed. Lesbian and gay sexuality, whether enacted upon or implied in types like the "butch" female or the "pansy" male, was easy to spot and so became among Breen's easiest targets.

Less than twelve months after Will Hays appointed Joseph Breen as the Code's enforcer, Samuel Goldwyn hired Lillian Hellman to join his screenwriting stable. Hellman had her initial run-in with Breen's office when working on her first major film for Goldwyn, the sentimental wartime melodrama *The Dark Angel* co-written with Mordaunt Shairp, incidentally the writer of a recent Broadway play, *The Green Bay Tree*, controversial for its gay undercurrents.

Though generally spoken of as a footnote in Hellman's career, *The Dark Angel* was a commercial and critical success that boosted Goldwyn's confidence in Hellman, leading directly to his purchasing *The Children's Hour*. *The Dark Angel* was also essential in opening Hellman's eyes to the Code's strictures. Breen had read Hellman's script in advance of production, and in a vaguely worded telegram from 1935, wrote that the film was "basically in violation [of] production code and impossible from standpoint . . . unless basic story is changed [sic]." After fighting and witnessing censorship battles in Boston, Chicago, and London, all of which refused to stage *The Children's Hour*, Hellman complied, toning down her first draft's sexual innuendo.

Hellman and Goldwyn's next project would require a lot more than toning down. *The Children's Hour* was too infamous to not attract attention, though by all accounts Goldwyn didn't know what he was getting himself into when Hellman persuaded him that they could, indeed, make a film from her blockbuster play, which was still running on Broadway. She convinced Goldwyn that the play was about "the power of a lie" first and foremost—as she would say throughout her career. She explained to him, "When I wrote *The Children's Hour*, I simply thought lesbianism was the most insidious lie the child could spread."

Does this paint the whole picture about Hellman's intentions with her work, or was this mere savviness? The play never would have been bought by Goldwyn, and certainly for nowhere near $50,000, if he felt that there was any question about its commercial prospects. The play's notoriety would seem to make it a household name for a shrewd industry type like Goldwyn. Though a successful businessman and an industry survivor during a tumultuous period for the movie business, Goldwyn was frequently given to malapropisms and confused proclamations. There is an amusing anecdote, often shared and likely apocryphal: told by colleagues that he could never make *The Children's Hour* because it centered on lesbians, he responded, "We'll make them Americans!"

Months before Goldwyn had even considered a film of the play, the Hays Office had already started a file on *The Children's Hour*. Hollywood studios were snatching up the rights to theater productions and novels left and right, and the PCA knew it was only a matter of time before someone went sniffing around the offending property. As early as November 21, 1934 (one day after the play's Broadway premiere), Breen, six months in his official position, described *The Children's Hour* in a memo to Hays: "A stark tragedy which deals with an alleged unnatural affection of one girl for another, culminating in a confession by one of the girls that she has had a mental unnatural feeling for her friend, is the daring theme of the play." The word daring here indicates an awareness on Breen's part of the play's ambition and, perhaps, in some other context, worthiness. Nevertheless, he concluded, "Thematically it is unfit material for the screen." He continued, in a series of early dictates that would more or less provide the template for the film that came to be: "If picturization of this play is contemplated, even though in my mind it is thematically a violation of the Production Code, careful consideration must be given to the following: I: The insinuation the two girls are degenerates; II: The sadistic nature of the young student; III: The confession of the young woman that she has had a mental unnatural affection for her girl friend; IV: All profanity."

When Goldwyn eventually made the purchase, Will Hays immediately contacted the producer. The demands did not surprise Goldwyn, considering the extent of the Code's censorship in matters of alleged "perversion," but for the note to come so early, laying out a warning as a way of heading off any drawn-out battle, indicated the project's notoriety and wild improbability. If he was to go ahead with a film, he was not to use the title *The Children's Hour;* he was "to make no reference, directly or indirectly, in either advertising or exploitation" to the stage play *The Children's Hour*; and he was to remove "all possible suggestions of Lesbianism and any other matter which is to prove objectionable." The hope was that an apparently easily corruptible public would remain ignorant of the source material even as they watched an ostensible adaptation of it. This was unlikely considering that even months before the rights to Hellman's play were optioned, members of the press were bemoaning the possibility of a censored version. In a *Herald Tribune* article from December 16, 1934, the journalist Richard Watts Jr. wrote a lengthy broadside against an imagined film: "It is safe to say that if *The Children's Hour* were made into a film the apologetic shifts in story, mood, and idea would be so vast that those who object to certain details in the play would see what quibblers they would have been."

Breen's censorship before the fact was an approach that would come to define at least the next twenty-five years of American studio moviemaking. It was especially tricky for the Breen office when Hollywood would turn to less intensely censored media for inspiration, whether a risqué bestselling novel or an East Coast stage scandal. After a few years of Breen's outright rejection or intense reworking of such material (some of it bought by studios for a high price before the 1934 crackdown), producers began to know well the kinds of subject matter, imagery, words, and suggestions that would make a film unrealizable in the minds of those with the power. So, especially in the years leading up to World War II, rather than fight for themes or ideas with transgressive social value (exemplified by a squashed adaptation of Sinclair Lewis's seismic antifascist novel *It Can't Happen Here*), the studios simply changed course, redirecting their resources to stories and characters that had little risk of being silenced.

Hollywood, it must be remembered, was intended to work with the utmost efficiency—but its machine-tooled products for the next century would nevertheless be evaluated in terms of artistic excellence, a central and defining contradiction. And because the industry was only a few years away from the period that is generally considered its zenith (roughly 1939 to 1950, from *Gone with the Wind* to *Sunset Boulevard*, or *The Wizard of Oz* to *All About Eve*), when it had streamlined production, perfected technical craftsmanship in both sound and camera, and fully established a constellation of charismatic talking movie stars for audiences to not just obsess over but relate to, the genius of the system seemed unquestionable and therefore went largely unquestioned for many years.

The classical American movie is a fantasy; we know that now, and audiences knew that then too. That the movies elided the experienced reality of those who watched them, and certainly those traditionally marginalized within American society, was part of their appeal, just as they remain from the supposedly more sophisticated vantage point of later decades. Even as we look for emotional authenticity, we still expect to lose ourselves in *The Maltese Falcon* or *Cat People* or *Rebecca* or *Red River*, all of which have left breadcrumbs for queer viewers over the generations. The beautiful trick of the movies—and certainly the movies of this period—is that even while getting lost we can also often find ourselves. The unexpected moment of truth amid the illusion. The glint of awakening within the daydream. This is one reason why movies continue to creep into our subconscious and capture our imaginations. As the 1936 film of *The Children's Hour* would prove, the most neutered production can achieve sensitivity and tap a deep well of mystery. Any movie, the delicate handiwork of so many souls at odds, can be beautiful and insidious at once, even a film conceived as an irreconcilable shadow of itself.

· · ·

The intimacy between the women is unmistakable. Bosom buddies newly graduated from the same women's college, they are nearly draped over each other while they imagine a life together, dreaming big about their futures, their independence, their careers, their need to define themselves. In an almost classically romantic pose, the ravishing brunette crouches over her supine blonde best friend. "Take a chance with me and come," the woman implores, her eyes narrowing with possibility, ambition, excitement.

The dark-haired, beckoning one is Karen Wright, and the fair object of her affection is Martha Dobie, as reimagined for *These Three* and embodied by Merle Oberon and Miriam Hopkins. Their easy physical familiarity, which stops short of the erotic yet expresses a bond that goes past the sisterly, offers a tangible sensuality that would be entirely missing from the ostensibly corrected version of *The Children's Hour* in 1961. There's no doubt that *These Three* is a chaste film—it was conceived to be, in body and spirit—but the desire coursing through it expresses much about how queerness made its way into the contours of cinema even at its most eradicated. When we look closer, we desire more; watching these incarnations of Martha and Karen, the viewer can pick up on signals that later, post-Code films more directly telegraph, dulling the erotic imagination.

Completed in late 1935 and released in March 1936, *These Three* begins with more than a half hour of fully dramatized backstory, entirely invented for the movie or only hinted at in Hellman's source material. In an effort to open the play for the screen and try to mitigate the stage-bound theatrics of its single setting, Hellman gives shape to her heroines' lives before their decision to open a school together. We meet the women on graduation day in caps and gowns, clutching diplomas and singing devotional hymns to their alma mater. Already they're warding off the chirpy advances of selfish and prattling Aunt Lily, who's clearly an unwanted presence, considering Hopkins's withering glances. With thirty-eight bucks between them, the women plan to move into a New England farmhouse left to Karen by her late grandmother.

However rudimentary these early scenes feel, and however reflective they are of Hollywood's penchant for clarifying psychological motivation to earn audience sympathy and reduce emotional ambiguity, it's remarkable how much work they do in establishing the women's ambitious, adventurous spirit and how they're strengthened by their bond to each other. In many crucial ways, the women of *These Three* feel more united (in sisterhood, in friendship, in devotion, and in professional endeavor) than the Karen and Martha of *The Children's Hour*. The moment they arrive at Karen's inherited dilapidated home, however, they meet-cute with Joel McCrea's local doctor Joe, introduced in a beekeeper's outfit, stealing honey from a swarm that's taken up residence in a busted thatch in the abandoned farmhouse's roof. A fount of unthreatening masculine energy, he's irresistible, and those two quickly become these three.

The choice to transform the inciting lie of *The Children's Hour* into an accusation of heterosexual promiscuity was staring Hellman straight in the face. She already had her three main characters, two women and a man, and in her original script they were indeed the three points of a love triangle. It took just a few tweaks from Hellman's pen to readjust her text so that the offending implication was erased yet a scandal remained.

Before the property was officially bought, Goldwyn had a conversation with Geoffrey Shurlock of the Hays Office in July 1935, certifying the removal of any inference to lesbianism. Not simply satisfied with the verbal promise, the PCA then asked for their agreement to be put in writing before Goldwyn went through with the purchase. "In suggesting this," said Shurlock in an interoffice memo to Hays, "we had in mind not only the necessity of having the treatment square absolutely with the Code, but also the question of publicity and public reaction connected with the announcement of the purchase of the play for pictures, as well as the further question of the advisability, or otherwise, of the use of the title."

Sketching out her ideas for the adaptation, Hellman went significantly astray from her play, drafting an initial, unused treatment that transformed the all-American narrative into a case of intercontinental culture clash. In this version, Martha and Karen, bosom friends, "almost sisters" since childhood, are from England, "brought up in comparative luxury." Later, they come to America to open a school, where Mary Tilford "confesses" about an illicit romance between Martha and Joe, allegedly seen through the keyhole. Little of this remained other than the repositioning of the women's disgraceful conduct as heterosexual hanky-panky. Rather than harbor a secret crush on Karen, Martha hides profound romantic feelings for off-limits Joe, who has already made his choice and fallen for Karen. The diabolical Mary's plan, then, is to destroy Karen and Martha's reputations—and secure her release from boarding school—by exposing the schoolteachers' illicit behavior, occurring right under the kids' noses.

To change the lie from one about the unspeakable—lesbianism—to one about the horrors of sexual promiscuity perfectly reflected the philosophies of the newly enforced Production Code; what could be more appealing to Breen, after all, than a moral tale about the nefarious accusation that a woman is engaged in an affair with another woman's fiancée? As a solution to the "problem" of *The Children's Hour*, the change makes disappointingly perfect sense; the question then becomes, how can this comparatively tame besmirchment of character lead to the kind of compelling, full-throated drama that made Hellman's play such an armchair-gripping sensation? And even though the Code disallowed any reference to *The Children's Hour* in the credits or marketing materials, wouldn't most viewers know they were watching a bastardized version of a well-known play?

Before getting to questions of audience reception, Samuel Goldwyn would have to figure out how to make the movie in the first place, which meant assembling a crack team behind and in front of the camera. The highly competitive salary he was paying Hellman expressed his confidence in her abilities, though it would take more than an airtight screenplay to make *These Three* viable as drama. Looking for someone to film his "unfilmable" property, Goldwyn accepted a suggestion from Hellman. She had seen *Counsellor-at-Law*, Universal's 1933 adaptation of a Broadway play by Elmer Rice starring John Barrymore, and had been impressed by the way its thirty-year-old director, William Wyler, had sensitively treated the New York story of a Jewish lawyer who rises from Lower East Side tenement poverty to the heights of professional success and is beset by potential scandal. The producer set up a meeting with Wyler in summer 1935. The director recalled, "He couldn't have been more charming, but I thought he had lost his mind. He told me he wanted to make *The Children's Hour*."

William Wyler would go on to be one of the most important artists in Hollywood history, ascending to a level of critical and commercial success exceedingly rare within the industry, earning twelve Academy Award nominations as Best Director and winning in that category three times (at the time of this writing, John Ford is still the record holder, with four). The notoriously withering, hard-to-please Hellman would later call him "the greatest of all American directors." In 1935, he was not widely known, but he was hardly a beginner. Born Willi Wyler in 1902 to a Jewish family in the Alsace region, part of Germany at the time, Wyler took more after his refined, poet mother than his father, a textile and clothing merchant turned haberdasher. A lover of local theater and opera, young Willi was the benefi-ciary of a remarkable family connection—his maternal grandmother's first cousin was one of the founders of the movie industry: Carl Laemmle.

Like so many Jewish immigrants, the German-born Laemmle started out as a small-time businessman, managing a clothing store in Oshkosh before noting the opportunities in the burgeoning American leisure industry at the turn of the century. After opening a series of storefront nickelodeons in Chicago, he set his sights higher, financing movies himself. Laemmle was at the crest of every wave: he was among the network of independent producers intent on breaking up Thomas Edison's Motion Picture Patents Company, which monopolized the nascent movie industry; he was among the first film entrepreneurs to see the value in hiring stars—such as Florence Lawrence and eventual icon Mary Pickford—at high rates; and he was among the first movie pioneers to go west—along with Samuel Goldwyn, Adolph Zukor, and Louis B. Mayer—and take advantage of California's perennial sunshine and temperate weather, both conducive to the demands of filmmaking. Buying a tract of land in the San Fernando Valley in 1915, Laemmle established Universal City, which would become one of the most resilient and internationally recogniz-able studios in the history of the business.

Laemmle gave his first cousin's grandson his big break, hiring Willi Wyler, freshly arrived from Europe in 1921, for the mailroom of the Universal's New York office. Insisting he was destined for more creative work, the nineteen-year-old took the train out to California in November of that year, arriving in Hollywood at the moment of its first enormous moral crisis, with the Roscoe "Fatty" Arbuckle trial in full swing and the pervasive rumors in the press of Hollywood's rampant adultery, prostitution, and drug-fueled orgies. For Wyler, then, Hollywood was a place of enchantment and productive disillusion from the start. He wasn't there to make dreams come true, but to ply his trade. Wyler would be known for a no-nonsense, demanding attitude, but he was also an eminent professional whose deliberate, workmanlike approach and almost preternatural grasp of realist aesthetics portended an astonishing career longevity.

The kid from Alsace started out in California as an errand boy for Universal's chief casting supervisor before convincing his superiors (including Laemmle, already a hardened, skeptical fifty-four years old) that he had more to offer. By the mid-1920s, Wyler was the youngest director on the Universal lot, with almost two dozen two-reel westerns under his belt. In 1927, the year of the talkie's inception, Wyler got his first contract at Universal, for $200 a week. Over the coming decade, as the industry went through its various irrevocable and often painful transformations, Wyler kept his head above water while honing his craft on a succession of features that ranged in tone and genre from the mostly silent, part talkie boxing picture *The Shakedown* (1928) to the prestige dramas *A House Divided* (1931) and *Counsellor-at-Law* to the romantic comedies *The Gay Deception* (1935) and *The Good Fairy* (1935), the latter featuring an early script by Preston Sturges. None proved newsworthy enough at the box office to put Wyler on the A list, but his quiet craftsmanship garnered crucial attention from Hellman and Goldwyn.

Despite his doubts about making a film of *The Children's Hour*, Wyler agreed to direct Hellman's script, at this point titled *The Lie*. Goldwyn and his story department were enamored of Hellman's work, considering her reimagined draft one of the best scripts they'd had. Putting aside the judicious elimination of offending elements, Hellman's reconstituted version maintains a fleetness of storytelling, an urgency of tone, and a thick vein of antipuritanism that feels entirely of a piece with the author's artistic and moral perspective. For a viewer who doesn't know the original story, the experience of *These Three* might feel histrionic yet dramatically undimmed; for a viewer fully aware of what was altered, it might prove a frustrating yet even richer experience. What cannot be seen on the page but sings on the screen, thanks to the input of so many intelligent cinematic collaborators, from director to cinematographer to editor to composer to actors, is its subtextual desire and the way it unavoidably toys with the memory of its expunged material.

Hellman said of Wyler. "He knew how to pack so much into a shot that I felt I could leave certain things unsaid, knowing Willy would show them." While she was talking of Wyler's pictorial sense in general, Hellman also might as well have been referring to the ability of a fine director to use film form to reveal the unrevealable. The glorious chasm between what is said and what is shown speaks to cinema's aesthetic and thematic possibilities (the world's most acclaimed, beloved films, from *Vertigo* to *2001: A Space Odyssey*, from *Beau Travail* to *In the Mood for Love* bear this out), and Code-era directors became prime practitioners of ambiguities that could never manifest on the page. In *These Three*, one can bear witness to a form just evolving, barely perceptible behind a newly straitjacketed production mode. Because of the nature of the original play, frequently referred to as that play "about lesbians," the film offers a metatext that helps it stand out among the hundreds of films that were simultaneously being shepherded through the PCA's new regulatory processes at all the major studios.

Wyler signed a lucrative three-year contract with Goldwyn (starting at $88,000 annually), with *These Three* as his first project. Casting had already begun, and Wyler was initially displeased that Joel McCrea, an industry stalwart who had never quite become a major leading man, would be Joe, fearing the affable, lanky actor lacked the proper gravitas. The two female leads already hired would prove less of a problem for Wyler. Films during the Code era would often rely on casting to communicate the dangerous eroticism below the surface, and unlike McCrea, with his aw-shucks demeanor, the women, Miriam Hopkins and Merle Oberon, were less inherently wholesome, figures already known, respectively, for their earthy sensuality and sylphlike exoticism.

Hopkins, like Hellman, was born in the South (Savannah); the two women had mingled among the same New York social circles, each counting Dorothy Parker as a confidante, though their paths never crossed until California. A stage break-through at twenty-four in an acclaimed adaptation of Theodore Dreiser's *An American Tragedy*, Hopkins entered the movie business when producer Walter Wanger offered her a five-year Paramount contract after seeing her on Broadway in *Lysistrata*. Hopkins said yes only because she was able to work by day in Paramount's East Coast studio in Astoria, Queens, and commute to Broadway in the evenings to rehearse or perform—an arrangement that appealed to many a stage actor poached by a movie industry newly desperate for vocally trained performers. Hopkins's ascendance paralleled the industry's rising Depression-era turmoil, and when Paramount was forced to close its New York studio, she was required to relocate to Los Angeles, curtailing a stage career she was far from ready to give up.

Hopkins embodied Hollywood's precarious "pre-Code" permissiveness with a knowing glint in her eye while never devolving into winking self-consciousness. She made her mark in a series of hits that gave the pre-1934 Hays Office apoplexy, films of barely concealed lust and undercurrents of genuine perversity. Her first Hollywood project, Rouben Mamoulian's virtuosic *Dr. Jekyll and Mr. Hyde* (1931), in which she plays the love interest/terrorized victim of Fredric March's mad scien-tist, was cut to size by censors, mostly because of Hopkins's undressing scenes and the intensity of her erotic flirtations. Her follow-up, *The Story of Temple Drake* (1933), which Joseph Breen, then Hays's assistant, called "sordid, base, and thoroughly unpleasant," was among the most controversial films of the decade. An adaptation of William Faulkner's *Sanctuary*, *Temple Drake* was, like *The Children's Hour*, based on source material so notorious that they changed the title in order to hide its origins. Post-PCA, it's unlikely that this story concerning rape, kidnapping, and murder, centered on the sexual debasement of a free-spirited Mississippi woman, ever would have made it past the first script stage. Even after the Hays Office enforced cuts—mostly as a result of Hopkins's character being raped off-screen, in a scene that evokes the book's infamous suggestion of the horrific use of a corncob—the film was still met with outraged reviews from offended critics and was banned from reissue for decades.

Hopkins's popular 1933 screwball comedy *Design for Living*, directed by Ernst Lubitsch, also would be the object of much consternation, based as it was on a property considered too hot—and queer—to touch. The movie had to tiptoe around the implications of the hit Noël Coward play on which it was based: namely that the "gentlemen's agreement" into which Hopkins had entered with her two handsome artist paramours (played by Gary Cooper and Fredric March) was in any way bisexual. Ben Hecht's script rewrote Coward's original so drastically that one could neatly claim the homosexual overtones to have been eliminated, yet there remains in Lubitsch's film—and certainly in Hopkins's sly performance—a charmed awareness of what's really going on in this ménage à trois. *Design for Living* is a film about erotic possibility overcoming the chastisement of moralizers, of living a life outside the normal codes of romantic and professional conduct. At the film's devil-may-care denouement, Hopkins, perched in the back of a cab squeezed between Cooper on the left and March on the right, kisses them on the mouth one at a time. "Boys, this is very important. There's one thing that has to be understood," she instructs. The three of them make a pact to maintain their "gentlemen's agreement" and shake hands giddily.

Both Hopkins's star persona and the sultry physicality of her technique—her voice is a sly, deep purr—would bring a crucial extratextual layer to her work and point toward decades of screen actors transcending sexually limited parts, communing directly with any sympathetic, knowing viewer who might be watching. Hopkins had seen *The Children's Hour* performed in New York and so was aware of the subject matter; this hardly deterred her when she ran into Hellman on the Goldwyn Studios lot and eagerly asked if she could read the script. Hopkins, a recent Oscar nominee for Mamoulian's *Becky Sharp* (1935), the adaptation of

Thackeray's *Vanity Fair* that is best remembered as Hollywood's first three-strip Technicolor feature, was a new Goldwyn acquisition. Goldwyn encouraged Hopkins to take the part of Martha, though what cinched the deal for the actress was discovering that the producer had courted Merle Oberon for Karen.

By 1935, Hopkins and Oberon had become close friends and neighbors, even owning adjoining beach houses. Oberon was a personal favorite of Goldwyn's; he had negotiated with British producer Alexander Korda to bring her to Hollywood, where she proved her mettle on *The Dark Angel*, Hellman's first script. Its director, Sidney Franklin (whom Hellman had detested), had balked at Oberon's casting, deeming her too sexual for an otherwise wholesome romantic melodrama that required someone with a "virginal quality." The line of thinking that Oberon was "dark" and "exotic" today seems undeniably coded language for a woman who throughout her career hid her mixed-race heritage. Oberon, born to a mother of Sri Lankan ancestry and a white father, would be the only actress of Asian descent to receive a Best Actress Oscar nomination (for *The Dark Angel*) until Michelle Yeoh in 2023.

Though she is often discussed in terms of "passing," matters of identity and heritage in the oppressively white atmosphere of Golden Age Hollywood merit more nuanced discussion and terminology. As Oberon scholar Mayukh Sen says, "There were very heavy speculations about Merle having 'Eurasian' heritage or being 'half-caste,' to borrow the parlance of that era, once she came over to Hollywood in late 1934—and in many of those interviews from 1934 and 1935, she'd flat out deny that she was South Asian. But those murmurs began to quiet somewhat around the time Goldwyn took her under his wing and helped pasteurize her image for *The Dark Angel*." The truth about Oberon's origins was somewhere between a rumor for the gossip mill and an open secret, talked about in a way that acknowledged and refuted her identity at once. The studios promoted her chosen story, that she was born to aristocratic white parents in the Australian island state of Tasmania, which lent her an air of otherness without sullying her rising star with the truth of her biracial, impoverished background. Yet Oberon, whose complexion was markedly darker than the lily-white screen stars of the thirties, was trailed by barely veiled suspicion. A September 14, 1935, newspaper article in *Literary Digest* extolling the release of *The Dark Angel* breathes a sigh of relief that "Merle Oberon has abandoned her tiresome Oriental sleekness," both gesturing to the unknown—or unknowable—and inferring that thus far her career had been cheapened by unrespectable exotic airs.

With two leads often regarded for forthright, risky sensuality, *These Three* cannot completely expunge its material's erotic promise—apt for a film that's still, at heart, about forbidden sexuality. The scholar Patricia White has proposed that the conspicuous absence of lesbianism from the film only enhances it for its viewers, especially considering the gingerly way the film's less scandalous "secret" is handled: "Making the accusation unspeakable, or unshareable as a public utterance, conflates it with, refers back to, lesbianism itself." Some have bought into the theory that Hopkins was willfully playing Martha as closeted: William Wyler's biographer Axel Madsen wrote that "Hopkins acts as if her desire is for her companion and not the man whom Merle Oberon loves, leading the audience to a conclusion at variance with the script." It's a plausible reading, but it also insinuates a measure of intentionality a sympathetic queer viewer of the film doesn't require. *These Three* is at its best as a lush cinematic expression of repressed desire, which is keenly felt throughout, regardless of how explicitly its hovering homoeroticism appears to whoever watches it.

The film offers a centerpiece sequence of intensely felt longing that is an exquisite showcase for the talents of all involved, especially the remarkable abilities of Hellman, Wyler, and cinematographer Gregg Toland—the innovator who only five years later would shoot *Citizen Kane*—to condense crucial narrative information and worlds of emotions to a few simple gestures and visual phrases. On a wintry evening, Joe has come to the farmhouse, now a fully operating school, looking for Karen, who's not home. Instead, he goes to a small upstairs sitting room and joins Martha, who's in the midst of painting a wooden stool. It's a comforting, cozy scene, with a roaring fireplace in the back. As she waxes altruistically about her reasons for going into teaching, dog-tired Joe falls asleep on a sofa. Martha watches him, gently touching the lapel of his coat, before resting in an armchair by the fire, her eyes never leaving the sleeping man. Toland's camera pans from her over to a window; after a dissolve to frosted-over glass, indicating time has passed, the camera pans back to Martha. The fire is now an ember, but she's awake and still watching Joe—her expression reads as comfort, desire, and appreciation at once. Carried along by Alfred Newman's plaintive score and Toland's hypnotic, deliberate movement, the scene establishes Martha's hidden love for Joe in a purely cinematic manner which could never be as effectively etched onstage, while also centering Martha's secret inner world as, once again, a driving force of the drama.

This idyll will be quickly interrupted when Joe awakens violently from a dream and, thrusting out his arm, knocks over and shatters a glass of milk on the side table—a coded evocation of violent sexual release that is gratifyingly unmistakable. A quick cut informs us that young Mary, in a nearby bedroom, has been jolted awake by the noise; the story's other antagonist, Aunt Lily, has also been roused to investigate, instantly suspicious that Joe would be visiting Martha at this late hour. After Joe pulls himself together and leaves, Martha collapses into a chair and cries, the camera panning out to the hallway to catch a glimpse of Mary, sinister as she watches from the shadows. From this point forward, the film will follow the general structure and narrative of Hellman's play. Finally, at the 32-minute mark, *These Three* abandons its backstory preface and the central story begins, with the scene of Aunt Lily's lesson, interrupted by Mary's entrance and her bouquet of flowers filched from the garbage.

Perhaps it was inevitable for such a gleefully fiendish character, but, recalling the sensational media response to Florence McGee in the stage production of *The Children's Hour*, the actress who played young Mary on-screen, thirteen-year-old Bonita Granville, threatened to steal the show. Mary, quite contrary in every way to the rest of the cast—in stature, in dress, even in performance style—becomes in *These Three* a ruthlessly appealing alternative to Martha, Karen, and Joe's unblemished goodness. This Mary is different from the Mary of Hellman's play, whose implicit if childish knowledge of lesbianism—indicated by her sly references to Gautier's subversive nineteenth-century novel *Mademoiselle de Maupin*—isolates her as a locus of perversity: does Mary's accusation in *The Children's Hour* confer upon her a burgeoning self-awareness of her own lesbianism manifest as an accusation against others?

With the homosexual narrative element deleted—and without Martha's final revelation of her own lesbianism—*These Three* creates an entirely different dynamic, in which Granville's Mary is the sole embodiment of social maladaptation. The "perversity" has been displaced solely onto the child. She's a malignant narcissist, but perhaps also an erotofascist, judging by the way she forces the other girls to pay tribute to her, having Rosalie vow loyalty to her as "vassal." She's also a potentially queer figure, existing outside the normal family structure, living with only a grandmother (Alma Kruger) and a housemaid (Margaret Hamilton) and all too eager to destroy Karen and Joe's heteronormative happiness. Costumed in a black skirt contrasting with the mostly lighter colors worn by her classmates, her dark, frizzy hair tightly pulled back, her plainly featured, makeup-free face locked in either phony beseeching or twisted rage, Mary has a notable butch air about her. When she collapses into an armchair, her legs are spread apart gracelessly; when she leans forward, she rests her elbows on her thighs; when she intimidates her easily duped peer Rosalie (the more traditionally angelic Marcia Mae Jones) into lying for her, she twists the kid's arm with practiced boyishness. In a cut scene of an early draft from October 1935, Mary even shoves a girl during a game of field hockey. Mary's rejection of the trappings of girlishness puts her in stark relief not only to her young classmates but also to an era in which Shirley Temple was the most popular movie star in the cosmos. Looked at through a different lens, Mary, as treacherous as she is, becomes a kind of stealth protagonist, a queer disruptor intent on shaking up the status quo.

Wyler may have come to *These Three* after the trio of leads had been cast, but he had a hand in finding Bonita Granville, selecting her after testing dozens of teenage girls with Goldwyn. The daughter of vaudeville actors, the Manhattan-born Granville had been in show business since she was very young and had appeared in small roles, including in George Cukor's *Little Women*. *These Three* would be her first major part, and Wyler devoted a great deal of attention to her while shooting. It became clear to both Oberon and Hopkins on set that the thirteen-year-old was becoming even more central to the film than they had expected, sharing a fear that the girl would walk away with the movie and frequently voicing their concerns to Wyler and Goldwyn. Hopkins and Wyler's relationship had already grown strained following his demand for multiple takes. After the film's release, Hopkins continued to fight for attention, even walking off the set of Louella Parsons's radio show while doing publicity for the film when Granville and little Marcia Mae Jones were getting too much airtime. Hopkins and Oberon's worries proved to be founded, at least in one major way: Granville became the only actor in the film nominated for an Oscar, vying for Best Supporting Actress in the category's very first year, added partly to appease a disgruntled Screen Actors Guild. (Granville gets hers in the film's final scene, however: a satisfying slap across the face from Margaret Hamilton, the future Wicked Witch of the West herself.)

Competitive streaks aside, *These Three* ultimately works so remarkably well because of the actors' passionate commitment and Wyler's elegant direction, which often favors single takes and medium shots for a sense of heightened realism. The radical redirection of the scandal that unravels the two women's lives to one of a rumored love triangle might make all the panic seem illegible in comparison to Hellman's play, especially when the horrified parents swoop in one by one and scurry their children away from these alleged monsters. "One of you ladies has been carryin' on with the other's fiancée," exclaims a nosy cab driver escorting a kid from school. Yet there remains an essential truth to Hellman's revisions: the writer, who loathed prudes and conservatives, was savvy in her target of American puritanism, a bedrock of her country's civilization. *These Three* becomes a story not simply about how quickly a life can be undone by a lie—and how keen gossip-hungry hordes are to believe it—but also, and perhaps more trenchantly, about small-minded American moralizing. "Whatever went on in your school may be possibly your business; it becomes a great deal more than that when children are involved," tsk-tsks Mrs. Tilford. In this way, the film functions as an implicit response to the priggish finger-wagging of the Production Code, purporting to care first and foremost about the welfare of America's children.

One revealing constant between the play and film is that Martha remains a figure of isolation and romantic unfulfillment. For Karen and Joe, it's a different story: in a somewhat dumbfounding reversal of *The Children's Hour*'s tragic ending, Karen tracks down Joe, who has escaped New England's gossip and judgment to Vienna of all places. A strange exemplar of urbane tolerance, maybe, even in the pre-Anschluss period, but nobody knows them in Austria, so as they embrace in a little café, the locals look on approvingly, laughing and smiling, a positive mirror image of the scornful glances back home. Martha receives no such absolution, as Hellman's revised screenplay doesn't dare invent a happy romantic conclusion for her. As in the play, there had been truth in Mary's lie (Martha is indeed in love with Joe), a revelation that's wistful and relatable rather than sick and dirty, leaving her noble in her outsider status.

A November 1935 draft of Hellman's script ends quite differently: Martha and Karen emerge together from the front door of Mrs. Tilford's house, after Mary's lies have been admitted and the old woman has recanted her accusation. Martha implores Karen to "Go back to Joe, wherever he is." Hellman writes that the women hold hands, before Martha says, in a moment of noble sacrifice, "I'm going to leave you, Karen." Karen shakes her head to protest her going. "It's the way it should be. I'll be all right now. I'm sure of that. Very sure." The women look at each other "with understanding and friendliness." FADE OUT. In a subsequent draft, these pages are crossed out in pen, with supplementary papers added to replace it with the Vienna epilogue.

In this unused version, the plot's emotional fulcrum is redirected to the relationship between Martha and Karen, underlining the emotional and implicitly erotic bond between the women established at the film's outset, bringing the film full circle. In either case, Martha would have remained a nomadic, solitary figure, yet by positioning the women as the true, equal protagonists, it would have deepened and enriched the underlying queer subtext. In either case, the film ends on two people, not the three of the title, thereby denying the possibility of a romantic trio (notably unlike the ménage à trois of Hopkins's pre-Code *Design for Living*). Martha is instead destined for loneliness.

These Three was a box office success and a critical darling, admired both for Wyler's nimble direction and, for those who knew its uncredited origins, its miraculous reinvention as a viable, Code-friendly drama. Hollywood giant David O. Selznick wrote to Goldwyn in appreciation, praising the "handling of this most difficult subject with little or no loss of the value of the original play." "I have seldom been so moved by any fictional film," Graham Greene effused in his *Spectator* review. "After ten minutes or so of the usual screen sentiment, quaintness and exaggeration, one began to watch with incredulous pleasure nothing less than life... Never before has childhood been presented so convincingly on the screen, with an authenticity guaranteed by one's own memories." Sound cinema was not even a decade old, and it had been only four or five years at most since filmmakers had begun using the camera in harmonious concert with recording technology, which had been clunky and intrusive. For Wyler to present "nothing less than life" on-screen was critical, expressing the director's ability to harness cinema's facilities for an unprecedented realism, gesturing toward a hallowed era of filmmaking of which Wyler would be one of its foremost practitioners.

It was a transitional time in Hollywood, and thanks to her confederation with Wyler and Goldwyn, Hellman was now an essential cog in the industry's evolution to well-oiled machine—one less prone to breaking down and less commonly attacked by religious moralizers. Thanks in part to her savviness in censoring her own work, she had proven herself an impeccable player of the Hollywood game. "We had to become friends, because we were the only two people in the Goldwyn asylum who weren't completely loony," Hellman said of Wyler, and sure enough they were collaborating again just one year later on *Dead End*, also shot by Toland. A tough-minded, New York–set proto-noir starring McCrea, Sylvia Sidney, and a breakthrough Humphrey Bogart, *Dead End* would be nominated for Best Picture, cementing the Hellman-Wyler-Goldwyn collaboration as a mighty triumvirate of post-Code Hollywood. The trio's greatest, most lasting gift to film history would come with Wyler's riveting 1941 adaptation of Hellman's play *The Little Foxes*, the 1939 Broadway success of which officially catapulted Hellman into the first ranks of American playwrights. A triumph of wit and ice-cold faux Southern gentility, inspired by Hellman's complicated relationship to her New Orleans family, *The Little Foxes* gave Bette Davis one of her most scintillating screen roles and Hellman her first Oscar nomination for writing.

Between *These Three* and *The Little Foxes*, Hellman had made her mark in Hollywood in other, more forthrightly political ways. An ascendant figure in the rising left-wing movements of late-1930s Hollywood that were increasingly emboldened in the face of fascism's cancerous spread throughout Europe, Hellman wasn't shy about her Communist leanings, along with other New York transplants like Donald Ogden Stewart and Ring Lardner Jr. She adapted her principles to a local cause when she joined and helped rally for the Screen Writers Guild, which had been formed in 1920 but had been fighting, like so many other Hollywood unions, for fair treatment amid the industry's evolution throughout the 1930s. A fateful trip to Moscow in 1937 would make Hellman more sympathetic to the Russian cause—and a prime target for the increasing number of Red-baiters in Los Angeles and Washington over the coming decades. Hellman would be historically defined by her leftist convictions and associations, which, unlike those of so many others in the industry, would remain unwavering even amid the persecuting forces of the right-wing politicians who would try to lay waste to liberal Hollywood in the late forties and early fifties.

Hellman's beliefs remained steadfast. Yet among the various liberal causes that captured the political imaginations of Hollywood in the 1930s, there was no incipient movement toward the acceptance of homosexuals, and there wouldn't be for decades. Though it was understood by most people in the industry that gay men and women worked in all aspects of Hollywood, their statuses running the gamut from hidden to open secret to quasi-uncloseted, they were a sexual underclass rather than people with a shared social or political identity. The application of the Production Code made their sexuality even more of a stigma, as what could be shown on-screen would have implications about what could be said or even implied behind the scenes. To ruthlessly maintain the Hollywood illusion that lives off camera were as unsullied and straight-arrow as those in the movies, the industry would put forward an image of white, heterosexual, Christian conformity. The depiction of homosexuality as a potentially dangerous social identity aligned with the Left would gain traction during the Red and Lavender scares of post–World War II America, which lassoed rumored gays right along with suspected Communists.

The Children's Hour was a political-minded, intentionally antifascist play, though its writer maintained, at least publicly, that its breakthrough gay content was nonradical and nonpolitical. It's thus a singularly apt text to jump-start an inquiry into an era of moviemaking defined by contradictions. *These Three* is similarly knotty: a film that exists only because of the sensational queerness of its origins but which is mostly remembered today for what *isn't* in it. Unlike most of the Hollywood films that are still discussed for their simmering queerness, and that laid the groundwork for a gay cinematic expressivity beloved by viewers well into the twenty-first century—which will be examined in this book—*These Three* was not, by all accounts, the product of gay artists. Yet it's not reducible to the product of a blinkered straight industry either, however truncated at inception. As with any work of art, it is a phantom of what the viewer sees, reads, experiences along with it. It's what she knows is there, and what she knows isn't there. What's happening in a movie is often just off camera.

3

Suitable Women

Among the dozens of handwritten notes tucked away in Lillian Hellman's collection of preserved personal correspondences, there is a short letter dated December 30, 1934, from her friend Laura Perelman, writer and the wife of humorist S. J. Perelman. After congratulating Hellman on the runaway Broadway success of *The Children's Hour*, Perelman's note ends on a sly eyebrow-raise: "Mother too enjoyed it and much to my surprise knows what a Lesbian is. I bet you don't dare wear a tailored suit anymore."

Brief and chummy as it is, the letter is revealing for how it reflects a certain—probably not at all rare—response of sophisticated heterosexual culture to female homosexuality in the 1930s. Even aside from Perelman's tongue-in-cheek reference to her modern mom, the note serves as a kind of warning to Hellman. The sensational subject matter of *The Children's Hour* might lead people to *mistake* Hellman—by no means a traditionally feminine woman—for a lesbian. Most telling of the way lesbian culture was identified and stereotyped at the time is Perelman's winking reference to a "tailored suit" as the dead giveaway.

The image of the "mannish" woman was prevalent throughout much of the nineteenth century. Not always related to an assumption of sexual habit or preference, it was often a disparagement for a type of woman, usually an ambitious professional, who might aggressively assume a man's appearance to be taken more seriously, and an attempt to impose standardized contradictory gender definitions on an individual in evident defiance of cultural norms. At the turn of the twentieth century, following influential studies by male psychologists such as Richard von Krafft-Ebing and Havelock Ellis, the stereotype of the "mannish lesbian" (later to evolve into the more enduring term "butch") began to circulate, effectively combining questions of dress, manner, and physical bearing with clinical discussions of female sexual identity: namely, as a psychopathology.

Because lesbianism was so widely discussed by medical professionals during the Victorian era, it came to be culturally regarded as a sign of psychological deviance, an effort to estrange, alienate, and mark women who should otherwise stay in their place. According to the historian Carroll Smith-Rosenberg, "The years immediately preceding and following the First World War saw women's greatest professional visibility and political activism. The number of women receiving advanced degrees and entering the professions reached a peak not to be equaled again until the late 1970s." Naturally, then, she goes on, "During these same years, male politicians, aided by male physicians, sex reformers, and educators, launched a concerted political attack condemning female friendships as lesbian and separate female institutions—whether educational or political—as breeding places for 'unnatural' sexual impulses."

As would be the case for most of the twentieth century, lesbianism was mentioned as a wink or teasing joke, indicative of political and social aberrance. In literature, such fascinating, almost mythic creatures, who refused to assign themselves to their "given" gender through dress, appeared in the works of Radclyffe Hall (*The Well of Loneliness*) and Virginia Woolf (*Orlando*), while in life women who dared wade into the radical, decidedly "unladylike" waters of art or politics—socialists, suffragists, downtown poets—constantly found themselves fending off the social stigma that came with dressing in clothes considered masculine. "From about 1900 on," the queer anthropologist Esther Newton writes, "this cross-gender figure became the public symbol of the new social/sexual category 'lesbian.'"

By the midthirties, Laura Perelman's mother wouldn't have been alone in her awareness of women who loved women. And the image of "the mannish lesbian" would have been firmly established in American cosmopolitan life. Hellman's schoolmarmish and provincial character Martha Dobie, about as likely to have her own "tailored suit" as she would legally adopt Mary Tilford, did not fit the urban stereotype, with her no-nonsense, nonfeminine bearing. Yet there was at least one "mannish lesbian" that Hellman, soon to be a major Hollywood player, certainly would have known about, and one for whom tailored suits were both a statement of identity and a form of armor.

. . .

Looking at most photographs of director Dorothy Arzner throughout her Hollywood heyday, from the late twenties into the early forties, one cannot help but notice, first and foremost, the cut of her jib.

It's not only that Arzner dressed frequently in men's clothes, but that in these photos, most taken on the studio sets of her films, her style stands in such sharp and remarkable contrast to that of the women beside her, often her leading ladies. In a pair of 1927 images, for instance, Arzner is paired with Esther Ralston, the angel-faced star of her first two features. The blonde actress appears traditionally feminine and soft in dresses and furs; Arzner, with a short-cut, slicked-back mane of jet-black hair (a point of pride), dons angular men's coats, hanging loosely and confidently over broad-collared dress shirts emboldened by the resounding pendulum of a striped necktie. In a 1933 photograph, she consults with her friend and repeat collaborator, the character actor Billie Burke (*The Wizard of Oz*'s eventual Glinda the Good Witch), from under a low-tilted panama hat. In 1943, directing *These Three*'s glamorous Merle Oberon, who's looking expectantly at her director with her chin resting on crossed arms, a suited Arzner appears with her hair pomaded into an arresting pompadour. Most alluring is the 1929 picture of Arzner, reclining on a chair in a sherpa-lined jacket and white fedora, with megastar Clara Bow, America's "It Girl," perched on the director's lap. In the foreground, Arzner's extended hand rests on Bow's leg, directly below the knee, and right above where her dress rides up to reveal bare skin.

While the positioning of the two women's bodies in this most provocative photograph connotes a certain playfulness, there's also a transgressive seriousness to it. Arzner's masculine persona was neither a put-on nor a calculation to be admitted acceptance into an industry increasingly preoccupied with standards of traditional masculinity. She may have had style, but her sartorial choices reflected something deeper. She was hardly the only woman to wear men's clothes in glamorous early-1930s Hollywood, either off- or on-screen—Marlene Dietrich, Katharine Hepburn, Greta Garbo—but she *was* the only woman director regularly working during the classical Hollywood period, so the way her image was used by the studios and press is significant. After all, most photos of Arzner we see today weren't surreptitious candid snapshots or suppressed images but composed publicity stills. Arzner wasn't caught with her hand on Bow's leg—they were posing for a photographer behind the scenes on a film shoot. However playful the intent, it's a rare and unambiguous display of Arzner's sexual forthrightness that goes far beyond the reversal of gender roles. No less than Dietrich or Garbo, Arzner was controlling her image. Looked at today, these shots are remarkably powerful in their ability to reject our modern gaze, to overturn our expectations about how a woman is supposed to present herself. Similarly, Arzner's films remain complicated objects of desire, thwarting any longstanding biases or conjecture we may have about who's looking from behind the camera and who is the willing recipient of that look.

It's difficult to point to many Hollywood figures as singular, however prominent or profoundly their work or image was imprinted upon the American consciousness; Arzner stands alone in this way, yet she achieved her singularity not by being a rebel but by playing the game. By all accounts she was respected, eliciting the admiration of actors, directors, and studio heads. She was so well-liked by many of her male superiors that they all but fought over keeping her in their employment. Early in her career, in the mid-1920s, when she was working as a "cutter" in the editing department at Paramount, she threatened to leave for a full-time screenwriting gig at Columbia Pictures, then an independent "poverty row" studio where she might also have the chance to direct. When Paramount's head of production, B. P. Schulberg, got wind of this, he became incensed, convincing her to stay by promising to let her direct. And though she appeared comfortable integrating into the firmly established man's world of the Hollywood system as it transitioned to sound, it would be reductive and inaccurate to call her "one of the boys." Arzner's career, unlike those of practically all her male contemporaries who had weathered years of Hollywood scandals, technological advancements, and industry ups and downs, would come to a definitive and premature end.

By 1943, she had sixteen directorial credits to her name. This was the year Arzner would make her final film, *First Comes Courage*, a war picture starring Oberon as a secret agent married to a Nazi commander; it would have to be completed without her after she came down with a serious case of pneumonia on set. Sixteen films would seem an impressive haul for such a span, though the churn-'em-out nature of Hollywood often resulted in more than a film per year for directors (for example, George Cukor, who began a few years later than Arzner, banked more than twenty films in essentially the same length of time). Arzner's slowdown and eventual abandoning of the industry strikes one today as an immense lost opportunity. It doesn't seem a coincidence that her career in movies ended when it did: following the Second World War, the gender norms of American culture drastically changed yet again, making a figure like Arzner even less likely.

Before Arzner, in the silent era, when the industry was still coalescing, there had been a flowering of women making films in the United States, including a handful of genuine pioneers who have long been all but erased from mainstream movie history: Lois Weber, Cleo Madison, and French-born Alice Guy-Blaché. After Arzner, the landscape would be parched. Even the pitifully few Hollywood woman directors in Arzner's wake were not operating at the same level of studio functionality; all were in one way or another outsiders. In the 1950s, the British-born actress and director Ida Lupino (*Outrage*) was largely working in a B-movie vein, making scrappy films for American audiences that were the products of her own independent production company. In the 1970s, during the hallowed New Hollywood resurgence that resulted in a new generation of ragged male antiheroes, Elaine May directed films for Paramount and Twentieth Century-Fox but was constantly battling male studio heads over final cuts, while the quirky, unmistakably personal films of Joan Micklin Silver (*Hester Street*) appealed to a sliver of the moviegoing audience. Along with a handful of directors working in independent production (Barbara Loden) or "exploitation" film (Doris Wishman, Stephanie Rothman), these women essentially created the corpus of female-helmed cinema that existed by the time of Arzner's death in 1979 at age eighty-two.

Considering this history, the successful but ultimately stunted career of Dorothy Arzner summons a host of what-ifs and alternate realities. If she had remained in Hollywood, amassing more credits and gaining rightful legend status, could she have mentored young women who also wanted to work in a directorial capacity?

There's another crucial hypothetical here. Arzner had been finished with her movie career for more than a decade when the critics of the French film journal *Cahiers du Cinéma* began articulating the ideas that would lead to the auteur theory—a revolution in cinematic analysis. The basic principles of auteurism position the director as the author—the voice, the perspective, the *soul* of the picture. Before these critics, including Jean-Luc Godard, François Truffaut, and Jacques Rivette, became the medium-altering filmmakers of the French New Wave, they were singing praises of the likes of Alfred Hitchcock, Charles Chaplin, Otto Preminger, and Howard Hawks as artists; in the past, studio directors had more commonly been thought of as competent practitioners. Crucially, these filmmakers were still all working in the 1950s when these revisions were taking place in the critical landscape, and by the early 1960s auteurism had been adapted to American criticism by the *Village Voice*'s Andrew Sarris. If Arzner had still been working, would she have benefited from this new way of thinking about film artistry? Or would sexism have still won out?

As with so many studio directors, it's easy to demystify Arzner as a cog in the machine, applying her skills to a variety of pictures of varying tones and genres. Yet even if we don't define auteurism strictly, or if we at least allow for the limitations of the single-author theory of the inescapably collaborative medium of cinema, it's difficult to dismiss the notion that movies boasting Arzner's directorial credit were marked in some way by two strong and complementary factors: her gender and her lesbian identity. The former would seem self-evident: she was seen as the maker of "women's pictures," movies that both starred women and were intended to appeal to female audiences; her status as a "woman's director" was the centerpiece of any of the dozens of newspaper and magazine articles written about her during her Hollywood tenure. Her lesbianism, often referred to today as an "open secret," is connected most explicitly to her long-term relationship with the modern dancer Marion Morgan, with whom she lived for forty years until 1971, when Morgan died.

Complicating any serious treatment of Arzner's life is that not much is known about her private world, encouraging writing on her to be mostly broad biographical outlines and close film readings, as acknowledged in Judith Mayne's indispensable *Directed by Dorothy Arzner*. The lack of concrete "evidence" remains true of so many influential gay Americans whose lives and careers were often dependent on remaining secretive. The facts of their emotional, psychological, and domestic existences remain to a certain extent guessing games, reliant on photographs, personal letters, and hushed accounts of those who knew them, all of it, like the work itself, defined by the vagaries of secondhand words and whispered pasts. In discussing these heavily circumscribed histories, the writer and filmmaker Andrea Weiss reminds us that "it is this insistence by the dominant culture on making homosexuality invisible and unspeakable that both requires and enables us to locate gay history in rumor, innuendo, fleeting gestures, and coded language." To this day, Arzner is marked by her historical privacy as much as by her queerness: long-term cohabitation with another woman, persistent lack of femininity in dress and manner, and perhaps most relevant for our concerns, a filmic oeuvre distinguished by a markedly ambivalent attitude toward heterosexual relationships.

. . .

Dorothy Arzner hated being called a "woman director." We can adequately reckon with her legacy only if we take her off the pedestal of exceptionalism that she so resented. The sustained, rather desolate image of Arzner as a monolithic figure in classical Hollywood film history—the *only* "woman director," the *only* "lesbian director"—is to a certain degree dependent upon isolating her and her work from cultural realities. But any discussion of Arzner's cinematic importance must situate her within the social landscape of the 1930s, the era when she was at the crest of her professional wave, capped by the 1940 release of *Dance, Girl, Dance,* her most popular and fascinating film.

One mustn't ignore that lesbian audiences were crucial—if statistically unquantifiable—elements in the box office numbers for Hollywood movies, and in the 1930s they turned out for pictures starring women, especially Dietrich, Garbo, and Hepburn. These stars of the pre-Code era were not only known or rumored to be lesbian or bisexual, they also often appeared in roles that playfully hinted at their off-screen personas. Studio filmmakers may have exploited such imagery for their own ends, titillating male viewers with lesbian flirtation and sensuality, but lesbians, a crucial part of the moviegoing ecosystem, were aware that these stars were catering to them as well.

The visibility of lesbianism in the pre-Code era has often been deemed inextricable from style. This view is likely based on cinema's most famous and glamorous moment of "lesbian chic": Marlene Dietrich kissing another woman in Josef von Sternberg's *Morocco* (1930). As Amy Jolly, a sultry, disillusioned cabaret singer working in a Mogador nightclub, Dietrich makes an astonishing entrance in tuxedo and top hat. While prowling the room, she catches the eye of a pretty female audience member and approaches her. She pulls a flower from the brunette's hair, sniffs it while maintaining electric eye contact, and then, in front of everyone, unabashedly bends over and plants a peck on the stranger's lips. It's brief yet charged, wonderfully unexpected, and even if it elicits approving laughs from the woman's tablemates, Dietrich's dead-serious sensuality expresses something other than a joke. She's not just alighting upon this woman, she's drinking her in. So strong is the whiff of eroticism that even when, a moment later, she tosses the flower at Gary

Cooper's handsome French Foreign Legionnaire, setting off the film's central romance, a sense of pansexuality hovers over the rest of the heterosexual love story. It's the ultimate example of what Hollywood films were able to get away with in this brief window in the early sound years, when homosexuality was technically forbidden, yet the nascent Code rules weren't enforced. About this famous scene, Dietrich scholar Gaylyn Studlar wrote, "With an absence of evidence in the PCA files as they now exist, we can only speculate that perhaps these sophisticated, wordless hints at the transgression of gender and sexual norms were tolerated because they were contextualized as being part of the heroine's 'performance.'"

For Dietrich, though, the performance was everything, and inextricable from her "real" persona. With the help of Hollywood stylists like Paramount's Travis Banton, who was gay—like so many of the studios' other costume designers of the era—Dietrich was staking out her own territory. She was so enamored of Banton's broad-shouldered tuxedo silhouette for *Morocco* that she requested him to design a masculine suit for her private use. Dietrich was assuming authorship of her filmic image, despite the mythic pull of Sternberg, one of the dreamiest image makers ever to work in motion pictures. Dietrich had become a screen star when Sternberg cast her in *The Blue Angel* (1930), which the already successful director made while temporarily working in Berlin. *Morocco* was American audiences' much hyped introduction to Dietrich, and it was a box office and critical triumph, landing Dietrich an Academy Award nomination in the ceremony's fourth year of existence. Dietrich proved herself more than an exotic new oddity. Even without knowledge of Dietrich's personal life, this scene would be legendary for moviegoers; Dietrich's sexual fluidity, her affairs with both women and men, her frequent visits to Berlin's drag clubs and gay bars lend the moment a greater power, allowing its star control and agency while also implicitly evoking the sexual permissiveness and vibrant, soon-to-be-eradicated gay culture of Weimar-era Germany.

"The woman all women want to see!" *Morocco*'s ads trumpeted. Paramount's publicity push for Dietrich upon the film's release reflected an awareness of a certain segment of its target audience, one that was growing. Dietrich's ascendance was concurrent with the interwar gay subculture that had risen in urban American areas in the twenties and thirties. New York, Chicago, and Los Angeles became down-low epicenters of gay parties, cabarets, and elaborate drag balls, communities established in concert with the rise of an expanding commercial leisure culture looking for ever more customers. Especially in the years before the end of Prohibition—when urbanites flaunted rebellious behavior as almost a matter of course—gay venues thrived as one more underground pleasure of city living. Hollywood didn't explicitly reflect this reality of queer culture so much as evoke it by gesturing toward decadence, which would prove impossible for an industry increasingly guarded by moralizers.

Dietrich wasn't alone in providing brazen thrills for lesbian audiences in the first half of the 1930s. Her mantle was taken up by stars like Garbo and Hepburn. The former offered a sphynx-like mythic grandeur, the latter an earthy tomboyish virility, but they were each knowingly engaging viewers by cultivating an ambiguous allure. Garbo, the rare star to have successfully transitioned from silent films to talkies, is known to have been involved in multiple affairs with women, including poet and playwright Mercedes de Acosta (also romantically linked to Dietrich) and Canadian actress Fifi D'Orsay. Awareness of this isn't necessary to perceive the dense homoerotic appeal of her films, especially Rouben Mamoulian's *Queen Christina* (1933), in which Garbo ups Dietrich's ante by kissing another woman flush on the lips—and this time it's not a cabaret tease.

Queen Christina may have largely erased the real-life homosexuality of Sweden's powerful monarch in favor of a traditional hetero-historical romance, but the brief yet passionate kiss between the Queen (while dressed in pants) and her devoted lady-in-waiting Ebba Sparre (Elizabeth Young) is a clear attempt to maintain a level of homoeroticism in the text. Confirming the film's placement in the constellation of Hollywood lesbian cinema—and further highlighting the intimate community of women artists these films forged—is the fact that its screenwriter, Salka Viertel (Garbo's devoted friend), acknowledged that she was directly inspired by *Mädchen in Uniform* (1931). This groundbreaking and scandalous German film, depicting a young student's obsessive love for her female teacher at an all-girls school, had recently received an American release, and Viertel had been personally acquainted with the director, Leontine Sagan, from the Berlin theater world. According to Viertel, even producer Irving Thalberg encouraged her to play the kinds of lesbian feelings and evocations associated with *Mädchen*. Joseph Breen sensed danger, deeming *Queen Christina* in violation of the Code and trying to stop its release. Yet this was mere months before he consolidated power and formed the PCA, so a jury of studio executives voted unanimously to overrule his objections.

Though the kind of winking, erotic audacity exhibited in *Morocco* and *Queen Christina* would come to an end with the enforcement of the Code in 1934,

Hepburn would offer her most confrontational gender role-playing in a film released in 1935: *Sylvia Scarlett*. An already highly respected star of the sound era, Hepburn had been developing her on-screen persona throughout the early part of the decade; her brand was brassy and boyish, whether as a daring, dashing aviator in her second film, *Christopher Strong* (1932), directed by none other than fellow trousers lover Dorothy Arzner, or as Jo March in George Cukor's *Little Women* (1933). Hepburn reunited two years later with Cukor, whose successes as a Broadway director had already made him a hot item when he arrived in Hollywood, and where his known homosexuality became an open secret. One of the queerest films ever made in Hollywood, Cukor's *Sylvia Scarlett* is a tonally schizophrenic cross-dressing farce that zips along on Hepburn's sensual yet gender-ambiguous charms, used to delicious effect as a young Frenchwoman who chooses to disguise herself as a boy so that she and her embezzler father (Edmund Gwenn) can escape to England.

What young Sylvia, now Sylvester and resembling a young, leonine Leonardo DiCaprio, couldn't have predicted are the pinballing sexual energies that her new identity sets in motion. She's on the receiving end of overtures from both handsome men—Cary Grant's Cockney crook Jimmy and Brian Aherne's sensitive aesthete Michael—and mercurial women, from an imperious Russian adventuress (Natalie Paley) to a Buckingham Street housemaid (Dennie Moore), who plants an unreciprocated kiss on Sylvester's lips. Some of these characters are attracted to Sylvester for his impish charm, others for his clearly present femininity. In Shakespearean tradition, all this confusion will be "corrected" on the path to heterosexual—or at least bisexual—fulfillment, yet *Sylvia Scarlett* seems to embrace human sexuality's complicated lack of fixedness all the way to the end, leaving such provocations for viewers to chew on.

Neither critics nor audiences had the jaw strength. The reviews weren't kind, though *Time* magazine's critics admitted the film "reveals the interesting fact that Katharine Hepburn is better looking as a boy than as a woman." An outright bomb, *Sylvia Scarlett* lost RKO the huge sum of $363,000 and forever poisoned the relationship between Cukor and the studio. There were reports of mass walkouts, hoots and hollers from theater patrons, and groans at the kiss between Hepburn and Moore. Today it's difficult to know if these anecdotes have been exaggerated over the years or were used to further bludgeon the filmmakers at the time. Either way, they would seem to reflect a cultural sea change already taking place in the nascent Code era.

Regardless of its once scandalous reputation, *Sylvia Scarlett* registers to its many appreciative cult fans today as a happy accident that somehow skirted past the powers that be. There was so much conceptually repellent about the film to Joseph Breen that it almost overwhelmed him. He threw up his hands at the president of RKO upon reading the script: "It is difficult to make any specific criticism or suggestion, as it is the general flavor . . . which is open to objection . . . We suggest that thought be given to the danger of overemphasizing or playing upon any possible relationship between Sylvia and another woman based on the fact that she is masquerading as a boy." One crucial moment in the final film appears to be a victim of censorship: immediately after Hepburn pulls away from Moore's kiss, the film cuts with a swift wipe effect—the only one in the film—to a moment just minutes later, with Hepburn positioned in a different spot in the same room. Yet there was something so intrinsically queer about this film that there was no way to fully straighten it out.

Hepburn brought *Sylvia Scarlett* to Cukor as a potential project for collaboration, and the film remains the prime example of Hepburn's androgyny as both comedian and erotic force. Though farcical and released in a newly censorious environment, Cukor's confection can be situated on a continuum with *Morocco* and *Queen Christina*. Their images were in part catering to female viewers in the know, women who were to gain pleasure rather than panic from them. Each of these films is imbued with a sensuality that exists in the interplay between the women on-screen and those in the audience, serving as reminders that it's not just men who look at women as embodiments of desire. According to Weiss, "the cinema's contribution toward the formation of lesbian identity in the early twentieth century should not be underestimated." The primal power of Dietrich, Garbo, and Hepburn, each inhabiting an on-screen sexual ambiguity enhanced by rumors of private sexual habits, exerts a pull over viewers well into the twenty-first century, where they stand in sharp and seductive contrast to largely risk-averse film and television celebrities.

Dorothy Arzner's films offer a lesbian perspective in an entirely different manner. Both before and after the Code's enforcement, the queer element in her work is perhaps imperceptible on a literal level. As Arzner scholar Mayne puts it, "Lesbianism affects her films in diffuse ways. There are no lesbian plots, no lesbian characters in her films; but there is constant and deliberate attention to how women dress and act and perform, as much for each other as for the male figures in their lives." Her filmography constitutes a lesbian cinema less concerned with revealing desirous undercurrents than about repositioning the viewer's perspective. Arzner's films assume a female viewer, creating a sense of companionship and conspiracy, pushing the Hollywood term "woman's picture" into complex depths of camaraderie and emotional connection, reasserting the perspective of women as both subject and object, star and viewer, the one who is looked at and the one who is looking. No film of Arzner's better expresses this constant negotiation than *Dance, Girl, Dance*, which explicitly articulates questions of gender, viewership, and the gaze more than three decades before feminist film theory would change the way we all talk about movies.

. . .

The various photos of Dorothy Arzner on the set buttoned up in dashing male attire become ever more fascinating when viewed alongside the personal photographs in which she's dressed as "Garth." Taken when she was a teenager, they show Arzner looking dapper and entirely comfortable in dark suit, pants, and plaid pageboy cap. In one, she's nonchalantly reading the newspaper, in another she's standing outside in a dryly masculine pose, hands in pockets, head cocked to the side, looking confidently at the camera. The pictures, tagged "Garth for a Night," indicate not just a costume but a male alter ego. According to Mayne, it was young Dorothy's penchant for tomboyish behavior that led her stepmother to send her to the private Westlake School for Girls, which she graduated from in 1915.

Arzner was a California native, born in San Francisco, raised in Los Angeles, and the movie industry had been in her peripheral vision from an early age. Her father and stepmother were restaurant proprietors, and one of these establishments, the Hoffman Café, was a hangout for early Hollywood bigwigs like Charlie Chaplin and D. W. Griffith. Nevertheless, Arzner's interest in movies wasn't truly kindled until she was in her early twenties and in 1919 was given a set visit to the Famous Players–Lasky studio, soon to be renamed Paramount. Her invitation came from the writer-director William DeMille (brother of Cecil), who during the First World War was head of the Los Angeles Emergency Ambulance Corps, where Arzner was volunteering. She had studied for two years at University of Southern California, planning for a medical career. The movie studio tour was entrancing, and, finding the technical operation of filmmaking appealing, she immediately applied for work, starting out as a script typist, essentially the movie studio's basement level. After three months she was script supervising on sets, and throughout the 1920s she steadily rose through the studio's hierarchies, gaining expertise in almost every aspect of the process.

After years of cutting pictures (which would remain her favorite job for the solitary creativity it demanded), she was promoted to chief editor. While working on the Rudolph Valentino vehicle *Blood and Sand* (1922), she was tasked with shooting the superstar in full toreador outfit, to be spliced into stock footage of the bull-fighting arena. Director James Cruze, wildly impressed with her nimble, intuitive work on *Blood and Sand*, hired her to edit a pair of large-scale historical epics, *The Covered Wagon* (1923) and *Old Ironsides* (1926); Arzner was on location for both, the first of which was shot in Nevada and Utah and the other on Santa Catalina Island, and which required the wrangling of enormous casts. Entrusting her with *The Covered Wagon*, a major production and huge moneymaker for the studio, indicated her rising reputation. In his memoirs, Jesse L. Lasky Jr., screenwriter and son of the studio founder, recalled a triumphant early screening of the film in their home's private projection room, attended by "a young, dark, extremely serious woman in tweeds and flat golf shoes, named Dorothy Arzner."

Old Ironsides, with its seafaring spectacle, shot partly in a process called Magnascope, a proto-wide-screen lens format that predated CinemaScope by nearly thirty years, wouldn't be as successful, but it was a crucial learning experience for Arzner, who felt kindly and rigorously mentored by Cruze. Full of sweep and masculine bravado, it was the kind of film that Arzner would never direct. Whether by choice or gendered default, Arzner's beat would be women's pictures: not just movies intended to appeal to women in terms of genre (the melodrama, for example, has always been marked as a "feminine" genre, even from its nineteenth-century stage origins), but movies that were often about the interactions between and among women.

Arzner's rise in power at the studio was hardly under the radar. Almost immediately the studio's PR machine kicked into high gear, promoting her as an exotic distaff Tinseltown commodity. Under the headline FORMER SCRIPT GIRL IS CINDERELLA OF MEGAPHONES, the *Los Angeles Daily Times* touted in December 1926, "Not only is Miss Arzner the first woman in the history of Paramount to be given a directorship, but she is the only woman in the industry to be assigned to a directorial position within the past ten years." The clippings in Arzner's bursting scrapbook, preserved at the UCLA archives, show that her ascendance was gushed over in nearly every newspaper and studio trade. Her gender is almost always the centerpiece: the *Daily Mail* referred to Arzner as "a strikingly handsome woman"; the *Boston Globe*'s headline proclaimed ONLY WOMAN MOVIE DIRECTOR! And though she would tell the *L.A. Daily Times* in September 1928, "I never think of myself as a woman director," Arzner would rarely be referred to in the press as anything else.

After Arzner graduated to director, love stories would out of necessity be baked into her films' narratives, yet these romances often took a back seat to tales of female friendship and professional pursuit. Her first feature, *Fashions for Women* (1927), helped make a leading lady out of silent star Esther Ralston. Two years later, the frisky *The Wild Party* (1929), a tale of female camaraderie set at a girls' college, was the first talkie for both Arzner and star Clara Bow, who immediately had to combat skepticism about her nasal Brooklyn accent. Heterosexuality was persistent in Arzner's films, but it was hardly aspirational. In many of her most successful sound films—from *Honor Among Lovers* (1931), a comic-tinged drama with Claudette Colbert as a capable secretary and Fredric March as her amorous boss, shot at Paramount's Astoria Studios in Queens; to the brilliantly cynical *Merrily We Go to Hell* (1932), with March and Sylvia Sidney as a couple struggling with professional disappointment and crippling alcoholism; to *Craig's Wife* (1936), with Rosalind Russell as a destructive and duplicitous housewife—marriage was depicted as a corruptible or poisoned institution.

Even her box office failures register today as anything but off-the-shelf product. After she had left Paramount in 1932, following Schulberg's resignation from his role as head of production and her refusal to take a company-wide pay cut, Arzner went freelance, and was soon hired by Samuel Goldwyn. Her relationship with the fearsome producer indicates her ability to navigate Hollywood's male-dominated backrooms with aplomb. Said Arzner, "I liked working for Sam Goldwyn. Oh, he would blow his top and the writers would be carted off to the hospital with ulcers, but I'd just wait for him to settle down and then I'd explain why things couldn't be the way he wanted them. You have to learn how to handle producers." Goldwyn wanted her for his high-profile Émile Zola adaptation *Nana* (1934), with which he was dead set on making a superstar out of Ukrainian-born, Stanislavski-trained actress Anna Sten.

"Goldwyn gave me everything I wanted in the way of sets, lighting, cameramen, and costumes, but he also gave me the job of making Anna Sten look like a great actress," said Arzner. "He had spent a year grooming her, telling everyone that she would be greater than Dietrich, greater than Garbo, and then when she opened her mouth, out came these monosyllables. The only thing I could do was not let her talk so much." The film failed to turn Sten into a household name, leaving the general audience cold while also alienating Zola fans by sanitizing his grimy, sexually explicit, and tragic novel about an impoverished sex worker. However, the film, shot by Gregg Toland (future cinematographer of *These Three* and *Citizen Kane*) and flaunting costumes for Sten by Dietrich's fashion guru Travis Banton, is one of Arzner's most stylistically bold movies, retaining a proto-feminist brashness in its depiction of a woman attempting to maintain dignity in an abusive, male-dominated world.

Most of Arzner's women are working girls of one sort of another, frequently focused more on their careers than on romance or male companionship. Arzner's penchant for stories of women's persistence is perhaps the clearest indicator of her authorship, the natural expression of someone who rose through the ranks at her place of work, from apprentice to captain, and ascended to the top of her field. *Dance, Girl, Dance* is the purest version of this theme, subordinating conventional heterosexual love to more pressing matters of professional ambition. On the page, one could see how this amusing yet emotionally substantial story of two formidable friends turned foes, played with fervid drive by Maureen O'Hara and Lucille Ball, might be dramatized as a tale of man-hungry careerists—after all, a fella does come between them, exacerbating dormant resentments. Yet through direction, performance, editing, and an attention to emotional detail that sharpens the women's perspective at every turn, *Dance, Girl, Dance* reduces or abstracts the love triangle to the point of inconsequence, even ludicrousness. Arzner's movie is about women, full stop: how they're perceived, how they perceive one another, and how they choose to tangle with the world around them.

. . .

Art doesn't have to be good for you. Cinema isn't a shorthand for morality, just as, despite its legions of religious worrywarts, it was never an expression of a culture's immorality. Art can't be reduced, and neither can commercial entertainment, given as it is to the whims and contingencies and shortcomings of living as a human being in a commodified world. Too much analysis is focused on justification (Why was this made? Whom does it benefit?) when perhaps what it requires instead is consideration and common sense. Mainstream American movies, traditionally the product of entertainment studios less interested in nurturing the soul than in augmenting the bottom line, are made up of contradictions that defy easy political readings.

Dance, Girl, Dance might strike a twenty-first-century viewer as remarkably progressive, the work of a filmmaker way ahead of her time, encouraging viewers to think about their status as spectators decades before any movies did. If it were released today, we would likely assume a film that explicitly addresses its audience, and specifically takes its male viewers to task for their complicity in objectifying the female body and demeaning the female spirit, was trying to be instructive while also positioning itself as on the right side of history. In 1940, when *Dance, Girl, Dance* did just that, decades before the term "male gaze" made its way from academia to overuse in the general parlance, Arzner was just telling it like it is.

The scene, jarring and cathartic, comes near the end of the film. Maureen O'Hara's character, Judy, is a wannabe ballerina who has too long endured being a professional punching bag for the cruel delectation of auditoriums full of hooting men. As the dancing "stooge" to Lucille Ball's Bubbles in a low-class Broadway burlesque, Judy is called upon to warm up the audience. Judy and Bubbles have a professional connection that goes beyond this one hit show. They both are protégées of the same dance instructor, the late Madame Basilova, who had encouraged Judy to follow her dreams to perform in a respectable ballet company and bemoaned the bump-and-grind of the burlesque circuit that Bubbles unapologetically joins. When Bubbles, now going by the stage name Tiger Lily White, gets Judy a part in her new show, her offer seems generous to the down-on-her-luck ballerina. Yet Judy is there only to be mocked: twirling in a tutu, she is laughed at while pointing and pirouetting, tossed off the stage to make room for Tiger Lily, known for her take-no-guff sass and far less classy acts of seduction, which border on stripteases.

Fed up with Bubbles, who has reduced Judy's professional pursuit to a distorted funhouse mirror of itself, Judy reaches her breaking point. In the moment, she decides to take her ire out on the faceless rows of men who have delighted in her humiliation. Stopping the show, she saunters to center stage and does the unthinkable: she looks right back at them.

Provoking immediate discomfort from men who have too long enjoyed their status as invisible gawkers, Judy's words are extraordinary and damning: "Go ahead and stare ... I know you want me to tear my clothes off so's you can look your fifty cents' worth. Fifty cents for the privilege of staring at a girl the way your wives won't let you. What do you suppose *we* think of you up here—with your silly smirks your mothers would be ashamed of?"

Judy's arms are crossed as she confidently scans the crowd for satisfying signs of discomfort. "We'd laugh right back at the lot of you, only we're paid to let you sit there and roll your eyes and make your screamingly clever remarks. What's it for?

So's you can go home when the show's over and strut before your wives and sweethearts and play at being the stronger sex for a minute? I'm sure they see through you just like we do."

As a contemporary viewer of the film may be, the burlesque audience is momentarily gobsmacked and silent—except for one woman in a reasonable suit and hat (the queer-coded, no-nonsense secretary of a local dance impresario) who immediately jumps to her feet and applauds. Finally, the rest of the audience follows suit. Perhaps they're cowed, perhaps they're enlightened. Perhaps Arzner's film itself won't let the moment pass without calling attention to such revelation. There are more onstage confrontations to come, including a farcical knock-down altercation between Judy and Bubbles that both complicates and elucidates Judy's *j'accuse*: What could be more delectable to a house full of catcallers than a catfight? But Judy's words are the true climax of the film. For she's not merely addressing the theater of anonymous, mostly male thrill-seekers: she's also talking to the viewers in the dark of the movie house. We are watching, looking at her, as moviegoers are invited to do with all women. "I'm sure they see through you just like *we* do." The *we* is particularly powerful here, as it shows that Judy is not simply defending herself as an artist but as any woman who demands professional respect. Delivered in a film by Hollywood's most ambitious and successful woman director, Judy's magnificent refusal to be her audience's plaything is powerful and luminous.

The fleetness of tone that Arzner maintains throughout *Dance, Girl, Dance* can obscure the film's cynical core: these two dancers may be on divergent career paths, but they are both drawn into acts predicated on consensual humiliation. This is true not only for Judy, whose performance turns "respectable" dance into a kind of maniacal masochism, but also for Bubbles, whose main number in the show, "Mother, What Do I Do Now?" finds her beset by wind machines that blow her dress up at inopportune times. The song climaxes with a (chaste, Code-approved) clothing snafu in which, after hiding behind a cardboard tree, Tiger Lily White sees her dress and bloomers yanked from her body one by one and soar to the rafters on a string. After this embarrassment, Bubbles peeks her head out and cries to the audience, "Hey, Mom, what do I do now?" Illusorily naked, she delivers the line in a baby-doll voice that's less coquette than little lost girl.

Because Bubbles's objectifying vaudeville of mock mortification is always followed by Judy's demeaning stooge dance, *Dance, Girl, Dance* conveys an overall queasiness around the question of women's professional options. In terms of ambition and aesthetic, Judy and Bubbles are in stark opposition, yet they are undoubtedly united by the film's perspective on an essentially demeaning system that gives women only one of two slots to fill: the sexless killjoy or the wiseass tramp—a show business variation on the virgin and the whore. Yet in Judy's climactic speech, the film lays blame for the women's humiliations at the feet of the men in the audience, signaling their complicity in a system of sexism and dehumanization. Crucially, her monologue also takes the onus off the women, who may have willingly embodied these vulgar stage roles but who also need to work to survive. "What are you going to do now, *cry?*" a man heckles Judy, right before she launches into her jeremiad—a moment of attempted infantilization and the last straw.

Dance, Girl, Dance fires back at a male-dominated world that demands traditional femininity from its women and then punishes them for it. In this way, it's particularly fascinating as a project for Arzner, who rejected conventional feminine signifiers in her profession, an approach that both secured her acceptance into a systemically macho environment and forever cast her as an outsider.

.   .   .

Arzner's ability to invest a protofeminist perspective and a queer sensibility into her work is especially noteworthy considering that her films rarely originated with her. This was the case with *Dance, Girl, Dance*, which offers a pure jolt of Arzner's bold individuality. It's worth recounting the film's journey to the screen—and the many creators who had their hands on it—as a way of certifying the strength of Arzner as auteur. The film began as a personal project of Erich Pommer, a German émigré producer who oversaw such expressionist masterpieces as *The Cabinet of Dr. Caligari* (1922), *The Last Laugh* (1924), *Metropolis* (1927), and Dietrich and von Sternberg's *The Blue Angel*. Arzner wasn't Pommer's first choice as director. The film was assigned to Roy Del Ruth, a Hollywood workhorse whose career stretched back to the silents and whose experience directing spirited musicals (including MGM's *Broadway Melody of 1936* and *Born to Dance*) and crime dramas (James Cagney's *Lady Killer*) would seem to make him a perfect fit for the material's mixture of street-smart sass and elaborate dance numbers. But Pommer removed Del Ruth soon after going into production, leaving an opening for Arzner, a freelancer since departing Paramount.

Her previous film, *The Bride Wore Red* (1938), had been a major box office disappointment for MGM. Yet the arbitrary winds of success and failure in Hollywood were as mysterious then as today: this effervescent yet slyly cynical rags-to-riches romantic drama, starring Joan Crawford as a working-class bar singer in Trieste who finds herself in the lap of luxury after posing as a wealthy countess, plays beautifully as a class satire. Nevertheless, the film flopped, and Arzner was looking for a quick resuscitation, seeing potential in the script for the RKO production, a largely female-driven affair then titled *Have It Your Own Way* (or *One of Six Girls*), co-written by Hollywood scribe Tess Slesinger and her husband, Frank Davis. Their script was based on an original story by Vicki Baum, an Austrian Jewish novelist who had emigrated to the United States in the early thirties to work on the screenplay for MGM's film version of her book *Menschen im Hotel*, which would become Best Picture winner *Grand Hotel*—the script that Lillian Hellman had been proud to discover in the slush pile while working as a "reader" during her first Hollywood adventure. Intrigued, Arzner demanded significant changes to the screenplay before restarting the film's halted production.

"I decided what should be said from the script at hand from some rewriting," as Arzner explained her process years later. "I decided the theme should be 'The Art Spirit' (Maureen O'Hara) versus the commercial 'Go-Getter' (Lucille Ball)." In elucidating the central philosophical conflict of the film as being between the women, Arzner moves the film away from the heterosexual romantic triangle among Judy, Bubbles, and Jimmie (Louis Hayward). A rich, alcoholic playboy who's going through an acrimonious divorce and whose predominant personality trait—other than drinking—is a childlike obsession with his Ferdinand the Bull stuffed animal, Jimmie is a grievously unappealing love interest. Arzner's noticeable de-emphasis of the character is a successful method for audience reorientation; despite second billing, above Ball, he's left off-screen for sizable chunks of the film. The queer theorist Alexander Doty proposed that Arzner "used Jimmie in the narrative in the same way women characters are traditionally used in 'straight' male narratives, that is, as a public vehicle for transgressive erotic exchanges between same-sex characters." Jimmie's marginalization allows the professional, homosocial interactions between the two women to take up primary narrative space—especially welcome considering the winning performances from O'Hara and Ball, each at the outset of an illustrious career. Even in black-and-white, these redheads are vivid spitfires with contrasting acting styles—O'Hara redirects her passionate "art spirit" inward, while Ball is all extroverted ambition, confidence with an alluring, sneering shrug.

There were other trims demanded by Arzner, including the elimination of a superfluous B-plot romance for Judy and Bubbles's roommate, further centering the two women. Yet her most decisive and important alteration was changing the gender of a crucial figure, which would both add an Arzner-like character to the mix and allow for a casting coup. Basilova, the women's Russian dancing teacher, was originally written as a man called Basiloff. In transforming this character into an imperious yet loving mother hen, Arzner gave the film's first half a crucial female center. Judith Mayne has remarked that the character's changed name sounds suspiciously like the surname of Alla Nazimova, the Russian American actress infamous in 1920s Hollywood for openly carrying on lesbian affairs; throwing lavish parties at her estate, nicknamed the Garden of Allah; and even directing one of silent Hollywood's most unlikely queer epics: a homoerotic 1922 adaptation of Oscar Wilde's *Salome*, rumored to feature an entirely gay and lesbian cast. (Early in her career, Arzner had served as script supervisor on Nazimova's *Stronger Than Death* [1920], and while not much is known about their working relationship, George Cukor gave a gossipy interview in 1986 in which he flat out stated that the women had been lovers.)

By casting the legendary, Stanislavski-trained Maria Ouspenskaya of the Moscow Art Theatre as Judy and Bubbles's instructor, Arzner evoked a lineage of mastery and expertise that lends a layer of seriousness to this story of artistic pursuit. Along with Richard Boleslavsky, Ouspenskaya had run New York's American Laboratory Theatre acting school, which Lee Strasberg and Stella Adler attended in the mid-1920s. The school's head teacher, she focused on concentration and affective memory, physical approaches to stage acting that would be passed down for generations, part of the suite of techniques that would form what we commonly refer to as "the Method." Ouspenskaya had first come to America in the touring company of Stanislavski's Moscow Art Theatre; rather than accompany the troupe back to Russia, she stayed in New York and set up shop with Boleslavsky. Her petite stature was in distinct contrast to her reputation among her students. As Isaac Butler writes, "Ouspenskaya cultivated a severe persona, smoking thin black cigars and wearing a monocle. In class, she was famous for her terrifying manner . . . You came dressed to move and work, and you approached acting with a pious seriousness."

In the midthirties, financial troubles led Ouspenskaya to relocate to Los Angeles, where Boleslavsky had been trying his hand at the movies, making period dramas and screwball comedies, directing Irene Dunne to an Oscar nomination for the riotous *Theodora Goes Wild* in 1936. That same year, Ouspenskaya received a Supporting Actress nomination for her brief yet indelible first screen role in William Wyler's *Dodsworth*, competing against Bonita Granville in *These Three*. She would receive another nomination for her similarly small but integral part as Charles Boyer's sweet-souled grandmother in Leo McCarey's *Love Affair* (1939), cementing the Russian grand dame as a character actor of rare command. In *Dance, Girl, Dance*, as in so many of her film roles, the sixty-four-year-old Ouspenskaya has limited screen time: she unceremoniously dies after being hit by a car while escorting Judy to a ballet audition. Yet she makes an undeniable impact. One cannot miss the sartorial and dispositional resemblance between Arzner and Ouspenskaya's Basilova—both are typified by wearing mannish clothes and wielding sober professionalism while overseeing companies of more classically feminine starlets. In the film's first half hour, the camera is often wedded to Basilova's point of view as she watches her troupe of women dance, literalizing a female perspective.

The diminutive Ouspenskaya carries tiny roles with monumental import. When she's in the frame, you look at no one else. At the same time, you want to look *with* her, see what she's seeing. In casting Ouspenskaya as *Dance, Girl, Dance*'s central teacher, a woman who believes in dance as a valid lifestyle as much as an artistic pursuit, Arzner allows us to consider the world through her discerning eyes. There's a brief sequence in which Basilova secretly, quietly watches Judy dance from a staircase; she looks with admiration, power, protectiveness, and even a little melancholy. She had just watched her girls do a "hula" dance during an audition for a dead-eyed cigar-chomping local producer, who is captured by Arzner in cutaways that heighten his grotesquerie—the kind of lascivious male animal Judy will later take to task in her stage smackdown. Only Bubbles fully commits to the sensuality of the dance, tossing and smacking her hips to the delectation of the producer, whose eyes scan her up and down with wolfish delight. She secures a job, but Basilova is unhappy with the sell-out. "Hula is not dancing. It's nothing but oomph," she later cries. For the teacher, Judy represents potential beyond the crassness of modern entertainment, a purity of desire that reminds Basilova of her own idealism.

A film about two women pursuing their dreams as dancers might seem uncontroversial, even rote for this era of Hollywood filmmaking; wannabe showgirls hoofing their way to theatrical stardom had been a story template since the advent of sound, as typified in Busby Berkeley's *42nd Street* (1932) or Gregory La Cava's

Stage Door (1937), the latter featuring a major early role for Lucille Ball. An inspection of RKO's correspondence with the PCA, however, reveals that the film had already begun to ruffle Joseph Breen's feathers before Arzner took over. "We regret to report," began Breen in his sobering, war-department-like tone in a letter from March 21, 1940, "that in its present form, it is not acceptable from the standpoint of the Production Code." The script was, on the page, an entirely too sexual affair, stoking Breen's fear and loathing of anything that might arouse the interest of one's nether regions. He and his PCA associates were horrified by "the sex suggestive scenes in the burlesque theater, specifically the striptease numbers." The constantly soused Jimmie was also unacceptable to Breen, aghast that "the leading male character is drunk throughout most of the story." Among the litany of other complaints, he insisted that a reference to "panties" be changed to "pants" (it ultimately became "stockings") and that the word "lousy" be deleted. But Breen's biggest demand, returned to again and again in letters back and forth with RKO over the coming months, was ensuring that "there must be nothing whatever sex suggestive about Bubbles' dance." One cannot forget that Bubbles's entire character arc is built around her becoming a burlesque star.

Lucille Ball herself further provoked the PCA's ire—and the public's curiosity—by doing her own personal research for the character in some of the city's seedier neighborhoods. In a March 23 article in the daily industry paper *Hollywood Citizen-News*, just two days after Breen wrote his first response, an article with the headline MOVIE PLAYER EYES ART OF STRIP TEASE declared: "To Los Angeles' incredible Skid Row, which is today what New York's Bowery must have been 40 years ago, went Lucille Ball late last night to learn from experts the art of the strip tease." The article is prime evidence of the willingness of the press and certain Hollywood players to tease the Hays Office and lightly mock the tenets of the Production Code Administration—criticism which would only grow more pointed as the years passed. The brash Ball herself is quoted in the article: "I've got to do the strip tease all right . . . but I've got to learn how to do it for Will Hays."

The next month saw a series of starts and increasingly heated stops, with Breen at first giving his stamp of approval in late March, then rescinding it in April, mere days before production was to start. His greenlight was contingent upon the complete elimination of the strip tease dance, for which "a type of 'hula' will be substituted." (Traces of this compromise ended up in the hula audition.) Angered by a new draft of the script, he wrote on April 9, "I wish to repeat our thought, again, in this matter: We cannot approve a motion picture, in which there is a strip tease dance, or any possible suggestion of a strip tease dance, and we cannot approve scenes showing characters offensively drunk." He was also offended by the insinuation of the men's leering gestures in the theater scenes, forcing them to cut such lines as "Go on . . . tear it off!" and "Show us something!" At this point, Roy Del Ruth was still directing the project; though by mid-May, after another round of demanded revisions, and the title had officially changed from the more provocative *Have It Your Own Way* to *Dance, Girl, Dance*, Arzner had been brought in as replacement.

One could easily envision a version of *Dance, Girl, Dance* directed instead by Del Ruth. With our knowledge of Arzner's changes to the project, one can suppose the elements that would have remained in place: a paternal male dance instructor, a centered comic romantic love triangle, another romantic subplot with a minor character that would have pulled focus from Judy and Bubbles. But there are also the more abstract, ineffable qualities a filmmaker brings to her work that are connected to perspective, philosophy, and control. In these pre-auteurist days, the producer was still viewed as a film's primary creator and personality. This is evidenced by *Dance, Girl, Dance*'s reviews upon release, which focused greatly on producer Erich Pommer, often mentioning Arzner only to dismiss her input. *The Hollywood Reporter*'s negative review insists that "Pommer was given a pretty tough assignment for his first RKO production . . . The picture's fault . . . rested mostly at the feet of Dorothy Arzner, who gave the script either old, stilted direction, or, in many cases, no direction at all." Befitting the period, even in its positive reviews, the director is treated as second banana, as in the *Variety* critique: "Erich Pommer is the producer and there's a definite continental flair about the picture, making itself felt even in Dorothy Arzner's direction."

Debates remain today about the centrality of a director to a film's authorship, and whether one can attribute the sensibility of a film—the product of writers, producers, stars, composers, cinematographers, costumers, editors, production designers—to a director at all. To downplay Arzner as an artistic force in order to herald the smooth factory-like functionality of Hollywood would risk further erasure of the system's solitary lesbian director. Arzner's agency can be affirmed only by admiring and analyzing the details that make her cinema so endearing. Or maybe take it from Arzner herself, who in 1976 seemed to have come up with a strong personal working definition of the director's job: "A director must realize what is inside a person, bring it out, and eliminate the flaws . . . The director is the only one who knows what it's all going to look like in the end. It's pictures, after all—the actors' faces, the composition, the movement, how the whole thing is orchestrated."

It's crucial to note especially Arzner's expert direction of Lucille Ball, who at this point in her career was a firecracker sputtering from one project to the next without ever fully sparking. Nearing thirty, the Jamestown, New York, native had been fired from Columbia Pictures before becoming a contract player at RKO in 1935, a steady paycheck keeping her from packing up and heading back east. Her roles at RKO throughout the thirties were small, mostly flower girls and dancers; even the minor breakthrough of an ensemble role in the hit *Stage Door* didn't raise her profile enough to get her out of the "B-movie" racket. In *Dance, Girl, Dance*, Arzner perfectly exploited Ball's singular ability to embody insolence, sensuality, vulnerability, and galumphing self-parody at once, while always remaining likable. Just a little more than a decade later, she would bring that same mix of neuroses and confidence to Lucy Ricardo, whose misplaced drive and inability to fit into predetermined domestic roles made her—inarguably, in this writer's opinion—the funniest character to ever appear on television.

Even if reviews of *Dance, Girl, Dance* downplayed or dismissed Arzner, Ball was indisputable. Wrote *Variety*, the studio "has a very important player on the lot in the person of Miss Ball, who may require special writing. But whatever the requirements, she has the makings of a star." *Dance, Girl, Dance* would prove important to Ball for reasons more than just reviews. The day Arzner filmed the knock-down, drag-out stage scuffle that follows Judy's withering monologue, Ball and O'Hara showed up in the RKO commissary for lunch. Ball, still wearing her torn gold lame dress, smeared makeup, and mock black eye, went over to say hello to George Abbott, the director of her next picture, *Too Many Girls*. Sitting beside him was a young Cuban bandleader, rehearsing for a small part in the movie. The two were introduced, and she shook hands with Desi Arnaz.

Dance, Girl, Dance was released to decent box office and reviews that ranged from positive to polite to disparaging. In other words, it was just another movie. In 1973, however, thirty-three years later, Arzner and this film would be recouped by a new generation. "From Edinburgh, Scotland, to Toronto, Canada, wherever women have gathered at festivals to re-examine their film heritage, the movie of the year has proved to be an obscure RKO comedy of 1940, rescued miraculously from the vaults, rescued from its original total dismissal," wrote the critics Gerald Peary and Karyn Kay in the journal *The Velvet Light Trap*. "The film is *Dance, Girl, Dance*, the next to last feature of Hollywood's most employed and probably most talented woman director, Dorothy Arzner—herself rediscovered and becoming a new star of the women's movement as she enters her 70s."

As is clear from this passage, the reason for Arzner's resurgence thirty years after she left Hollywood is inseparable from the seismic cultural shifts taking place in the United States. The rise of second-wave feminism in the mainstream was leading many to reconsider the long suppressed or devalued roles women played in various popular media, especially cinema. While experimental or independent women filmmakers had become increasingly visible (the 1970s would see works by Chantal Akerman, Barbara Loden, Joan Micklin Silver, and Margarethe von Trotta released in American theaters), the studios remained as male-driven as ever, perhaps even more so, considering that the heralded New American Cinema resuscitating the industry was propped up by a masculinist mythology—embodied by the likes of Michael Corleone, Randle Patrick McMurphy, Ratso Rizzo, and Frank Serpico. Movie lovers scouring the screens for powerful women often had to focus on the past. The feminist critic Molly Haskell would write, "Scanning cinema history for unheralded trailblazers and untold stories, 1970s feminists hit paydirt with the discovery of Hollywood director Dorothy Arzner ... She made the films she wanted to make, and through a whole range of gesture, composition, emphasis, and selection of stars, expressed distinct feelings for women that constitute a kind of signature." At the same time, academics in the still relatively nascent field of film studies were applying new lenses on cinema history, encouraging radical ways of seeing through a feminist perspective. The influential theorist Claire Johnston was an early progenitor of Arzner analysis, writing in 1973 that Judy's cathartic speech at the end of *Dance, Girl, Dance* "has the effect of directly challenging the entire notion of woman as spectacle."

No work of feminist film criticism would prove more lasting—or, to this day, contested—as an essential retraining of *how to look* than Laura Mulvey's epochal 1975 essay "Visual Pleasure and Narrative Cinema." Film criticism bolstered by psychoanalytic theory, Mulvey's piece has so long been a foundational argument and citation, and has been so embraced by subsequent generations of moviegoers, that it braves cliché when raised. Mulvey's essential point is, in a nutshell, that the images of women in American moviemaking are conceived, shot, and stylized for the voyeuristic pleasure of the allegedly male, presumably turned-on viewer, and that this is as much an unconscious manifestation of existing power structures as it is a systemic intentionality. "Unchallenged, mainstream film coded the erotic into the language of the dominant patriarchal order," Mulvey wrote. "It is said that analyzing pleasure, or beauty, destroys it. That is the intention of this article."

Without explicitly erasing the possibility for other types of viewers (lesbians, straight women, gay men), the theory assumes a male, straight, white spectator as the creator and receiver of the image, leading to a subject-object transference predicated on the idea of the viewer's control. The "male gaze" has been leveled over the years as an accusation at most filmmakers whose work tends toward artifice and violence, from Hitchcock to Tarantino to De Palma, as well as a term of basic formal analysis. The theory has remained so central in part because it's simple to apply. When Rita Hayworth makes her ravishing first appearance in *Gilda* (1946), in a shot that exquisitely defies spatial sense, appearing from the bottom of the frame and tossing her hair back, who is she performing for? When Robert Forster first sees Pam Grier in *Jackie Brown* (1997) and Bloodstone's "Natural High" drifts across the soundtrack, and the scene cuts between his eyes and her figure in long shot, whose perspective are we aligned with? De Palma explained a primary goal of his career in 2012 by stating matter-of-factly, "People have been looking at beautiful women since the beginning of time. All you have to do is look on your television screen or go Googling or pick up a magazine, and what do you see? Women, dressed or undressed. That's what people are interested in."

By this point in the twenty-first century, many critics have taken steps to remedy what they perceive as Mulvey's own limited vision, including, powerfully, Janell Hobson, whose essay "Viewing in the Dark: Towards a Black Feminist Approach to Film" tries to account for the placement of Black women in film history, as their almost complete invisibility makes questions of the presumed viewer's pleasure so knotty: "Whereas the construction of the white female body in film can be viewed, studied, deconstructed, often in Hollywood cinema there is no black body that we can analyze. Or so we think." Andrea Weiss problematizes Mulvey by pointing at the many lesbian or lesbian-rumored stars of the thirties who may have been consciously performing erotically for women audiences, who did not have to identify with a male perspective to gain pleasure: "It is clear that, for a lesbian who perceived herself as 'butch,' identification did not require what film theorist Laura Mulvey has called a 'masculinization of spectatorship' in order to connect with the male star."

So durable has Mulvey's theory proven that one might assume it to have always been there—a constant of cinema's conversational landscape. Fascinatingly, Arzner's films would seem to both confirm and refute the idea of the "male gaze" as effectively as those of any filmmaker who ever lived. By virtue of being the only woman to direct in Hollywood during the classical period that Mulvey interrogates, Arzner, whose work focuses on and occasionally eroticizes women, becomes either the exception that proves the rule or the potential bee in Mulvey's bonnet. It's a little of both: Judy's monologue near the climax of *Dance, Girl, Dance* offers a remarkable distillation of Mulvey's essay *avant la lettre*, a condemnation of male viewership as essentially violent and sexualized ("Go ahead and stare . . . Fifty cents for the privilege of staring at a girl the way your wives won't let you"). At the same time, Arzner inherently destroys the idea of a man at the helm; she is both maker and viewer, the constructor of images made not for men's pleasure, but for that of women and other lesbians just like her.

The reemergence of Dorothy Arzner as a topic of discussion in the 1970s moved beyond the discussions of academics. Now that the director had definitively usurped the producer as the brains and heart of the operation in the minds of film lovers, Arzner was finally getting her due. In addition to touring retrospectives and appreciative write-ups in film journals, Arzner was honored in Los Angeles in a 1975 tribute by the Directors Guild of America. The celebration dubbed her a "pioneer director," but as it was organized by the DGA's Committee of Women Members, the evening necessarily focused on her exceptionalism—an ironic, or at least bittersweet, ceremony for a filmmaker who, in her time, didn't like being referred to as a "woman director."

Arzner would inspire future generations of filmmakers, including those aware of her sexual identity, which was still more an open secret than a spoken fact even after her death in 1979 at age eighty-two. Just one year later, the German filmmaker Katja Raganelli touched down in the Coachella Valley city of La Quinta, where Arzner had moved with her lifelong romantic partner, Marion Morgan, building her a house in 1961 so that the desert air might improve her failing health. Here, Raganelli shot the short documentary *Dorothy Arzner: Longing for Women*, a poignant testament to her career and work as well as to the air of mystery around her personal life. It's an attempt by one filmmaker to make sense of another, one who had been defined by absence, privacy, and invisibility. Because of this, rather than moving as a straightforward documentary, the film flits through time and space like a ghost. Patiently filming Arzner and Morgan's stucco-roofed house surrounded by Southern California hills, the filmmaker says it "looked lonely blazing in the sun, with a sun porch reminiscent of ancient architecture, like a temple from another world." Upon Raganelli's second visit, the house had been razed, and the property was in the process of being turned into a series of rental bungalows for L.A. vacationers, further erasing a past that had existed only for these two women.

Arzner had first met Morgan in 1927 on the set of her first film, *Fashions for Women*, which the accomplished modern dancer had been assigned to choreograph. She would remain Arzner's most steadfast partner throughout her touch-and-go career in Hollywood. After her collapse from pneumonia during the making of *First Comes Courage*, Arzner would be bedridden for a year, during which Marion tended to her health and took over the household chores. Though she would never return to film directing, Arzner's impact on the movie world did not end here. To subsequent generations, she would be known as a teacher, building the first filmmaking course at the Pasadena Playhouse, and in the 1960s instructing at the UCLA School of Theater, Film, and Television, where Francis Ford Coppola would be among her pupils. Her remaining years in La Quinta were marked by caregiving and heartbreak, as Morgan, Arzner's senior by more than a decade, died in 1971 after a long illness. Arzner's collection of personal letters received during this period overflows with a love and concern specific to one who has lost a life partner: "I think of you across the miles which separate us and wish that I might be there to give you solace and support. Always your strength has been Marion's true sustaining gift of love," writes one friend; "My heart goes out to you for the loss of your beautiful 'Blythe Spirit.' I cannot tell you how much I wish I could comfort you, if only to be near you in silent understanding," writes another.

Even if her name remains, as Mary Murphy would write in the *L.A. Times* in 1975, "as obscure as John Ford is famous," Arzner's posthumous reputation has continued to grow. In March 2018, Paramount paid tribute to the director by naming a building after her. At the dedication ceremony, her former student Coppola told an anecdote: "She stopped, and she handed me a box of crackers that she always had with her for her hungry students, and she said to me, 'You'll make it,

I know, I've been around and I know.' Then she disappeared into the shadows like the ending of one of her movies."

Coppola's image of Arzner fading off into darkness is enormously poignant, considering the truncated trajectory of her career as well as the state of the industry at the moment of her departure. Arzner's sixteen years of filmmaking create a sort of bridge between highly distinct eras of lesbian representation. The careers of Dietrich and Garbo, singular evocations of lesbian and bisexual glamor, never regained their mythic luster after the code, and Hepburn never again embodied her androgynous appeal as fully as in Arzner's *Christopher Strong* and Cukor's *Sylvia Scarlett*. And Arzner's films carried their own unspoken queer eroticism, by virtue of the lesbian behind the camera, yes, but also the invitation to the female spectator to enjoy homosocial bonds over heterosexual ones. By the time Arzner's directorial career was in its final stages, the on-screen lesbian figure had ever so delicately shifted to something more sinister. With any direct representation or inference of lesbianism eradicated by the Code's enforcement, same-sex desire among women had become the province of the invisible, the unseen, and the unclean: the perfect formula for gothic mysteries and ghost stories, narratives fueled by questions and doubts of human perception. (Sexuality, like an unembodied spirit, is largely imperceptible, after all.)

Alfred Hitchcock's influential, Best Picture–winning adaptation of Daphne Du Maurier's *Rebecca*, released in March 1940 as *Dance, Girl, Dance* was going into production, contained subtle yet, for those really watching, unmissable evocations of queer female eroticism, in the form of Judith Anderson's obsessive, villainous housekeeper Mrs. Danvers, who holds a candle for the title character, her deceased former employer. In one of cinema's most memorable moments of repressed eroticism, while giving her new mistress a tour of Rebecca's untouched bedroom, she caresses the dead woman's gossamer nightgown, eagerly exhibiting its sheerness ("Look, you can see my hand through it!"). The early part of the decade also boasted two superb B-horrors from maestro producer Val Lewton featuring screenplays by gay writer DeWitt Bodeen: *Cat People* (1942), in which a sexually secretive Eastern European woman shows her sensual side by shapeshifting into a feral beast and terrorizing her husband's female coworker in a gym locker room, and *The Seventh Victim* (1943), in which a young woman tracks down her missing sister to a cabal of satanists, presided over by the butch Mary Newton, who, in a scene that predates *Psycho* by seventeen years, creeps up on the heroine in the shower.

The 1944 haunted house hit *The Uninvited* features the most startlingly overt phantom lesbianism of the era. As the Mrs. Danvers–like Miss Holloway, the masculine, intimidating Cornelia Otis Skinner speaks of her long-dead best friend, a presumed ghost now haunting a cliffside manner, with a reverence bordering on obsession: "Mary was a *goddess*; her skin was radiant, and that bright, bright hair . . . The nights we sat by that fireplace, planning our whole lives . . ." At one point, she turns to a portrait of her long-lost Mary and says, "They shan't ever find out, my darling, I promise you." The film sets Miss Holloway up as aberrant, the definition of, per the Code, perversity, yet the undeniable romanticism of the character captured the attention of the censors. Breen's office caught the queer inferences in the screenplay and warned Paramount not to make the nature of their relationship any more obvious.

A perfect example of the movies' ability to unlock its viewers' queer desires, *The Uninvited* spoke directly to a certain subset of its audience. Upon initial release, word of the film's content was passed around in a kind of whisper network among the lesbian community. Angered when they got wind of this, the Catholic Legion of Decency sent a letter to the Production Code Administration: "In certain theaters large audiences of questionable type attended this film at unusual hours. The impression created by their presence was that they have been previously informed of certain erotic and esoteric elements in this film." Paramount apologized profusely for the transgression, insisting they had no idea, and vowed to be more careful in the future.

"Lesbianism is the ghost in the machine, a sign of the body, desire, the other woman," wrote queer cinema scholar Patricia White, whose book *Uninvited* borrows its title from the 1944 horror film. By the time that lesbians had become ghostly nonentities in movies, Arzner had herself disappeared into the Hollywood ether. And her films have yet to attain anything like the brand-name recognition afforded so many of her male peers. Even *Dance, Girl, Dance*, despite its rediscovery in the 1970s and despite being an early career triumph for Lucille Ball, has never truly caught fire among movie lovers as an essential classic. In 2020, when the Criterion Collection selected the film for digital restoration and release in Blu-ray and DVD formats, the company discovered that its original nitrate negative had been languishing and slowly deteriorating in the vaults of Warner Bros., which had some years earlier inherited the RKO film library. If not for the restoration, the negative would have been on its way to irrevocable decomposition.

Arzner remains a kind of phantom presence in film history, a woman we know only from tantalizing photographs and the cinematic images she created, both of which rely on our interpretations and eager suppositions to make queer sense of. It's telling that her directorial career would end with *First Comes Courage*, a wartime spy narrative made and set during the ongoing war in Europe and featuring a heroic, Nazi-infiltrating woman at its center. As the decade wore on, women would often inhabit less trustworthy on-screen roles. With unprecedented numbers of women entering the workforce, taking the place of men fighting overseas, the boundaries between traditional male and female social roles and behaviors were blurring more than at any previous point in the twentieth century. As a result, new myths, new narratives, and new social fears were popping up in the movies.

Even more prevalent than the ghost stories evoking anxieties about strong women were films from an as-yet-unnamed genre featuring expressionist shadows and byzantine crime plots frequently initiated by formidable, malevolent females pleasurably emasculating male patsies and fools. Years later, such movies would be broadly categorized under the oddly French moniker *film noir*, but in the 1940s they were immediate, starkly fatalistic visions without precedent—and with their strong intimations of sex, violence, and immorality, they were the first films to consistently challenge the Code. Released during and after the war, a period of immense change and intense psychological tumult that began the gradual chipping away at entrenched ideas about gender and sexuality, these dark evocations of the American soul would reflect and indicate broader shifts in the way America and the film industry dealt with queerness. With women marked as a danger, it was only a matter of time before the nation, and our movies, began worrying about the men. Masculinity itself was now under threat, a perception that would have cultural, political, and cinematic consequences.

4

Capable Men

Even for someone who already held a jaded outlook on humanity, the view from here was sickening. Thirty-one-year-old Richard Brooks had enlisted in the Marine Corps in July 1943, but he would never serve overseas. His experience of the ongoing global conflict that was changing the course of history would be relegated to his barracks in Quantico, Virginia, where he was stationed following basic training at Camp Pendleton outside San Diego. A journalist who had begun to get noticed for his film and radio work before the United States' entrance into the European conflict, Brooks was one of the thousands of men deemed more valuable to the war effort for his writing and filmmaking skills than his potential in combat. At Quantico, Brooks was given the position of scenarist, writing scripts for military training films.

Spared the horror of battle, Brooks nevertheless had a front row seat to the ugliness of humanity. A proud member of the American liberal working class with a functioning bullshit detector, Brooks was sickened by the bigotry spewed by so many of his fellow servicemen, whether casually integrated into conversation or brutally applied to make a hateful point. His first novel, which would prove transformative not only for his career but also, later, for a film industry on the cusp of significant change, would pull back the curtain on the free-floating racism, sexism, anti-Semitism, and homophobia he witnessed during his military service.

The eternally pugnacious Brooks was born Reuben Sax in Philadelphia in 1912 to struggling Russian Jewish immigrant parents. His father, Hyman, worked twelve-to-fifteen-hour days as a cutter in textile factories, a job that exacerbated a respiratory illness and led to chronic bronchial asthma. A tough-minded, confident street kid who ran with gangs and excelled at baseball and football, the imposing and athletic Reuben was also a library hound who dreamed of becoming a writer. After graduating high school in 1929 and unable to find work in his hometown city, he rode the rails, discovering the country and its people and partaking in the occasional Salvation Army meal. This led to one-off writing assignments about his experiences on the road for newspapers such as *Kansas City Star* and *St. Louis Post-Dispatch;* when he returned to Philadelphia he received more steady writing jobs, first as a part-time sports columnist for the *Philadelphia Record*, which led to work as a reporter for the *Atlantic City Press-Union* and the *New York-World Telegram*. A real breakthrough for Reuben occurred when he landed a radio writing gig in New York at WNEW, telling of current events from a humanizing, often political perspective.

By 1940, he had moved, like so many curious neophytes of the booming entertainment industry, to Los Angeles. Though interested in plying his trade in the movie business, he ended up with another job in radio, but with a bigger megaphone: writing and reading aloud fifteen-minute short stories for NBC called *Sidestreet Vignettes*. Reuben filed a story a day, caked in irony and pessimism, purposefully deglamorized, and centering on the often futile pursuits of the American everyman, frequently topped with O. Henry-esque twists. The people Reuben met during his travels made him a staunch supporter of unions and left-wing political causes, and his *Sidestreet Vignettes* hinted at the politics that would eventually filter into his work.

On June 28, 1943, Reuben Sax legally changed his name to Richard Brooks, which he had already begun using professionally, a de-ethnicization so common at the time as to be pro forma. (John Garfield was born Jacob Julius Garfinkle; George Burns was Nathan Birnbaum; Danny Kaye was David Kaminsky). One month later, he enlisted in the Marine Corps. It had been a year and a half since the United States had entered the war following the Japanese attack on Pearl Harbor, and Brooks was at a personal and professional crossroads. His two-year marriage to the actress Jean Brooks had dissolved, and though he had been screenwriting for B movies, westerns, and serials, his radio output had outpaced his Hollywood work in volume and artistry. By officially entering the war, he was doing his part, but he was also running away from himself.

War without war wasn't what Brooks had anticipated, but instead of going into combat, he became a cog in the U.S. military's well-oiled moviemaking machine. Along with his fellow Marines, Brooks was tasked with writing training and propaganda films that would appeal to potential enlistees, promote confidence and patriotism, and function as basic training information—all while living within the confines and costumes of military life, with its uniforms, mess halls, and sleeping barracks. For those who had either been drafted or enlisted only to find themselves stuck stateside, used for essential duties other than battle, there was a strange, indescribable combination of relief, humiliation, and torpor, resulting in an antsy desperation that could contribute to feelings of inadequacy. These claustrophobic barracks, where trained soldiers often felt trapped in a kind of liminal zone, were nicknamed "brick foxholes."

It was here, bunked tightly with his fellow stalled marines, that Brooks heard alarming levels of hatred and prejudice. Virulent anti-Japanese sentiment was, of course, omnipresent during World War II, but, as Brooks discovered, there was a seemingly limitless amount of anti-Black racism and anti-Semitism as well. And that wasn't all: more than once he heard fellow soldiers bragging about weekends in D.C. that included beating and robbing homosexual men for sport.

Fueled by simmering rage at such displays of inhumanity, Brooks began furiously writing a novel while confined to Quantico. The book, titled *The Brick Foxhole*, is terse psychological portraiture that takes the form of a hard-boiled thriller, written in fiery, often declamatory prose. Though riddled with verbose internal monologues direct from the heads of its desperate characters—most frequently its wild-card protagonist, a stationed military man named Jeff Mitchell—the novel is kaleidoscopic. Brooks touches upon the various ways in which men bottle up or unleash their aggression, from casual to violent bigotry toward society's outcasts to the misogyny that manifests as jealousy and paranoia about wives and girlfriends back home. Jeff, a former animator for Disney (like a couple of Brooks's bunkmates had been), obsesses over suspicions of his wife's infidelity after hearing an unsubstantiated rumor about her, and thus embarks on a weekend of drinking, carousing, and self-pity in Washington, D.C. As wayward as Jeff is, the villain is his racist fellow serviceman Montgomery "Monty" Crawford, whose ultra-patriotic, pro-American rhetoric (he weeps when he hears a rendition of "God Bless America") barely conceals his intense fear and loathing of refugees, Asians, Blacks, and Jews.

As written, Monty leaves no doubt about the rot at the core of Brooks's novel, although there's no sense that he's one bad apple; rather Brooks makes it clear that Monty is but one extreme example of a widespread American dysfunction, reflecting the cultural tendency toward white supremacy, intensified by the all-male, racially segregated military and the dehumanization that's key to its training for killing in battle.

The central incident of *The Brick Foxhole* occurs when Monty and his bigoted lackey Floyd Bowers invite Jeff along on a nighttime ramble. They have picked up a mild-mannered and, in Jeff's estimation, "hungry"-looking man named Mr. Edwards, who invites them back to his apartment for a drink. Hardly the type of "guy's guy" one might assume to be in their company, Mr. Edwards—whom Monty and Floyd "affectionately" begin to call Eddie—plays the original cast album of *Oklahoma!* and displays on his wall a painting of a nude, muscular man aiming a bow and arrow (the "prettiness" of the image unsettles Jeff). It becomes uncomfortably clear to the reader, and to Jeff, that Edwards has been targeted by Monty and Floyd. Monty asks Edwards for a dance, coming on to him and holding him too tightly. After Edwards tries to toss them out, they refuse to leave; Floyd even takes off his pants. Edwards begins to cry, and Brooks writes, "Jeff didn't like to see Eddie cry. He liked Eddie. He thought Eddie was a swell guy." Upset by the escalating tension, a drunken Jeff decides to stagger out of Mr. Edwards's apartment, though Monty and Floyd do not follow.

It's worth pointing out the upsetting, heartrending details of the above scene. Brooks treats it with incrementally mounting horror—and he's careful to show that Monty and Floyd are entirely the aggressors. Inviting themselves to Edwards's apartment, fixing drinks, asking him to dance, removing their own clothes: these are men on a mission of entrapment, and, in Brooks's clear estimation, they are the aberrant monsters. Most chilling is Brooks's decision to stay wedded to Jeff's perspective; once the door to Edwards's apartment swings shut, we are not allowed to see the nightmarish death that occurs. Later in the book, the murder weapon is revealed: the porcelain top of the toilet water basin that "smashed Edwards's skull like a cantaloupe." At this point, Jeff, who had accidentally left his furlough satchel in Edwards's apartment, has been brought in under suspicion of murder. He learns of the killing from a front page headline: PROMINENT DECORATOR FOUND MURDERED IN SORDID SEX ORGY: SERVICEMAN BELIEVED KILLER.

Monty tries to pin the murder on Jeff, yet because his all-consuming homophobia radiates off him, he can't help but incriminate himself: "He was making goo-goo eyes at poor Jeff from the start. I don't blame Jeff. It serves Edwards right. They oughta kill every one of them fairies. There ain't a court-martial in the world would do anything to Jeff for that."

Jeff's last-chapter exoneration relies on verifying his alibi with a prostitute named Ginny, whom he was with at the time of the killing. Crucially, Brooks doesn't use Ginny as merely a plot device. Hard-bitten and no-nonsense in a way that feels radical rather than derivative, Ginny is resistant to sharing anything personal about her life to Jeff, yet she does tell a hair-raising story about a colleague in the bordello, a woman who is regularly beaten by a client—a "big hero from the navy" who comes once a month and carries a rubber switch in his satchel. Ginny says, "Every night he goes home and gets into bed with his wife and he don't even put the lights on because it isn't decent to look on a woman's body. But once a month he comes here with that suitcase and that damned rubber switch. And after he uses it, he kisses you where you bleed till his mouth is all covered with blood. And then he gets all excited. He's like a wild animal then."

With these descriptions of sexual violence, Brooks treats women and gay men as equal victims of male rage, the perpetrators in both cases enlisted men. Brooks was flirting with controversy, and indeed when the book was published by Harper and Brothers, while the author was still living in Quantico, he became the center of an internal firestorm. The military brass were incensed that he had submitted *The Brick Foxhole* for publication without soliciting their permission, which would have involved clearance from its public relations committee. Naturally, it never would have passed muster, with its incendiary depiction of U.S. servicemen stewing in their own paranoia and trapped by their own bigotry. While they hadn't been given a copy to read, the Marine Corps noticed the positive *New York Times* review that deemed the book's evocation of military life "shocking and revolting." Brooks was served with a court-martial summons, though perhaps owing to the Marines' reluctance to draw more publicity to the book, the case was soon dropped.

Amid the brouhaha, Brooks found that the book was bringing him positive attention as well. In anticipation of the court-martial, he had lined up the support of major writers, including *Native Son* author Richard Wright and Nobel Prize–winner Sinclair Lewis, who had reviewed it for *Esquire*, calling Brooks "a really important new writer." The playwright Clifford Odets approached Brooks to do a possible play adaptation, which never panned out. And while temporarily stationed back at Camp Pendleton, Brooks was sought out by rising Hollywood star Robert Ryan. A six-foot-four tough guy known for playing boxers and soldiers, Ryan had been living in his own "brick foxhole" for months with no end in sight. Ryan, like Brooks, was a liberal who had little time for pigs like Monty Crawford. "I know that son of a bitch," he told Brooks, emphasizing that he wanted to play Monty if ever there were a movie version.

After the war ended, Brooks was honorably discharged in October 1945 (though denied a Good Conduct Medal), returning to Los Angeles with a growing reputation as both novelist and inveterate truth-teller. Having written a book that commanded the attention of Hollywood folk, who were always looking for sensational source material, Brooks was embraced by the industry in short order. Following a stint working on the screenplays for a pair of feverishly cynical postwar dramas for the journalist turned producer Mark Hellinger, including the bruising Burt Lancaster prison thriller *Brute Force*, RKO came calling with an offer: the rights to *The Brick Foxhole* for $12,000. The purchase was made possible thanks to the interests of a group of social-minded upstarts at the studio, including producer Adrian Scott. When Dore Schary, a young, respected producer and former playwright who believed in promoting social realist dramas with virtuous liberal values, was promoted to head of production on January 1, 1947, he declared that Brooks's book would be his first project.

Considering the broad subject matter—American bigotry—making an adaptation of *The Brick Foxhole* would require significant finessing. The stipulations of the Code disallowed vulgar or racist language of any kind, and films were not free to depict the military in a negative light. The movies had until this point shied away from any serious tackling of prejudice, and the novel was as direct as a heart attack on that front. Considering the specificities of the plot—the brutal murder of a gay man—a faithful adaptation was out of the question. Gay men didn't exist, according to Hollywood. But the movie, unimaginably, was moving forward.

The eventual transformation of Brooks's novel into something deemed more palatably challenging for mainstream audiences shines a light on the limits of well-meaning liberal American values in the 1940s and the contested zone of masculinity in the postwar United States, where the trauma of battle and the reorganization of gendered social space and time allowed for a brief period of psychological reckoning. And the trajectory of *The Brick Foxhole*'s bumpy road to the screen would find fascinating counterpoint in another film, a concurrent late-forties production to be directed by a man who was already on the path to becoming a living legend: Alfred Hitchcock. One film would slyly dare viewers to deny the queerness staring them straight in the face; the other would disallow them from reckoning with the queerness that was once there.

. . .

Arthur Laurents had his own brick foxhole. But first he had a "broomstick army." This was the term for an underequipped military unit. According to Laurents, by the time he arrived as a draftee in Fort Monmouth, New Jersey, "there weren't enough guns to go around."

Like Richard Brooks, Laurents wasn't destined to see the battlegrounds of Europe. He was stationed stateside, from basic training to a stint as a truck driver for a photographic unit at Fort Benning in Columbus, Georgia. The entire company in Georgia would be sent overseas except for Laurents, who, thanks to the string-pulling of a fellow serviceman who had taken a shine to him (and who just happened to be the son of the U.S. secretary of commerce and presidential adviser), was sent north and ended up in Queens, New York City. In January 1942, the U.S. Army Signal Corps had set up shop in the borough's mammoth Astoria studios, the former site of Paramount Pictures's East Coast operations throughout the twenties and thirties. In this legendary spot, Gloria Swanson, Rudolph Valentino, Fredric March, Miriam Hopkins, and Maurice Chevalier had starred in some of their best-known films and hobnobbed in the commissary; the Signal Corps Photographic Center (SCPC) was repurposing its cavernous soundstages into a production and editing center for training and safety films as well as movies meant to entertain the troops. The most prolific film studio during wartime, the SCPC required large numbers of military-appointed staff; by 1945, more than twenty-one hundred men and women were working there to churn out films for the war effort.

Laurents was pleased as punch to be shipped back home. Born in Brooklyn in 1917, Laurents was the son of a Manhattan lawyer, a Reform Jew whom Arthur called "a humanitarian above all" and "the most tolerant man I ever knew." His mother, more staunchly observant of Judaism, harbored a general fear and resentment of gentiles, suspecting everyone harbored a latent anti-Semitism. A self-described combination of his parents' differing personalities, Laurents would become a writer for the stage and screen whose work juggled both idealism and pragmatism about the American twentieth century. Obsessed with New York theater since childhood, when his father's secretary took him on daytrips to Broadway matinees and opera productions, Laurents was fixated on the idea of writing for the stage. Years later, when he was studying playwriting at Cornell, his parents' sensibilities and his professional interests merged in a course he invented to examine prejudice and theater (the university allowed excelling students to come up with ideas for their own courses). His first professional breakthrough was writing plays for radio, including the popular CBS broadcast *Lux Radio Theatre*. The draft came just as Laurents's career was taking off.

The SCPC turned out to be a dream assignment in many ways. The old Astoria studios had come back to life, buzzing with creative activity; the military unit at times felt more like an Algonquin round table. Private Laurents found himself working alongside a stimulating mix of filmmakers, novelists, and playwrights, some established, others starting out, including John Cheever, William Saroyan, Irwin Shaw, and George Cukor, who would direct the first training film Laurents was assigned to write, *Resistance and Ohm's Law*. More than an unexpected entrée into New York's intellectual artist elite, Laurents's call of duty at Astoria also sent him on a journey toward sexual self-knowledge.

In the spring of 1944, while on assignment in Fort Aberdeen, Maryland, Laurents attended an "all-male, all-soldier" service club production of *The Women*, the Clare Boothe Luce play that Cukor had adapted to the screen in 1939. Luce's play famously has no speaking roles for men, as was also true for Cukor's film, a Hollywood anomaly. Male soldiers performing as women to entertain themselves and one another had become a convention during the war, both overseas and stateside, officially approved by the United Service Organizations (USO) and American Red Cross as morale-boosting entertainment. In Laurents's eyes, this performance of *The Women* registered as not merely a burlesque to entertain stationed enlisted men and their wives or girlfriends but a revelation for the way the actors performed it "straight." In his memoirs, Laurents recalls the play with a still vivid astonishment: "They weren't drag queens or transvestites or Hasty Puddings or anything I had ever seen or heard of. They were girls, women, ladies who happened to have hair and muscles in masculine places."

The ease with which these soldiers performed as women, and the excitement of the soldiers in the audience, elicited a powerful emotional response in Laurents that he wasn't yet quite able to detect as a latent personal referendum. "If I'd had any sense, lonely as I was, I would have made a beeline for the stage door . . . I wasn't sure what queer was, I was too afraid of being caught and I didn't lose my inhibitions and throw my sexual hat over the dam until some months later." The men of *The Women* lit a fuse for Laurents. Though he'd had sexual experiences with other males growing up, the early twentysomething had yet to wed his erotic appetites to matters of romance or identity. Following the experience of seeing himself in the play's splintered mirror, he had another gay revelation of a sort, one that augured his future in even more direct ways.

En route back to Astoria, Laurents caught a movie during a stopover in Washington, D.C. Naturally, it was a war picture, like nearly everything else the studios were all but mandated to release at the time. *The Purple Heart,* by Lewis Milestone (the Oscar-winning director of the 1930 antiwar picture par excellence *All Quiet on the Western Front*), was a brutal piece of anti-Japanese propaganda that fictionalized a "show trial" enacted by the Imperial Army against American Air Force soldiers shot down over enemy lines; in defiance of international law, the men are brought to trial for murdering Japanese civilians. For Laurents, Milestone's heated courtroom drama was memorable for one reason: the face of a young actor named Farley Granger. His response was "instant infatuation." If fate—or, more pragmatically, the small circles of Hollywood—hadn't later brought Laurents and Granger together for both romantic and professional reasons, this "infatuation" might have been nothing more than a movie star crush. Yet the two young men were destined to collaborate, just four years after Laurents first glimpsed this beautiful stranger's big-screen visage, on one of the most indelibly queer movies of the Code era.

. . .

Private Laurents's puppy love for Farley Granger arose partly out of an idealization of the young star's image. "Not only was he handsome," wrote Laurents. "He was pure in heart." As the captured Sgt. Clinton in *The Purple Heart*, the dark-haired nineteen-year-old radiates an ethereal innocence; when he stares off into the middle distance with unblinking saucer eyes and full, distressed lips, gripping prison bars, he's an angel, an instant martyr. His one monologue—about getting lost as a little boy and being approached by a kindhearted policeman who instructs him to find his own way home—connects his character to an eternal boyhood, making it all the ghastlier when the young man is whisked away for an off-screen torture that leaves him mute (apparently even his torturers can't bring themselves to destroy his physical beauty, which remains unmarked.)

Granger's ripe, slightly crooked handsomeness was fresh to the screen in *The Purple Heart*, which was only his second film appearance. Four months earlier, November 1943 had seen the release of his debut, *The North Star*, another work of wartime propaganda directed by Milestone and written by Lillian Hellman. After a remarkable run of critical and box office successes in Hollywood following *These Three*, including two more films with William Wyler (*Dead End* and *The Little Foxes*) and Herman Shumlin's 1943 movie of her anti-Nazi stage drama *Watch on the Rhine*, Hellman's outspoken, pro-Russian stance led to her strangest creative project. *The North Star* was intended as an expression of solidarity with Soviet Russia in its war against the Nazis. Producer Samuel Goldwyn was persuaded of the idea's political efficacy, even if he wasn't aligned with Hellman's leftist politics. The sensible realist Wyler originally intended to direct the film, planning to shoot in a gritty documentary style, but when Wyler suddenly enlisted in the army and went overseas, the film was passed along to Milestone, whose old-fashioned, less vivid approach would ill-serve the film. Set in a charming Ukrainian village victimized by occupying German forces, *The North Star* operates under a seemingly willful naïveté, featuring a cast of villagers who look fresh as buttermilk, artificial-looking sets and costumes, cornball dialogue, and odd, incongruent musical numbers written by the otherwise illustrious Aaron Copland and Ira Gershwin.

Hellman, whose adoration of Wyler left little room in her heart for very many other directors, found Milestone uncooperative. His demand of script rewrites produced little more than a battle of wills between the two. Intended as an urgent dispatch from the frontlines of war, the film instead turned out a heavy dose of ersatz sentiment. Merely dismissed upon release, it was years later a professional liability for Hellman, cited as prime evidence of its writer's Russian sympathies when the industry began sniffing out "Reds," and a frequently referenced culprit in Hellman's FBI file. Nevertheless, the cast, which also included Anne Baxter, Walter Huston, and Walter Brennan, was exceptional. And in Farley Granger, Goldwyn, Hellman, and Milestone had found their revelation, the face of defiled innocence. (As in *The Purple Heart*, Granger is an angelic martyr; in *The North Star* he loses his sight instead of his voice.)

Granger was only seventeen when the talent scout Phil Gersh and Goldwyn's casting director Bob McIntyre saw him in a Los Angeles independent theater production. They immediately contacted him and whisked him away to a conference room at the Goldwyn studios. Here he found himself face-to-face with the intimidating trio of Goldwyn, Milestone, and Hellman, whom Granger recalled as "an ugly little lady wreathed in clouds of cigarette smoke." According to the intimidated and nervous young actor, she was unwelcoming and barely spoke during his audition; he later discovered she had preferred an up-and-coming stage actor named Montgomery Clift, but he had Broadway commitments. Nevertheless, after a month of waiting by the phone, Granger got the callback: *The North Star* would be his film debut, and it came with a seven-year studio contract, paying $100 a week.

Right after *The North Star* wrapped, Granger turned eighteen and enlisted in the navy. After a deferment to shoot *The Purple Heart*, deemed important for the war effort, Granger shipped off to Hawaii, where he was assessed and given shore duty. Like Richard Brooks, Arthur Laurents, Robert Ryan, and so many other men who were either called up or volunteered to do their part, Granger would never see battle, working as a clean-up crew member and short-order cook for an enlisted men's club before being reassigned to the Honolulu unit of the Army Special Services Division, where he bonded with stationed musicians and actors—despite warnings from his unit's lieutenant that "they are all fucking pansies up there, and I don't want any of that rubbing off on you." Granger's years serving in the military were integral to his emotional, moral, and sexual coming-of-age. In his memoir, he recalls with vivid, romantic detail his erotic awakening to both men and women while stationed in Hawaii, losing his virginity to a beautiful local female sex worker and on the same night sleeping with a handsome Air Force flight instructor.

Granger's lucid, tactile memories of that night might come across as idealized embellishments, but they speak with a rare crystalline clarity to the wartime experiences of so many men. As the gay historian George Chauncey writes, "By freeing men from the supervision of their families and small-town neighborhoods and placing them in a single-sex environment, military mobilization increased the chances that they would meet gay men and explore their homosexual interests. Many recruits saw the sort of gay life they could lead in large cities and chose to stay in those cities after the war." It's an alternative narrative to the one that defines the era in the popular imagination, of the shell-shocked soldier returning home from abroad and unable to reintegrate into civilian life. For many men and women, possibilities were opened up, leading to new forms of social networking and urban living, gay bars, restaurants, and publications that would function as both meeting places and emotional support groups.

When Laurents and Granger returned to work after the end of the war, they were changed men, but not because of scars sustained in battle. During the war, each had forged new intimacies and confronted truths about his own sexual prefer-ence and identity. Their paths crossed when Laurents first arrived in Hollywood. He had decided to move out west following an initial success on the New York stage. Like Brooks, Laurents had furiously written while stationed in his military outfit, completing his first play, *Home of the Brave*, which opened on Broadway December 1945. As with *The Brick Foxhole*, it concerned the psychological effects of bigotry and prejudice on the American soldier, though here, rather than a stateside barracks, the character was trapped in the South Pacific jungle (an experience Laurents never had), and instead of homophobia, the play focused primarily on anti-Semitism. After the less stellar reception of his follow-up play, *Heartsong* (1946), Laurents relocated to California, securing a rental house in Beverly Hills. He had only just arrived when he found himself face-to-face with Granger, the beauty who had so captured his lust and attention in *The Purple Heart*, suddenly in the flesh, a guest of a friend and sometime lover who had invited Laurents to dinner. The two began seeing each other casually before Granger, looking for a way out of his parents' house, decided to move in with Laurents.

Laurents and Granger's love affair was commonly understood and tacitly accepted within their circles, though it was not known within the entire Hollywood commu-nity and certainly not to the general public. Soon enough they would collaborate on a film that would forever ingrain their relationship into Hollywood lore. No minor B-picture, *Rope* would be directed by none other than Alfred Hitchcock, the rare director for whom "perversity" was something to be sought after and embraced rather than eradicated from sight. Within the strictures of the Production Code, *Rope* would prove the trickiest, most elegantly gay film of its era, in which matters of queer visibility and concealment function as both literal narrative elements and symbolic gestures.

Hitchcock knew of Laurents and Granger's romance and cohabitation, which he saw as an asset rather than a liability. Unlike the filmmakers preparing *The Brick Foxhole*, who had to figure out how to get rid of the source material's gay content, Hitchcock, adapting a British play by Patrick Hamilton loosely inspired by the infamous 1924 killings by Chicagoans Nathan Leopold and Richard Loeb, was insistent on finding ways to make sure it stayed put against all odds. It would be the first and last film Laurents and Granger would work on together. *Rope* remains the quintessential queer film of the 1940s, mirroring the "open secret" nature of the two men's relationship—and that of any same-sex romance in the industry—while also symbolizing the simmering postwar anxiety around men and their social and sexual roles.

.   .   .

Laurents and Granger's experiences of sexual becoming were hardly unique. The gender segregation of the war upended traditional ideas of maleness, the homosocial bonds forged in barracks and bunks reconfiguring expectations of what constituted psychological and physical connection. Just as homefront women had been entering the workforce in large numbers, taking on traditionally male roles in both the professional and domestic spheres, and depending on one another for intimacy, men were learning to rely on other men for emotional, sometimes sexual comfort. The military's official policy during the war was explicitly antihomosexual (a discharge for homosexual behavior could potentially lead to imprisonment or, more likely, psychiatric hospitalization) and would remain so well into the twenty-first century; men were interrogated about their homosexual experiences or feelings during induction physicals—a patently ludicrous way of psychologically rooting out gay men, whose perceived femininity was considered a liability on the battle-field. Yet once they were serving, there was a tacit understanding that sexual activity would occur between men or between women, stationed together stateside or overseas.

Homosexual activity was widespread during the war, leading not only to individual erotic awakening but also, ultimately, to sociopolitical legitimacy. The historian Allan Bérubé writes, "The massive war mobilization forced many American women and men to discover their homosexuality for the first time, to end their isolation in small towns and find other people like themselves, and to strengthen their identity as a minority in American society." The "safe" spaces of gay postwar American nightlife, from cruising spots to bars and nightclubs, would often be visited by soldiers on weekend furloughs. With the rise of surreptitious queer activity came a concurrent escalation in antihomosexual violence—the sort of gay-bashing that Richard Brooks detailed in *The Brick Foxhole*.

As a result of these significant shifts, postwar American culture was primed to embark on an era of hand-wringing over masculinity and the looming specter of homosexuality deemed a threat to it. Compounding fears that the war had altered traditional definitions of American maleness was the publication of Alfred Kinsey's *Sexual Behavior in the Human Male* in January 1948. A biologist with a PhD from

Harvard who had spent the early part of his career studying the gall wasp, Kinsey seemed an unlikely figure to initiate a revolution in the way people thought about their minds and bodies. Before he had begun studying human sexuality in the late thirties, while teaching a course on marriage and family at Indiana University, studies of sex were largely conducted by physicians like Havelock Ellis and written in such a way as to be inseparable from questions of hygiene and morality, with homosexuality always branded as an illness. Kinsey's findings, based on years of sweeping research made possible by a 1941 grant from the Rockefeller-funded Committee for Research in the Problems of Sex, were merely descriptive, avoiding the moral judgment that leads to stigma. In addition to revealing the normality of such taboo acts as masturbation and extra- or premarital sex, Kinsey insisted that homosexuality was nondeviant, providing the statistic that 37 percent of American men had orgasmic sexual experience with other men—a whopping number for most to be faced with. All male sexuality, he related, existed on a sliding scale between homo and hetero, rather than as a strict binary, denying the mainstream notion that homosexuality was unnatural or aberrant. The study's effect was incalculable, and the book was an official bestseller. With an initial printing of just five thousand, by spring it had sold more than two hundred thousand copies.

With men back from the war and reentering society amid an economic boom predicated on their buying into the heteronormative "American dream," the Kinsey Report—for those who believed it—was just more evidence of the need to entrench standards of behavior. In the government, this led to policy changes concurrent with the growing frenzy around possible Communist infiltration. Throughout the late forties and early fifties, known and perceived homosexuals working in government were rooted out by the State Department along with suspected Reds in what would later be dubbed the "Lavender Scare." It was commonly held that homosexuals, whether actively Communist or not, were a liability because they were susceptible to blackmail: in other words, if they could be manipulated into doing anything to hide their identity, they could also easily be coerced into working against their country—not just aberrant but also a security risk. Between 1947 and 1950, more than four hundred federal employees lost their jobs under suspicion of being homosexual.

The governmental purges in the 1940s found parallels in a growing number of zero-tolerance firings at college campuses. In June 1948, two students at the University of Missouri were discovered by a police officer being intimate in a car, leading to a campus-wide investigation to root out homosexuality; because of a state law already in place, this resulted in the expulsion and arrest of nine men. More students suspected of engaging in undesirable behavior would be expelled and/or put on trial; one of the arrested students, Keith Pritchett, had been a decorated war hero in the Air Force and was now also an official sex offender. That same summer, the university fired a tenured professor and former dean of the School of Journalism under suspicion of being the leader of a homosexual "ring" that included faculty, students, and locals. The university thereafter established a committee that would help identify suspected homosexuals and force them into therapy sessions that would reveal their "true" nature, making their dismissal from school all the easier.

The rooting out of gay students and faculty in higher education would lead to a wider panic in the nation's elementary schools, where, as the gender scholar Jackie Blount writes, "communities quietly purged educators who were thought to be homosexual or who transgressed gender norms . . . Typically, the purges were described euphemistically in newspapers or in sealed court proceedings." From today's vantage, one would be mistaken to look back at this postwar climate as unusually hysterical. Rather these extreme reactionary measures reflect a recurring, ever-persistent American puritanism that hides behind issues of "protection" (of our nation, of our children) to advance its agenda—something that Lillian Hellman knew in embryonic form when she wrote *The Children's Hour* in 1934. The failure of conservative forces to identify and then eradicate queer sexuality from our schools, our government, our military, or our entertainment is proven one generation after another. Yet the social and emotional effects of these restrictive and punitive efforts to the mental health and physical welfare of young Americans persist and are costly.

A society buffeted by such oppressive agents consequently produces popular art that's both a product of and a reaction to forces of control. American cinema of the second half of the 1940s subtly reflected a growing, if hesitant, interest in prodding at the truths that had been laid bare by the war and its aftermath. The journey of *The Brick Foxhole* to the screen provides a case study of the moment's schizophrenia. In daring to diagnose the rampant bigotry of the masculine, white American male without psychoanalyzing or excusing it, Brooks's novel appealed to Hollywood producers, actors, and writers determined to make something of raw emotional authenticity. Yet the actual content of the novel—which achieved its effects by making a homosexual male the sympathetic victim of shocking violence—was so utterly unthinkable in Hays Code Hollywood (or, we could say, in Joseph Breen's America) that the producers' intended righteousness was greatly compromised.

Years before RKO had bought the rights, the studio had gingerly tested the waters with Breen, sending him a copy of the book as early as July 1945 along with a memo acknowledging that "this novel will probably not pass muster under the Production Code." Breen's swift response, sent just one week later, was unqualified: "We have read the novel, *The Brick Foxhole*, and, as you can well understand, the story is thoroughly and completely unacceptable, on a dozen or more counts. It, also, goes without saying that any motion picture following, even remotely, along the lines in the novel, could not be approved."

After Dore Schary had come on board as head of production in January 1947, the studio put the adaptation on the fast track. Forced to reimagine how Brooks's book could be achievable on-screen, its producers wished to maintain their bona fides as makers of pictures with social virtue. Instead of tackling homophobia, the film would mutate into something more acceptable, but which was nevertheless previously unheard of in Hollywood: an exposé of anti-Semitism.

One might assume such subject matter would be fish in a barrel in an industry that had been largely founded, and was still mostly run, by Jewish men. And with widespread international knowledge of the atrocities committed against Jews during the war by the United States' Nazi enemies, one would think that brandishing anti-Semitism as a societal evil could hardly be controversial, or even an example of political side-taking at all. Yet never had an American studio film, so restricted in language and subject matter, directly tackled it as a "social problem."

Part of the issue was that under Breen's jurisdiction, Hollywood cinema was slow to respond to the war in the first place. Prior to U.S. involvement in the war, Hollywood saw itself as strictly a producer of entertainments for public consumption, a source of escapism. Thanks to directors and especially writers—like Hellman, Ben Hecht, Charles Lederer, Preston Sturges, and, in his early days in the industry, Dore Schary—movies with "messages" frequently squeezed their way through the system, but whatever political leanings they professed simmered beneath the surface, detectable only to those intent on sniffing them out. The idea that Hollywood would forthrightly produce films made explicitly and obviously for the wartime effort—propaganda—was initially considered dubious to many in the industry and was anathema to Joseph Breen. His Hays Office was strict in its refusal to allow films made pre–Pearl Harbor to show any kind of clear anti-Nazi sentiment—and therefore implied an anti-isolationist bent. As late as June 1942, even as the U.S. government's Office of War Information was coordinating the production of wartime propaganda, including in Hollywood, Breen was still voicing recalcitrance about getting into the business of war. In an interview with the *Motion Picture Herald*, when asked about loosening restrictions on using such words as "hell" and "damn" in war pictures to more authentically reflect soldiers' lives and experiences, he refused, insisting, "The war simply does not affect the Code or its application." Additionally, Breen's reputation for casual anti-Semitism—typified by personal letters to fellow Catholic laymen early in his career that often referred to his industry colleagues as "dirty Jews" or "kikes"—furthered the suspicion that his reluctance to allow the movies to "take sides" during the war was not based solely on an adherence to the Code's traditions. Yet by the time all three of Breen's sons were serving overseas in the armed forces, there was little question where his personal sympathies to home and country lay.

The frequent questioning of the Code's meaning, efficacy, and application during World War II, both in the industry trade papers and in pushback from the studios themselves, began to crystallize for many the idea that industry standards of censorship were in basic opposition to verisimilitude. The Code was making movies less *real*, and at this drastic and violent moment in history, viewers no longer demanded simple escapism but a reflection of what they were seeing and experiencing. Of course, wartime propaganda fiction films, typified by *The North Star* and *The Purple Heart*, were no more real than anything else produced by Hollywood, often artificial in emotional effect, with Japanese and German enemies depicted as grotesque cartoons. A film about anti-Semitism during peacetime was an entirely different matter: to identify the widespread hatred of Jews as a pervasive American social ill rather than as an aberrant toxicity endemic only to our enemies was to interrogate one's own country and people and to suggest, once and for all, that racism and bigotry are woven into the fabric of everyday American life.

By 1947, the Hays Office had little recourse on this point. The postwar world had irrevocably changed. Two studios with dueling pictures about anti-Semitism were in the works, and they had industry muscle behind them. Though uncomfortable with the material—which was mercifully drained of references to homosexuality—Breen could only pick nits. When Schary got wind of Darryl F. Zanuck's upcoming Twentieth Century-Fox production *Gentleman's Agreement*, with the major new star Gregory Peck as a gentile reporter going undercover as a Jew to expose insidious cultural anti-Semitism, he moved full speed ahead to get his adaptation of *The Brick Foxhole* made, shot cheap and quick on a $500K budget and existing studio sets.

On February 19, 1947, Schary and producer Adrian Scott sent a final script, written by RKO house scribe John Paxton, to the Production Code Administration. The script maintained the general structure and fatalism of Brooks's book, yet with changes large and small throughout. Even the press wanted in on the ground floor: in her influential column, the gossip journalist Hedda Hopper announced, "Dore Schary has wasted no time at RKO. He'll have *The Brick Foxhole* (now called *Cradle of Fear*) before the cameras any day now. It's a rugged, tough murder story, but the contents of the yarn have been changed." The notoriously conservative Hopper makes no explicit mention of what those "contents" were, but the changes would be legion. In addition to the gay-bashing that once formed the plot's centerpiece, any references to racism against Black Americans—or indeed Blackness itself—would be eliminated to conform to the PCA dictum against racial slurs. Another significant alteration was that the film's soldiers had returned from overseas battle. In addition to making the original title's reference to their entrapment in stateside barracks meaningless and therefore necessary to change, this insinuated that the men were suffering more traditional forms of PTSD, which might help "explain" their violence, specifically the murderous actions of Monty and Floyd. Further, the book's minor character of Finlay, the police captain who solves the case, was promoted to a main role, giving this poisonous atmosphere a center of uncomplicated decency.

Breen responded to the new script on February 27, writing "the basic story seems to meet the requirements of the Production Code," yet he also puts forth a host of items to be changed, including references to adultery, instances of "kike" and the "n" word, two uses of "lousy" (still considered filthy), excessive displays of liquor, and "any flavor of prostitution" around Ginny, a character who in the novel was unmistakably a sex worker. Recalling the already wildly altered source material, Breen added, seemingly as a warning, a note about the murder victim: "It is understood, of course, that there will be no suggestion of a 'pansy' characterization about Samuels or his relationship with the soldiers."

After final changes certifying to Breen that this film, the first Hollywood picture that would explicitly grapple with hatred and bigotry, would feature no references to homophobia or racism against Black Americans, the film went into production on March 3, to be directed by Edward Dmytryk, who had worked throughout the thirties editing movies by filmmakers such as George Cukor and had graduated to directing, first at Columbia, then at RKO. Dmytryk, best known for the Raymond Chandler noir adaptation *Murder, My Sweet*, was something of a B director, heralded for his economy of visual storytelling and known throughout Hollywood for running in leftist circles. Now titled *Crossfire*, the production was touted in the press; as early as March 16, the *New York Times* sniffed out a trend: "The American cinema is apparently preparing to face questions of racial and religious prejudice with more forthright courage than audiences have been accustomed to expect. Two major companies, RKO and Twentieth Century-Fox, are competing over anti-Semitism as a screen subject." The article then notes, "The novel dealt, incidentally, with anti-Semitism, but the crucial murder in the plot was explained by homosexuality." It's a detail that would later be almost completely elided in the copious press about *Crossfire*, destined to become one of the most talked-about, critically admired, and commercially successful pictures of the year. The movie industry was finally ready to "face" discrimination head-on, yet *Crossfire*'s Hollywood version of justice for one marginalized group of people could be achieved only at the erasure of another.

. . .

When one recalls the films of Alfred Hitchcock, one does not summon narratives of social import, explicit political messaging, or images that seek the Holy Land of realism. His is a world of the internal, of hidden pictures and concealed messages, of deviant pursuits and bodiless longing, of humans curdled by avarice, voyeurism, or self-abnegation. If the man in the shadows who oversees all this glorious folly is indeed, as so many have long believed, the greatest popular practitioner the cinematic medium has ever known, then one reason might be the special anxiety he creates in the viewer. I don't just refer to his ability to *produce* anxiety through his suspense narratives or the terrifying precision of his compositions, camera movements, and succinct cutting, but the special relationship one has to his work and the almost familial discomfort that comes with getting lost in one of his films. To watch a Hitchcock film is to feel you're being directly communicated with by the director himself, to become complicit in his way of seeing—to be engaged in a constant moral conflict with the screen and the self.

Since at least the 1950s, when *Cahiers du Cinéma* critics like François Truffaut and Claude Chabrol began to recognize him as an artist and the undeniable *auteur* of his work, rather than a "mere" director functioning successfully within a factory, Hitchcock has been puzzled over by critics and historians trying to ascertain the source of his unparalleled brilliance. He had a seemingly preternatural ability to use photography, sound, performance, and editing as constant expressions of where, why, and how the audience will look, and either indulged or upended our expectations based on that knowledge. How did a filmmaker whose talents are so clearly visible in the technical aspects of the medium so consistently create works of such deep, abstract, even spiritual rupture, movies that tapped into some well of darkness that was also inseparable from pleasure?

The answer might come in the ways we define "perversity," that ever-mutating, highly personal word that means something very different when we talk about Hitchcock than when we talk about Joseph Breen, but which is essential to understanding both of these men and the shifting currents of Hollywood and America at this moment. For Breen, "perversity" is a legible, literal word with terrible finitude, a marker of difference and an indicator of sexual aberrance; for Hitchcock, the perverse is a subject of inchoateness and great fascination, an appeal to base instincts and erotic possibility and somehow a reminder of our essential humanity. Breen sees perversity as an external contaminant; Hitchcock sees it as an inherent human trait. Breen sought to uncover the perverse in a script like *Crossfire* and expunge it; Hitchcock sought to uncover the perversity in a script like *Rope* and then do his damnedest to get it up on-screen despite the industry's gag orders—in a sense, to find its soul.

The notion that perversity itself could be eradicated from the work of Alfred Hitchcock is hilarious at best, like imagining an egg without a yolk. He was classical Hollywood's most prolific peddler of coded perversity, and no discussion of his infinite career can exist without calling attention to the way he provokes discomfort through notions of sexual depravity, or at least instability. His worlds are heteronormative, but knowingly so, on the surface; roiling below are disruptive forces that put into relief the fragility of the bonds and boundaries of our everyday existence.

Too often, the gayness in Hitchcock's cinema has been critiqued as being purely in the maleficence of his characters, as if one can circle them with a red pen and move on. Yet the queer aspect of Hitchcock's cinema is bred in the bone, so inextricably a part of his work that it's rudely insufficient to simply rattle off the list of closet-case monsters that speckle his oeuvre as some kind of *evidence*. Judith Anderson's domineering Mrs. Danvers may be one of American cinema's most striking lesbian-coded villains, but she's also the tragic, beating heart of

Rebecca's gothic melodrama. Robert Walker's Bruno Antony, the fussy, murderous, mother-loving dandy of *Strangers on a Train*, may be an unrepentant murderer, but his obsessive friendship with the film's nominal hero (Farley Granger, as the perfectly named, normal Guy), indicates a pure, extreme version of love with which we might all identify. In killing Marion Crane in his motel's shower, *Psycho*'s hapless cross-dresser Norman Bates may initiate *the* primal scene of horror cinema, the triggering trauma of all our movie nightmares, but doesn't the fact of his psychotic break—indicated in the blunt title—only reinforce that he may be the film's most sympathetic character? Even *Vertigo*, crowned the greatest film ever made in the 2012 world critics' poll in *Sight & Sound* magazine, is at heart a necrophile's fantasy, a film that makes one awkwardly identify with a man trying to refashion a living woman into a dead one who he *thinks* lives only in his memory. The clearest testament to Hitchcock's use of perversity—with a form of love rather than condemnation—is that his films are at their swooniest, their most lush and loving, when they're at their sickest.

Rope coils around the dark heart of Hitchcock's filmography, and despite the overflow of gleeful queer perversity to be found throughout the six decades of his career, it was and would remain his *gayest* film. "Privately I had assumed Hitchcock had hired me to write *Rope* because it was to be filmed as a play and I was a playwright, and because its central characters were homosexual and I might be homosexual," said Laurents. At the time Laurents recalls that he was "constantly worried whether anyone, everyone knew of my affair with Farley. It was always on my mind." Yet Laurents became aware that Hitchcock, who had already cast Granger as one his leads, knew of their relationship when he and his wife Alma invited Laurents and Granger to dine with them at a table for four at Romanoff's the Saturday night before the start of shooting. Over steak, red wine, cigars, and brandy, Hitchcock made it clear—without ever saying it out loud—that their affair was of crucial importance both to the conception of the film and was of clear interest to him. According to Laurents, "It tickled him that Farley was playing a homosexual in a movie written by me, another homosexual; that we were lovers; that we had a secret he knew; that I knew he knew—the permutations were endless, all titillating, not out of malice or a feeling of power but because they added a slightly kinky touch and kink was a quality devoutly to be desired."

Though Laurents claims, "Initially I thought he was a repressed homosexual," the source of homosexuality's allure for Hitchcock seems to be of a piece with his camera-eye: his need to dig deeper and find the unorthodox beneath the mundane. "Sex was always on his mind; not ordinary sex, not plain homosexuality any more than plain heterosexuality," said Laurents.

The dark nature of homosexuality in *Rope* makes it a particularly tricky proposition, especially for contemporary gay viewers. For many, *Rope* offers little more than nasty, retrograde gay villainy. Its two erudite, well-to-do, well-dressed, white collegiates, Brandon and Phillip, are clearly an unspoken couple, yet what's even less ambiguous, from the very opening shot, is that they are cold-blooded murderers, squeezing the titular weapon around the neck of a third handsome young man. Soon enough we find out why they've committed this heinous act, depicted with homoerotic intimacy: because they wanted to see how it would feel. This evocation of a murder as a sort of "joy-killing" would have evoked a familiar, terrible news story for many midcentury viewers. *Rope* was based on a play that recalled the 1924 "crime of the century" killing of fourteen-year-old Bobby Franks by Nathan Leopold Jr. and Richard Loeb, nineteen and eighteen respectively, in Chicago. To this day, *Rope* is often referred to as a film "about" Leopold and Loeb, even though their names are never mentioned and the cases are vastly different. The reason for this has more to do with the looming presence of Leopold and Loeb in the American consciousness, not just for their crime but also for their infamous status as perceived homosexual killers.

When writing the 1929 play on which Hitchcock's film would be based, English playwright Patrick Hamilton claimed not to have been directly inspired by the case. And yes, the particulars of the real-life Chicago killing and Hamilton's fictional London murder diverge greatly, not just in the settings: the play's killers, Wyndham Brandon and Charles Granillo, do not lure away and bludgeon to death a child neighbor, as Leopold and Loeb did, but rather strangle a fellow university student; they do not attempt a fake, failed ransom plot to try and lead the police off their scent, but rather stuff the body in a trunk, serve dinner over the ghastly hiding place for a group of unwitting guests, and get caught by a former professor, all in one night. Hitchcock's American version draws it only slightly closer to the sordid real-life story. By setting it in New York, the Leopold and Loeb connection remains opaque. Furthermore, *Rope*'s recasting of the killers—named Phillip and Brandon in Hitchcock's film—as WASPy country club types de-ethnicizes the characters, moving them away from the sensationalized Jewishness of the real-life murderers.

Yet for our concerns, the philosophical similarities the story evokes are more crucial than the literal differences it features. Like Leopold and Loeb, aka "Babe" and "Dickie," Phillip and Brandon are well heeled and connected, persons of taste and intellectual seriousness within their community. Their privileged social standing is crucial, as *Rope* is predicated upon a murder done out of a sense of moral certitude; its killers justify themselves by endeavoring to embody the ideals of the Übermensch, who in German philosopher Friedrich Nietzsche's definition exists beyond good and evil and is created in the absence of God. This connects *Rope*'s killers to Leopold and Loeb, whose murder was an act of intellectual hubris, an attempt to exist outside common definitions of morality and claim immunity to earthly consequence. The public's appetite for the sensationalistic nature of the case extended to the way the killers were talked about in the press, which defined their monstrousness by triangulating their bookish, Jewish homosexuality; all were deemed evidence of the same outcast abnormality. Leopold and Loeb were not just seen as predatory homosexuals but also as demonic social deviants, men whose aberrance ran deep, indicated by their knowledge and understanding of queer-tinged literature and art, especially the more mannered, "effeminate" Leopold's professed love of Oscar Wilde and Italian Renaissance poetry and his awareness of the writings on sexuality by Havelock Ellis. In the eyes of the public and prosecution, these were unnatural men whose intellectual pursuits were evidence of their perversion.

It makes sense that such material would again gain cultural traction in the postwar years, amid rising concern over shifting masculine roles in American society. *Rope* maintained just enough flavor and essence of the Leopold and Loeb narrative to make them legible for viewers, as though they're being called forth as phantom icons of the early twentieth century to play on the viewer's generalized knowledge of the killing. And just like Hamilton, Hitchcock would not claim any direct awareness of or interest in the historical events his work evoked. Laurents, for his part, would say Hamilton's play "stemmed from the Leopold-Loeb murder case in Chicago, but that was never acknowledged or discussed."

Hitchcock had been taken with the play since he first saw it performed years earlier in London, but by the time he had begun working on a film treatment in 1947, the killers' spouting of Nietzschean philosophy would take on a different meaning. By this point it was well known that Nietzsche was the presiding philosophical avatar of National Socialist ideology, though he had died in 1900, thirty-three years before Hitler's rise to power. The twisting and appropriation of Nietzsche's writing by the Nazis has raged throughout post–World War II history in debate, as his works have proven to inspire a seemingly limitless range of belief, from anarchists and leftists to extreme right fascists. Nevertheless, Austrian philosopher and Nazi ideologue Alfred Baeumler trumpeted his work as central to Nazi philosophy in his 1931 book *Nietzsche, Philosopher and Politician*—after Nietzsche's own sister and posthumous editor Elisabeth, a National Socialist herself, had been positioning him similarly. His writing, specifically the easily reducible concept of the Übermensch as the human ideal, has been entwined with Nazi ideology ever since, even if Nietzsche's ideas rejected nihilism rather than embraced it, as the Nazis did, as a justification for the murder of those deemed culturally inferior. The evocation of a murder case that inherently summons Third Reich ideology is further knotted by the homoeroticism of the Übermensch figure, replicated in Nazi imagery that exalted "pure" Aryan male.

Hitchcock's homo killers Brandon and Phillip thus commit murder for reasons that recall the American "crime of the century" ("we did it because we could") and the Holocaust itself (the Third Reich's extermination), both matters of ghastly intellectual justification. At the same time, *Rope* is quite literally not about either of these things, which is essential to understanding the shell-game beauty of the film and the hidden-in-plain-sight queerness that defines it. For depending on how one decides to view it, *Rope* is either the most clearly gay film of its era or the one that most consistently abstracts and elides its homosexual nature. Just as it *isn't quite* about Leopold and Loeb, and just as it's *not really* about the very recent trauma of genocide, it's also almost definitely but not really—but, yes, so clearly—a movie about two men who domesticate together and sleep together, just as they kill together. We see only the latter aspect, of course.

To fully see how *Rope* speaks to its historical postwar period, radically altered by the Holocaust, necessitates a closer look at Hitchcock's own experiences during the Second World War, which were distinctly different from those of Laurents and Granger. By September 1939, when Britain declared war on Germany, Hitchcock had already relocated to Los Angeles from his hometown of London. For some in the British film world, including his friend and former producer Michael Balcon, Hitchcock's defection to Hollywood felt like a betrayal—after internationally successful thrillers like *The 39 Steps* and *The Lady Vanishes*, he was their industry's most acclaimed export. So even amid preparing his first Hollywood productions in 1940, *Rebecca* and *Foreign Correspondent*, Hitchcock wanted to make sure his support for the British war effort was felt, even if from afar. Overweight and in his early forties, thus out of fighting shape and already too old for battle, Hitchcock worked on British propaganda films until 1945, a secondary career beneath his rising Hollywood one. Though it took more than a year of convincing Hitchcock's new producer, David O. Selznick, who didn't want to allow him to go to England, Hitchcock's work eventually included reediting the informational docudramas *Men of the Lightship* (1940) and *Target for Tonight* (1941) to make them more appealing for the American market; and in 1944, writing, producing, directing, and editing two French language shorts for the British Ministry of Information (MOI) that were in support of the French Resistance: *Aventure Malgache*, which proved controversial in its moral gray areas and its uncompromising criticism of the Vichy government and would be kept from circulation; and the espionage thriller *Bon Voyage*. The most troubling assignment was still to come.

In early 1945, Bernstein asked Hitchcock if he would oversee a team of editors and writers whom he had tasked with making a movie about the ongoing Nazi atrocities now coming to light. The film was intended as a work of global public education: a document that would graphically depict the evils perpetrated by Germany and provide visual evidence for Allied troops, civilians, German citizens, and German POWs. By June, Hitchcock, along with editor Peter Tanner and writers Richard Crossman and Colin Wills, was sifting through hours of raw footage shot by combat and newsreel cameramen at the liberation of eleven concentration camps, including Dachau, Buchenwald, and Bergen-Belsen, where Bernstein, armed with a camera, had borne witness to the aftermath. Though Hitchcock has been credited as the film's "treatment advisor," an internal MOI memo from Bernstein in July originally confirmed that he was "appointed to direct the film" and that "he will not take a fee for his work."

To this day, there remains a disagreement about Hitchcock's ultimate role. In a 2015 interview with *Cineaste*, the Imperial War Museums' senior curator Toby Haggith said, "The reason I don't believe he can be described as 'director' is that Hitchcock comes over in July and because of the delays in preproduction the MOI team is hardly at the stage to show him anything other than rushes or perhaps roughly assembled material." Whatever his final input, Hitchcock seems to have been integral in shaping and narrativizing the film, as well as contributing crucial aesthetic choices. Decades later, Tanner would relate, "Hitchcock's main contribution to the film was to try to make it as authentic as possible. It was most important that everybody, particularly the Germans themselves, should believe that this was true, that this horror had happened, that people had suffered to that extent . . . We tried to make shots as long as possible, used panning shots so that there was no possibility of trickery." (Though to different ends, Hitchcock's belief in the emotional effect of shooting scenes in single, uncut takes would continue to find outlet in his work, most famously and extremely in *Rope*.)

The film was not fated to have its intended effect in its day. Shelved and left unfinished, the result was deemed too upsetting by French, British, and U.S. officials, who felt the footage was best left out of the public eye. According to the historian Ulrike Weckel, "Had it been completed and screened around the time of the first anniversary of VE Day as planned, it would have been the only Allied film to arrange its footage into a story rather than stringing together horrific sights, one more disturbing than the next, as an exercise in the pedagogy of shock." Though some of the film was used as evidence for the prosecution during the German war crime trials at Nuremberg, it was housed for decades in the archives of the Imperial War Museum. In 1985, the same year that Claude Lanzmann finished and debuted his epochal nine-hour document of Holocaust testimony, *Shoah*, an episode of the PBS series *Frontline* incorporated extended portions of the film in its episode "Memory of the Camps." Yet the film wasn't completed until 2014, when it was screened in a new restoration at the Berlin Film Festival under the title *German Concentration Camps Factual Survey*.

Watched today, the film achieves the total clarity of vision and purposeful bluntness its makers were after. Perhaps we have seen the film's images decontextualized or edited into clip reels: emaciated corpses dumped into makeshift mass graves or piled into ovens; naked men and women reduced to living skeletons and barely able to walk; charred and mutilated corpses locked in eternal expressions of desperation; deposed German guards standing by and attempting to maintain an air of guiltless stoicism; idyllic local villagers existing right outside the camps' gates, insistently unaware. Yet all attain a greater power within the film's straightforward trajectory; this extraordinary confrontation with the unspeakable works because of the inexorable, linear motion of its construction, from Bergen-Belsen to Dachau to Buchenwald to Ebensee to Mauthausen to Auschwitz and beyond, and the escalating sense of horrific discovery, the magnitude of man's inhumanity to man.

Hitchcock never spoke in any significant way about the film or the impact it may have had on him throughout his career. Yet it's impossible to imagine that the experience of scanning through hours of such footage, witnessing atrocities most of the world had yet to see, would not have a profound effect on anyone and certainly on someone so preoccupied with thinking about the meaning and consequence of moving images. In June 1945, Hitchcock had already been in the midst of a long preproduction for David O. Selznick on *Notorious*, which featured Ingrid Bergman as the daughter of a convicted German spy going undercover for the U.S. government to help catch a Nazi (Claude Rains) hiding out in Rio de Janeiro after the war. However, for all its wry drawing room repartee and clever technical experimentation, one might see *Rope* as Hitchcock's true response to the Holocaust, a dramatization of the philosophical rationalizations that can lead one to murder: an act of inherent self-superiority.

Rope was to be the first film made for Transatlantic Pictures, Hitchcock's new production company, formed after the director finally pried himself loose from Selznick's iron grip. Transatlantic was a dream Hitchcock shared with Sidney Bernstein; with Hitchcock as the name and Bernstein as the money man, this new venture would divide its creative and business operations between England and America, with the promise that Hitchcock could secure major movie stars in the United States and help land top investors and distributors. *Rope* was particularly appealing because Hitchcock originally shopped it to potential buyers as a vehicle for Cary Grant. Based on this information and the sensationalism of the thriller plot—the director's bread-and-butter—Warner Bros. agreed to distribute.

Grant ultimately passed on the role of Rupert, the cynical philosophy professor whose lectures justifying the murder of the intellectually inferior influence Brandon and Phillip in their dark deed. Written by Laurents as a homosexual, Rupert was too risky a proposition for Grant, already dogged by rumors around his own bisexuality. Similarly, Montgomery Clift, just graduating to film work from the stage, turned down the part of Brandon, leaving it open for up-and-comer John Dall, a gay actor in his midtwenties who had recently been nominated for an Oscar opposite Bette Davis in *The Corn Is Green*. The part earmarked for Grant would go to James Stewart, acting in his first of several epochal roles for Hitchcock that upended his nice-guy image. What the gentlemanly actor would distinctly lack in Laurents's hoped-for homoeroticism and fey intellectualism, he more than makes up for by the climax in expressing Rupert's conflicted, righteous fury at how his teachings have been perverted.

Patrick Hamilton, who had recently seen another play of his transformed into a major suspense picture, George Cukor's *Gaslight* (1944), turned down an offer to write the film adaptation of *Rope*. Hitchcock then hired his friend Hume Cronyn to work on it, even though it was the first screenwriting job for the actor and occasional short story scribe. It was from the resulting treatment, done between March and April 1947, that Laurents was brought in to write the actual screenplay; Laurents and Cronyn would never meet. The dictates of the job were clear to the young writer. For one thing, Laurents was to relocate the British play to a recognizable American idiom, which to him meant a very particular milieu: "I drew from some silver-and-china queens I had met briefly in New York who played squash and were raunchy after dinner in my effort to Americanize English homosexuality." In other words, Laurents was hired to make *Rope* authentically queer, even if that would or could never be issued explicitly as a directive.

Brandon and Phillip are hardly the first male dandies in major Hollywood roles (the early thirties, before the enforcement of the Code, is a wonderland of the brand of effeminate men that terrified Joseph Breen). But they are brazen in their status, however unbrokered—they are not in relationships with women, talk often about going upstate, and clearly live in this penthouse apartment together ("Couldn't we pretend we're not home?" Phillip pleads at one point to avoid an unwanted visitor). Granger recalled, "Arthur made sure that I was aware of what he felt was going on between the characters, and of course John Dall and I discussed the subtext of our scenes together. We knew that Hitch knew what he was doing and had built sexual ambiguity into the presentation of the material." But what was happening on set wasn't necessarily acknowledged at the executive level, as Laurents recalled: "At Warner Brothers studio in Burbank where *Rope* was shot, homosexuality was the unmentionable, known only as 'it.' 'It' wasn't in the picture, no character was 'one.' Fascinating was how Hitchcock nevertheless made clear to me that he wanted 'it' in the picture."

It's the simultaneous absence and presence of "it" that makes *Rope* the singular, thrilling, and, for many, baffling experience it is. In devising the production, Hitchcock envisioned a wildly audacious filmmaking method that would somehow both distract from and complement the story's themes of concealment and revelation. *Rope*, perhaps even more than its reputation as a bit of are-they-or-aren't-they queer trickery, is remembered for its singular technical experimentation. The original play takes place over the course of one evening's cocktail party, and Hitchcock wanted to preserve the passage of time in Hamilton's drama. To create the effect and feeling of real time on-screen, the director would go against the cinematic principles of montage he had always embraced, evoking the sense of the film as one long unbroken shot. Today, with the advent of digital cameras, which can record and store unlimited amounts of visual information, this would be simpler to pull off, albeit with much rehearsal, and our contemporary cinema is riddled with single-take calisthenics designed to draw the viewer's attention to the filmmaker's technique (see *Birdman* or *1917*). With traditional film processing, however, each cartridge could hold only about ten minutes of footage, so *Rope* would have to be stitched together from a succession of elaborate single shots.

Hitchcock, uninterested in making just a filmed play, would complicate matters by having the camera tell the story with as much vigor as his well-rehearsed actors: each of *Rope*'s ten-minute shots is full of bold tracking and dolly moves, with the camera either subtly calling attention to or explicitly zeroing in on something in the frame and therefore sinuously maneuvering around the fairly small soundstage. The resulting shots—eleven in all—were then edited together, alternating with "hidden" cuts (most frequently with a figure passing in front of the camera, briefly blacking out the action) and hard cuts or reverse shots that would correspond with projector reel breaks and would come at particularly gripping moments in the action—in other words, during moments when the viewer would be so caught up in the story that they likely wouldn't notice.

This was all possible only thanks to elaborate schematics and intense rehearsal for actors, camera, and lighting. With its extremely mobile camera, a dolly was necessary, which made shooting even more complicated. Recalled Granger, "The rehearsals were grueling. Since there were no cuts, as one walked through the apartment, walls had to be pulled out of the way, lights had to follow and/or precede you, and furniture had to be removed and replaced, and this activity had to be silent because of the sound recording." Stewart would later say, "By the time it came to the actual shooting of a full reel, I was practically in a state of nervous collapse. I was having nightmares, the kind I had not known since my first days in the theater."

Making things even trickier, *Rope* was the first Technicolor film of Hitchcock's career, and as the director had been distrustful of the format (he found color lighting flat, without the depth of image that black-and-white provided), he proved fussy about it. Of particular annoyance to him was the elaborate New York city-scape visible through the apartment's huge expanse of window, intended to make the viewer aware of time passing by subtly progressing from daylight to evening to nighttime. However, the orange sunset image looked "like a lurid postcard" to Hitchcock, so he would force the cast and crew to shoot five reels over again with a new lighting scheme.

Rope's high-concept approach to shooting is hardly high-wiring for its own sake—even if Hitchcock would call it a "stunt" in his later interviews with François Truffaut. Flamboyant though it may be, the technique of *Rope* makes for one of the most marvelous marriages of theme and formal experimentation in cinema. The film persists as an object of study and fascination for film academics, Hitchcock aficionados, and queer scholars for how it guides the viewer to look at its images while at the same time insinuating that what's *not* on-screen is just as important as what *is*, if not more so. *Rope* is a film about the closet—represented literally in this case as a trunk—and the bizarre dance of estrangement and fear that gets performed around it. A film about the denial of what's right in front of our eyes—whether, for the characters, it's a hastily concealed dead body or, for the audience, the self-evident fact of two men's sexuality—*Rope* is made all the richer and more enticing by a cinematic technique that calls attention to its own artifice and fakery: the "invisible" cuts.

The film begins with a climax—of a sort. After a brief shot of a New York City street—the outside world we will not be privileged to see for the remainder of the film—the camera pans to an apartment window, its curtains drawn. We hear a petrified scream, and Hitchcock cuts to a close-up of a man being strangled to death. It's macabre, but the innuendo of Laurents's dialogue soon clues us in that it's something more. The camera tracks out and we see the victim flanked tightly on either side by two elegantly suited young men, hardly the usual screen killer types. On the left of the frame is John Dall's Brandon, still gripping the rope with which he snuffed the life out of David Kentley; on the right is Farley Granger's Phillip, wearing a pair of leather gloves and the expression of abject anxiety he will keep for the remainder of the film. They shove their victim into a capacious trunk and slam the lid. Phillip softly intones, "Let's stay this way for a minute," while Brandon lights a cigarette. In case the sexual undertones of the two men's words and actions aren't clear enough, in just a few minutes, this is how Brandon will describe the feeling of committing the murder: "His body went limp, and I knew it was over . . . then I felt tremendous exhilaration."

Laurents's suitably perverse, homoerotic opening portends the most abhorrent premise in any Hitchcock film: the two men subsequently cover the trunk hiding David's body with a tablecloth and candles and serve dinner off it to the victim's own friends and family. It's through such innuendo that Hitchcock's film decouples itself from both Hamilton's source material and the potential vise grip of its Leopold and Loeb reference points. Thanks to the clever evasiveness of Laurents's script, the knowing performances of Granger and Dall, and Hitchcock's unyielding fascination with the sexually and morally unconventional, queerness is embedded in the text with a gleeful eyebrow-raise.

Rope offers a prime example of the surgical, subliminal treatment filmmakers deployed to smuggle in sophisticated ideas about human lifestyles deemed deviant by the PCA. Because Joseph Breen and his colleagues at the Hays Office approved or rejected everything at the script stage, matters like performance style, directorial choices, and visual emphasis couldn't be as easily regulated. Therefore, dialogue with sexual undertones, which could be heightened while filming, often got by Breen. *Rope* would in many ways register as too subtle. Nevertheless, Breen had his antennae up about the source material. Though he had found Hamilton's play generally admissible when Hitchcock sent it to him in September 1946, Breen voiced some concerns, namely that the adaptation should unambiguously reaffirm human morality at the end. After he received Laurents's script draft on December 1, 1947, however, the Hays office's warning tone became more ominous. In a December 15 memo to Transatlantic Pictures's production manager, Fred Ahern, the PCA's Stephen S. Jackson reminds him, "We got a possible flavor in some of the dialogue that a homosexual relationship existed between Brandon and Phillip. This was heightened somewhat by the fact that there is some degree of similarity between these two characters and Leopold and Loeb, which was a notorious case here in America some years back . . . such a treatment could not be acceptable under the terms of the Production Code." He also reminds Ahern, "You agreed that you would be willing to change any specific lines of dialogue that might reflect a homosexual relationship between the characters."

The back-and-forth that ensued over such details between the PCA and Transatlantic Pictures paints a rather amusing picture of the sorts of words and tonalities deemed queer. Because it's never clearly stated in the script that the men are lovers, the PCA was on the lookout for indicators of dandyish irregularity or femininity. The word "lovely," for instance, should not come out of the men's mouths, it was insisted. Laurents recalled that in trying to lessen the evident queerness, "Sidney Bernstein had gone back in and added 'English-isms' like 'My dear boy,' which the Hays Office found too gay noting the HOMOSEXUAL DIALOGUE." The filmmakers became increasingly nervous that further tinkering from the PCA after production ended would put them in an impossible situation, considering the complexity of the film's single-take aesthetics. Wrote Transatlantic's Arthur A. Peers in a memo to the PCA on January 24, 1948, after shooting had begun: "Since we are photographing the picture one reel at a time without any cuts, any comments you might have to make when the picture is completed might well be calamitous."

Not only did Hitchcock's absurdly complicated approach to shooting *Rope* allow little leeway for postproduction corrections or demands, it also ended up boosting the film with a kind of inoculation against its troubling themes. By focusing on the novel technical achievement of the film in its press materials, the studio could ignore touting whatever story or character transgressions might upset certain viewers. Hitchcock's biographer Patrick McGilligan wondered, "Was the technique mainly his way of distracting journalists and censorship from subject matter as daring and provocative as anything he had done?"

Indeed, it's hard to find a Golden Age Hollywood movie whose hype was so centered on its radical technological merits at the ignorance of its themes. To celebrate the film's release, Warner Bros. published an elaborate "Photographic Production Notebook," which focuses exclusively on the technical apparatus and labor-intensive process of rehearsing and shooting. "To every one who worked on the production, the *Rope* assignment was a great challenge and a tremendous responsibility. For them this was more than just another picture," says studio head Jack Warner himself. The booklet, which unabashedly trumpets the film's "place in the historical development of a vital art," is divided into four sections: The Camera: Narrative Technique, Backgrounds and Lighting, Still Photography and the Motion Picture, and Color. Not a word, not a whisper, about Brandon and Phillip. But would audiences see what was—or wasn't—there?

· · ·

RKO began preview screening *Crossfire* in summer 1947. Riding a wave of press focused on its honorable social messaging, Dmytryk's film had been effectively divorced from the memory of *The Brick Foxhole*. It was now the scrappy, economically shot anti-Semitism drama that had beaten Fox's *Gentleman's Agreement* to the punch. Still, for the studio, there was no guarantee that general moviegoing audiences, unaccustomed to being confronted with the realities of bigotry and racism, would welcome the experience. And making the film at all became a point of contention between producer Dore Schary and RKO's then president, N. Peter Rathvon. In February 1947, weeks before the film was to start production and while script details were still being hashed out with the PCA, Rathvon sent an interoffice memo to Schary highlighting the ways in which the project was not only potentially ineffective but dangerous.

"I doubt sincerely that it has the least value as a document against racial intolerance and I think there is a chance that it might backfire and have an effect opposite to that intended," Rathvon warned. A problem area was the character of Monty, whose unrepentant anti-Semitism made him too despicable for a mainstream audience. He was an unrepentant creep, "without one trace of decency," who would be difficult for viewers to identify with (a strange concern about a murderous villain), worried Rathvon, who further wondered, "How often in America does a Jew-hater go out looking for a Jew to kill? In this matter the picture has even less motive for the killing than has the book." Rathvon's concerns may betray both a naïveté about anti-Semitism and a clear homophobia, though he has an undeniable point about the script's simple replacement of the murder motivation. In his book, Richard Brooks incorporated the routine weekend gay bashings he heard fellow stationed soldiers boasting about. In the film, the beating and murder of a Jew becomes more of an artistic expression of a social evil—no less powerful but more metaphorical than literal. However valid his critique of the changeover, Rathvon goes on to state that the murder in the book was accidental (not true) and therefore implies Monty is more sympathetic. "I think it will do more harm than good," Rathvon concluded.

He wasn't alone in his fears. Many, including representatives from Jewish organizations, worried that to highlight anti-Semitism in a popular movie was to risk inflaming it. As producer Adrian Scott noted in an article published in *Screen Writer* in October 1947, "From the very beginning *Crossfire* has been the victim of a strong minority pessimism . . . Chiefly it stemmed from sources that had genuine anxiety about the project and thought it would be better left alone . . . if it were done badly it would cause more anti-Semitism."

The handwringers needn't have worried. In shifting the narrative from the entrapment and violent bludgeoning of a homosexual to the fatal beating of a Jew, they happened upon the right social message at the right time. Most of the reaction cards from the first preview screenings—"A subtle, well-needed lesson in democracy was brought to the screen," "A first for movies! The courage to use correct words," "It deals with a question that should have been handled more firmly a long time ago"— indicate that the film industry under Joseph Breen's watch was needlessly anxious about viewers' responses to social issues, as well as two steps behind the moviegoing public. One viewer's note, referring to a "queer sense of embarrassment of hearing the word Jew said out loud and a deep sense of shame that we should all need this," expresses the gulf between the worlds experienced on-screen and off.

When the film was officially released, reviews were ecstatic; the film was lauded high and low for its bravery. Practically from day one, *Crossfire* had been positioned as Hollywood's first—though, with Kazan's film on the horizon, not last—word on anti-Semitism. *Variety* trumpeted, "RKO can really do some whooping and hollering about *Crossfire*. Picture is an exciting, daring exposé of intolerance in the U.S. that skillfully blends pamphleteering for a worthy cause with tense dramatics," while *Time* proclaimed it "emerges first in the field in Hollywood's anti-anti-Semitic sweepstakes." Unsurprisingly, Richard Brooks's original novel is mentioned only in the most passing fashion in reviews, though the extent to which it's dismissed is rather remarkable. In the *Hollywood Reporter*, Jack D. Grant wrote, "An absorbing crime drama has been made from a novel which caused a great deal of attention under the title of *The Brick Foxhole*"—and then said nothing else about the book. The *New Republic*'s Shirley O'Hara insists, "John Paxton wrote the scenario of *Crossfire* from a novel inferior to it, called *The Brick Foxhole*"—and that's it. In the *New York Times*, Bosley Crowther teasingly stated, "Incidentally, the motive for murder which was brought out in the book has been changed for this present film version—and to remarkably advantageous effect." He declines to describe, or even imply, what that motive might have been, indicating that in the late forties, mainstream film critics still followed Hollywood's lead when it came to the existence of homosexuals.

The studio and press angle was that the film took a risk yet ultimately proved itself a noble work of social importance, and this ensured its shelf life throughout all of 1947. Dmytryk wrote a letter published in the *New York Times* in August about the decision to use the character of Captain Finlay to talk directly to the audience about the evils of anti-Semitism in a final monologue: "For purely democratic reasons, it was necessary to prove racial prejudice is so dangerous that . . . it could lead to murder." In October, Schary wrote an op-ed for the *National Jewish Monthly* about his convictions that movies can have positive influence on the world, insisting that "the men working on this picture were consumed by an ideal." And in December, *Variety* reported on a non-industry-sponsored study of *Crossfire* made under the supervision of the director of research at the NYU School of Education and the national program director of the Anti-Defamation League of B'Nai Brith. Based on samplings from high school and adult audiences in Ohio, Denver, and Boston, "the film resulted in a more tolerant attitude not only to Jewish persons but Negroes and other minority groupings as well."

The preoccupation with *Crossfire*'s unimpeachable social urgency and liberal messaging, from both journalists and studio publicists, makes it sound merely medicinal, which detracts from the aesthetic accomplishments of the film and the atmospheric, postwar melancholy that suffuses it. However neutered from Brooks's cynical tirade of a novel, which dredged up a specifically American fear and loathing, *Crossfire* packs a wallop, using the era's ascendant film noir conventions (loathed by Breen for the encroaching permissibility of violence and sex they represented) to dramatize intolerance as a shadowy, devouring urban evil.

The film's political righteousness—that it's trying to "right" a wrong—may disallow it from being a pure shot of fatalistic noir, but *Crossfire* effectively strips away the book's meandering subjectivity for the pure pummel of a B-picture, all meat and bone. Brooks's protagonist Jeff "Mitch" Mitchell is largely abstracted to the background; here he is introduced as just one of the three men who were in the room where Samuels was killed. With the film reconceived as a murder mystery, Mitch, played by wan, baby-faced George Cooper, doesn't even appear on-screen until fifteen minutes in. He becomes little more than a pawn in a game of survival played by a trio of sturdier movie stars, all named Robert: Young as Captain Finlay, now the film's heroic center, an upstanding Irish Catholic police officer; the up-and-coming Mitchum as Keeley, using his mysteriously passive, heavy-lidded decency to fill out the third-wheel role of Mitch's loyal friend; and Ryan as Monty, the glowering murderer who can feign incredulous innocence for only so long.

Dmytryk's direction and Paxton's script move away from some of Brooks's toughest implications, such as that war exacerbated rather than created a hatred already bred in the American psyche. Yet in changing the film to the immediate postwar moment and centering on returning soldiers rather than stationed ones, they do alight on some hard truths. Samuels, here a veteran who had served in

Okinawa, speaks to the film's simmering despair in the bar scene when he meets Mitch, articulating the difficulty of having come back to civilian life after battle: "We're too used to fighting. But we just don't know what to fight. You can feel the tension in the air. A whole lot of fightin' and hate that doesn't know where to go . . . Maybe we'll stop hating and start liking things again." The implication here that these men are united by an intractable hatred best reflects the philosophy of Brooks's book. The most self-reflective character of the film, Mitch responds to Samuels's words; the two immediately bond, though the film is quick to confirm that Samuels has a girlfriend (Marlo Dwyer), which helps reduce the residual "pansy flavor" one might have sensed when Samuels then invites him up to his apartment.

As *These Three* had proven a decade earlier, traces of queerness can linger even in the most rabid attempts to de-homoeroticize cinematic material. The connection between Mitch and Samuels remains subtly sensual, and despite the addition of a female companion for the Jewish victim, an inescapable sense remains that he might be seducing the young veteran, who, as played by doe-eyed Cooper (appearing in his first movie after a stint in the navy), registers as naïve and open to persuasion. Furthermore, there's an implication of Mitch's inability to sexually perform with Gloria Grahame's Ginny, transformed from the book's hard-bitten prostitute into a no-nonsense yet emotionally tremulous dancehall girl, all the more glaring considering his equal physical estrangement from his wife, Mary (Jacqueline White). Throughout, *Crossfire*'s narrative also highlights the homosocial bonds between soldiers, forged in battle and maintained in civilian life, with Keeley's loyalty to Mitch the latter's saving grace when he becomes the prime suspect. Even the book's sense of Monty as a potential closet case—suspiciously willing to lure a man into a sexual trap—remains present in the interpretation of Ryan, whose persistent physical bearing is an obsessive, intensely physical intimidation of other men.

Much of the postrelease press for *Crossfire* had coalesced around Ryan, the former Marine who had approached Brooks at Camp Pendleton about playing Monty years before an adaptation even existed. A brawny former boxer and outspoken, Dartmouth-educated left-wing WPA worker, Ryan would be hyped as the ruggedly handsome face of the film, in essence humanizing a character who couldn't be redeemed on-screen. *The American Hebrew* ran an interview with Ryan, lauding his gutsiness in taking the role of the Jew hater Monty. "I was worried about this Montgomery guy. He's just an unrelieved villain with not a single nice thing about him . . . He's just a nasty guy. Even his mother couldn't love him." Dmytryk described Ryan as "the most liberal man on the set," but Ryan convincingly embodied the malevolent bigot, having done his own personal research into anti-Semitism, both as a cultural tradition and as a twisted ideological mindset.

For Ryan to have been the face of *Crossfire* reflects a shift in American popular movies, where untouchable good guys were less and less at the center. During the war, with the rise of sardonic, disillusioned crime narratives conspicuously devoid of traditional heroes, such as *Double Indemnity*, *Scarlet Street*, and *Detour*, films were increasingly headlined by men whose lack of moral compass made them dupes, often to conniving women; the sense of disaffection became only more pronounced in the immediate aftermath of the war, in *The Postman Always Rings Twice*, *Gilda*, and *Out of the Past*. Often one doesn't root for these films' protagonists so much as shake one's head at their impulse to submerge themselves in miasmas of their own making, led by sexual obsession or financial desperation or both. In a major alteration from the book and a studio-imposed change that was not screenwriter Paxton's original intention, Monty is shot in the back by Captain Finlay at the end of the movie. This effectively gets rid of the "bad apple," though he remains in many ways the twisted protagonist, giving unsettling voice to all the social evils the film wishes to diagnose and correct.

Ryan received an Oscar nomination for Best Supporting Actor for the film, which also received a Best Picture nomination, no mean feat for a film with such a modest budget—it is often called "the first B movie" to earn such an honor. In a battle royale of the anti-Semitism pictures, it would lose to the more prestigious *Gentleman's Agreement*, but *Crossfire*'s ability to cause a stir is nothing to dismiss, especially since 1947 marked a crucial moment in the history of American movies, when box office began to show dramatic, irrevocable decline. This may have been barely perceptible, considering that in the previous year, American movies were more popular than they had ever been. Today, when going to the movies is increasingly a niche activity for a public with its attention dramatically split among various modes of entertainment, and people are most likely to venture to theaters for megabudget spectacle, it's difficult to quantify or describe just how essential film attendance was as an American pastime in the years before the widespread accessibility of television.

According to the historian Robert Sklar, by 1946, the decade's first full peacetime year, "Total weekly attendance climbed to nearly three fourths of their 'potential audience'—that is, the movie industry's estimate of all the people in the country capable of making their way to a box office, leaving out the very young and very old, the ill, those confined to institutions, and others without access to movie theaters." Just one year later, though, attendance was starting to dwindle, a reality that would grow ever starker in the coming decade—the monoculture paradise of classical Hollywood cinema was already beginning to come to an end. Beyond the rise of television, Hollywood would find itself at the center of various public disillusions by the end of the 1940s, including the 1948 Supreme Court case known as the Paramount Decrees, which broke up the studios' vertical integration model, separating distribution, production, and exhibition; and the industry-rattling investigations by the House Un-American Activities Committee (HUAC), charged with rooting out suspected Communists. That process, which would continue for the better part of a painful decade, claiming a wide swath of casualties that spared no known leftist (including Lillian Hellman, whose coming decade would be defined by her battles with HUAC), officially began in 1947.

Crossfire's legacy remains forever tied to Hollywood's embattled political left. With the effective erasure of *The Brick Foxhole*, its derivation as a rare takedown of American homophobia has been all but forgotten. In its immediate aftermath, *Crossfire's* self-congratulatory exposé on anti-Semitism would become evidence of what its right-wing detractors saw as liberal propaganda. In late 1947, while the film was still in theatrical release, HUAC, steadily gaining in power, summoned Dmytryk, along with *Crossfire* producer Adrian Scott, to Congress. With eight other Hollywood leftists suspected of long-standing Communist ties, including the writers Dalton Trumbo and Ring Lardner Jr., they were deemed uncooperative and tagged as "unfriendly" witnesses. Placed on a list that would forever be known as the Hollywood Ten, Dmytryk and Scott served time in prison for contempt of Congress, were fired from RKO, and found themselves blacklisted from making movies in Hollywood.

Dmytryk relocated to England and directed films there for the remainder of the forties. In 1951, he reappeared before Congress, this time as a "friendly" witness, turning his professional fortunes around by naming names—among them Scott's. For his part, however, Scott stayed staunchly opposed to HUAC's tactics, remaining outspoken about the politically motivated purges throughout Hollywood and the U.S. government. In an editor's letter to the *New York Herald Tribune* in the mid-1950s, Scott wrote about the unjust practice of firing men and women under suspicion of homosexuality, calling it "an uncivilized practice, one which does not advance us prominently as an understanding people." The producer who had helped excise any inference of queerness from *Crossfire* was then quick to remind the reader, "I am not now, nor have I ever been a homosexual, nor do I intend to be."

. . .

When executives at Warner Bros. finally laid eyes on *Rope*, many were aghast at the grotesque subject matter. They had been so focused on Hitchcock's intricate aesthetic technique throughout its complicated production that they had barely noticed he had made exactly the film he had wanted to make all along. Bad word of mouth was permeating the industry. When Paramount president Barney Balaban got wind of the film, he even contacted Jack Warner and tried to convince him not to release such perverted, inappropriate entertainment.

Warner Bros. stood by the film, although it would prove only a minor hit, perhaps resulting from its general air of esoterica, reflected both in the purposely alienating elitism of its nefarious protagonists and in the "hidden" audacity of its technique. Fixated on the single takes, invisible cuts, and back-breaking rehearsal processes touted in the studio's publicity machine, some critics were quick to act unimpressed. The *New York Times*'s Bosley Crowther wrote, "The novelty of the picture is not in the drama itself, it being a plainly deliberate and rather thin exercise in suspense, but merely in the method which Mr. Hitchcock has used to stretch the intended tension for the length of the little stunt . . . the unpunctuated flow of image becomes quite monotonous." *Variety* supposed, "The continuous action and the extremely mobile camera are technical features of which industry craftsmen will make much, but to the layman audience is of a distracting interest . . ." *Motion Picture Daily*'s critic conceded that "in point of artistry and craftsmanship it is a shining milestone in the distinguished career of the producer and in the development of production technique." Though he was quick to add, "In theme it is a film of extremely questionable appropriateness for entertainment purposes."

Though the evident homosexuality of *Rope*'s main characters goes as unremarked upon in reviews as it does in the film itself—save one eyebrow-raise in *Variety* cheekily referring to "lavender overtones"—the insistence on separating the film's aesthetic approach from its "themes" has consistently missed its central point and brilliance. The artful, neurotic precision of the filmmaking functions as an expression of Brandon and Phillip's highly aestheticized perfection. Everything about their dandyish behavior—the elegance of their dinner party, their neatly tied piles of books, their tailored suits, the exquisite simplicity of the murder itself—is self-conscious and obvious, even as it conceals plain truths about the men (as homosexuals, as killers) that one might notice only if we really *looked* at them. This stratagem mirrors Hitchcock's bold, bratty cinematic endeavor, an attempt to create a flawless evocation of reality (a film with no cuts!) that regards its own impossibility (you'll notice all ten of its cuts if you just keep your eyes open). When Granger snaps at Dall, "You'll ruin everything with your neat little touches," he might as well be yelling to Hitchcock behind the camera.

Rope is extraordinary for how it calls attention to its own making while remaining at every moment dedicated to the "real-time" anxiety of its situation. Whenever I've shown it to an undergraduate class, it has received roomfuls of hearty applause at the end; one young student exclaimed, "That was the most suspenseful movie I've ever seen!" Fascinated, I asked why he felt that way, initiating a classroom conversation about what we want, expect, or fear as audience members. We know from the very beginning that David Kentley is dead and who killed him, so there's little in the way of a traditional mystery or a race-against-the-clock narrative to save the life of an innocent. Instead, we watch as James Stewart's Rupert slowly pieces together the possibility of what has happened, captured in sly, revelatory glances and wonders. Yet Rupert, who inspired their crime with his cynical Nietzschean teachings and who also proves to be their undoing, is an abstract character at best, hardly our identification point. Instead, we are tethered to Brandon and Phillip, and the suspense is based on whether they will be found out—which summons the question of whether we *want* them to be caught. Once the trunk (closet) is opened, all will be revealed—a tantalizing and frightening prospect.

This ambiguous form of suspense provides the narrative engine, while Hitchcock's aesthetic boldness encourages an unusual, gratifyingly active viewership. *Rope's* insistence on navigating a highly mobile camera within such a tight space and then letting it run out the clock on each of its ten-minute increments produces the kind of visual daring that looks unlike anything made then or now in a Hollywood film. The most exciting expression of this is also the most intentionally static: at one point late in the film, after dinner has been consumed, the camera stops and lingers on the far end of the chest while the harried maid Mrs. Wilson begins cleaning it off. She moves the plates one stack at a time, walking into the kitchen at the far end of the apartment, which is two rooms away, through a door beyond the foyer. Then she puts out the candles and removes the tablecloth, still walking back and forth though the apartment. All the while, the camera stays fixed in place; the chatter of the party guests is happening entirely offscreen—we see only Mrs. Wilson at work. The narrative purpose is clear: the more she clears off the serving table and returns it to its former use as a chest, the more likely she is to open the lid—and reveal a freshly murdered corpse in front of the entire party. Before Brandon arrives into the frame at the last moment to stop this from happening, we assume it's only we who have been watching the entire time—Hitchcock has given us the false feeling of privilege that comes with being a viewer, the sense that we alone are the voyeurs. Do we want Mrs. Wilson to open the chest, thereby revealing Brandon and Phillip's nasty secret and likely bringing this narrative to its conclusion? Or do we want to attenuate the suspense and perhaps save our antiheroes from exposure?

This is the true source of Hitchcock's brand of "perversity"—his desire for us to identify with it, however uncomfortable that makes us, or however morally antithetical it feels to our beliefs when we're outside the movie theater. It's a variation on what Laurents called Hitchcock's fascination with "perverse sex, kinky sex," redirected and reconstituted in a thriller framework. One can detect it in Hitchcock's career as early as his 1927 silent breakthrough *The Lodger*, which starred the not-so-secretly gay matinee idol Ivor Novello as an English dandy who may or may not be a Jack the Ripper–style serial killer. Throughout, Novello's character is an object of fascination and sympathy more than of outright fear. As the landlady of the boarding house where he's lodging defends him to a suspicious detective: "Even if he's a bit queer, he's a gentleman."

There's no doubt about the guilt of *Rope*'s gentlemen killers, which situates them firmly in Hitchcock's gallery of grotesque main characters, from *Strangers on a Train*'s frighteningly earnest Bruno to *Vertigo*'s almost inhumanly obsessive Scotty. We're even desperately wedded to Norman Bates's perspective as he submerges shower victim Marion Crane's body in the bog behind the motel—when at first the car doesn't disappear under the water, we panic right along with him. Rupert uncovers the terrible truth and in a sudden fit of seething self-righteousness becomes, for the first time, a lecturer on goodness and truth, rejecting his past reliance on "logic and superior intellect." His words have eye-stinging force, yet we might feel just as Brandon and Phillip likely do in this moment: it's too late. David is rotting, and Rupert is simply trying to clear his conscience. Our two killers, on the other hand, show no remorse, just disappointment at being discovered. The camera, always watching, pulls back one last time, surveying the desolation of Brandon and Phillip's world, once scrupulously maintained, now a shambles.

. . .

In terms of queerness, *Rope* is all about lingering presence; *Crossfire* is all absence. The fey indirectness of *Rope* conceals what is fairly direct and clear; the gut-punch directness of *Crossfire* hides the elision that made it possible. Together they create a single, Janus-faced narrative of postwar cinematic masculinity: Hitchcock and Laurents's desire to imbue their film with a homosexual sensibility the flipside of Dmytryk, Schary, and Scott's drive to remove any trace of the same. (It's worth noting that, whether in response to *Crossfire*'s elisions or not, Dmytryk's later career would be dotted with films today often referenced by queer scholars, from the 1959 western *Warlock*, drenched in gay subtext, to 1962's *Walk on the Wild Side*, with Barbara Stanwyck as a lesbian bordello madam.)

Rope's reputation upon release as gruesome, amoral entertainment and *Crossfire*'s status as a therapeutic social message picture with the power to effect positive change may have made these violent stories of murder seem opposites, but I see them as united by the obscured queerness that both defines them and remains at their peripheries. Both are, in a sense, impossible pictures.

Amid this discussion of Hollywood movies and the restrictive forces that made homosexuality an invisible but permeative specter within it, one ought to acknowledge that another, more clandestine American cinema was being born, emerging from the same postwar anxieties around masculinity. In this case, however, the filmmakers were working far from the centralized national film industry and could not be touched by the censoring tendrils of the Production Code Administration. Progenitors of what would come to be known as underground cinema, young filmmakers like Kenneth Anger, Curtis Harrington, and Gregory Markopoulos were using self-purchased 8mm and 16mm cameras in the late 1940s to construct personal visions of psychological turmoil that did what mainstream studio films like *Rope* and *Crossfire* could never dream: use the cinematic form to create a subjective expression of the anxiety of living with homosexual desire. It's an alternate cinema in the truest sense of the word, providing a distinct yet thematically comparable form of expression. Influenced by the work of the pioneering L.A. experimental filmmaker Maya Deren, whose 1943 *Meshes of the Afternoon*, shot on a Bolex for less

From left, Florence McGee, Anne Revere, and Katherine Emery in a posed publicity photo for *The Children's Hour* (play), 1935. PHOTOFEST

"Lillian Hellman, youthful author of the play 'The Children's Hour,' is pictured here as she arrived in Los Angeles via TWA Sky-Chief. Miss Hellman has a writing contract with the Samuel Goldwyn Studios." NEW YORK WORLD-TELEGRAM

Publicity still of *These Three* cast, from left, Merle Oberon, Joel McCrea, and Miriam Hopkins, 1936. UNITED ARTISTS/PHOTOFEST

Left: Clara Bow and Dorothy Arzner, 1929.
SPECIAL COLLECTIONS, UCLA: UNIVERSITY RESEARCH LIBRARY
Right: A teenaged Dorothy Arzner dressed as "Garth for a Night."
SPECIAL COLLECTIONS, UCLA: UNIVERSITY RESEARCH LIBRARY
Below: Arzner and Maureen O'Hara on the set of *Dance, Girl, Dance,* 1940. EVERETT

Above: Steve Brodie and Robert Ryan in *Crossfire*, 1947. ALAMY/FILM COMPANY RKO
Below: Farley Granger, John Dall, Alfred Hitchcock, and James Stewart on the set of *Rope*, 1948. ALAMY/THE FILM COMPANY

Above: Judy Garland performing "Lose That Long Face" in *A Star Is Born*, 1954. ALAMY
Below: James Mason and Garland in *A Star Is Born*, 1954. ALAMY

Kerr and Kerr (no relation!) in the forest in *Tea and Sympathy*, 1956. EVERETT

Liz Taylor in a publicity still for
Suddenly, Last Summer, 1959.
ALAMY

The devouring of Sebastian
Venable in *Suddenly, Last Summer.*
PHOTOFEST

Above: William Wyler and Hellman, 1961. EVERETT
Below: Wyler directing Audrey Hepburn and Shirley MacLaine on the set of
The Children's Hour (film), 1961. ALAMY/THE MIRISCH CORPORATION

than $300, used free associative imagery and repetitive symbolism to represent its maker's internal landscape and reflect on the nature of the subconscious, Anger, Harrington, and Markopoulos created works of psychological portraiture focused on the socially repressed minds of queer men living in 1940s America.

In stark contrast to Hollywood's treatment of the postwar male psyche, these honest, insolent searches for identity and evocations of erotic dreams rejected the popular storytelling techniques and the presiding film grammar of the forties. Expressing entrapment and freedom, embracing sexual forthrightness, and rejecting linear narrative and clear causal linkages between scenes, dialogue-free short films like Harrington's *Fragment of Seeking* (1946), Anger's *Fireworks* (1947), and Markopoulos's *Christmas USA* (1949) are responses to and rejections of mass culture and would prove instrumental in setting the scene for the American avant-garde. All three films position their makers as men in search of socially aberrant identities: in *Fragment of Seeking*, Harrington—a protégé of Deren's—plays a young man pursuing a female phantom through a labyrinthine house, only to finally discover that he *is* her; in *Christmas USA*, Markopoulos, a USC grad living back in Toledo, Ohio, enacts a symbolic liberation, suffused with Christian guilt and sexuality, from the stultifying drudgery of heteronormative suburban life; in *Fireworks*, the cockiest and most influential of the bunch, Anger sets forth on an explicitly erotic, slyly humorous sadomasochistic journey, expressing the unique alienation of homosexual American life and the psychic split that occurs when you're scared of the thing that you're also attracted to (in this case, a pack of homophobic sailors who mete out violent, homoerotic punishment on the young protagonist). *Fireworks* was first shown in a midnight film society screening at the Coronet theater in Los Angeles, where it was reportedly attended by the 1930s gay Hollywood director James Whale (*The Bride of Frankenstein*) and none other than Alfred Kinsey, who, according to Anger, purchased a print of the film for his Institute for Sexual Research archives.

Unlike the shrewd *Rope* and the expurgated *Crossfire*, these films aim to evoke the experience of life from inside the closet, teasing at questions of separatism versus assimilation that would define the gay liberation movements in the subsequent decades. As such they also reflect a transitional moment. These works pointed toward the 1950s, when homosexual communities began to rise in urban centers across the country, whether united by the desire for political action, such as the men of the clandestine Mattachine Society, which first met in 1950, or the women of the

Daughters of Bilitis in 1955; or coming together for the purposes of communal entertainment in film societies, midnight screenings, or bars. Reaching full flower in the 1960s, the underground cinema movement would remain a necessary counternarrative to mainstream American movies, and in its embrace of camp would prove to have a symbiotic relationship to Hollywood: movie stars such as Bette Davis, Mae West, and Judy Garland would be embraced and recouped as gay icons for the disenfranchised, an appreciative, fun-house mirror of American movies aimed back at itself.

In the 1950s, as public gatherings of gays and lesbians proliferated, the sense that there could be such a thing as a queer "community" rose, a natural outgrowth of the anxious 1940s and a stark contrast to a reactionary era recalled most typically for clichés of white-picket suburban conformity. So even as conservative forces continued to rise, and the Red and Lavender Scares threatened livelihoods, the seeds of queer liberation were being planted. Throughout the decade, some Hollywood producers and directors would become ever bolder in pushing back against the restrictions of the Production Code, trying, ever so slightly, to untangle the knots of traditional gender roles. Whereas *These Three* and *Crossfire* left only barely discernible traces of their homosexual source material, *Dance, Girl, Dance* abstracted its maker's queerness into a homosocial scenario, and *Rope* was content to play winking parlor games, a handful of bold 1950s Hollywood movies would attempt to make direct inquiries into masculinity and heteronormative social codes. They wouldn't all successfully achieve these ends, but these artists, influenced as ever by the enviable permissibility of the theater and spiritually encouraged by that guiding light of the perverse, Tennessee Williams, would rewrite the rules of engagement in their battles with the PCA. By the beginning of the 1960s, film history would be altered, forever changing the representation of gay characters in popular culture in ways that continue to resonate with our modern conception of queerness.

5

Musical Interlude

It's a shame a book can't sing. Because it's as difficult to evoke in mere words the tenor and meaning of this chapter's star as it is obvious to include her in this book. Just as any endeavor to describe the contours, discernible or not, of queer cinematic history would be incomplete without her, attempts at trying to understand her evidently immortal grip over American gay culture can come up short. A writer is doomed to fall back upon platitudes or conjecture as a means of characterizing the ineffable emotional core of human identity and sexuality to which she's forever tied.

This is a figure who has long served as an unofficial mascot, emblem, and guiding spirit for gay people, an image and idea to congregate around, an eternal maypole. As such, she's also long been reduced to an easy punchline, both for what she represents and because of the trickiness of describing what she represents. And this is the right moment in the book to briefly croon about her, because the gradual manifestation of visible postwar gay urban communities coincides with the unofficial creation of her queer status, which is impossible to extract from the appearance of her richest, queerest film, *A Star Is Born* (1954). I sing, of course, of Judy Garland, whom legions of gay men have long held close to their hearts like a jewel eternally in danger of being stolen.

Some years ago, I was researching an article for a film magazine about a film magazine. I had long been *intrigued*, let's say, by the pictorial content of a niche

British periodical titled *Films and Filming*, which had been published between 1954 and 1990. Stacks of lovingly sorted back issues had been available to me in two separate workplaces where I was employed during the first decade of my career in the New York film world: on the shelves at *Film Comment* magazine, which were in the offices of what was then called the Film Society of Lincoln Center, and in a series of binders in a conference room at the Criterion Collection. The magazine's presence in these establishments affirmed its exalted status among serious cinephiles, and the way the issues were cataloged and protected hinted at their out-of-print preciousness. Yet was it just me, or was there a startling abundance of beautiful male actors, frequently shirtless (and even more unclothed as the magazine slid into the late sixties), a nearly drunken display of homoeroticism illustrating otherwise sober articles about film culture by consummate critics?

Of course it wasn't just me (it never is). Nevertheless, when I first discovered *Films and Filming*'s treasure trove of exploited torsos, flaunted alongside rigorous movie criticism, it felt like my own dirty secret—which is of course how growing up gay feels. Here was a magazine that seemed uncannily, unabashedly tuned in to the voyeuristic pleasures cinema afforded men who like to look at men. My feeling that the magazine, with its unerring gaze on performers like Marlon Brando, Paul Newman, Alain Delon, and Terence Stamp, was sending out signals to a specific demographic was somewhat confirmed when an informal poll of straight cinephile colleagues familiar with the magazine led to quizzical stares about what was to me its self-evident eroticism.

Indeed, as I would learn in my research, the magazine's founder, Philip Dosse, who ran a small empire of other publications with unassuming, workmanlike titles (*Dance and Dancers, Music and Musicians, Records and Recording*), was gay, and the magazines were intentional down-low communiqués to a segment of the population that were not only marginalized but criminal: sex between consenting adult men in England was illegal until 1967. This makes the magazine's section of coded personal ads particularly poignant: see the "YOUNG MAN, 25" in the November 1957 issue who "seeks male correspondents (similar age)" and is into "films, swimming, dancing." Yet the magazine was not focused solely on British cinema, nor did it cater exclusively to London readers. As queer film scholar Justin Bengry writes, "*Films and Filming* was widely circulated, affordable, available internationally and accessible to virtually anyone." This was meaningful for gay readers in the United

States, where explicitly queer, politically minded magazines like the *Mattachine Review* or the Daughters of Bilitis's *The Ladder* were underground publications.

Delving into back issues at the New York Public Library for the Performing Arts, I was not disappointed by the amount of male skin, but stoking more than my prurient interest, the magazine revealed its gayness in another fascinating way: an inordinate focus on Judy Garland. In *Films and Filming*'s very first year, *A Star Is Born* is given pride of place in three separate issues, including a cover story for Garland in Christmas 1954. The hype for this major Warner Bros. production was not the sole province of Garland aficionados, as the film was her long-gestating comeback project after her heavily publicized emotional breakdown, which had led to the end of her long-standing relationship with MGM in 1950. Yet the adoration and lofty language with which Garland was spoken of in a magazine whose readership today registers as unambiguously gay communicates a great deal about both Garland's growing queer fan base and the communities of like-minded gay people that were becoming more prevalent in postwar America—people united not just by their social invisibility and disenfranchisement but also the devotional relationship to and recapitulation of mainstream pop culture inherent to so much of gay identity as we'd come to know it.

The mystique around Judy Garland begins for most of us in childhood, with a special pride of place to *The Wizard of Oz* (1939). Dorothy, who journeys, undaunted, from her drab, black-and-white Kansas farmland to the Technicolor grandiosity (and pull-back-the-curtains theatricality) of the Land of Oz, is a powerful source of identification for those just beginning to wend their way through a confusing, intimidating world beset by dreamers and hypocrites, defined by arbitrary rules of conduct. Oz is a fantastical alternate reality, yet it requires wisdom and courage to brave its very real perils; Dorothy, armored only with a blue and white gingham dress and wicker basket, comes across as more than up to the task because of the young actor embodying her. Garland, who was sixteen at the time and had been in show business almost since she learned to walk, plays Dorothy with that singular contradiction of vulnerable indomitability that would define her career. The exquisite tremor in her singing voice only enhances its power. The wide-open, emotional transparency of Garland's Dorothy is an invitation for all children to see themselves in her. She imprints herself on the consciousness, encourages a kind of unbearable intimacy. For some of us, and especially for gay men, that imprint lasts a lifetime, a stamp that becomes a self-affixed mark of a romantic gay exceptionalism.

Garland will likely mean something different to each person who cherishes her for her films, her songs, or her general persona, but she's also unavoidably monolithic in her meaning, in her ability—miraculous in its unintentionality—to have created generations of enthralled gay worshippers and to have become a community avatar that appears to require no explanation. Her inextricability from gay culture has led to mythmaking, including that her death at age forty-seven on June 22, 1969, fomented the anger and anxiety that led to the Stonewall riots in New York six days later. (No evidence exists of what is essentially a white gay fiction, sidelining the Black, Latine, and trans queers who initiated the resistance, though one can surely understand the appeal of such a romantic and depoliticized notion.) Garland's cultural legacy as a gay stereotype has also led to her own form of cultural exile, or at least marginalization. The mighty tether binding Garland to gay men creates a narrative so culturally prevalent that at some point in our lives we might have denied our own feelings for her, either for fear of being "found out" or to avoid being stereotyped.

The qualities that make Judy Garland an eternal figure of fascination, even obsession, are worthy of serious consideration. Like the other films and artists discussed in this book, she deserves to be better understood for her place in a specific midcentury evolution of queerness, and for the connection she continues to make with contemporary viewers. Judy Garland is such a crucial, all-consuming figure in evaluating queer Hollywood legacies that, for fear of her overwhelming this book, let's just allow her this short musical interlude. And what better conduit is there than Garland for trying to understand the strange cadences of the Hollywood movie musical itself, whose seemingly self-evident yet textually hidden queerness remains one of cinema's great gay conundrums?

· · ·

In a 1986 essay titled "Judy Garland and Gay Men," certainly the most persuasive one I've read about her, Richard Dyer analyzes Garland's queer meaning in a concrete, evidential way that remains respectful of its elusiveness. Cataloging gay men's ecstatic responses to Garland as a performer via magazine articles, letters, and his own personal correspondence, and offering close readings of films she made as an adult, Dyer summoned three categories that might help explain her appeal to a particular subset of her audience. The first is ordinariness, specifically the disparity between the every-girl normality of her movie roles and the extraordinary depths and problems of the woman behind the screen, which became more acute as her personal travails were sensationalized in the media. The second is androgyny, meaning the perceptible embrace of clothes and style in her performances that were either more commonly thought of as male or just generally shapeless and nonsexual, such as the figure of the "tramp" she inhabited onstage. Finally, there's camp, a word of slippery, still-debated meaning, inextricable from queerness, and which in Dyer's case referred to the knowing self-awareness in many of Garland's roles, and the source of much of her distinct humor. This creates a winking, conspiratorial distance for the viewer in such films as *The Harvey Girls* (1946), *The Pirate* (1948) and in some scenes of *Meet Me in St. Louis* (1944).

It's this latter film, directed by Garland's future second husband, Vincente Minnelli, that's maybe most responsible for my own reverence. I'm sure I watched *Meet Me in St. Louis* at least as many times while I was growing up as I did *The Wizard of Oz*. And this film, a rendering of turn-of-the-twentieth-century Americana, Technicolor but with just enough darkness trimming its borders, contains an element of Garland's queer persona that I would modestly add to Dyer's tripartite illumination. Let's call it *hunger*.

There's an aspect of longing to all her roles, and while this is a quality of many an American movie protagonist—after all, identifying with the desires that fuel a film's plot allows for emotional engagement—with Garland there's something especially intense about how that longing is represented and embodied, and especially graspable to gay men. In that first song in *The Wizard of Oz*, the one that became her career-long anthem, she sings with aching need to go to "a land that I've heard of once in a lullaby": she looks beyond the clouds, almost as though she's trying to will herself into the sky. In *Meet Me in St. Louis*'s "The Boy Next Door," Garland's Esther Smith is pining for something fleshlier, if seemingly just as unattainable: her handsome neighbor, John Truitt, although "he doesn't know I exist, no matter how I may persist." In a long auburn wig and blue-and-white-striped pinafore, she registers as more than a lovelorn teen. Garland's ability to make her desperation so deeply felt and accessible transcends character and allows her to speak to all those young people—young men included—who have felt tragically invisible to their handsome boys next door.

Meet Me in St. Louis's most heartrending Garland performance is saved for the film's emotional climax. On Christmas Eve, Esther serenades her weeping little sister Tootie (Margaret O'Brien), who's upset that the family will soon relocate to New York from their beloved Victorian home in St. Louis. To lift her spirits, Garland sings "Have Yourself a Merry Little Christmas," and has there ever been a more intensely pained expression of hope than her agonized protestation of "Someday soon we all will be together, if the fates allow / Until then we'll have to muddle through somehow"? The word *somehow* is sustained with enough fire to power a jet engine. Esther may have intended to cheer up Tootie, yet Garland, with her agonizing intensity of feeling, fails. Tootie's response is to run outside in the middle of the night and smash the snow family she and her siblings spent all day making—a frightening form of symbolic familial destruction that feels perfectly apt in the aftermath of a Judy Garland performance.

A consummate performer who was able to turn it on and bounce into a song or dance from an extremely young age as a result of her vaudeville family training, Garland was also tapping into something genuine and unfalsifiable within her. Her biographer Gerold Frank wrote that her personal life was defined by romantic longing, "an exquisite and vulnerable sensibility in search of its complement in another." Constantly compared to the more conventional beauties and glamor girls surrounding her in Hollywood, she grew tumorous insecurities that would extend past the professional world and into her own love affairs. According to Frank, "Her relationships with men were always fraught with peril because of her deep-seated doubt of her desirability."

Garland's persistence as a figure of fascination for the public in the twenty-first century is undoubtedly related to the transparency with which her performances communicate her evident, highly sympathetic humanity, especially poignant considering the carefully crafted, sanitized nature of celebrity today. Under the watchful eye of the twenty-four-hour social media cycle, in which the slightest misstep could relegate one to the dustbin, screen actors rarely allow much of their mysterious selves—their hidden emotional landscapes—into their roles. This, paired with the decline of moviegoing in general, and with studio heads unwilling to take risks on character-based, nonfranchise properties, is partly to blame for the death of the movie star: celebrities are as gawked at, lusted after, and lovingly mocked as ever, if not more so, yet they're no longer bankable assets for motion picture studios more obsessed with the intellectual property of creators. A figure like Judy Garland, whose emotional baggage was part and parcel of her screen presence, is unthinkable now. Perhaps such a star could exist only at a time when actors were cogs in a factory that was supposed to be a model of efficiency. Garland's breakdown within that mechanism was a simultaneous liberation from it—a contradiction that harbors appeal for the queer movie viewer historically left on the peripheries.

A Star Is Born was manufactured as her cinematic restart after that breakdown. The harrowing conclusion to the first movement of Garland's career occurred between 1949 and 1950, amid swirling rumors of her pill addiction and suicide attempts and bad press about her unprofessionalism. She had been fired from the lead role of the hot property *Annie Get Your Gun* and was erratic on the tortuous shoot of *Summer Stock* (1950), which would be her last film for MGM before being released from a contract she had had since age thirteen. *A Star Is Born* would reintroduce Garland to moviegoers. In the intervening four years, she had been reestablished as a touring stage performer in Europe with a hugely successful run at London's grand Palladium in April 1951. As a result, the gallant impresario Sid Luft, whom Garland would wed in 1952 after the gradual dissolution of her marriage to Minnelli, brought her act back to the United States. To help Garland reconnect with the audiences who had been dazzled by the depth and excitement of her voice since she was an adolescent, Luft produced shows for Garland that nostalgically evoked the vaudeville era of her youth and highlighted signature songs featured in her films ("Over the Rainbow," "The Trolley Song" from *Meet Me in St. Louis*, "After You've Gone" from *For Me and My Gal*) to keep in rotation for new generations—an irony considering the trauma those years represented and the ebullience with which she'd have to continue digging back into them.

The idea had legs. Garland opened her new act that October at New York's Palace Theatre, once the fabled peak on the vaudeville circuit, since fallen into disrepair after having been converted into a movie theater by RKO. Rejuvenated for Garland, the Palace proved the poignant backdrop for a concert that was, according to Frank, "the beginning of the legend." Lasting nineteen weeks, the Palace engagement reinvigorated her career in seismic fashion, creating legions of newly obsessive fans and engendering a cult-like fandom. It was a spectacle of reclamation, and it's certainly not surprising that Garland's rediscovery of her personhood in this moment marks her functional beginning as an idol for gay men.

A Star Is Born would be part and parcel of this extended resuscitation campaign. An update of the hit 1937 melodrama of the same title with Fredric March and Janet Gaynor, the project originated with Luft, who knew the remake rights had been sold at auction to a producer acquaintance, Eddie Alperson. After Luft got to work pitching the film to studios, Warner Bros. bought the rights from Alperson, and despite Garland's reputation for volatile behavior and her ongoing mental health issues, she attached herself to the project. In the character of Esther Blodgett, the small-time nightclub singer remade into a movie superstar with the more appealing name of Vicki Lester, there were inescapable similarities to the life and career of Judy Garland, née Ethel Frances Gumm. Garland's addiction struggles were recast onto the character of her husband, Norman Maine, a major star whose career is on the decline. The crux of the drama lies with Norman, who by the film's gutting end will kill himself in act of attempted selflessness, while his wife's fame ascends.

This tale of tragic love and sacrifice has proven durable and popular across multiple generations (the 1976 and 2018 remakes with Barbra Streisand and Lady Gaga, respectively, proved massive hits), allowing its female star to suffer beautifully while her male partner self-destructs. The narrative thus becomes a story of her self-actualization while she remains forever connected to his legacy, her eternal devotion also signaling a notable loss of her independence. It's such a primally compelling arc that it would require little in the way of emoting to produce an effect in the viewer. Yet Garland's performance is so potent that it practically removes the invisible scrim between audience and performer and between the performer and her character, so that *A Star Is Born* seems to collapse all reasonable boundaries of melodrama. If it sounds as if I'm engaging in the kind of irrational idolatry that befits a Garland fanatic, then so be it.

There is a swirling host of reasons to consider *A Star Is Born* an essential work of gay American cinema. In addition to being the comeback film that would confirm Garland's survivor status and make her a queer kindred spirit, the narrative itself paralleling and intensifying the travails of her own life, the film also marked the debut of "The Man That Got Away," an uncharacteristically hard-driving blues ballad that was written by the composer Harold Arlen, who in 1939 introduced "Over the Rainbow" into our hitherto grayer world. With lyrics of rhapsodic despair by Ira Gershwin—brought on after "Rainbow" lyricist E. Y. "Yip" Harburg had been blacklisted during the Communist witch hunts—the song was destined to live on as a kind of gay anthem; you can hear the ascending introductory notes of "The Man That Got Away" in the triumphal opening to the overture for Garland's legendary Carnegie Hall performance in 1961, the event that would cement her legacy of indomitability. Further crowning its queer royalty, *A Star Is Born* would be directed by George Cukor, Hollywood's most successful living gay director to those in the know—which, in Hollywood, was practically everyone.

· · ·

George Cukor's queer status—or nonstatus, depending on how you look at it—exemplified the condition of gay identity in Hollywood's Golden Age. Despite his fearsome reputation and career longevity, Cukor, who directed films from 1930 to 1981, worked during a distinct period that never granted him the confidence to come to public terms with his homosexuality. Even into his eighties he was giving interviews in which he skirted the issue, yet in a way that made his every word on the subject seem like conspiratorial winking. In 1981, the interviewer Boze Hadleigh confronted him by saying, "When a public figure—and I'm speaking in general, not of anyone in particular—who is gay pretends to be straight, it *is* other people's business, because the message they're sending is that it's still not okay to be gay." Cukor responded, "I know what you're saying. And it's true. All I know is *I* wouldn't want to be the one to sacrifice my career to the New Honesty."

To those in the industry who acknowledged it, Cukor's reputation as a gay man rested upon both the known facts of his personal life and the presumptuous interpretation of his professional one. Yes, he was known for the wild parties at his luxe mansion, especially the more exclusive all-male soirees, but he also became tagged as a "woman's director," which in the eyes of colleagues connected him to the stereotype of gayness being unmasculine. "George was a better woman's director because he was more feminine by nature," said Joan Fontaine, expressing the kind of unfounded analogy many took as gospel. "We all knew he was homosexual. He made no bones about it . . . He cared about detail, about clothes, about ambiance. These are feminine traits . . . a sense of chic and style." Ben Hecht's dismissive evaluation of Cukor's talents verged on the homophobic: "He didn't know anything about stories, he didn't know anything about directing, sets, technique. He had a flair for women acting. He knew how a woman should sit down, dress, smile." This was common code. Mitchell Leisen, another hugely successful gay director who worked throughout the same period in Hollywood, was described by Billy Wilder thusly: So, while it was true that he would be most revered for his astonishingly fruitful work with stars like Katharine Hepburn, Greta Garbo, Joan Crawford, Ingrid Bergman, and Judy Holliday, Cukor was never able to shake what amounted to a stigma within a culture that prized masculinity above all. Even in his early days as a stage director, Cukor was known for discovering and molding female talent, such as *These Three*'s future star Miriam Hopkins, who got her first big break at the Lyceum Theater in Rochester in Cukor's 1927 production of the comedy *Applesauce*, when she stood in at the last minute for the lead actress, thereafter becoming a regular player in his troupe.

Though Cukor vowed to keep his personal life a secret when he moved from New York to Los Angeles in the late twenties, cautiously staying away from gay hangouts and unwilling to be seen publicly with the known gay crowd, he regularly brought men home. It wouldn't take Cukor long to be established as surreptitiously gay. Legend has it Louis B. Mayer, the fearsome head of MGM, where Cukor was employed during part of the 1930s, asked him point blank about his sexuality and turned a deaf ear when Cukor gave him the honest answer he dreaded. (He was too successful too quickly to dismiss, even to known intolerants like Mayer.) Soon enough, Cukor would become a central figure of the gay community in L.A., however under the radar he was committed to remain, a den mother to the city's new gay arrivals. "Homosexuals would call George as soon as they arrived in Hollywood, and if he liked them, he would introduce them to other members of his elite," said Joseph Mankiewicz. His parties became legendary. Wrote Cukor biographer Patrick McGilligan, "There was a flow of distinguished homosexual guests from around the globe, and particularly from England: the author Somerset Maugham, playwright and actor Noël Coward, the noted *Vogue* photographer George Hoyningen-Huene, the photographer and designer Cecil Beaton . . . and many others."

His personal and professional lives stayed separate; there was no room on Coded Hollywood screens for what might be regarded as flamboyance. Cukor's awful experience in 1935 with the reception of *Sylvia Scarlett*, his passion project with Katharine Hepburn which dared to depict fluid sexuality and question entrenched social gender roles, only led him further back into the professional closet. After the humiliation of the film's failure and his resultant blackballing from RKO, never again would he feature such explicitly queer material on-screen (though his 1949 Katharine Hepburn–Spencer Tracy comedy *Adam's Rib* contains a famously queer-coded character, Hepburn's sidekick Kip, performed by David Wayne with sparkling, irremediable cattiness).

Cukor had been originally assigned to direct *Meet Me in St. Louis* at MGM in the early forties, but he had eventually ceded to Vincente Minnelli after being enlisted (and ending up at Astoria's Signal Corps Photographic Center alongside

Arthur Laurents). By the time he had come to *A Star Is Born* a decade later he had still never worked with Judy Garland—nor had he shot a film in color or directed a musical. So when Sid Luft invited him to lunch at Romanoff's in Beverly Hills, Garland's husband barely got a word out before Cukor, according to McGilligan, blurted out, "If you want me to do a picture with Judy, I will."

A Star Is Born had become a hot property by the time Cukor signed on to make it for Warner Bros. in the summer of 1953, and was granted a large budget at $6 million. These were the days of a newly ascendant kind of cinematic spectacle, when the astronomic rise of television and the resultant decline in movie ticket sales were frightening Hollywood studio heads, who were devising new methods to coerce moviegoers back into theaters. The previous year had seen the release of *Bwana Devil*, the first 3D feature film, and *This Is Cinerama*, which introduced a much-hyped three-projector process using an enormous wraparound screen, both designed to turn moviegoing into a kind of simulation thrill ride. By 1953, the idea of wide-screen spectacle was being wedded to conventional narratives, with films like Twentieth Century-Fox's biblical epic *The Robe* and their Marilyn Monroe–starring candy-colored romantic comedy *How to Marry a Millionaire* leading the charge, utilizing a process called CinemaScope, boasting an elongated frame with a 2.55:1 aspect ratio. Once the novelty of these processes wore off, films in widescreen format would become the industry standard, yet by the time *A Star Is Born* went into production, it was still, for many veteran filmmakers, untested. Warner Bros. was intent on using its new WarnerScope process, and Cukor, expanding his horizons in terms of color and genre, was skeptical of the 'scope format's ability to maintain the emotional intimacy that was, for him, cinema's reason for being. The film's screenwriter, Moss Hart, agreed, writing to Cukor in September 1953, one month before the beginning of production, "I do hope you can talk them into doing it large-screen and not WarnerScope. It may be vital, that choice. I have a horrid suspicion that CinemaScope or WarnerScope might drain the emotion out of so personal a story as this."

Cukor's innate ability to wring complex pathos and deep human connection out of nearly any scenario and Garland's presence, a special effect equal to any new technological advance, made Hart's fears unwarranted. *A Star Is Born* may stand as the most emotionally compelling, least visually austere widescreen American film of the 1950s. Though conceived from the beginning as a comeback vehicle for Garland, *A Star Is Born* was a tragic two-hander and would live or die on the chemistry between Garland and her romantic co-star. Cukor and Garland both wanted Cary Grant for the part of Norman Maine; though he was actively courted for the role, Grant, as he had proven when he refused to take the part of the gay-coded philosophy professor in *Rope*, was watchful and apprehensive about his star persona. In the case of Norman Maine, he was fearful that audiences would see too many parallels to his own career, which was currently experiencing a downturn, and he politely declined. Though other men were considered, including Humphrey Bogart, Laurence Olivier, and Frank Sinatra, the role of the crumbling alcoholic former star would go to respected British actor James Mason, whose dissolute yet gentlemanly demeanor proved apt for Norman's tortured attempts to keep up appearances.

Norman sets the rhythm of the narrative with his addiction swings, but Mason is also there to be dazzled and swoon in the presence of Garland, a compelling audience surrogate. Despite the use of the 'scope frame, the vivid Technicolor, and the tragic drama of the plot, the real spectacle is Garland. In *A Star Is Born*, she performs numbers in the ripped-from-the-guts style that had become part of her new persona following the triumphant Palace Theatre stint. Both because of its "comeback" nature and the full-throated maturity with which Garland tackles it, *A Star Is Born* seems like a vehicle for a middle-aged performer, though she was only thirty-two when she made the film—just ten years after she played a high-schooler in *Meet Me in St. Louis*, and only fifteen years after she was whisked away to Oz.

What a difference those years made: "Over the Rainbow," once a lullaby of yearning, had been transformed into a soul-baring torch song in Garland's recent one-woman show. In her 1950s performances of the song, customarily performed as a curtain call, with Judy dressed in her recurring Chaplinesque "tramp" outfit, perched on the edge of the stage with legs dangling, gone is the wistful girl longing for the clouds. When she sings, "If happy little bluebirds fly beyond the rainbow, why, oh, why can't I?" with that desperately attenuated final note, Garland now articulated the unlikeliness of transcendence rather than the childish hope for escape. A song that once looked to the future became a melancholy journey to the past, to a moment of youth when the road, yellow brick or otherwise, was still paved with possibility.

Her relative youth as the been-around-the-block chanteuse of the fifties feels especially unfathomable in *A Star Is Born*, considering the depths Garland plumbs. When in "The Man That Got Away," she sings, essentially to herself, "No more that all-time thrill, for you've been through the mill," there's no doubting the considerable mileage already expended in her life. It's in this performance, which occurs startlingly early in the film, before we know anything about the character, that Garland reestablishes her place as a movie star, four years after reports of her on-set breakdowns and hospital stints left her a Hollywood vagabond. When Norman watches Esther, a nobody band singer and chorus girl, rehearse after hours at a nightclub, we are, like Norman (and Mason), transfixed, and also, like him, we would do anything to help Esther (and Judy) succeed.

The casualness with which Garland slides into a run-through of "The Man That Got Away" as she pals around with her bandmates is amusing considering the shattering perfection with which she serenades the mostly empty room. The performance is more of a pile driver than anything she did at MGM: the vocal arranger Hugh Martin, who had also worked with Garland on *Meet Me in St. Louis*, had wanted the song kept in Garland's lower range, but she wanted more vocal razzle-dazzle. The filmmaking forgoes obvious flourish, except for one breath-catching instant when Garland emotes so close to the camera that she momentarily goes out of focus. Cukor captured the whole thing in a single take, all but reaching through the screen and yanking out your heart. The spontaneous little giggle she gives when the song is through is almost hilariously incongruous. Yet these are the unspoken tenets and blissful unrealities of the movie musical: at any moment we might suddenly and easily slip into virtuosity, a better version of ourselves, proclaiming our love or, in Judy's case, heartbreak to a world that, for a few shining moments, might actually listen.

Dog-tired yet vocally proud, "The Man That Got Away" is a surrender to impossible love, and it might be the great gay anthem of the movie musical. One would be forgiven for assuming there are plenty of competitors for such a title, yet the great irony of the Hollywood musical, despite its unofficial status as an inherently gay genre, is how surface-level straight it is—even in the years after the coded Golden Age. The narratives of musicals are largely predicated on fantasies of heterosexual coupling. Because musicals promise a utopian other world, they are designed as a response to the mainstream social order; the genre's gay viewers are legion, but we produce our own meaning from them. This is, of course, common to queer perspectives on cinema, which historically rely on gay spectatorship and reading to imbue films with queer subtext, as opposed to actual gay themes or characters on-screen, which at the time were impossible. Yet the movie musical was a special case, as these films were often the result of intense labor by gay craftspeople and workers.

This was particularly true during the forties and fifties at MGM, where Arthur Freed, who had worked his way up from Tin Pan Alley songwriter to major producing force (first proven with his uncredited work on *The Wizard of Oz*), headed a legendary company affectionately known as the Freed Unit. The married Freed was straight, but the number of homosexuals employed by him led some to call his company, less affectionately, the "Fairy Unit." Here Judy Garland was surrounded by gay men, including the pianist and songwriter Roger Edens (a creative and personal support to Garland since she had come to the studio barely in her teens), the choreographers Robert Alton and Charles Walters, and the music orchestrator Conrad Salinger. It was a bustling hive of creativity that set the stage for such dazzling talents as Gene Kelly, Cyd Charisse, and Lena Horne to reach the screen, and it paved the way for Fred Astaire's comeback in the late 1940s.

All classic exemplars of the form, like *For Me and My Gal* (1942), *Meet Me in St. Louis*, *The Harvey Girls*, *The Pirate*, *On the Town* (1949), *An American in Paris* (1951), *Singin' in the Rain* (1952), and *It's Always Fair Weather* (1955), may predictably end with the unification of their central opposite-sex romantic partnerships, yet the integration of musical numbers—song and dance—within these narratives adds an element of supernal expressivity outside normal human function. If musicals, in essence, circumvent reality to express something inexpressible, then they have the ability to speak (or sing) to the deepest reservoirs within their viewers, especially those unable to vocalize their truth within everyday social circles.

Musicals are formally driven by a feeling, which is that something inside has to *come out*. This is as true of the musical onstage as on-screen. The film scholar D. A. Miller has written, "The true content of show-tune transcendence is simply the strength to endure a repressive status quo." Yet the sui generis quality of the movie musical is more easily highlighted when set in relief to other film templates. There are all types of catharses in cinema, though in various genres they're usually hinged to violence, whether physical (horror, westerns, action pictures) or emotional (melodrama, tragedy); in the musical the catharsis is redirected to moments of self-actualization, yearning, or confession. In some numbers, like Garland's "Over the Rainbow" or "The Boy Next Door," or Kelly's roller-skating paean to egomania "I Like Myself" in *It's Always Fair Weather*, or Doris Day's "Secret Love" in *Calamity Jane* (1953), there's the sense that we the audience are being let in on a secret, a glimpse into a deeper version of a character that never would have been revealed if not for music. In others, supportive collectives of characters trade stories of hardship and hope for better days, revealing the genre as the most dramatic cinematic expression of utopian promise. Is there a more apt song title for a musical than

"There's Gotta Be Something Better Than This" from *Sweet Charity* (1969), sung by a trio of New York City women dreaming of life beyond sex work?

Dance numbers essentially function the same, especially in the "integrated" movie musical, which became the generic standard after Minnelli's *Cabin in the Sky* (1943) and *Meet Me in St. Louis*. Previously, in the backstage musicals of the 1930s, films such as Busby Berkeley's *42nd Street* and *Gold Diggers of 1933*, the musical performances would be couched within the narratives as stage performances, however fantastically the filmmaking would explode the numbers themselves into spatially fanciful formation. By the height of the Freed Unit's output at MGM, characters embodied by such wildly talented performers as Garland, Kelly, and Astaire would not necessarily be dancers, actors, or singers, but "regular" folk (tradespeople, waitresses, painters), their performance skills manifesting on-screen only within show-stopping asides or dream ballet sequences. Somewhere in the incongruity between the presented self and the fantasy self lies the musical's appeal for the queer viewer, the sense that everyone has two identities—the more fantastical, seemingly artificial one being, ironically and excitingly, the more honest.

There's no other movie genre so completely reliant on its characters' being able to "code-switch" between the public and the private, itself a classical definition of the gay experience within homophobic culture. These characters, however much they are written to conform to traditional standards of socially acceptable masculinity or femininity in their "real" worlds, are all but forced by the dictates of the musical to occasionally shed their skins and show their concealed selves. In this way, they are hidden in plain sight, but unlike Brandon and Phillip of *Rope*, they are allowed to prove their artistry—fly their freak flag—by singing and dancing rather than, say, committing murder. Music encourages us to express something that nothing in our grim, ordinary world would ever make space or time for. According to Miller, "Every lyric becomes a figure for present-day metropolitan homosexuality which no lyric has ever cared, or dared, to literally mention."

Since a musical number functions more or less autonomously, with its own beginning (verse or overture), middle (chorus and/or bridge), and end (climax and resolution), a movie musical provides one catharsis after another. Maybe this accounts for the genre's persistent divisiveness among viewers: like horror movies, which also exist to "get a rise" out of you, people tend to either love them or hate them. In horror, the refrain for the uninterested often goes, "Why would I want to put myself through that?" One disinclined toward the movie musical might as well ask the same thing, for the genre requires a certain emotional surrender that some simply aren't willing to give. An intense dose of normally concealed human expression, the musical is defined by a lack of fidelity to reality and therefore to the hetero status quo. I'm not going to go so far as to say that to vehemently dislike musicals is homophobic, but . . . it's difficult to deny that the reasons often weaponized by the genre's detractors as "personal taste" tend to conform to the masculinist societal standards that keep gay people closeted. (Bemoaning the unreality or inauthenticity of the musical by saying that people just *don't* break into song sounds perilously close to saying that they *shouldn't*.)

Judy Garland, the most lasting avatar of the genre, exemplifies all this emotional signification to a remarkably poignant degree. She both embodies and transcends the movie musical. The extraordinary power of her singing voice—what one would customarily define as a "gift," given the maturity of her tone and control from an early age—and the grand tragedienne narrative of her life that still haunts any discussion of her to this day combine to create a star that is both untouchable and unbearably human, an incongruity that recalls the discontinuity built into the form of the musical. There is an ease with which most of the great musical movie stars boast their skills: though the result of muscle-aching, tendon-testing practice and rehearsal, the graceful athleticism of the eternally smiling Gene Kelly, Cyd Charisse, and Fred Astaire would lead you to doubt they ever break a sweat; while the winsome vocal stylings of the likes of Kelly, Horne, and Debbie Reynolds likewise give the sense of simple, painless pleasures.

By the time of *A Star Is Born*, such manufactured false humility is left by the side of the road. Having moved on from being MGM's girl-next-door to the music hall powerhouse of her career's second act, Garland appears no longer afraid to show effort. In the film's two most extraordinary musical numbers, she exhibits her fearsome vocal range. As "The Man That Got Away" reaches its impassioned pinnacle, she gesticulates as though she might be able to catch the notes with her hand and squeeze them to death. At the close of the film's centerpiece sequence, the fifteen-minute "Born in a Trunk" medley that charts Vicki's (and, implicitly, Judy's) rise from vaudeville kid to music superstar, she hits a note of such otherworldly power that the otherwise innocuous closing lyric "When I was born in a trunk at the Princess Theatre in Pocatello, Idaho" becomes a wrenching rallying cry for all wannabe stars trying to crawl out of their own personal nowheresvilles.

. . .

The code-switching of the musical—between "realism" and fantasy but also between the melancholy of the real world and the escape of music—is embedded in *A Star Is Born*. As a Hollywood movie about Hollywood, it's remarkably bleak, drawing upon sad truths about its star's personal life to tell the story of a fictional star's decline. The inescapable central idea of *A Star Is Born*, in all its incarnations, is that one person's ascent will always be mirrored by another's downfall. Mason's alcoholic, self-sacrificing Norman Maine is the film's tragic figure, undone by his own demons, addictions, and the looming shadow of professional failure. Yet he is not given any song or dance numbers with which to escape. Unlike in most other musicals, there is no sense of community or collaboration—characters do not work together toward a shared purpose, like those putting on a show in *The Band Wagon* or saving the farm in *Summer Stock*. Instead, the musicality is centered on Garland. And it's a huge burden to bear.

Cukor's *A Star Is Born*, made just two years after the joyous metamusical *Singin' in the Rain*, could be seen as its own deconstruction of the form, in that it acknowledges the escape hatch that movie singing and dancing provide yet concludes that in the face of real-world pain, it might not be enough. The film's most brutal expression of this comes when Vicki performs "Lose That Long Face," a number featuring Garland in a newsboy outfit with torn pants and straw hat, her face painted with freckles, cheering up adorable city kids during a thunder and lightning storm. "If you want trouble double-crossed, don't give into a frown," she sings with a smile. "Turn that frown upside-down and get yourself that long face lost." On the page, it appears to be your average "buck-up, buddy" number, recalling Garland's signature "Get Happy" from *Summer Stock*, yet what's directly before and after reveal the moment's transgressive conceit. In the prior scene, Vicki experiences an unimaginable public humiliation when, after winning her first Academy Award, a drunken Norman climbs up onstage next to her, not only obscuring her spotlight but also accidentally whacking her in the face with the back of a flailing hand. In the moment directly after she stops singing "Lose That Long Face," Vicki is shown in her dressing room, barely able to hold back sobs as she tries to articulate her simultaneous love for Norman and hate for his inability to stop drinking. The scene is among American cinema's most direct and honest expressions of what it feels like to negotiate a loved one's addiction. As she wipes the tears from her cheeks, the painted-on freckles go with them. Of course, Vicki will have to get right back on set for another take and plaster her smile back on.

A Star Is Born's acknowledgment of the simultaneous thrill ("Born in a Trunk") and falseness ("Lose That Long Face") of the movie musical as escape makes it, to these eyes and ears, the ultimate queer movie musical, just as much as the presence of the gay icon at its center or the gay director behind the camera. Further marking the film with a kindred queerness is the history of its mistreatment. Though produced with a hefty budget, hyped by its studio as Garland's epochal comeback event, and met with ecstatic raves in advance screenings, *A Star Is Born* would be famously abused by studio head Jack Warner and would be the cause of decades-long resentment between Cukor and Warner. In early 1954, the director delivered a nearly three-and-a-half-hour cut before trimming it down to 181 minutes for the New York and Los Angeles premieres. Warner, believing that audiences wouldn't sit through this epic length for an intimate film with only a few major characters, took a heavy hand in editing it further, hoping to eradicate the need for an intermission and having it run continuously rather than as a special "road show" event. In a May 1954 letter from Jack Warner to screenwriter Moss Hart, Warner calls the film "way over length" and boasts that he's "personally cut out about 1500 feet."

Cukor had been traveling and starting preparations for his next film while Warner was messing around. By August, when Cukor had seen Warner's cuts, he wrote to Hart: "He snipped here and there, seemingly without reason. He succeeded in muddying things up, making scenes pointless and incomprehensible." There was no such thing as a director having "final cut" in those days, and the battle over *A Star Is Born*'s running time would continue until the film was put into general release missing a half-hour of footage, excising crucial narrative details that better established Vicki and Norman's romantic relationship, and cutting two musical numbers, including "Lose That Long Face." Reports of studio infighting and a tampered-with product resulted in disappointing box office returns. Angry letters, especially from Garland fans, arrived in Warner's mailroom. One read, "Congratulations! It isn't very easy to foul up a great picture, but you people out at Warner's seem to be doing a bang-up job." And another: "I've been a Judy Garland admirer for about 17 years, but the picture didn't move me. I kept thinking, 'Something's wrong, what is it, there's something wrong here.' It seemed to jump too fast from one scene to another, no build-up, and I realized I was missing much of what I had expected to see. The whole trouble was, I was seeing the cut version, and I was very angry." And another, a French fan of Garland who had seen the premiere in Milan: "The long-awaited *A Star Is Born* was served up with Garland singing just two songs of all the ones we have read about . . . I hope that something can be done in time for the showing of the film in Paris."

Neither Garland nor Cukor, who later called the film "mutilated," would live to see preservationist Ronald Haver's restored version, which received a glitzy Radio City Music Hall premiere in July 1983. The reconstructed version of the film, which incorporates black-and-white archival production stills and unearthed soundtrack recordings from missing scenes to help patch crucial sections of the narrative back together, is the version commonly available now. These static photographs and disembodied audio elements not only forever identify *A Star Is Born* as abused and incomplete but also give it a quality of ghostly emanation. It's somehow fitting for a film that often feels lonely and vulnerable but which, like its star, has proven indomitable.

A Star Is Born has primal staying power. In addition to the Streisand and Lady Gaga remakes, echoes of Cukor's film would be found even more directly in Martin Scorsese's melancholic 1977 *New York, New York*, starring Garland's daughter Liza Minnelli and Robert De Niro as a singer and saxophonist suffering through the extended, violent dissolution of their marriage. Scorsese explicitly references *A Star Is Born* in structure and theme, and so his film, a direct homage to the MGM musical made in the postmusical era, is the rare instance of a deconstruction of a deconstruction, with Minnelli uncannily embodying the performing-through-tears audacity of her mother. There's even a midfilm number that, echoing "The Man That Got Away," gifts Minnelli her own gut-wrenching single-take ballad: in John Kander and Fred Ebb's scorching "And the World Goes 'Round," Minnelli's post–World War II big band singer Francine Evans, having been abandoned by her husband after giving birth to their son, sings of the need to live with pain. Minnelli, also a performer of intensity, sings the lyric "Sometimes your heart breaks with a deafening *sound*!" When she hits the word "sound," she clutches at the sides of her head as though experiencing a cataclysmic head rush: the thrill of agony, the sensational, brutal, magnificent intensity of the movie musical in a single word. (*La La Land*, the 2016 Oscar winner, a reworking of the general themes and structure of *New York, New York*, is the rare case of a deconstruction of a deconstruction of a deconstruction, which was already a remake.).

That Minnelli would prove to be a powerful gay icon in her own right speaks to more than the queer legacy of one family. Minnelli's star was born in a markedly more permissible era. Her 1972 breakthrough role in Bob Fosse's *Cabaret*, set in decadent Weimar-era Berlin on the cusp of the Third Reich, explicitly centered its characters' bisexuality, its unprecedented naturalistic eroticism a product of the ongoing sexual revolution. There is no trace of outward sexuality—or even physical sensuality—in Garland's films; one can only speculate what a movie star like Judy Garland might have looked or moved like without the dictates of the Production Code era. The identification gay men have felt toward her for decades is nevertheless unbroken. The invisible tether that exists between this performer and her legions of devotees remains perfectly legible in theory yet somehow still mysterious as a phenomenon. Nevertheless, one can be assured that Garland would not be the gay icon she was in life and remains in death if she had not been a musical star—or *the* musical star—at a moment in history when the form was at its height, when hidden dreams and secret lives were the domain of songs, breaking through the diaphanous border between the real and the imagined, the discord and the harmony.

6

Back to School

On Sunday, December 14, 1952, the *New York Times* arts section touted the return of "an old drama hit." The cobwebbed play in question was *The Children's Hour*, making its first Broadway revival eighteen years after it had premiered and, per the lede of Harry Gilroy's article, "turned a nice quiet young woman named Lillian Hellman into one of the best-known modern playwrights."

The *Times* profile allowed a woman few would have dubbed "nice" or "quiet" to bask anew in the professional glow the play had first bestowed upon her. She also had the chance to reiterate her oft-spoken belief that "this is really not a play about lesbianism, but about a lie." Her insistence that *The Children's Hour* was most centrally about the damage inflicted upon an individual who becomes the target of malice implies the play's usefulness as sociological rather than psychological drama—while also protecting her from being targeted as overly sympathetic to homosexuals at a moment when such allegiances would have no professional benefit. Yet *The Children's Hour* had undoubtedly gained newfound meaning from recent events, personal and political, that had all but transformed Hellman's life.

Just six months earlier, a subpoenaed Hellman had appeared before the House Un-American Activities Committee, grilled on her leftist affiliations and outspoken sympathies for the Russian causes that had captured her political imagination in the late thirties and early forties. Her forced testimony, which she had long anticipated with deep anxiety, had been the culmination of several years of feeling like a target was on her back, beginning with being blacklisted from Hollywood in 1948. (She had first discovered her outcast status when barred from writing the screenplay for a screen adaptation of Theodore Dreiser's *Sister Carrie* for her old *These Three* collaborator William Wyler.) Then, in early 1951, her longtime romantic partner Dashiell Hammett was pursued by the FBI for being a member of the Civil Rights Congress, an organization established to protect the voting rights of the disenfranchised that had recently taken on the cause of funding bail for convicted Communists. When four of the country's most-wanted Communists disappeared after jumping bail, the FBI questioned Hammett. He pleaded the Fifth, a decision the judge deemed as contempt, and he was sentenced to six months in prison. By the time he was released in early 1952, Hellman had had to sell her beloved Hardscrabble Farm, where the two had been living, both to help cover Hammett's legal expenses and because paying the bills had become more difficult after her blacklisting cut off the flow of Hollywood money that had been her main income for more than a decade.

Hellman's refusal to name names before the House Un-American Activities Committee in May 1952 was one of the events that would come to define her, in terms of both the historical record and her own self-mythologization. (Her 1976 book *Scoundrel Time*, an account of her tussles with the conservative powers of the period, incited accusations of aggrandizement and, as frequently was the case with Hellman, truth bending.) Hellman was an unabashed grandstander whose taste for sweeping, ideologically driven political gestures frequently rubbed her adversaries the wrong way, yet during a moment in history when so many of her peers either threw their colleagues under the bus or opportunistically capitulated for fear of losing their own professional standing, Hellman's steadfast refusal to play by HUAC's rules grants her a sizable amount of historical credibility. She had been an outspoken critic of the Right's witch hunts as early as 1947. After the original Hollywood Ten—which included *Crossfire* director Edward Dmytryk—were cited for contempt of Congress, she wrote a scathing editorial for *Screen Writers' Magazine*, a publication of the Screen Writers Guild, that called out Hollywood figures Gary Cooper, Robert Taylor, Leo McCarey, and Adolphe Menjou for their status as "friendly witnesses" for the committee and wrote of "the horror of seeing politicians make the honorable institution of Congress into a honky tonk show; of listening to craven men lie and tattle, pushing each other in their efforts to lick the boots of their vilifiers."

In 1952, after Hellman was finally subpoenaed to Congress following nearly five years of witnessing industry colleagues systematically lose their livelihoods, she penned a letter to John S. Wood, chairman of HUAC. Marked May 19, two days before she was set to appear in person, the letter stated, "I am most willing to answer all your questions about myself. I have nothing to hide from your Committee and there is nothing in my life of which I am ashamed." But she refused to answer any questions about others: "To hurt innocent people whom I knew many years ago in order to save myself is, to me, inhuman and indecent and dishonorable. I cannot and will not cut my conscience to fit this year's fashions, even though I long ago came to the conclusion that I was not a political person and could have no comfortable place in any political group."

Hellman's insistence on not being "a political person" may have been disingenuous, but in using this tactic to distance herself from HUAC, an organization for whom politics had become synonymous with self-righteous indignation and the disempowerment of those who didn't share their beliefs, she makes a philosophical point as much as casts a light of innocence on herself. Hellman's letter would be her most lasting statement on the affair during that period; in her sixty-seven-minute interrogation, she did little more than decline to answer questions about alleged Communist affiliations. Unwilling to admit—or deny—past party membership while also refusing to incriminate others, Hellman stood her ground, shaky but defiant. Hellman's accounts of her own heroism would later become a cause for annoyance with the writer's many personal detractors, but there's no denying its effectiveness. According to biographer William Wright, "At her hands, [the HUAC committee] suffered one of its most severe and long-remembered public relations defeats."

The Children's Hour was back on the New York stage that December, in a production directed by Hellman herself, no less. It was difficult not to see Hellman's angry tale of two women ruined by an accusation through a new political lens. Gilroy's *Times* article made no mention of Hellman's recent ordeals with HUAC, but Brooks Atkinson, in his review in the same newspaper just five days later, states, "Now we know that lives can be destroyed by other types of slander . . . the implications are much broader now and have new political overtones." Atkinson's meaning would have been clear to anyone reading the *New York Times* arts section. The theater world had largely been untouched by the congressional committee's tendrils, which were tightening around Hollywood, ever the locus of alleged bad influence, but the entertainment industry at large had been agonizing over the Right's anti-communist rampage for nearly half a decade. "The period of anti-Communist madness in American life was a time when accusations without proof were immediately granted the status of truth," wrote the historian Robert Sklar. "When guilt was assumed, and innocence had to be documented . . . a perverse kind of democracy was practiced: all accusations, no matter from whom, were taken equally seriously."

Kim Hunter, cast as Karen in the new revival of *The Children's Hour*, had been a victim of the Hollywood blacklist, even after winning a 1951 Academy Award for Elia Kazan's film of Tennessee Williams's *A Streetcar Named Desire* for the role of Stella, which she had originated on Broadway. Patricia Neal, a future Oscar winner for 1963's *Hud*, had read for both parts and chosen Martha for herself, a telling difference from 1934, when so few women could be persuaded to even read for the role. The analogy between *The Children's Hour* and recent political events might not hold up to scrutiny. The "lie" told about Martha and Karen leads to Martha's deeper self-realization but is nevertheless the creation of a spiteful child, whereas those accused of Communist sympathies were not necessarily the victims of false testimony but rather were persecuted for their beliefs or past affiliations—guilty by association. And there was opportunism in Hellman bringing back her play: the hit revival, playing for 189 performances, helped pay her HUAC lawyer fees. Nevertheless, Hellman's play felt right at home in the early fifties, an era when homosexuality and Communism were regularly conflated as equally untrustworthy markers of social disease. The revival of *The Children's Hour* would be followed on Broadway in quick succession by the January 1953 debut of Arthur Miller's *The Crucible*, whose Salem witch trial backdrop was immediately understood as an indignant response to the McCarthy hearings—in their perversion of American justice, a more apt comparison to the moment.

The renewed political relevance of *The Children's Hour* validated the play for a new generation. Atkinson concluded, "Things have changed a lot in eighteen years. But *The Children's Hour* is still taut and pertinent." Yet it also further estranged the text from the themes of homosexuality at its center, once again reassuring viewers that the subject of lesbianism is symbolic, a means to an end rather than a central feature of its humanist inquiries. In this way, *The Children's Hour*'s revival functions provocatively amid the ongoing "Lavender Scare," as suspected gay men and lesbians, especially those working in government and education, were routinely subject to professional ruination and risk of exposure, all under the guise of some vague idea of "protecting national security." In April 1953, President Eisenhower issued an executive order that barred known gay and lesbian people (and those suspected of being gay and lesbian) from holding any federal jobs. For hundreds of men and women, being outed meant ruin, as it did for Martha Dobie.

Less than half a year later, another Broadway drama premiered that was part of this response cycle to the McCarthy era. This play would more directly associate anticommunist sentiment and bullying tactics with the fear of homosexuality, preoccupied as it was with American society's distrust of unconventional masculinity. It would also lead to one of the most contested Hollywood productions of the decade: a movie so queer to the bone that not even the most judicious censorship could stop it from being the gayest studio film of the 1950s.

. . .

Too genteel to be revolutionary, too provocative to soothe, Robert Anderson's *Tea and Sympathy* has long risked fading into the nether space between its conflicted sensibilities. Opening in September 1953, Anderson's play depicted the torment of a seventeen-year-old named Tom Lee (performed by John Kerr). He's marked as a "sissy" by his boarding school peers for all the ways he doesn't subscribe to traditional ideas of maleness: he enjoys the friendly company of women, knows how to cook and knit, plays and sings gentle folk music, and prefers his hair a little shaggier. In other words, he's the nightmare boy of postwar American conformity, and Anderson's play charts how he becomes a pariah to everyone except the kind wife of the school's headmaster, Laura Reynolds (played by Deborah Kerr, no relation to her co-star), who, as a woman, embodies another kind of eternal social outsider.

The stage was the province of psychological realism for Anderson. Born to a middle-class family in New Rochelle, New York, he survived prep school at Phillips Exeter Academy in New Hampshire and attended Harvard University as both an undergraduate and a graduate student with a focus on theater studies (his thesis was titled "The Necessity of Poetic Drama"). His veneration of twentieth-century dramatists like Maxwell Anderson, Moss Hart, and Robert Sherwood anticipated an interest in the kind of successful mainstream theater deemed middlebrow by detractors. Following a stint in the navy during the war, Anderson returned to the northeast, teaching theater studies at women's colleges, cofounding writing workshops, penning theater reviews for local newspapers, and instructing playwriting courses for veterans. Anderson's approach to playwrighting was disciplined, literal and emotional, with little room for abstraction. "All good playwriting is, in a sense, the dramatization of a diary," he wrote. "Playwriting is highly personal, not necessarily autobiographical in details, but certainly derived from the author's attitudes and points of view, which are in turn derived from his 'experience.'" Finding his greatest success in the 1950s, a period in which the American theater, rocked by postwar titans Arthur Miller and Tennessee Williams, was increasingly given to provocation and incendiary themes, Anderson exemplified a dignified stage tradition that had been in vogue since the 1920s, of the forthrightly intellectual, "well-made" play whose ultimate goal was to elucidate some idea of psychological truth and a universalization of the author's feelings.

In its first draft, finished in 1948, *Tea and Sympathy* took the more discernible form of a love triangle, between a boarding school housemistress, widowed by the war; a newly arrived housemaster and war veteran whose wounds have left him sterile; and a delicate, shy student embarrassed by a deformed clubfoot. Anderson's fascination and sensitivity for social outcasts, evidenced in this early version, would remain palpable in the final play, in which the always sympathetic Tom is seen by everyone as different: to Bill, Laura's husband and the school's suspiciously über-masculine headmaster, he is an "off-horse"; to his father, Tom is a disappointment for not being a "regular fella." *Tea and Sympathy*'s inciting incident occurs when Tom, already distrusted by his peers for showing no interest in girls or sports, is spotted swimming naked at the beach together with the school's young, good-looking teacher, Mr. Harris. "I told them all along he was the wrong sort of man to . . . Well, the wrong sort of man to have at a boys' school," Bill explains to Laura. "He's what I always said he was, right from the start. It's not a very nice word, Laura, but he's a queer."

Mr. Harris, more of a concept than a flesh-and-blood person, is summarily fired offstage, and Tom is left to take the brunt of the accusation, in an example of guilt by association closer to the political climate of the Red Scare than anything in *The Children's Hour*. The swimming incident ultimately fades into the background; it's Tom's nature—his individuality—that marks him as other and therefore dangerous. The possibility that his effeminacy and sensitivity equal homosexuality hovers over every unsettled comment made about him. His gentility is anathema to everyone except Laura, drawn to Tom by a kindred loneliness. We come to learn that Laura notices a resemblance in spirit and soul between Tom and her first husband, who was quite unlike the boisterous, masculine Bill and who died in the war trying to prove his bravery. Her continued devotion to the memory of her first love and her protective feelings toward Tom, which walk the line between maternal and sexual, make her the teenager's only genuine confidante and, in the play's last moments, his initiator into the world of adult sexuality. Laura enters the boy's bedroom and, according to Anderson's stage directions, "unbuttons the top button of her blouse, and moves toward Tom." He brings her hand to his lips in a gesture of desperate intimacy. Her final words before the lights slowly dim: "Years from now—when you talk about this—and you will—be kind."

Despite the still provocative ambiguity of this ending and the extravagant emotional uncertainty of the notorious closing words, *Tea and Sympathy* is by nature a staid play, a pallid cousin to the more genuinely transgressive theater by Tennessee Williams that had galvanized Broadway in the postwar era. Williams was gay and Anderson was not, an essential difference between the playwrights considering that Anderson does everything he can to quell any thoughts of Tom's difference making him perverse, while Williams, in *A Streetcar Named Desire* (1947) or *Cat on a Hot Tin Roof* (1955), refuses to deny perversity, even regarding it as an essential aspect of the American psyche. Fascinatingly, Elia Kazan, whose career took off after his epochal staging of *Streetcar*, also directed *Tea and Sympathy* in its original Broadway incarnation at the Ethel Barrymore Theater, further entrenching it as sort of Williams-lite. *Tea and Sympathy* may ask us to rally around Tom for his essential humanity, but it constantly positions that humanity within social bounds of normalcy rather than difference. This makes sense for a play keyed into the political moment, when so many were fearful of being tagged as other—of losing one's social position. *Tea and Sympathy* may plead for individualism and acknowledge the philosophical rightness of "marching to the beat of a different drummer," but it doesn't revel in Tom's outsider status. Its characters want to be on the inside, as conservative and oppressive as it may be.

Anderson scholar Thomas P. Adler has written that "Anderson is emphatic in his attempts to counter the myth that *Tea and Sympathy* has anything at all 'to do with homosexuality,'" further quoting him as having said, "It has to do with an unjust charge of homosexuality and what follows such a charge." This sounds jarringly like how Lillian Hellman would regularly discuss *The Children's Hour*, putting into relief how the framing of political content and "homosexuality" were considered by mainstream America as two separate, unbridgeable zones throughout the first half of the twentieth century. There's of course an insincerity and transparent self-preservation to Anderson and Hellman's persistence in claiming homosexuality as beside the point in works for which it is so completely, irreducibly central. Part of the game for artists of the period, even ostensibly straight ones, was a meticulously managed public denial, not unlike that of gay people themselves. Using homosexuality, or the threat of it, as a metaphor for social disenfranchisement was one way for more liberal-minded writers to sneak uncomfortable ideas and characters into their work.

The insinuation that homosexuality functions as a mere symbol for wider, more politically "meaningful" social ills in these two plays implies that you could somehow extract the homosexuality from their narratives and still offer up the same points. This proves historically insufficient at best, considering how these texts have proven catalytic flash points in the discussion of gay dramatic representation. Despite their calculated protestations, the proof is in the pudding. *Tea and Sympathy* and *The Children's Hour* are unusual for how matters of homosexuality are on the surface—this isn't the teasing territory of *Rope* or the sly antihetero readings of Dorothy Arzner's work. The queerness is right here, in the text, spoken of, wrestled with, in ways that theater could, and movies still could not.

Young Tom Lee may not be or become a gay man—the play ends abruptly at the point of a sexual encounter that could be revelatory or, frankly, a flop. Yet *Tea and Sympathy* speaks directly and movingly to the experience of gay men oppressed by imposed codes of acceptable masculinity and the systematic loss of individuality in the name of conformity—as much a part of American society in the twenty-first century as it was during the 1950s. It's little surprise that Anderson's play has taken on a life of its own in the American queer consciousness.

The playwright Tony Kushner, whose *Angels in America* would help transform the formal possibilities and political nature of gay theater in the post-AIDS era, recalls meeting Robert Anderson in the early nineties: "I joined the executive council of the Dramatists Guild, right after *Angels* was on Broadway, everybody was on the committee, Arthur Miller, [Betty] Comden and [Adolph] Green, Sondheim, and Robert Anderson was there for the first meeting. I met him and said, 'I can't believe I'm meeting you! *Tea and Sympathy* is such an important play.' And he smiled and said, 'Really? I'm so surprised that you think so,' and sort of drifted away. I thought that was interesting." Anderson's bemusement that a major new gay voice in theater would attest to his play's importance speaks to the unsettled, curious nature of *Tea and Sympathy*'s meaning and legacy. The film that would finally be wrested from it would follow suit. Depending on one's perspective, it's a revolution or a liability, a major inspiration or a mild embarrassment.

.   .   .

The tortured, at times exasperating story of *Tea and Sympathy*'s journey to the screen puts the lie to Anderson's disavowal of his own play's gayness. Since the Production Code banned even the minutest reference to homosexuality—after all, homosexuality didn't *exist* in Hollywood's on-screen "reality"—*Tea and Sympathy*, with its near constant inferences or accusations of its main character's "sissy" nature, would seem unadaptable. And indeed, after MGM snapped up the rights to Anderson's hit play, the studio found itself in the predictable situation of being told that the material was too risky to even consider. So, despite what Anderson himself would say, the homosexual content was so intrinsic to what *Tea and Sympathy* was about that adapting it would seem a profitless endeavor. What Hellman and William Wyler had accomplished in eradicating the source material's queer content for *These Three* in 1936 was possible because *The Children's Hour*, with its thriller-like structure, dramatized the gripping fallout from a baseless accusation. *Tea and Sympathy* was purely psychological in tone and structure, with Tom's queerness—imagined or real, and never confirmed either way—the incitement to everything that happens.

Why would anyone in Hollywood even try to make this potentially hazardous material into a movie? Though twenty years had passed since *These Three* when *Tea and Sympathy* was finally released in 1956, the industry was going through familiar growing pains. In a strange mirror to the early 1930s, when movie producers were scooping up the rights to scandalous books and plays to entice dwindling audiences—and laying the groundwork for Joseph Breen's ascendance—studio heads in the early 1950s found themselves in another slump. Movie theater attendance had fallen a full 50 percent from 1946, the peak of American moviegoing, to 1954, following the rapid rise of television. Aside from the various attempts at spectacle and splendor to lure people back to the movies (CinemaScope, 3-D, Cinerama), Hollywood executives were also on the lookout for more "adult," envelope-pushing material that television, in its heavily regulated infancy, could never beam into millions of households across America.

Hollywood was constantly glancing back east. Following the war, the New York theater had become a breeding ground for an astonishing new generation of talent: actors, writers, directors who were obsessed with methods for approximating a newfound authenticity in art, brazenly questioning commonly received cultural ideas and self-consciously plumbing psychological depths. The film industry's reliance on established theater work, and the subsequent "movie effect" it would have on playwrights, was a long-standing concern for stage people. Lillian Hellman had predicted Hollywood's overreliance on Broadway in the 1930s, when she first began toggling between the two modes, telling the *Herald Tribune* in 1935, "If the present tendency of Hollywood to buy into Broadway is not arrested somehow in the next five years, the theater is going to be in an awful mess . . . Pretty soon it will be impossible to put on a show that Hollywood doesn't like or can't use in its own business. Broadway will merely become a try-out ground for Hollywood."

The air of prestige that haloed the theater hung heavy around the necks of movie producers, who knew that their products, however popular, would rarely be placed in the domain of art. Says Tony Kushner, "To be a successful playwright, at that point, still had an enormous amount of highbrow cultural capital in it. Back then, in terms of modern American drama after Eugene O'Neill, there was really no way to make a bigger cultural impact than to write an important American play. Part of the talent of Hollywood moguls like Louis Mayer was figuring out what counted as highbrow culture, figuring out what culture people would want to consume."

By the 1950s, producers in Hollywood were envious of what New York playwrights could get away with, especially in their frank discussions of sex. Playwrights like Williams, Miller, Anderson, William Inge, and Calder Willingham picked at the scabs of long-encrusted social mores, and often bereft of their own ideas, movie producers increasingly aspired to the evident maturity and emotional complexity of theater. That this frequently meant turning to plays with gay themes or characters— *Streetcar, Cat on a Hot Tin Roof, Tea and Sympathy*, Wallingham's *End as a Man* (which would become the Ben Gazzara-starring *The Strange One*)—led to the kinds of obfuscations and reorientations that would define the 1950s cinema.

A crucial reason why Hollywood was so keen on stealing Broadway's thunder was that the Production Code Administration was increasingly embattled from years of movie producers proselytizing for the loosening of its strictures. In October 1953, only a few weeks after *Tea and Sympathy* had opened on Broadway,

Joseph Breen received a frantic letter from his old friend Martin Quigley, the *Motion Picture Herald* editor and Catholic layman who had been one of the original writers of the Code way back in 1930, warning him about *Tea and Sympathy*: "The homosexuality angle might be dealt with ala [sic] Goldwyn's *These Three* . . . If the headmaster's wife's solution of the boy's difficulty is an essential part of the story, I for one do not know what could be done about it." Breen wrote back summarily with reassurance and, as always, no small measure of the kind of excitement that masks titillation: "It is our considered judgment that this is, possibly, one play wherein we will be compelled to withhold any consideration for it . . . You can be sure that we are quite alive to the seriousness of this situation!"

Troublesome material though it may have been, *Tea and Sympathy* would be pursued by executives at Paramount, Twentieth Century-Fox, Warner Bros., and Columbia, as well as Samuel Goldwyn, despite the constant stream of warnings from the Production Code Administration that it would be foolish to try. It was a hot property, and studios were entering a new era of intentionally pushing the PCA's buttons. The adaptation's foolhardy shepherd would prove to be Dore Schary, MGM's new head of production, who had taken over the studio in 1951, following the retirement of Louis Mayer. Schary, who had made *Crossfire* his pet project at RKO, believed movies had the potential to reflect and even foment social change and that the liberalization of American culture only indicated how backward Code-ruled Hollywood increasingly seemed. At the same time, Schary was less a radical than a game player who saw the efficacy of working with the Breen Office to get what he wanted. Schary and his team had willingly expurgated all explicit homosexual character and connotation from *The Brick Foxhole* when adapting it into *Crossfire*, nevertheless seen—and heavily marketed—as a work of liberal reform in its depiction of violent anti-Semitism within the macho ranks of the American military.

Six years later, in trying to get *Tea and Sympathy* off the ground, this time for the most hallowed of all A-list movie studios, Schary found himself in the opposite position, trying to maintain the integrity of a project for which the inference of homosexuality was its pulsating, inoperable center. Once again, Schary would come up with what he felt were novel solutions to working within the Code. In a September 1949 article in *Motion Picture Herald*, the trade publication that was effectively a trumpet for Martin Quigley, Schary is quoted as saying, "I can assure you I have never had any trouble with the Breen Office—that all subjects can be put on the screen under the Code provisions. I can't go along with the idea of a Code revision to bring it up to date. I happen to know how hard Joe Breen works, and how conscientiously he examines every questionable project to see what adjustments can be made." The timing of the article wasn't coincidental. In the years following the war, the Code had been coming under fire by an escalating, vocal opposition in the industry, including *These Three* producer Samuel Goldwyn, who stated in a 1949 address to the Theater Owners of America, "It is my firm belief the time has come to bring the Code up to date, to conform to the changes that have taken place during the nineteen years since it was first adopted. It needs overhauling, revamping, renovating." Breen remained intractable; throughout the early fifties, he would be playing constant offense. "Not only has there been no relaxation of the standards of good taste and decency represented by the Code, but there will be none," Breen would say in 1952. "Hollywood, as it has done in the past, will continue to provide clean and wholesome entertainment."

Breen's digging in his heels meant that internal battles would continue for some time. No matter the changes in the American psyche wrought by the Second World War; no matter the near decimation of the industry by television; no matter the explosion of the grim and violent crime dramas (later to be dubbed "film noir") that were slowly changing standards of permissibility; no matter the increasing appeal of sophisticated foreign art films, mostly imported from Europe and Japan, which made American films look suspiciously sanitized—the Production Code Administration would remain desperately wedded to the same values they wielded in the 1930s. Breen's Office increasingly seemed like the addled, grizzled grandpa still slouched over the dinner table after the plates had long been cleared.

A monumental change was in store, however. In October 1954, Breen retired from his post as the head of the PCA. By the time MGM bought *Tea and Sympathy* and was deep in negotiations about the best way of getting around the Code while still adequately representing the material, Breen had handed the reins to Geoffrey Shurlock, his sixty-year-old former assistant. Shurlock had been with Breen from the beginning; he had been the one to send the July 24, 1935, interoffice memo to Will Hays himself, alerting the Code's creator to the "attached treatment of *The Children's Hour*, removing all suggestion of lesbianism and substituting a straight love triangle." While Shurlock, certainly no liberal reformer, was set in his ways about the important moral prerogative of the Code after decades of working alongside Breen, he would be easier for the studios to push around. His tenure, taking place during an era of rising social unrest and a growing political left, would ultimately short-circuit the Code's power, leading to its amending and, by the end of the sixties, its dismantling.

Tea and Sympathy would become a rancorous battleground on which the Code's proponents would fiercely and successfully defend their turf, as well as an early test for Shurlock. The process of bringing such contentious material to the screen would reveal the anxieties and promises of an industry perched on the edge of transformation. Even more than *These Three* twenty years earlier, the film of *Tea and Sympathy* that would finally be released in 1956, following more than two years of negotiations and haggles, rewrites and alterations, stands as an extraordinary example of the domineering, imposed morality of the Production Code. Despite all this, the film, to be directed by Vincente Minnelli, brought on board only after the property had been argued over for years and sufficiently tweaked to meet Code standards, is one of classical Hollywood's most remarkable and striking interrogations of routinized American masculinity and the homoeroticism that's part and parcel of it.

. . .

In subsequent decades, *Tea and Sympathy* has been an object of fascination and even occasional ridicule more often than a focus of serious consideration. The title describes Laura's feminized position at the all-male school boarding school, where she's expected to occasionally give the boys nothing more than a little "tea and sympathy." This remains cultural shorthand for a sort of hapless politesse, which extended, naturally, to the film's treatment (or lack) of homosexuality. Eminently courteous and respectable, like Laura herself, the film has never attained the exalted space in cinephile circles reserved for other Technicolor American melodramas of the 1950s that similarly traffic in tortured masculinity (Nicholas Ray's *Rebel Without a Cause* and *Bigger Than Life*), domestic angst (Douglas Sirk's *All That Heaven Allows*), or postwar suburban alienation (Minnelli's own *Some Came Running*). In *The Celluloid Closet*, Vito Russo devotes ample space to the film, yet largely to discuss the negation of its homosexuality and hold it up as an example of what *wasn't* there. Russo believed that the film "pleads tolerance . . . not for sexual deviation but for unfortunate heterosexuals who happen to be less than 'masculine.'" How Minnelli's film interrogates socially acceptable forms of maleness, however, are just as fascinating as the ways in which tenable expressions of homosexuality were silenced in its making.

For a film destined to stoop to censorship, it's noteworthy how much emotional currency *Tea and Sympathy* retains. In the classes I taught at NYU and The New School, students responded to it with a remarkable favorability, which I found refreshing and revealing for a film that had for decades been discussed primarily in terms of its datedness. Yet I might have realized how *Tea and Sympathy* could appeal to people still in the throes of youth, when the search for one's identity isn't necessarily attuned to an easily determined or applied sexuality. In Tom's inability to adequately conform to the standards of maleness, in his tender outsider's kinship with Laura, in the embarrassment Tom's unwittingly abusive father voices for his son, many students admitted to feeling a twinge of familiarity and were fascinated by the incongruous yet historically apt mixture of conservatism and progressiveness. The ambiguity of Tom's sexuality has long been a liability for many gay scholars, especially those, like Russo, seeking to elucidate a narrative of invisibility over decades of cinema lacking in any viable representation. For many younger queer viewers of today, Tom doesn't need to be identified in any kind of binary fashion: the indeterminacy of his identity is more relatable than any certainty might have been.

Confirming Tom's homosexuality is something that neither Anderson nor the film's makers ever would have been interested in doing. Yet in his play, Anderson also refuses to clarify his heterosexuality. The Production Code would insist on another story, though the way they went about doing it would be via a new narrative wraparound that might as well have been affixed with Scotch tape—so clumsy that it would be easy for the viewer to psychologically excise it from the experience of the film. (The film's *New York Times* review would suggest the viewer should do just that.) After MGM had signed the deal, paying a then whopping $400,000 for the rights, Anderson was brought on board to write his own adaptation, and there began a lengthy process of adding and subtracting to get the script to a place that would be deemed acceptable but that would also retain the human drama that had appealed to Dore Schary in the first place. For nearly two years, Shurlock and the PCA had been telling every interested studio that two major alterations would have to be made if a film were ever produced of *Tea and Sympathy*, and they were non-negotiable: there would be no mention, inference, or implication of homosexuality; and, since, per Shurlock, "this treatment of adultery is also a definite Code violation," Laura could not be celebrated for the adulterous transgression she initiates in the play's closing moments.

At first, Schary had come up with elaborate solutions to convince the PCA that there was a possibility of making the film within the Code's boundaries and therefore justifying the hefty price tag of the play's rights. Many of his outlandish ideas to rework the play, in memos in the PCA archives, didn't stick, such as a very *These Three*-esque notion that the character of the headmaster Bill "will be persecuting the boy because of suspicions of adultery, not homosexuality. He is jealous of the boy." This would lead to a heavily reconceived climax in which the final bedroom embrace between Laura and Tom would be interrupted by Bill, resulting in fisticuffs. Thankfully, this wouldn't come to pass, yet there are traces of Schary's initial thoughts that do make their way to the final film: "As for the character of the boy himself, Mr. Schary protested that he did not wish to bring up the question of homosexuality. He wished, rather, to center the boy's problem on the fact that he was an 'off-horse,' who liked long-hair music, who did not date girls like other boys did, who was reticent, and pretty much of a 'sissy.'" Code officials responded that creating such a character would be "an extremely risky and difficult task, particularly in view of the fact that the Code forbids even the inference of sex perversion. We secured a copy of the Code and insisted that he read it in black and white."

The memo anticipated the absurdity in creating a character who was conceived by his author for the sole purpose of being perceived as "queer" . . . and then denying that he could be perceived as queer. This is precisely what would come to pass following years of scalpel-like alterations and trims and pointed word changes. As for the equally alarming matter of Laura's decision to give her body to Tom, which Breen and Shurlock believed was dramatized by Anderson with not just tacit acceptance but also commendation, positioned as a gift of unusual compassion—this would have to be even more harshly reconsidered. There was certainly no way that the finished film would let Laura "get away" with adultery; only if her deeds were characterized as morally wrong and she were sufficiently *punished* could this ending, so integral to Anderson's vision, remain on-screen.

The latter of these two perceived major problems would ultimately be addressed in the most transparent way possible, with the addition of a prologue and epilogue. Otherwise, the general structure of the finished film would adhere closely to the play, though a read of Anderson's original manuscript reveals the bounty of shifts in language and focus that de-emphasize the playwright's more direct interrogations of gender expectation and sexuality. The swiftest and simplest cut was Mr. Harris, the schoolmaster Tom is seen swimming naked with on the beach. Tom's character doesn't need Mr. Harris to be further incriminated as an "off-horse," and, after all, the teacher's presence makes it more difficult to deny the centrality of homosexuality to the story's themes. Without Mr. Harris, the film would also lose one of the play's connecting threads to *The Children's Hour*, which is the manic fear of the corruption of youth by teachers suspected of being gay.

Anderson was working on a Code-suitable adaptation as early as January 1954, years before the film would go into production. Though his initial notes retain the character of Harris and the intimation of the nude beach jaunt, as witnessed by Bill and a group of aghast schoolboys, Anderson is already trying here to hold on to his story's meaning while transforming the words he had used to create that meaning. "The whole thing is done by implications," writes Anderson. "The scene with the father which would follow leaves out the words, but keeps the meanings." Knowing the final scene is his most controversial, Anderson wonders if changing the setting will de-emphasize the sexual implications. "Instead of playing this in the boy's bedroom, I would play it out in a wooded patch off a field."

At this point, Anderson's proposed script still ends on the play's famous final line. But by July, Anderson's revisions begin to incorporate versions of the possible wraparound sequences that the PCA and a conciliatory Schary believe would solve the essential "moral" problems of *Tea and Sympathy*. Now, the script begins as the film eventually will, with a sequence in the present day, a decade after the events of the play, with a suited, well-adjusted Tom, now a successful writer, returning to the boarding school for a reunion celebration. In this first conception of the scene, which would then flash back to the story's main action and the site of Tom's youthful trauma, Tom runs into his sympathetic former roommate, Al, in front of the dorm. While catching up, Tom fingers a woman's brooch attached to his keychain—we come to learn this was the top button of Laura's blouse, implying that Tom keeps a flame kindled for Laura. (Neither the reunion with Al nor the device of the brooch ended up in the film.) When the action proper of the original play ends—culminating in Laura's sexual gift to Tom—and the script returns to the present day, Tom goes to pay his respects to Bill, still the housemaster, though fallen into lonely disrepair. He tells him: "Two years ago when she died, they got in touch with me. I had to go out and take care of . . . of everything. There was no one else to do it. She was absolutely alone." Then he hands Tom a letter. "Among her things when I went out there was this letter addressed to you, care of your publisher, I imagine. She never sent it, or even stamped it."

The letter indicates the blatantly, almost parodically moralizing tone in which this enforced sequence trafficked. "Ever since I left you that afternoon, you have been on my mind, on my conscience," Laura writes. "These years I have been trying to justify myself to myself. And I have failed. I have awakened in the night, filled with self-condemnation and remorse. And then when I read your book, and that last line, I realized that instead of saving your life as I had intended, I had ruined it ... I meant to do the right thing. I thought it <u>was</u> right. Now your book tells me what I feared so long ... I was wrong. If you ever receive this ... forgive me." In a January 1955 draft, she would add: "Now that I re-read this letter, I am a little ashamed at having written it. It almost seems as though I am asking you to share a blame which is wholly mine." By the time the film would reach the screen, the words in this final scene would be pored over, changed, and rearranged many times, and would even feature alterations suggested directly by the Legion of Decency's Reverend Thomas F. Little. There was clearly no way Laura was going to "get away with it," and the audience would not be allowed any ambiguity over this whatsoever, whether the character ended up dead or not. (In the final draft, she lives, her voice emanating as voiceover from an undisclosed location, unknown even to Bill.)

Punishing the woman would prove easy; de-queering the queer wouldn't be so simple. Tom's speculated homosexuality is embedded in its nearly every interaction. Words like "queer" and "fairy" were, of course, not allowed, though one of the film's lingering sore-thumb changes was the bizarre attempt to split the bill by changing the word "sissy" (a bugbear for the PCA since the thirties) to "sister-boy," a taunt that becomes more ludicrous the more frequently it's used. Tantalizing efforts by Anderson in early drafts to come up with coded indignities for Tom include the nickname "Grace"—derogatory, it's explained, because it refers to Tom's outspoken devotion for the opera singer Grace Moore, indicating, interestingly (and interestingly known to Anderson), that male identification with a female diva was a "tell" in postwar American culture.

In the absence of the Mr. Harris character, the film would need a triggering incident that tips off Bill and his fellow students to Tom's unsettling unmanliness. By July 1955, Anderson had come up with the idea that Tom, rather than spotted nude at the beach, would be spied upon by his sportier, football-clutching peers doing something even more incriminating: sitting with Laura and other faculty wives on the sand and helping with their knitting. In the final film, it would become sewing, slightly less feminine for being more functional. Excising Mr. Harris, avoiding a guilt-by-association narrative, and shifting toward such signifiers as giveaways of Tom's inadaptability to standards of American maleness orients the viewer's thoughts more directly around Anderson's critique of social codes. In losing the character, the film also avoids what might have been a troubling implication about hierarchies of acceptable male behavior: the point would likely have been that Tom might not be "all man," but at least he's not a queer like Harris.

By doubling down on what he believed *Tea and Sympathy* was truly questioning—the social definitions of manliness and how they're often in opposition to one's human nature—Anderson wrote a film that poked holes in (and fun at) macho culture, to a degree that would prove unusual for Hollywood of this or any era. As early as his July 1955 draft, he was adding insightful moments that satirized American male behavior, including having Tom's braggadocious, athletic peers taking a goofy magazine quiz titled "Are You Masculine?"; a sequence in which Al fruitlessly tries to teach the put-upon Tom how to "walk like a man" (in certifying its own ridiculousness, the scene anticipates similar, and similarly parodic, ones in the gay-themed hits *La Cage Aux Folles* [1978] and *The Birdcage* [1996]); and the narratively crucial addition of the "bonfire pajama fight," an annual public hazing ritual in which the boys ritualistically tear off a chosen student's pajamas. In such moments, Anderson perspicaciously reveals the homoeroticism at the core of American male machismo and therefore at the center of homophobia itself. After all, Bill, the most virulently bigoted character, is framed by Anderson as a possible closet case. (In a line that didn't make it to the screen from the play, Laura's friend Lilly says curiously, "Even before he met you, Bill never gave me a second glance. Frankly I didn't think he was susceptible to women, till he brought you home . . .") After Minnelli had been asked by MGM to take on the film, Anderson wrote to him, "I stump for essential manliness which is something internal, and consists of gentleness, consideration, and other qualities of that sort, and not just of brute strength."

While Anderson was scrupulously working to play by the rules of the game, the producers were in the midst of battling to make sure the film could be made at all. As 1955 began, they were no closer to an agreement with the PCA. In a March 25 letter, Geoffrey Shurlock wrote to Dore Schary: "We read the treatment dated January 13th of the play *Tea and Sympathy*, and note the changes and improvements made therein. We regret, however, to have to say that we feel that, in spite of the work that has been done, in an effort to remove the Code objections, the present version still appears to be in violation of the Code. It seems to us that in spite of the rewriting the problem of the boy is still his fear that he may be a homo-sexual [sic].

And the wife's giving herself to him in adultery still appears to us to violate the Code inasmuch as her adultery would seem to be justified in view of the fact that it solves the boy's problem." In a subsequent follow-up letter to Schary from April 18, Eric Johnston, the president of the MPAA, insists in no uncertain terms that there's no way forward. He writes of a long talk with Shurlock: "He says the entire staff that has gone over this matter in great detail a number of times feels there is no change that can be made that will effectively meet the Code requirements and still keep the story of *Tea and Sympathy* as presented on stage." On April 29, a special meeting of the MPAA's board of directors was held in New York to hear an appeal by Schary and Loew's Incorporated, the parent company of MGM, after the decision to reject the screenplay draft of *Tea and Sympathy*; the studio would continue to try to get it right.

Shurlock was not simply voicing disapproval but genuinely trying to dissuade this picture from getting made. The vehemence with which *Tea and Sympathy*'s detractors spoke of its cinematic impossibility speaks to the anxiety of the era's cultural gatekeepers, who feared they were falling into irrelevance. The writing had been on the wall at least since 1953, when filmmaker Otto Preminger had battled publicly with Breen over *The Moon Is Blue*, one of the most fiercely contested films of the decade. *The Moon Is Blue* had been refused a Code seal for its sexual brashness, specifically for its discussion of a young woman's loss of virginity and use of such scandalous words as "pregnant" and "seduce." Rather than entertain Breen's demands for censorship, United Artists released the film anyway. Denied official Code approval and publicly condemned by the Legion of Decency and the *Motion Picture Herald*, who said the film's makers and distributors showed "contempt" to audiences and all decent people, the film was a hit, grossing more than $4 million, thanks in part to the brouhaha, and leaving the PCA with egg on its face. The incident indicated the sea change to come in terms of permissibility. In Preminger the PCA had found a formidable and consistent adversary: throughout the remainder of the decade, he would righteously battle the Code over such proudly scandalous films as the drug addiction drama *The Man with the Golden Arm* (1955) and the courtroom procedural *Anatomy of a Murder* (1959), the latter of which had the audacity to refer to a woman's "panties." With Breen out of the picture, Shurlock appeared desperate to take up his former boss and mentor's mantle. If he allowed *Tea and Sympathy* to be made, would Shurlock appear weak—a sign of a lack of control and, echoing the themes of the film in question, forceful masculinity? In one fell swoop, could he dash decades of punctilious regulations that kept Hollywood in its grip?

On August 4, 1955, Anderson came up with an entirely new option for *Tea and Sympathy*'s ending. Tom would be established as a well-to-do writer, seen in a small study, "possibly in a duplex in Greenwich Village." A letter from Laura arrives amid a pile of mail, sent from his publisher at Random House. He rubs his fingers over his totem of devotion, the tell-tale brooch, lights up a cigarette, and reads the letter, propelling the viewer back in time. At the end, we dissolve back to Tom, who, after having finished Laura's self-lacerating screed, looks up and sees his wife and three-year-old daughter in the doorway. The last line, from Tom to the child: "Come along, *Laura*." Though undeniably reassuring that Tom's been properly straightened out and healthily procreative, this ending perhaps too clearly romanticized Tom's feelings for Laura and even enhanced her legacy by giving the child her tributary name; it ended up on the trash heap. The PCA opted for the original wraparound, which appeared to leave no hint of ambiguity about the evils of Laura's "good deed."

A final set of stipulations from Shurlock on August 26 were accompanied by the ludicrous warning, "These changes are to be so definitized that there should be no spot where it could be inferred that anybody is afraid he is homo-sexual [*sic*]." Somehow, Anderson's subsequent tweaks in response to these frankly impossible demands resulted in a letter from Shurlock on September 1 letter officially approving the script, punctuated by the eternal signoff: "You understand of course that our final judgment will be based on the finished picture." A huge wrinkle was still to come. A September 25 article by Thomas M. Pryor appeared in the *New York Times* with the headline MGM SOLVES ITS "TEA AND SYMPATHY" SCRIPT PROBLEM. In the article, the film's producer, Pandro S. Berman, states: "We didn't put anything over on the Code office. That wasn't our intention. Geoff Shurlock wasn't fighting us. As a matter of fact, he was very patient and helpful." Yet he also is quoted, tellingly, as stating, "We never say in the film that the boy has homosexual tendencies—I don't believe the word 'homosexual' was actually spoken in the play either—but any adult who has ever heard of the word and understands its meaning will clearly understand the suspicion in the film."

Berman's admission immediately provoked the ire of the National Catholic Legion of Decency. Two days later, an angry letter arrived in the inbox of Loew's president, Nicholas Schenck, from the Legion of Decency's executive secretary, the Reverend Thomas F. Little, voicing "serious concern over the reported story changes" as seen in the *Times*. While the Legion was customarily only allowed to pass judgment on the morality of movies once completed and ready for release, the specter of a *Tea and Sympathy* film was so appalling that they demanded inclusion in the process. Responding to Little, Shurlock disavowed any inference in the *Times* article that the movie would maintain the flavor of the play. As a result, Schary, under the pressure of Shurlock by way of Little, would have to entertain suggested revisions in the coming months, specifically in the phrasing of Laura's final letter.

Now the Catholics were doing their own rewrites. Even after Anderson had turned in a completed script in March 1956, the Legion of Decency was invited to suggest alterations: "These are terrible things to write to you, Tom, about guilt and right and wrong" was asked to become "*sin* and guilt and . . ." They wanted to embellish Laura's revelation that "I have come to realize I showed a lack of faith in you, in your ability to meet a crisis by yourself and come through it alone" so it would read "come through it *manfully* alone." And they wanted the already burdensome line "You are old enough now to know that when you drop a pebble in the water, there are ever widening circles of ripples" to feature the addition ". . . ripples that may carry afar a burden of *good or of evil*." While such biblical warnings didn't make it into the final cut, their suggested climactic kicker did: "Dear Tom, I was so pleased to hear that you were married."

By the time *Tea and Sympathy* was ready for release, enough public ink had been spilled about its production that its reputation preceded it. The film was less an entertainment unto itself than a symbol of Hollywood's obsolescence. In October 1956, the *New York Times* critic Bosley Crowther used it as an anchor for an article that had bigger industry fish to fry: "That long-time formidable obstruction to morally controversial material in American films—we speak of the operation of the industry's own Production Code—is slowly and quietly being loosened to accord with what is obviously a change in social attitudes. And the industry is much better for it, as is certainly the medium of films." The article then critiques the suspicious epilogue: "Obviously this poignant postscript suggests that the woman has 'paid.' And it states a moral judgment of adultery in preachy platitudes. It comes as a purely incidental addition of information to the play." Nevertheless, Crowther concludes, "The fact that *Tea and Sympathy* could be put upon the screen for all the mature values in it is fair token of the broadening of the Code." In his official review,

Crowther called the end "prudish and unnecessary . . . we strongly suggest that you leave after Miss Kerr has reached her hand gently toward the boy and spoken the unforgettably poignant line, 'Years from now . . .'"

The film's other reviews would be uniformly positive, yet what's most fascinating about them is their ability and willingness to say outright what the film hadn't been allowed to—indicating the increasing liberality of the mainstream press in the midfifties, which would only grow bolder as the decade wore on. Wrote the critic in *Weekly Variety*: "First, let Metro be congratulated for not being discouraged and for going ahead with a box-office proposition that presented unique problems right from the start . . . The spotlight is on clearly implied homosexuality—and what was explicit to the stage play's plot." MGM's expensive ad campaign for the film played off the film's reputation as a stage play in a way that the publicity for the expurgated *These Three* never would have been allowed two decades earlier. "Even the MOST DARING STORY can be brought to the screen . . . when done with COURAGE, HONESTY, and GOOD TASTE," breathlessly proclaimed the trailer script from October 1956. It concluded: "Years from now when you talk about this movie, and you will, be kind."

. . .

Now, almost seventy years later, let's be kind about *Tea and Sympathy*. The laborious process of getting the film produced, and the often ridiculous alterations made to appease Hollywood's censors, can easily and understandably eclipse the film itself, obscuring our ability to watch it on its own terms. Yet the film is particularly powerful and emotionally rewarding for the exceptional care and craft bestowed upon it by director Vincente Minnelli. In the subsequent decades, when the auteur theory had burrowed its way out of academic circles and into mainstream critics' evaluations of cinema, Vincente Minnelli would come to be recognized as one of the most exacting and gifted practitioners the classical Hollywood form has ever known.

In its day, when critics or studio representatives spoke of the "sensitivity" of *Tea and Sympathy*, it was usually to signal its timidity and overly cautious approach to its subject matter—a way of reassuring potential viewers that they couldn't possibly be offended by a film they heard had uncomfortable material. Yet in Minnelli's hands, we can now see that the term "sensitivity" also—and quite wondrously—refers to the ways in which questions about the nature of sexuality and identity, and socially imposed ideas of masculinity and femininity, can be handled in a complex, humane fashion even amid a framework of inevitable censorship. In another director's hands, *Tea and Sympathy* very easily could have been a screed against difference, aligning itself cinematographically with its teenage character's desire for conformity by overvaluing straight white heteronormativity. Minnelli's film consistently does the opposite, positioning Tom Lee and Laura Reynolds as lights in the darkness of an uncaring, hypocritical society that distrusts and punishes anyone who steps out of their designated places.

Minnelli was brought on late in the process to direct *Tea and Sympathy*, once the undulations with the PCA, MPAA, and Legion of Decency had ebbed, but the project was as perfectly tailored to him as his impeccable blazers and turtlenecks. The midwestern-born Minnelli had begun his career as a showman when he was hired at Marshall Field's department store in Chicago, working as apprentice to the chief designer, with a focus on its famously elaborate window displays, which featured, in Minnelli's words, "voluptuous statuary." "I was never told that creativity was unmanly," Minnelli wrote in his autobiography decades later. "Talking to the other display men who were all married and raising families, I saw by their example that one could happily function as the male animal and still give vent to his so-called feminine traits. As a result, I wasn't cowed at this impressionable age into more conventionally male avenues of expression. I'm thankful for that. I'd make a miserable football coach."

Minnelli would bring his aesthetic muscularity to his subsequent work in theater, initially as head of the costume department at the Chicago Theatre, where he first made a name for himself in the city's insular show business circles, and then in New York, where he moved in 1931, cutting his teeth on the gaudy, escapist musical revues that were bedazzling the theater world at the height of the Great Depression. In 1933, Minnelli got a significant boost, landing a job costuming, production designing, and finally directing spectaculars at Radio City Music Hall, the Rockefeller Center behemoth that had been open for less than a year. From his work staging musical extravaganzas at Radio City, Minnelli was soon rubbing shoulders with the New York theater glitterati from George and Ira Gershwin to Moss Hart to Lillian Hellman and Dashiell Hammett. It was Hellman, in fact, who set the stage for Minnelli's first, albeit unsuccessful, entrée into the movie world, encouraging him to take a meeting with her new boss from out west, Samuel Goldwyn. One can only imagine the precise and proper Minnelli's repulsed response to the famously crass, malaprop-prone Goldwyn, whom Minnelli would find, in his own words, "unduly aggressive and presumptuous." They didn't hit it off, and Goldwyn found Minnelli's preference to stay in New York misguided at best ("He looked at me as if my IQ was minus three," recalled Minnelli).

Paramount eventually lured Minnelli to California in 1937, the studio hoping he could help them enliven the moribund movie musical of the 1930s, which Minnelli found lacking in "taste, substance, and style," professing to be more a fan of European cinema. This was in keeping with Minnelli's air of pan-European cultural dandyism and his reputation as a snob. His only assignment for Paramount turned out to be an advisory role on a single musical number for the Jack Benny vehicle *Artists and Models*, a trying experience that had him on the first train back to New York. Three years later, Arthur Freed, the visionary whose production unit at MGM would revitalize and make forever mythic the musical movie form, seduced Minnelli back to Hollywood. "Whenever film cultists point to my contributions in the progress of the movie musical, I plead not guilty," Minnelli would write. "The true revolutionary was Arthur. He, more than any one man, made it possible."

One cannot argue with Minnelli's point: Freed's output at MGM provides one of film history's clearest indications of the essential shakiness of the theory positing director as singular auteur. Unparalleled in his ability to corral talent, Freed convinced Minnelli to give another go at Hollywood, promising him leeway and flexibility and providing an irresistible learning curve—he'd advise, assist on edits, direct musical numbers, get to know the studio's panoply of stars. By 1943, he had become a fixture, and Freed entrusted him with directing *Cabin in the Sky*, the first Hollywood musical with an all-Black cast since the late twenties. Though it remains the subject of debate for its often stereotypical representation of a Southern Black community (the main male character is shiftless and lazy; the glamorous object of his affection is a gold-digging jezebel), the film is a rare showcase for such legendary talents as Eddie "Rochester" Anderson, Ethel Waters, and, in one of her few major roles before being sidelined by a racist industry, Lena Horne. As would be the case more than a decade later with *Tea and Sympathy*, Minnelli's sensitivity to and alignment with outsiders registers throughout *Cabin*. The small-scale, black-and-white film also pointed toward an approach to musical moviemaking that never allowed spectacle to overwhelm the people—even in such visually dazzling, Technicolor productions as *An American in Paris* and *Gigi*, Minnelli ensures that the psychological realities of his characters take precedence.

It had been in 1940, while visiting the set of Busby Berkeley's *Strike Up the Band*, that Minnelli first met Judy Garland, then eighteen and fresh off the astronomical success of *The Wizard of Oz*. He was immediately entranced by her talent and sincerity, although it would be four years before the two were paired on *Meet Me in St. Louis*, initiating one of classical cinema's most renowned and speculated-about romantic and creative partnerships. By the time Minnelli was assigned *Tea and Sympathy*, he and Garland had been divorced for five years, with Garland granted legal custody of their daughter, Liza, who would spend six months of the year with her father. Coming after Garland's emotional breakdowns and suicide attempts, and the highly reported dissolution of her MGM contract in 1950, she had claimed emotional abandonment from Vincente. ("He secluded himself and wouldn't explain why he would be away and leave me alone so much," she was quoted as saying during the divorce trial.) While she was rejuvenating her career with her stint at the Palladium in London, Minnelli was also ascending to new heights post-divorce, with *An American in Paris* winning the Best Picture Oscar in March 1952. One can detect a newfound darkness or cynicism creeping into his work at this time, augured most distinctly by the release of *The Bad and the Beautiful* (1952), a biting-the-hand-that-feeds-you melodrama about a vindictive and vile movie director (Kirk Douglas) that's anything but a love letter to Hollywood.

The psychologically acute, compositionally complex melodramas that Minnelli would make throughout the 1950s would prove essential to his legacy; one can read more thematic and aesthetic consistency in them than even his well-loved musicals. The meticulous construction of Minnelli's melodramas, from *The Bad and the Beautiful* to *The Cobweb* (1955) to *Some Came Running* (1958) to *Home from the Hill* (1960), is wedded to their characters' psychological angst—without the catharsis of a musical number or a slapstick set piece, these films are given freer rein to burrow into the darker corners of the 1950s postwar American psyche. They are often centered on men whose masculine repression reflects an inability to fully commit to social and domestic expectations. Even Minnelli's superlative biopic of Vincent van Gogh, *Lust for Life* (1956), also starring Kirk Douglas, seems keyed into a desperately Minnellian disillusionment: fear of professional failure, the dissatisfaction of creative endeavor, the alienation of a life whose goal is aesthetic perfection. Within the continuum of Minnelli's oeuvre, *Tea and Sympathy* can be seen as a pungent condensing of the director's dramatic interests—his fixation on lives on the precipice of estrangement—and, in its inquiry into standards of masculinity, perhaps his most achingly personal film.

"I made the first homosexual picture while I was at MGM. That was *Tea and Sympathy*," Minnelli would state publicly at a film festival in the 1970s, according to biographer Mark Griffin. The comment is fascinating for a seemingly unlimited number of reasons: the unabashed proclamation of something the studio had been desperate to hide twenty years earlier; the ambiguity of whether "homosexual" related, in Minnelli's estimation, to the film's main character or its aesthetic approach; the claim that *Tea and Sympathy* was "the first" picture with homosexual content, even though it was forced to play hide and seek with its queerness, as so many pictures before it; Minnelli's sudden willingness to talk about homosexuality in his seventies, especially considering the decades of rumors about his bisexuality.

The stories of Minnelli's sexual encounters with men and the status of his gay identity in New York in the 1930s remain a matter of dispute (another Minnelli biographer, Emanuel Levy, claims he was more openly homosexual in the years before moving to Los Angeles, while Garland biographer Gerald Clarke asserted that "Vincente was indeed homosexual, or at least largely so." This makes the frequent assumption of his homosexuality, often tied to the highly aestheticized, aggressively nonmasculine way Minnelli presented, all the more applicable to the themes of *Tea and Sympathy*. Certainly, the director never explicitly equated himself with Tom Lee, but it's difficult not to see a reflection of Minnelli in a character who prefers gentle serenades to rock 'n' roll, the elegance of tennis over the roughhousing of football, and who is emotionally devastated when his father forbids him to cross-dress to play Lady Teazle in a student production of *School for Scandal*. The lingering uncertainty of Tom's sexuality—save the dismissible, Code-appended postscript—serves as a kind of biographical parallel to the way we still talk about Minnelli, whose queerness was free-floating and all-encompassing rather than specific or quantifiable.

When producer Pandro S. Berman officially asked Minnelli to direct *Tea and Sympathy*, the production was largely ready to go. Anderson's script had gone through its parade of intense revisions, and the PCA had finally signed off. The studio had cast the three principals: Deborah Kerr, John Kerr, and Leif Erickson would reprise their roles from the Broadway production as Laura, Tom, and Bill, respectively. Minnelli had already worked with John Kerr on *The Cobweb*, in which he played another fragile young artist, this one a patient at a mental institution unsettled to the point of derangement by a change in window drapes. *The Cobweb* might be Minnelli's most direct and perverse statement about his own obsessive-compulsive approach to set design, and it even seems to have inspired an indirect reference in *Tea and Sympathy*, when Tom's father learns, much to his chagrin, that his "off-horse" son has spent his allowance on nicer curtains for his dorm window. It's worth noting that Minnelli uses this window as a kind of gossamer portal between the past and present that takes us away from and back to the otherwise clunky wraparound.

Minnelli had yet to collaborate with Deborah Kerr, who'd been performing the show on and off for more than three years, in New York and touring productions, creating a character of uncommon compassion and basking in the narrative in an almost empathic glow. Delighted by the possibility of Minnelli's coming on board, she wrote him a letter in early 1956 which reflects the protectiveness she felt over the material as well as a certain exasperation over the labyrinthine process of getting it this far: "I had a very nice talk with Bob Anderson on Saturday night in Philadelphia—and he has some really quite interesting and unusual ideas about scripting it—and making it a 'whole' thing if the Breen office are very difficult about the homosexual angle—which is I understand their objection—adultery is o.k.—impotence is o.k.—but perversion is their bête noir!! But as you will see when you see the play—it really is a play about persecution of the individual, and compassion and pity and love of one human being for another in a crisis. And as such can stand alone I think—without the added problem of homosexuality."

At this point, that "added problem" had already been dutifully subtracted and would become the film's structuring absence. In the hands of such a discerning composer of psychologically loaded imagery as Minnelli, however, that absence would reveal itself within a detailed mise-en-scène that explores the trappings and hypocrisies of social oppression. In the film's early beach sequence, after Tom has been spotted sewing with Laura and the other wives, Minnelli crowds the frame with a bevy of shirtless, muscular boys, romping and wrestling with Bill as they read the "Are You Masculine?" magazine quiz—a visual indication of codified, socially normative male behavior in opposition to Tom's alleged weakness, but also, more transgressively, an image that lays bare the latent eroticism in both homosocial interaction and cinematic representations of male bodies. Even in the era of Marlon Brando and James Dean and Rock Hudson, whose bodies were topographies of sensuality and machismo, objectified in fashions unseen throughout the thirties and forties, such pointed homoerotic horseplay is unusual, at least outside the decade's popular, skin-baring biblical epics like Cecil B. De Mille's *The Ten Commandments* (1956) and William Wyler's *Ben-Hur* (1959). The era's homoerotic beefcake magazines, such as *Physique Pictorial*, targeted to a subterranean gay readership, now appear blatantly gay, yet their surreptitious nature meant that their photographs of muscular, scantily clad sailors, athletes, and handymen could be plausibly passed off as simply celebrations of masculinity. In moments like this, *Tea and Sympathy* acknowledges and plays with these hidden-in-plain-sight ways of seeing, in which the pleasure of looking at men is inextricable from taking part in male camaraderie and horseplay. Tellingly, it's a world from which Tom is excommunicated.

Minnelli is also careful to visually convey the straitjacketing domesticity of Laura, framed at crucial points within shadows or interior spaces in opposition to male characters. In an exquisitely composed scene, Laura is shown moving about the house while preparing drinks for Bill and Tom's visiting father, who are discussing the "situation" of Tom in the backyard; though all the dialogue is drifting in through the window from the men in the garden, the camera stays fixed on her as she listens—a visual ("deep-space") reminder of the heavily circumscribed boundaries in which Laura is expected to stay. This makes the cinematic reimagining of Laura and Tom's communion all the more satisfying: rather than place their sexual trespass in Tom's bedroom, as in the play, Anderson came up with the idea to situate them in a secluded spot in the woods. Minnelli visualizes this as a kind of forest primeval, with shafts of ethereal light poking out from behind fairy-tale trees—a natural setting made fantastical. Rather than just a backdrop for Tom's sexual initiation, it's an escape for them both from a world of repressive masculinity.

The sensitivity and attention Minnelli shows to Laura, and the poignant humaneness with which Deborah Kerr plays her, make the film's grafted-on epilogue all the more galling. "We gritted our teeth, and decided to handle that problem when we had to," Minnelli said of that sour final note. Yet in Minnelli's hands, even this enforced misogynist moralizing is made devastatingly beautiful. As Tom sits in Laura's abandoned garden, now gone to seed, he reads her letter, its self-excoriation made bearable by Minnelli's moments of grace: gentle, high-angle crane shots that glide on the breeze as Deborah Kerr's voice emanates from her unknown place in the void; an out-of-focus shot of a single standing flower that mimics Tom's bleary, tear-stained perspective. There's an almost soaring tragedy to Minnelli's interpretation of his Code-imposed mandate, which only serves to make Laura *more* sympathetic. Laura's cruel banishment ironically ensures her eternal presence, and a sequence intended to mollify the moralizers somehow, in its wild incongruity, serves to put the film's more subversive elements into sharper relief.

Minnelli would later write, "In retrospect, it wasn't a very shocking picture, but it might have set up a brouhaha at the time. Ostrich-wise, the censors refused to admit the problem of sexual identity was a common one." Considering the cloud of dust kicked up around *Tea and Sympathy*, it's remarkable that only three years later, another Hollywood adaptation of a controversial New York play with overtly gay themes, discussed in the next chapter, would make it to the screen—and this one with *far* more salacious, vigorously provocative material. By the late fifties, the desire to poke and prod at the censors had become commonplace, yet Shurlock, even without Breen breathing down his neck, was still an obstacle—just an easier one to volley over. In its alterations—which we might call moral failures—*Tea and Sympathy* stands as one of the Production Code's last successful battles. It's to the great contradictory credit of Minnelli's film that, however tampered with, its provocation—the reason its producers fought so hard to make it—lingers so many decades later. Or perhaps that speaks more unfortunately to our moment, when expressions of social identity that exist outside entrenched gender binaries are still fodder for sociopolitical warfare.

"I would just like to say how much I loved this movie. It is rare for me to find something so referential toward my own life and having the source material so detached from our current time. It felt oddly surreal and comforting at the exact same time." This is part of an email that one student wrote me in response to our class screening of *Tea and Sympathy*. There were other such responses indicating that the undergrads were somehow hardwired to understand Tom. At this moment, something crystallized in me, something I hadn't been able to feel from years of academic and historical readings of a film long dismissed as agonizingly polite: Tom's indeterminacy is what makes him beautiful, sympathetic. There is no definition of Tom that could be satisfactory, just as there is no single way of bifurcating human sexuality. Suddenly, Minnelli's film seemed to expand out in so many places where I once thought it had narrowed. Like so many films in this book that have been twice rejected, first for being too queer and years later for being not queer in the right ways, *Tea and Sympathy* refuses our easy moralizing categorizations. Whatever is imposed upon Tom—whether by us as viewers or by the Code—only serves to fortify the lie that each of us needs to be strictly defined at all.

7

America's Nightmare

I f you find yourself googling "Elizabeth Taylor pinup" or "Elizabeth Taylor cheesecake"—and why not—it's always one of the first images to appear. It's a black-and-white photo, or maybe it's been colorized. The pose and outfit are vivid, classic. The brunette movie star, the dream girl whose unfathomable beauty never precluded her ability to persuasively inhabit complex roles in serious dramatic pictures, is at the beach, crouching in the shallows of the ocean. Swirls of water around her bare legs indicate some low tide rushing in, but she's unperturbed, staring straight ahead into the camera, her dark mane teased into a sturdy helmet. The left shoulder strap of her milk-white bathing suit inches ever so slightly down her arm, further teasing the cleavage that's already implicated the viewer in the act of looking. The raven-haired alternative to Marilyn getting her dress steamed up over that New York City sewer grate, it's a seduction meant for any true red-blooded American male of the fifties. If a man doesn't want this, then *what* could he want?

The photo was taken as a publicity still from the production of the 1959 film *Suddenly, Last Summer*, Joseph L. Mankiewicz's hit adaptation of the notorious play by Tennessee Williams that even today would be an improbable project for the screen. Decontextualized from its source, the image is standard poster girl fare, yet for anyone who saw the film—and at the time that was a great many people indeed—it would doubtless summon all kinds of strange, likely unwanted associations. The meaning of the scene in which Taylor dons this bathing suit entirely subverts the heterosexual desire that would seem to fuel such an image—as does the whole film around it, the most shockingly queer studio release of the decade, a work so unsettled in its depictions of gay anxiety and identification that it may never outrun its eternal status as an object of contention and debate.

In *Suddenly, Last Summer*, Taylor feasts upon the meaty role of Catherine, the desperate, embattled niece of a wealthy and eccentric New Orleans dowager named Mrs. Venable, played by a brittle yet scarily incandescent Katharine Hepburn. Catherine is in the process of being committed to a mental institution following an emotional breakdown, and Mrs. Venable has begun beseeching the hospital's head surgeon, Dr. Cukrowicz (Montgomery Clift), to perform a frontal lobotomy on the younger woman, still an experimental and highly controversial procedure in the late 1930s, when the story is set. After she dangles the promise of a hefty donation to the doctor's struggling hospital in exchange for the operation, Mrs. Venable's motivations for wanting to see a piece of her niece's brain surgically removed become gradually, disturbingly evident: Catherine knows something— something terrible—about Mrs. Venable's beloved son, Sebastian, who died under mysterious circumstances while on vacation the previous summer with Catherine in an unidentified Spanish-speaking country. With Catherine's involuntary surgery looming, the film revolves around the ultimately sympathetic doctor's extraction of truth: What happened to Sebastian, and who *was* he? And why does Mrs. Venable want this information cut out of Catherine's brain?

One of American cinema's most puzzled-over queer figures, Sebastian Venable is dead when the story begins yet the center of everyone's attention from first frame to last. Sebastian is never fully seen on-screen, even in the film's climactic flashbacks, when he appears from the back, a solemn, faceless form in a white suit or seen from the waist down in a pair of small bathing trunks, hovering ominously over Catherine at the beach. Though everyone effuses or muses about Sebastian, referred to by his proud mother as a poet of rare artistry and sensitivity, so much about him— everything, really—remains unspoken even by film's end. Even a passing knowledge of Williams's life and prior work such as *A Streetcar Named Desire, Cat on a Hot Tin Roof,* and *Sweet Bird of Youth* makes it unsurprising that Sebastian is very strongly implied to have been homosexual. Furthermore, Mrs. Venable's ecstatic reveries ("My son Sebastian and I constructed our days, each day, we would carve out each day of our lives like a piece of sculpture...") strongly imply a bond that verges on incest. Yet the moral character of Sebastian—and what it means to the ultimate revelation of his death—is so much more complicated and discomfiting than even this initial outline might suggest.

This is not simply the story of a phantom gay man whose past is about to be erased from his family's memory and the official record. Hardly a congenial figure, Sebastian is less an identifiable human being than a succubus who exploited and used people as objects for pleasure, and whose carnal and material appetites led him to an inevitable, shockingly violent end. In one of the most exalted passages of Williams's career, Mrs. Venable presages the circumstances around Sebastian's death in an early monologue to Dr. Cukrowicz, recalling their trip to the Encantadas in the Galapagos Islands, where Sebastian, then a child, witnessed with dread and fascination the revolting death of a flock of newly born sea turtles by a "sky full of savage, devouring birds," swooping down and picking at their "soft underbellies." In this moment of luxurious horror, Mrs. Venable claims that Sebastian "saw the face of God."

Sebastian's own gruesome death is revealed to the viewer only in the play and film's final minutes, during Catherine's sodium-thiopental-triggered recollection: under the "hot, white" skies of the beach at Cabeza de Lobo he was overtaken and *devoured* by a group of impoverished young men and boys, representative of those he had been sexually and economically exploiting. Williams gives Sebastian a grandly violent dispatch that evokes the monstrous fate of Pentheus, torn limb from limb by a frenzied mass of women as punishment for hubris in Euripides's *The Bacchae*. This provides the basic narrative outline for *Suddenly Last Summer*'s lurid scenario, in which madness, liberation, and sexual deviance are not matters of morality but ways to investigate human beings' relationships to one another, their bodies, and the gods.

Yet the play also articulated Williams's unconscious fears, recently dredged up in a period of intense psychoanalysis. In expressing the playwright's deepest anxieties around his own sexual insatiability and his increasing professional and mental fragility, *Suddenly Last Summer* could be handily misread as Williams's homophobic self-laceration by those who so desire absolutes.

With Sebastian left unseen on-screen, Elizabeth Taylor's Catherine is easily reconfigured as the film's erotic center. This was helpful for marketing purposes, of course: part of the film's success had to be attributed to the use of Taylor's bathing suit shots in the film's posters, billboards, and other promotional materials. Yet it also helps emphasize one of the play's central provocations of gay misdirection. Late in the film, before the reveal of the unspeakable truth, Catherine tells of the provenance of that white one-piece, and it's the film's second most shocking revelation. Sebastian bought his cousin this skimpy lisle bathing suit and insisted she wear it at the beach, against her wishes. The outfit was so indecent and tight and see-through that when she emerged from the water, Catherine says, she looked practically naked. Asked why her cousin wanted her to attract so much attention, she responds, with frustrated insistence, that she *"procured* for him . . . don't you understand?!"

The revelation—that Sebastian used Catherine as bait to lure and arouse men and then use them for his own pleasure (only after his aging mother was no longer able to function as bait herself!)—not only adds a perverse twist to Williams's story, his most scandalizing yet, but also recasts and recontextualizes the meaning of Elizabeth Taylor's body within the film and its marketing. After all, any male viewer who lusts after and pursues Taylor might as well be prey for Sebastian. Catherine's embodiment of queer displacement makes Williams's central conceit of gay erasure (the disappearance of Sebastian's "truth") further compelling: an ostensibly heterosexual woman becomes a potential proxy for the monstrous medical punishments to which homosexuals were commonly subject throughout the twentieth century, in her case lobotomization rather than electroshock "therapy" or chemical castration.

Horrific but juicy, *Suddenly, Last Summer* leans into notions of gay monstrosity with relish. Yet it's not just the fact of its writers' gayness—Williams as well as the screenwriter, his friend Gore Vidal, who did the adaptation—or even the queer icon status of co-stars Clift and Hepburn that complicates its essential, provocative homophobia to the point of short-circuiting it. Sebastian may be the personification of gay amorality, and the communication of this during preproduction was partly how the film got past the church's censors, but the film is also abuzz with exciting frissons of homoerotic desire and genuine transgression. The guttural shock of Williams's text isn't tied to teasing the audience with contemporary sexual abnormality (as in *Rope*) or overturning traditional ideas of American masculinity (as in *Tea and Sympathy*), but rather in asserting sexual rapaciousness and the artist's pursuit as primitive, ancient, ineluctable.

It's helpful to have established the sheer chutzpah of *Suddenly, Last Summer*'s plot from the get-go, as the briefest summary cannot help but beg the question of how its mad makers got this material past the Production Code, even amid the

PCA's diminishing powers in the post-Breen years. This has everything to do with the odd, singular status of Tennessee Williams as a cultural figure throughout the 1950s, and the paradoxically lofty space to which he had ascended by the time he had written *Suddenly Last Summer* (titled onstage without the film's emphatic comma), his grimmest, most violent play, produced off-Broadway in 1958. Williams, who had first won over the New York theater world in 1944 with *The Glass Menagerie*'s dreamlike, personal portrayal of familial dysfunction and then given the stage a galvanizing charge of sexual danger with *A Streetcar Named Desire* in 1947, became the dark heart of Hollywood throughout the 1950s, a decade also marked by the rise of postwar conservatism, red-baiting, and out-in-the-open homophobia. Williams was a catalyzing, generational voice; fifteen of his plays and stories would be adapted into films between 1950 and 1970. He was a sui generis agent of change for the movies as industry standards and policies liberalized throughout the decade.

Williams was so entrenched in mainstream American culture by 1959 that upon *Suddenly, Last Summer*'s release in December of that year, the *Los Angeles Times*'s Philip K. Scheuer wrote, "Tennessee Williams, it occurs to me suddenly more than gradually, is exerting more influence on our stage and screen than any other living playwright. He is our dream-world author . . . not the dream of America in its age of innocence, not of one's own childhood, but the nightmare." This was a precursor to a 1962 *Time* magazine cover story by Ted Kalem calling Williams "the nightmare merchant of Broadway" (as well as "the greatest living playwright"), but it's important to note the wider audiences connoted once the word "screen" is invoked alongside "stage." By the end of the fifties, Williams's appeal was hardly limited to the New York commercial theater world. Movie audiences were turning out in droves to see his grotesque neuroses made flesh, interpreted by some of the most beloved film stars seeking roles they could sink their teeth into, works that announced their seriousness of intent and for which they could potentially win awards.

The nightmare of *Suddenly, Last Summer* was clear, at least to Scheuer: it came with "fancy names like homosexuality, cannibalism, the death wish, the Oedipus complex, and dementia praecox." Yet that dream world went deeper and longer than the monstrosities of *Suddenly, Last Summer*. Williams's tormented losers, romanticists, and vagabonds had been unleashed upon American screens like some id gurgled up from a primitive chasm, and they had allowed audiences to partake in disillusionment, to lift the crinkled corners of American society for a peek at our "soft underbellies." The perversion, the self-recrimination, the sensuality, the transgression, the estrangement—these were films that had the veneer of cultural cachet and importance, because of their origins on the New York stage, but their unerring focus on their characters' sexual hang-ups and unfulfilled needs and frustrated longings also excited viewers' prurient streaks. Williams's *A Streetcar Named Desire* and *Cat on a Hot Tin Roof* were cathartic for movie and theater audiences alike, dramas whose plots were subordinate to psychological portraiture. The gay subtexts and gay-coded side characters in those films would be scraped away by the time they reached screens, but their essential queerness could still be detected and discussed by those who had their antennae properly placed.

It's likely that no queer figure of Hollywood's classical era was more responsible than Tennessee Williams for fomenting the change in perception that would lead to the end of the Code. Awareness of Williams's sexuality was likely variable with the American public, but the constant stream of film adaptations of his work was creating an implicit, unspoken dialogue with viewers, quietly readying them for the eventual revolution in permissibility in mainstream entertainment. *Suddenly, Last Summer* is the perfect indicator and symbol of that change, a full-throttle work of horror and a blithe middle finger, a movie with dead serious intent that feels constantly on the verge of jaw-dropping camp.

Hollywood was still two years away from making crucial—and anything but altruistic—changes to the Code in terms of the representation of "perversity." Yet here is a film so unapologetically perverse and clearly queer that it would be foolish to not see it as its own historical marker. The film's central contradiction is mind-boggling: Sebastian's gayness is never explicitly spoken of, but the entire film is premised on the unspoken fact of Sebastian's gayness. In this way, it's reminiscent of Hitchcock's *Rope*, also a film written in part by a gay man in which gay men are beautiful, evil dandies. Yet *Rope* was never a work of its author's psychosexual excavation; *Suddenly, Last Summer*, on the other hand, is personal in ways that are entirely alarming, fully amusing, and, finally, unsettled. In Sebastian, movie audiences were granted a figure whose homosexuality was acceptable because he is ultimately vanquished for his misdeeds and his intrinsic, aberrant nature. If Williams's own personal neuroses did indeed help fuel the "nightmare" world of the American fifties, then his effect on the culture requires a close look: the implicit rules and standards around homosexuality in the movies would be in part a result of his cinematic adaptations, for better or worse. The way we think about the legacy of queerness on-screen might be more connected to Williams's work—and therefore his psychological interiority—than many have noted or cared to admit. Though he would be considered by many to be a less than radical voice in the coming liberation post-Stonewall, Williams was, simply by nature, the gay firebrand 1950s popular culture needed.

. . .

The indecorous attractions of *Suddenly Last Summer* illustrated a turning point in Williams plumbing his own past for his art. *Suddenly Last Summer* is a real scream, hysterical in its louche ghastliness, yet it's also a work of psychological rupture and catharsis that exposes wounds. With no room for propriety or platitude, its story harbors shock value that remains undiluted. You could lose your mind imagining the social media "discourse" it would erupt a half century later. Williams hadn't reckoned with his own familial traumas so deeply since *The Glass Menagerie*, yet the central conceit of *Suddenly Last Summer* allowed him to exorcize particularly hellish demons. Framing the grisly mania of *Suddenly Last Summer* around Williams's traumatic biography risks reducing the play to a therapy session or exalting it to the grandiose status of serious autobiography. This quite delirious work is more playful and idiosyncratic than either reading would allow, yet its connection to Williams's life is central to understanding it.

The dysfunction of Williams's childhood, in Mississippi and later Missouri, was attributable to many factors, including the fact that his domineering, alcoholic father Cornelius and overbearing, paranoid mother Edwina were given to willful retreats from reality. In his journal on January 25, 1937, a twenty-six-year-old "Tom" Williams wrote, "We have had no deaths in our family but slowly by degrees some-thing was happening much uglier and more terrible than death." The festering sadness had coalesced around his older sister, Rose, whose mental illness—and his family's response to it—would haunt him for the rest of his life.

Rose had been Edwina and Cornelius's problem child since the onset of puberty, suffering from derangement and paranoia that frequently manifested as verbal attacks on her parents, tongue-lashing them with provocative vulgarity and accusing them of adultery and "sexual immorality." Starting in March 1937, Rose, in her late twenties, would be shuttled around various institutions and homes, from the Missouri Baptist Hospital's psychiatric ward to a Catholic convalescent home to, finally, the Farmington State Hospital, where she would live for decades and where her delusions and hallucinations initially increased under a regimen of insulin injections. A hospital report indicated her worsening condition by detailing: "Smiles and laughs when telling of person plotting to kill her . . . Masturbates frequently. Also expresses various somatic delusions, all of which she explains on a sexual basis." She would shock her visiting parents with stories designed to repulse in their graphic sexual nature. Williams recalled, "Rose said, 'Mother, you know we girls at All Saints College, we used to abuse ourselves with altar candles we stole from the Chapel.' And Mother screamed like a peacock! She rushed to the head doctor, and she said, 'Do anything, *anything* to shut her up!'"

As Williams would reiterate throughout his life, the prefrontal lobotomy performed on Rose in January 1943 was approved entirely by his mother, who broke the news in a letter: "Now that it's over, I can tell you about Rose who has successfully come through a head operation." Though in later years Edwina would try to correct the narrative in her favor and blame Cornelius for the decision, claiming the psychiatrists convinced him of the procedure's necessity, Williams held his mother in contempt for the decision and carried an enormous sense of guilt and helplessness throughout his life. A haiku in Williams's diary from late March 1943 reads, "Rose. Her head cut open. / A knife thrust in her brain. / Me. Here. Smoking."

Though he admitted that her situation had become unbearable ("Her talk was so obscene—she laughed and spoke continual obscenities"), Williams had held out hope for his sister's recovery and believed that the lobotomy was a monstrous solution. He wrote in his 1975 *Memoirs*, "I regard that as a tragically mistaken procedure, as I believe that without it Rose could have made a recovery and returned to what is called 'normal life,' which, despite its many assaults upon the vulnerable nature, is still preferable to an institution existence." Making things more difficult for Williams was the fact that he saw Rose as a kindred spirit, someone who harbored the same neuroses and "the same precarious balance of nerves that I have to live with." That identification, and the guilt of having survived his own perceived deficiencies, followed him all his life. In subsequent decades, Williams devoted himself to Rose's care. After she was discharged from Farmington on New Year's Eve 1956, Williams found her a tranquil, river-view home at Stony Lodge Hospital in Ossining, New York. So central was Rose to Williams's psychological self-conception that his *Memoirs*, idiosyncratic, expansive, and frequently given to frank descriptions of his gay sexual desires and encounters, ended with the following two sentences: "You couldn't ask for a sweeter or more benign monarch than Rose, or, in my opinion, one that's more of a lady. After all, high station in life is earned by the gallantry with which appalling experiences are survived with grace." She would outlive Williams by thirteen years, dying in 1996 at age eighty-six.

A year after Rose was released from the state hospital, Williams began drafting *Suddenly Last Summer*, a play centered on an older woman ordering a lobotomy on a younger woman in order to silence her "dreadful, obscene babbling." Yet his sister's condition wasn't the only factor in his ability to summon these long untold horrors into his work. Williams had recently entered Freudian analysis with a psychotherapist named Dr. Lawrence Kubie, the experiences of which had a rattling effect on his plays and personal life. Though there were positive initial results— alleviated panic attacks and claustrophobia—many of Kubie's therapeutic methods were anathema to Williams, specifically his insistence that Williams take extended breaks from writing and sexual interactions with men. These were nigh impossible demands for Williams, who was addicted to work and for whom sex was among the few pleasures life afforded—however much guilt was part and parcel of it. Many Williams scholars have interpreted his sessions with Kubie as homophobic and creatively stanching, and they were not to last. Nevertheless, his trips with Kubie down the well of his unconscious produced enough self-inspection, anger, and resent- ment to spark something new and deeply personal in his work—a wild, metaphor- ical examination of the various fears and desires that were all but devouring him.

Suddenly Last Summer was originally presented as the second of two one-act plays titled *Garden District*, both set in the New Orleans neighborhood of the title. It was staged at the Upper East Side theater the York, according to Williams "one of the first important Off-Broadway houses" amid a decade of flourishing alterna- tives to mainstream Broadway productions. *Suddenly Last Summer* was visually defined by an elaborate living jungle set that is both intensely symbolic and narra- tively literal: this was the backyard garden that Sebastian tended when he was alive, a thriving, primitive green world inhabited by serpents, birds, and carnivorous plants, and a backdrop against which the savage nature of the Venables comes into inexorable view. In three extended scenes, Williams sketches out the drama economically, and with some of the most exquisitely brocaded dialogue of his career. Mrs. Venable extolling the artistic and intellectual virtues of her deceased son to Dr. Cukrowicz while explaining the necessity of "helping" to correct her niece's madness; the arrival of Catharine (spelled with an *a* in Williams's original text and an *e* in the film) and her first encounter with the sympathetic doctor, who administers "truth serum" to her in order to better understand what really happened to Sebastian; and Catharine's agonized final revelation of the events the previous summer at Cabeza de Lobo. After the "truth" comes out, the play, like a therapy session, or like a terrible dream, comes to a quick, brutal end.

Williams anticipated a negative, potentially even violent response. In a *New York Times* essay in early 1959, he wrote, "I think I was surprised, most of all, by the acceptance and praise of *Suddenly Last Summer*, when it was done off Broadway, for which I thought I would be critically tarred and feathered and ridden on a fence rail out of the New York theatre, with no future haven except in translation for theatres abroad, who might mistakenly construe my work as a castigation of American morals . . ." Anne Meacham, who played Catharine, recalled that "Tennessee was absolutely terrified of this play," while Joseph L. Mankiewicz, who would later direct it for the screen, said, "*Suddenly Last Summer* is a play [Williams] would have liked to have back—as if he regretted writing it." But critics couldn't ignore that there was something persuasive and genuine in the play's furious, gory originality. It was "impressive and genuinely shocking," according to the *New Yorker*'s Wolcott Gibbs, and the *New York Times*'s Brooks Atkinson called it a "superb achievement," adding, "Although his world is tainted with corruption, it is beautifully contrived. No one else can use ordinary words with so much grace, allusiveness, sorcery, and power."

The seriousness with which critics took this seemingly heavy-duty material belies the amusement with which its most Grand Guignol shocks are dispatched. As gutting as *Suddenly Last Summer*'s personal aspects are, the play also shows Williams in mischief mode—the kind of material we might later characterize as "scaring the straights." The eventual film testifies to this paradox, toeing the line between horror and camp, and embracing the play's productive, therapeutic hysteria. The film may have literalized the playwright's metaphors in a way that displeased him, but his words remain timelessly propulsive, captured by the actors with a relish and mania that remain deliciously unsettling.

Despite the play's popularity and acclaim, Williams was highly dubious about the possibility of a screen adaptation. He felt the play functioned exclusively on the level of metaphor, and he believed the literalizing realism of cinema could ruin or even make a mockery of it. More practically, how could the subject matter, with its direct references to cannibalism, intimations of borderline incestuous intimacy between mother and son, and barely concealed homosexuality, be remotely permissible? Enhancing Williams's wariness around a film adaptation were recent, raw memories of his burdensome trials getting films made. If the Production Code Administration had been so recalcitrant about his prior works for their homosexual subtext, and considering MGM's recent battles over *Tea and Sympathy*, then surely any rational person would foresee a film of *Suddenly Last Summer* as a fool's errand.

Williams's first experiences with Hollywood came in 1943, when his newly acquired agent Audrey Wood, his confidante for the next thirty years, landed him a $250-a-week screenwriting job at MGM. Unlike Lillian Hellman nearly a decade earlier with *The Children's Hour*, Williams had not yet found success on the stage when he was hired by a movie studio. Williams's first produced play, *Battle of Angels* (1940), starring Miriam Hopkins—her film career flagging just four years after the success of *These Three*—had suffered a disastrous opening in Boston, which stopped the play dead in its tracks before making it to New York. Chastened by the experience, Williams went out west, though he found his MGM work polishing up existing B-movie properties intellectually numbing and devoted most of his attention to his next play, *The Glass Menagerie*. Echoing Hellman's initial reaction to Los Angeles, Williams said "the atmosphere makes you lazy. I only work in spasms." After six months, he was let go, allowing him to focus on his stage work and setting the scene for his sudden, astronomical success. Immediately upon *Menagerie*'s opening in March 1945, Williams became the toast of Broadway; by late 1947, when the curtain raised on *A Streetcar Named Desire*, he was hailed as its savior. The watershed production, directed by Elia Kazan, would win Williams a Pulitzer and a Tony.

In the meantime, Williams was dipping in and out of L.A., getting acclimated to the city's fetching yet hollow environs through work or pleasure travel, which included, as a matter of course, meeting the gay glitterati at George Cukor's notorious house parties. When the woebegone 1950 film of *The Glass Menagerie* went into production, under the supervision of old Hollywood workhorse Irving Rapper (the gay director who had introduced the world to *Rope*'s John Dall in *The Corn Is Green*), Williams, feverishly protective of his work and words, got his first taste of the Production Code's methods and its grip on the industry. Joseph Breen insisted that the final lines uttered by the main character Tom (played on-screen by Arthur Kennedy) evoked the possibility of incest between Tom and his sister, Laura (Jane Wyman). A disgusted Williams, uninterested in keeping up appearances for the sake of what he saw as a small-minded board of censors, wrote to the film's producers, "I cannot understand or acquiesce to this sort of foul-minded and utterly stupid tyranny, especially in the case of a film as totally clean and pure, as remarkably devoid of anything sexual or even sensual, as the *Menagerie*, both as a play and a picture. The charge is insulting to me, to my family, and an effrontery to the entire motion-picture industry!" It may seem pugnacious or even disingenuous in retrospect for Williams, of all writers, to defend his work as "clean and pure," yet this first head-to-head would establish a template that would continue throughout the decade: Williams, aghast, pointing the finger back at the censors to reveal *them* as ones with the dirty minds.

Though the early disappointment of *Glass Menagerie* would entrench Williams in opposition to the town's established authorities, it never scared him off. He was keenly aware of Hollywood's reach and the effect a successful film career would have on his legacy. He wrote to Wood in 1954, "Films are more lasting than play productions and I'm afraid that my plays will be remembered mostly by films made of them, and for that reason it is terribly important to me that I should get as much artist's control as possible in all film contracts." Though Williams would win the battle over the *Glass Menagerie* line that Breen had—perhaps willfully—misunderstood in its implications, the producers gave in to demands to lessen the despair of the play's ending.

There were more outrages to come during the volatile production of Kazan's 1951 film of *A Streetcar Named Desire*. No longer could Williams make the claim for his work being "devoid of anything sexual or even sensual." As rapturous and titillated Broadway audiences knew, the story of the fragile, aging Southern belle Blanche DuBois and her animalistic, brutish brother-in-law Stanley Kowalski coasted on the fumes of erotic compulsion and featured disturbing images and implications of sexual violation. *Streetcar* was intended to penetrate the flesh and the spirit, a psychologically supple depiction of the body's contradictory appetites, made physically intense by Kazan's intimate staging and the carnal volatility of its cast, especially the breakout star Marlon Brando, whose Stanley oozes enough earthy, dangerous sexual bravado to all but create a revolution in physical naturalism on-screen. Two aspects make *Streetcar* a quintessential queer text over and above its creator's identity: one is the overwhelming and unusual eroticization of the male body, with Brando's physique and swagger the frequent focal point for both the audience and other characters onstage; the other is the backstory of Blanche's first husband, Allan, who, she recalls with grief and regret, shot himself after she discovered him with another man. Like Sebastian in *Suddenly Last Summer*, he exists only as memory and rupture, an evocation of an unresolvable past; yet here he's the victim, where Sebastian is the aggressor. Both have the ability to haunt the present.

The tragic Allan was expectedly cited by the PCA in its initial warnings to Warner Bros., though Williams's play was deemed cinematically unacceptable for a variety of reasons, including Blanche's "sexual avidity" and its disturbing climax, in which Stanley rapes Blanche. This last was, to Williams, the emotional crux of it all and, as the ultimate expression of bodily and spiritual violation, its reason for being. Williams tried to appeal to the PCA by insisting that the film would be *less* moral without it, imploring in a letter directly to Breen in October 1950: "The rape of Blanche by Stanley is a pivotal, integral truth in the play, without which the play loses its meaning, which is the ravishment of the tender, the sensitive, the delicate by the savage and brutal forces in modern society." Breen kept insisting that Stanley should deny that he raped her, to maintain his innocence.

Earning a whopping $6,000 a week working on the script for Warner Bros., the Pulitzer winner had a modicum of leverage, but the power of the PCA was still absolute, and he was obliged to keep making changes, including an altered ending that implied Stanley would be left by his embittered wife, Stella, giving him more of a taste of moralizing comeuppance. Kazan and Williams both threatened to quit the project on account of all the headbutting with Breen and the PCA, which continued through to production. The Legion of Decency condemned the film after screening a cut, scaring studio head Jack Warner, nervous at the prospect of being denied a Code seal, into taking matters into his own hands. In a panicky move predicting his treatment of Cukor's *A Star Is Born* three years later, Warner canceled the film's high-profile premiere at Radio City Music Hall and trimmed the film without informing the director. Twelve cuts were made sans Kazan's knowledge, excising about four minutes of screen time deemed overly sensual or erotic. A month after it opened, in an unprecedented move, Kazan, already a major Hollywood player who had won a directing Oscar for his anti-Semitism exposé *Gentleman's Agreement*, and emboldened by *Streetcar*'s box office and critical success, penned an angry article in the *New York Times* about the changes: "My picture had been cut to fit the specifications of a code which is not my code, is not a recognized code of the picture industry, and is not the code of the great majority of the audience." Opposition to the PCA had been increasingly fashionable since the end of the 1940s and would continue to gain momentum as the 1950s wore on, especially as the motion picture business relied more on sensational, risqué material—much of it adapted from the New York stage—to entice audiences away from their television sets.

Williams and the Greek-born Kazan were simpatico as artists and willful iconoclasts. Their bond was not compromised by the differences in their sexual preferences. Kazan found Williams's homosexuality not a deficiency but a source of camaraderie, writing in his autobiography *A Life*, "What the gay world—then still largely closeted—was to him, my foreignness was to me. We were both outsiders in the straight (or native) society we lived in. Life in America made us both quirky rebels." Kazan's fascination with his friend's gayness extended to sex: "I was so square that I would still ask myself who does what to whom when faggots bed together. A year later I made up my mind to find out, so I double-dated with Tennessee in the company of a young lady, one couple to each of his twin beds, and my curiosity was satisfied."

The two remained close throughout the decade, even after Kazan's fateful decision to provide testimony against several accused peers to the House Un-American Activities Committee on April 10, 1952, a choice that allowed him to preserve his standing in the industry just one year after *Streetcar*'s release. Though disappointed in his friend's capitulation to HUAC, and dismissive of Kazan's acclaimed *On the Waterfront* (1954) as little more than apologia for his turncoat behavior, Williams stuck with him, believing Kazan was the American theater's foremost director, as well as the key interpreter of his work, able to unlock the writer's often metaphorical conceits with his intuitive, naturalistic direction of actors. No other director had more fully popularized the psychologically revelatory acting approaches readied for the American stage by the Group Theatre, influenced by the Russian acting guru Konstantin Stanislavski and further elaborated for an American idiom by such teachers as Stella Adler and Lee Strasberg. Williams's work, with its psychic fractures and wounded souls feeling their way through moral darkness, was indebted to that ability. It's impossible to imagine Williams's career without the looming presence of Brando's Kowalski. Through Kazan, Williams's work would be brought to fragile, sometimes barbarous life by such generative Method actors as Maureen Stapleton, Geraldine Page, Paul Newman, Eli Wallach, Ben Gazzara, and Jo Van Fleet, all at the heights of their powers, thrilling stage audiences and sending ripples of envy through Hollywood.

Williams and Kazan continued to be among the most famous (notorious, to some) collaborative teams in the business. Kazan would direct several of Williams's best-known plays throughout the 1950s, including *Camino Real* (1953) and *Sweet Bird of Youth* (1959), and for the screen would direct the sexually frank Southern folies à trois *Baby Doll* (1956), from an original script Williams adapted and revised from a pair of one-acts he wrote in the forties. *Baby Doll*, which was intentionally "grotesque and gothic," according to Williams, and which was infamously advertised with a behemoth Times Square billboard showcasing star Carroll Baker's nineteen-year-old title character suggestively sucking her thumb while reclining in an infant's crib, would ignite the most public firestorm of any Williams adaptation (the actress was in her midtwenties). Though it was passed by the Production Code Administration, *Baby Doll* was condemned by the Legion of Decency, and Cardinal Francis Spellman himself lobbied to have it removed from theaters (efforts that were partially successful), fracturing the already eroding relationship between the PCA censors and Catholic authorities in the post-Breen regime.

Among Williams's most subtextually queer plays of the era was 1955's *Cat on a Hot Tin Roof,* which Williams desperately appealed to Kazan to direct. Unconvinced of its worth, Williams knew that Kazan would see something he could not in this Mississippi Delta–set story of familial and sexual dysfunction whose main character is an alcoholic former football hero named Brick, eternally under the thumb of his plantation-owning Big Daddy and no longer sexually attracted to his wife, Maggie. Williams was fearful that elements of *Cat* would too much echo Robert Anderson's *Tea and Sympathy*, the play that Kazan had directed into a hit the previous year, but which Williams saw as overly polite and earnest as a depiction of masculinity in crisis. In a letter to Kazan about *Cat* in 1954, Williams wrote, "You are on the threshold of your richest creative period. There were unmistakable signs of this in *Waterfront* and in *Tea and Sympathy*. In both cases you triumphed over scripts which I personally don't care for and invested them with values without which they would have been red caviar: I mean salmon roe, not shad. All you need now is a thing that can rise when you rise, with the same sort of lift that you give it, and I am still hoping that something of mine will be it." After he was convinced to direct it, Kazan encouraged Williams to lengthen the play from its initial conception as a one-act. Wringing his hands over a new ending, the playwright worried to Wood, "Do you think it contains an echo of *Tea and Sympathy*? . . . Here is another case of a woman giving a man back his manhood, while in the original conception it was about a vital, strong woman dominating a weak man and achieving her will."

As in Anderson's play, the homosexuality of the main character in *Cat on a Hot Tin Roof* is both an unmissable centerpiece and an ambiguity, the unanswered question around which the entire story revolves. Unlike Tom in *Tea and Sympathy*, Brick doesn't have to fend off accusations of being a "queer," but his obsession with the memory of his best friend and fellow football player Skipper, who killed himself after Brick sexually rejected him (shades of *Streetcar*'s Allan), paired with his lack of physical interest in his wife, has long led to the interpretation of Brick's own homosexual repression. This view would be corroborated by Williams in a revealing November 1954 letter to Kazan: "I now believe that, in the deeper sense, not the literal sense, Brick *is* homosexual with a heterosexual adjustment: a thing I've suspected of several others, such as Brando, for instance . . . Their innocence, their blindness, makes them very, very touching, very beautiful and sad. Often they make fine artists, having to sublimate so much of their love, and believe me, homosexual love is something that also requires more than a physical expression. But if a mask is ripped off, suddenly, roughly, that's quite enough to blast the whole Mechanism, the whole adjustment, knock the world out from under their feet, and leave them no alternative but—owning up to the truth or retreat into something like liquor." Crucial to *Cat*'s affecting portrait of the constraints of societal expectations around heterosexual monogamy and procreation is Maggie's complexly empathetic embodiment of the simultaneous practical and emotional need for familial stability—if Brick cannot perform in bed and impregnate her, she will tell his wealthy family that she is with child, in order to confirm their inheritance.

Kazan was uncommonly adept at humanizing Williams's essential nihilism, evoking sympathy for his unhappy, insatiable characters agonizing their way to something comfortingly like—and simultaneously mocking of—heteronormative coupling. But he was unavailable when Hollywood beckoned *Cat* from Broadway. In his place, MGM hired Richard Brooks, who in the near decade since the success of *Crossfire*, the film based on his novel *The Brick Foxhole*, was becoming a major Hollywood director in his own right. Brooks had his breakout with 1955's *The Blackboard Jungle*, a hard-boiled juvenile delinquency drama set at an inner-city Bronx vocational high school and featuring a crucial early supporting role for Sidney Poitier. Based on Brooks's unusual willingness to acknowledge homophobia as a crucial component of American bigotry in *The Brick Foxhole*, as well as his iconoclastic nature, he was a fitting Kazan replacement for *Cat on a Hot Tin Roof*, even if the adaptation would still be impeded by the lingering biases of the Code as it entered its twilight.

Brooks's declawed *Cat on a Hot Tin Roof* would offer a mild, though engaging, rendition of the play's more subversive takedown of the moral superiority of the heteronormative American family unit. For Williams, the nuclear family passes down its miseries and seeded dysfunctions through generations as readily as it procreates. Williams's fears about his own play during his writing process—that Brick's "problems" could be seen as "solved" by the love of a good woman, à la *Tea and Sympathy*—were realized on-screen, as Brooks's version, capitulating to many of Shurlock's PCA demands, finds resolution in its characters' journey toward a normal domestic life. As had been the case with *Tea and Sympathy*, the implications of the play were too much to handle for an industry whose watchdogs intended to extinguish any inference of "sex perversity," and also like Anderson's play, many possible film versions of *Cat* were imagined by prospective producers.

Dore Schary, who had doggedly pushed so many years for his film of *Tea and Sympathy* by scrupulously chiseling away at its implications of homosexuality to make Anderson's play more clearly about non-normative masculinity under fire, initially worked on a treatment for *Cat*. According to a memo from Shurlock, this version would "stress the father-son relationship as its central theme. It would omit any inference of homo-sexuality [sic]. The son's problem would be that he had idealized the older football player, and looked up to him as a father." Schary ultimately passed on producing, but traces of this reframing remain in Brooks's final film for MGM, which could easily make the case that Brick's apparent impotence was related more to drinking and patriarchal oppression than to his repressed attractions. *Cat* would be headlined by two of the industry's most glamorous and beautiful stars in roles that toyed with the erotic allure of their star power: an up-and-coming Method-trained actor from the New York stage named Paul Newman would be the impotent, antiheroic Brick; Elizabeth Taylor, already one of Hollywood's most popular actors, if still regarded more for her offscreen marriages than her film roles, would be the undesired, ignored Maggie.

For Taylor, it was the first of two consecutive film roles based on Williams plays in which her sex appeal would be both emphasized—especially in marketing materials—and subverted, an image of ravishing all-American beauty that only serves to remind the viewer of her insufficiency as an erotic object for men on-screen. In *Cat on a Hot Tin Roof*, Taylor is desperate to be desired by her presumably gay husband; in *Suddenly, Last Summer*, she is desperate to escape the memory of her gay cousin, who used her beauty to lure men to him and, ideally, away from her. There's an odd psychic connection between Taylor wanting to be seen in *Cat* (insisting to her unmoved husband, "Maggie the Cat is alive! I'm alive!") and wanting to be unseen in her "transparent" bathing suit when corrupted as Sebastian's bait in *Suddenly, Last Summer*. Elizabeth Taylor cast as an unwanted or discarded woman remains among the most acute of the many perversities that Williams gifted, advertently or not, to American cinema.

. . .

Increasingly disappointed with the neutered cinematic adaptations of his work and exhausted by the battle royale of *Baby Doll*, Williams responded to the prospect of a *Suddenly Last Summer* movie by essentially taking the money and running. Sam Spiegel, who had ascended to the highest ranks of American film producers after winning Best Picture Academy Awards for both Kazan's *On the Waterfront* and the World War II drama *The Bridge on the River Kwai* (1957), was instantly tantalized by the challenge of making a film of Williams's scandalous, perhaps unadaptable play, which he had seen performed during its initial run. Receiving a call directly from Spiegel inquiring after the rights while at his home in Key West, Williams quickly wrote up the terms himself, asking for $50,000 plus 20 percent of the profits. Spiegel agreed, leading to an improbably lucrative deal for the playwright. (Williams, no fan of the final product, wrote in his *Memoirs*, "The profits were as good as the movie was bad.")

Soon after this, Williams and Spiegel invited the young, gay writer Gore Vidal down to Miami to ask him if he would write the screenplay. Vidal and Williams had been friends since 1948 upon the publication of Vidal's *The City and the Pillar*, a breakthrough novel for featuring a sympathetic gay protagonist, yet their bond was not without its fractures and rivalries, and they could be witheringly honest about each other's work. About *The City and the Pillar*, Vidal recalled, "Tennessee didn't care for the ending. 'I don't think you realize what a good book you had written.' He found the fight at the end melodramatic—that from Tennessee, whose heroes, when not castrated, are eaten alive by small boys in Amalfi." Vidal agreed to write the script, but "only if Tennessee would have no hand in it. Later, Sam would talk him into taking co-credit for my screenplay on the ground, 'Baby, it will win the Academy Award.' As the Bird [Vidal's nickname for Tennessee was "the Glorious

Bird"] was ravenous for prizes, he put his name alongside mine on the script." Later, despite this credit, Williams would deny any serious involvement in its creation.

As *Suddenly, Last Summer*'s primary screenwriter, Vidal found clever ways to open up the text and more conventionally narrativize *Suddenly Last Summer* for the screen, while at the same time adhering to its pleasingly histrionic dialogue, metaphorical grandiosity, and thematic shocks. Anticipating intense pushback from the PCA, who would surely reject the premise sight unseen, and the always less forgiving Catholic Legion of Decency, Vidal slyly began to dig his own makeshift tunnels around the authorities, going directly to a well-regarded Catholic priest for biweekly check-ins to discuss drafts of his screenplay. The hope was not only that he was proving his due diligence in engaging the nonsecular powers that be but also that he was serious in his endeavors to make a *moral* film from such outrageous material. Vidal's approach would, on the surface at least, seem righteous, though to its unapologetically gay writer, engaging with the priest, whom he later called "one of the dumb ones, a Christian brother or something," was as much a joke as it was an act of ass-covering.

Vidal's savvy framing of *Suddenly, Last Summer* as a work of profound morality at heart, hinging on the punishment, rather than veneration, of its homosexual poet and libertine, may have been a way to get it past the censors, but it would also end up informing how the film would be discussed and received by a wide variety of parties—the PCA, producers, critics, audiences. *Suddenly, Last Summer*, despite being conceived and written for the stage as a morally ambiguous work of psychodrama, echoing Greek tragedy and existing in a symbolic realm, was and is still frequently, if simplistically, read as a film about the dangers of sexual deviance.

The back-and-forth memos between Spiegel and Shurlock, arguing over the screen viability of the play, reveal *Suddenly, Last Summer* as a test run for the convention of the punished homosexual. The battle began in the usual, even perfunctory way, with Shurlock stating in a memo from May 25, 1959, "The specific Code violation is the fact that your leading character is a homosexual. We also felt that the ending—cannibalism with sexual overtones—was so revolting that we did not feel justified in giving the Code seal." However, Shurlock's suggestion that "Mr. Spiegel should take his finished picture before the Appeals Board" represents a drastic change in approach from the days of Breen. By implying that there was still a chance for this material to be made into an approved movie—essentially washing his hands of the matter and leaving it for inevitable appeal—Shurlock lays bare the shifts that had taken place in the industry since the tortured wrestling matches over *Tea and Sympathy*. In a post–*Baby Doll*, post–*Cat on a Hot Tin Roof* world, it now seemed a fait accompli that some version of Williams's "gay cannibalism" play would become a movie. Spiegel helped move the film along on its path when, in his response back to Shurlock, he stated, echoing Vidal's line of thought, "The story admittedly deals with an [*sic*] homosexual, but one who pays for his sin with his life."

There would of course be more pro forma haggling over other sensational details, including the fact that Mrs. Venable and Sebastian's stated perspectives on God skirted blasphemy (Spiegel felt, though, "that there should be no offense on religious grounds because the mother and son are obviously psychopaths"); a reference to a character "losing her virginity"; and Liz Taylor's bathing suit, which the PCA insisted should by no means be, per the script, "transparent." On June 4, Spiegel responded, "I have taken note of all your specified suggestions on the script and the general code problems mentioned in our telephone conference. We shall, of course, have to handle these when the picture is finished."

Despite this relatively blasé response, the PCA continued to stay conspicuously quiet about *Suddenly, Last Summer*. After screening the finished film on October 30, Shurlock wrote, "It is the unanimous opinion of the PCA that this picture violates that section of the Code which states 'sex perversion or any inference of it is forbidden.' . . . In view of the fact that the dead man, Sebastian, is definitely indicated to have been a homo-sexual [sic], we are unable to issue the Association's Certificate of Approval." Yet this seemingly forbidding note proved to be little more than needing to be on the record. By mid-November, the studio had successfully appealed, and Shurlock was sending Spiegel an almost gleeful letter confirming the Seal of Approval, adding, "I don't need to tell you what a treat it is for us to meet you under all circumstances, and even in the melee of an Appeals hearing . . . And I must thank you again for getting me in to that magnificent performance of 'Figaro' at the Metropolitan."

Such chummy glad-handing would have been unthinkable in the intractable days of Joseph Breen. Yet even more reflective of the cultural shift taking place was the Catholic response from the Legion of Decency, for whom Vidal's efforts appeared to have worked like a charm: "This motion picture is judged to be moral in its theme and treatment, but because its subject matter involves perversion, it is intended only for a serious and mature audience. In view of the mass medium nature of American entertainment motion picture presentation, both distributor and theater owner are urged to manifest social and moral responsibility to the impressionable and immature in the exhibition of this film." In other words, time was marching on, the world was becoming more permissible, and rather than fight it, the industry's outlying religious abstainers, seeing the writing on the wall and afraid of losing cultural relevance, could twist the message to their own ends. Thus *Suddenly, Last Summer* was acceptable as something that Williams never intended: a cautionary tale. Furthermore, the Legion's response ("intended only for a serious and mature audience") predates wording of the revolutionary Motion Picture Association of America ratings system that was still nine years away from replacing the Code once and for all.

Positioning the film in such a way would have been far from the mind of Joseph L. Mankiewicz, the two-time Oscar-winning director whom Spiegel brought onto the project in early 1959. Rather than framing the story as a punitive portrait of homosexuality, Mankiewicz, whose wry, psychologically complex character studies such as *A Letter to Three Wives* and *All About Eve* left room for emotional ambiguity and refused to paint people as either wholly virtuous or villainous, cannily tried to move the conversation *away* from its controversial talking points. "It has nothing to do with cannibalism, incest, or homosexuality— any more than *Hamlet* with murder. It has to do with basic emotions, disturbed people, the possessiveness of a mother," he told the *New York Post*. "What impressed me was the chance of putting on the screen finally—there's the word—a real catharsis. So, that's why I can't agree with people who say this is about homosexuality or cannibalism. That's one of the injustices people to do Tennessee Williams. That's just his vocabulary."

In assembling the cast, Spiegel and Mankiewicz would inadvertently escalate the sense of disruption around already difficult material. Elizabeth Taylor, fresh off an Oscar nomination for *Cat on a Hot Tin Roof*, was willing to dive back into Williams, agreeing to sign with Spiegel on her first film after a longstanding contract with MGM. However, Taylor came with a specific and nonnegotiable demand: she would only accept the role—for the tremendous amount of $500,000—if Montgomery Clift was cast as Dr. Cukrowicz. Taylor and Clift had been the closest of friends since starring together in *A Place in the Sun* in 1951, and their bond had only grown more profound following the devastating car accident Clift had suffered in 1956 while he and Taylor were in the midst of shooting the historical romance

Raintree County (for *Crossfire* director Edward Dmytryk). Clift, like Taylor, known for extraordinary good looks as much as dramatic ambition, had driven his car off a steep hill after leaving a party at Taylor's house in Coldwater Canyon, breaking his nose and shattering his jaw, his face sliced open with shards of broken windshield glass. When alerted to the news, Taylor had rushed to his side, cradling his bleeding head in her arms. Already protective of Clift, whose emotional fragility, closeted sexuality, and health problems, including chronic colitis, would lead him to alcohol and pill abuse, Taylor fervently wished to aid in her friend's career resurrection.

Though Clift was seen by producers as no longer bankable and, worse, had the reputation for being unreliable postaccident, Taylor drove a hard bargain and prevailed. Clift wouldn't be the only volatile presence in the cast. Taylor, whose personal life had been the hot topic of scandal sheets and celebrity profilers for years, brought her own brouhaha to the set at Shepperton Studios in Surrey, England. (As movie audiences continued to dwindle throughout the fifties, many Hollywood productions were increasingly being shot abroad as international co-productions to help with financing.) Taylor left for London on May 15, 1959, only three days after marrying her fourth husband, the popular crooner Eddie Fisher. Her relationship with Fisher had made her, in the words of *Look* magazine, "the apex of a globally publicized love triangle": Fisher had left his wife, Debbie Reynolds, for Taylor, leaving Reynolds, in the eyes of the public, the wronged wife and Taylor a "homewrecker." Taylor and Fisher's relationship had begun just two months after the plane crash death of her third husband, the producer Mike Todd, which made her personal life even stronger catnip for the press. Rather than escape the firestorm, Taylor was hounded by press and paparazzi the moment she descended from her plane in London.

Rounding out the film's trio of mercurial performers was Katharine Hepburn, who claimed that she "loathed" the role of Violet Venable and found the play "disgusting," but she so highly respected Tennessee Williams that she was persuaded by Spiegel to take the role. Initially told by the producer that her dear friend and frequent collaborator George Cukor was considering directing, Hepburn was chagrined to learn of the appointment of Mankiewicz, with whom she had had a simmering feud for a decade (Hepburn held that some of the less flattering aspects of Margo Channing in Mankiewicz's *All About Eve* were based on her). Furthermore, she didn't want to travel to London, as she desired to stay near her dear friend Spencer Tracy, recently diagnosed with emphysema. From the start, Hepburn and

Mankiewicz had essential differences of opinion about the direction of her character; to distance herself from the monstrous woman and to make her actions more believable, Hepburn wanted to play her as though she were insane from the outset, while Mankiewicz wanted Mrs. Venable to be of sound mind until the final scene.

The resultant on-set fights between Hepburn and Mankiewicz were exacerbated by Clift's skittish and erratic behavior, which verged on unprofessionalism, from frequent tardiness to constant line flubbing to visible anxiety on camera. The left side of Clift's face, reconstructed after the accident, had been nearly immobilized; Hepburn would recall that Clift would have "the most peculiar expression on his face. Whenever we'd shoot a scene, big beads of sweat would pop out on his forehead." On only the second day of shooting, following the extended first garden scene between the doctor and Mrs. Venable, Clift broke down and had to be coached throughout his performance. After seeing the initial rushes, Spiegel talked of firing Clift, though Taylor's reported retort—"Over my dead body"—put an end to that.

Mankiewicz and Spiegel would prove less patient and understanding of Clift than the more nurturing Hepburn and Taylor. Vidal recalled, "Unfortunately, the director, Joe Mankiewicz, hated him. All one day, he made Monty repeat, over and over again, a scene where he must hold a document in a shaking hand. The result sounded like forest fire on the audiotape." Yet Mankiewicz ended up guiding Clift to a delicate and persuasive performance. The doctor is essentially hollow, a rough outline meant to evoke the memory of Sebastian. Described by Williams in the play as "very, very good looking," Dr. Cukrowicz is said to have the deceased's beauty and physicality, a constant reminder of the man we'll never see. Clift's tremulous bearing and perplexity add shades of sympathy and mystery to a character written largely as a device and an echo of a phantom. The actor's oddly recessive presence also validates Taylor's instincts about casting him, as he provides a crucial, numbing counterpoint to Taylor's escalating intensity and to Hepburn's imperious verbosity.

The filming of the climactic crescendo of dialogue, in which Catherine reveals the horrific fate that befell Sebastian at Cabeza de Lobo, filmed by Mankiewicz in multiple takes from five different angles, drove Taylor to near delirium. "After four or five takes I called a break," Mankiewicz later recalled; "we'd been close, but no cigar. Maybe a short rest would do it. Then somebody, one of the gaffers, I think, waved at me—and took me around behind the set. There, slumped on the floor beside a flat, was Elizabeth. Physically and emotionally exhausted. Sobbing in great dry gulps."

Stories about Taylor's weeping and running off the set made their way to magazine reports and profiles even before the film was released. The associative trauma Taylor appears to have experienced while filming *Suddenly, Last Summer* would prove beneficial publicity for such a high-decibel drama (as well as for an actor with designs on Oscar), but it was also thematically apt for a script that was, at heart, about the psychodramatic revelation of "truth" through performance. Williams's plays and film adaptations are all, in a way, with their heightened, hothouse versions of reality, *about* performance. The scholar Shonni Enelow shrewdly positions Williams's play as an extended metaphor for acting: "Catherine triumphs over the stage, playing out her emotional honesty not to cathartically expel but to theatricalize her trauma." As a theatrical performance, Catherine's final revelations feel necessarily unreal, even though they are relating to us the "facts" of what happened. But how can we—or anyone else onstage—unreservedly believe the elaborately grotesque atrocities of which she speaks?

"I think we ought to at least consider the possibility that the girl's story could be true . . ." This is the play's enchanted but far from definitive last line, inviting viewers to take her words as subjective—so possibly fantasy. In the movie, Vidal and Mankiewicz overlay Catherine's words with hazy flashbacks to the terrible events of the previous summer, superimposed on the screen as though memories half visible through a shroud of muslin. Sebastian remains forever obscured, seen only from behind, cutting a figure all the more imposing for not being seen full on. Yet these scenes go a long way toward literalizing the preposterous extremities of Williams's play, enhancing the text as melodrama and subduing its intended symbolisms. Furthermore, by visually embodying Sebastian en route to his gruesome end, the overwhelming queerness of the play, meant to permeate everyone and everything onstage, is localized in one human figure. The last image we see of him is a desperate, grasping hand poking up from a sea of devouring, crouching cannibals.

More than the addition of a comma, the distinction between the play *Suddenly Last Summer* and the movie *Suddenly, Last Summer* is thus crucially metaphorical, and essential to understanding why Williams disliked the film. Writing in *Life* two years later, Williams criticized its "unfortunate concessions to the realism that Hollywood is often too afraid to discard. And so a short mortality play, in a lyrical style, was turned into a sensationally successful film that the public thinks was a literal study of such things as cannibalism, madness, and sexual deviation." The film was indeed a hit when it opened, perversely, just in time for Christmas. The images of Taylor in her "transparent" lisle bathing suit helped make a potentially impossible sell appealing to millions of moviegoers. Pairing it with a mysterious horror element in the marketing campaign only further enticed: an advertisement in the December 20 *Los Angeles Times* depicts Taylor on the sand alongside Sebastian's outstretched hand, as though thrusting from a freshly dug grave, emblazoned with the tagline "Suddenly last summer Cathy knew she was being used for something evil!"

Most moviegoers would be surprised to learn that Catherine's "something evil" was procuring gay lovers for her cousin. Though *Variety* deemed it "possibly the most bizarre film ever made by any major American company," critics were generally kind, even many who clearly found the film repulsive by design, bestowing nearly unanimous praise on Taylor and Hepburn for daring to bring Williams's scandalous poetry to life with such expressivity. According to *The Hollywood Reporter*, "Adults will be forced to admit that it is done with a sensitivity and subtlety that absolves it from charges of crass commercial sensationalism," while insisting that "Miss Hepburn gives one of the truly great elocutionary performances in the history of movies." Gossip columnist Louella Parsons, in her column from *Modern Screen*, March 1960, happily clutched her pearls: "One of the best-acted films I've ever seen . . . but oh, oh, oh—the subject matter is a shocker!"

Even Williams, pursing lips around his distaste for the film, praised Hepburn as "a playwright's dream actress. She makes dialogue sound better than it is by a matchless beauty and clarity of diction, and by a fineness of intelligence and sensibility that illuminates every shade of meaning in every line she speaks." Indeed, Hepburn's magisterial ability to make every word sound haughty and sinister all but defines the first half of the film, giving Williams's words playful, ominous luster; one cannot ever forget the oddly counterintuitive way Hepburn emphasizes the syllables on the word *debris*. Williams would go on to praise Taylor as "probably the finest raw talent on the Hollywood screen," though adding, "It stretched my credulity to believe that such a 'hip' doll as our Liz wouldn't know at once in the film that she was 'being used for something evil.' I think that Liz would have dragged Sebastian home by his ears, and so saved them both from considerable embarrassment that summer." The actresses would end up competing for the Best

Actress Oscar, likely canceling each other out and paving the way for a surprise win by the French actress Simone Signoret in the British drama *Room at the Top*.

Some reviewers less delighted by the transgressions of the film were inclined to take it seriously as the morality tale Vidal had pitched to the Catholics. Henry Hart, a critic for *Films in Review*, tried to explain its monstrosities by delving into the playwright's personal life: "It is said that Tennessee Williams wrote the play on which *Suddenly, Last Summer* is based when a psychiatrist advised him that for his own sake—not to mention society's—he had better stop denigrating normality and begin exposing the evils in homosexuality and its allied forms of vice. The film version of *Suddenly, Last Summer* exposes clearly the foremost cause of male homosexuality, and does indicate, albeit unclearly, one of the horrible fates that can overtake a particular kind of sex pervert."

Such homophobia feels both imposed onto the film by the critic and a natural reaction to how Williams's cagey, ambiguous text was framed by so many, from Vidal to the producers to the strategically lenient PCA and Legion of Decency. It wasn't simply that the film could be recouped as a condemnation of homosexuality by the closed-minded but that one must actively work against the text to understand Sebastian Venable as something more than a threatening queer archetype, equally horrifying to Williams as to an ingrained homophobic culture. Though exalted by Mrs. Venable as an artist and aesthete, Sebastian's only recognizable human traits seem to be avarice, selfishness, exploitation, and delusions of grandeur. Says Tony Kushner, "One suspects he wasn't much of a poet. And that he's after rough trade, as are many of Tennessee's characters—drawn to people that will abuse them and hurt them, people who are the representatives, the manifestations of direct, phallic power in the world, and everyone is supposed to be drawn to them." Sebastian treated people, according to Catherine, "as if they were items on a menu." What makes him frightening is not his queerness but his nihilism; his aging vanity; his use of his economic class to make others grovel at his feet; his unshakable conviction in the nothingness of existence; and the amusement he took in lording over his tiny, privileged slice of a godless world.

In his Nietzschean belief in his own aesthetic and moral superiority, Sebastian has his strongest film antecedent in *Rope*'s semi-closeted gay killers Brandon and Phillip. Those two dandies, who also enjoy the finer things in life, may receive a more acceptable "law and order" kind of comeuppance, but they similarly exist within a purposely ambiguous, coded cinematic world in which their queerness is treated as just another unmentionable aspect of a deviant, elitist personality. Williams's language is, in a way, as cunning as Vidal's workarounds. Words like "queer," "homosexual," or "gay" do not appear in the play or film, and the viewer is invited to rely on inference to get the full picture of Sebastian's sexuality. While describing his insatiability at the outset of their fateful summer trip, Catherine notes that Sebastian was "famished for blonds"—a tricky use of a word that, when spoken aloud, sounds gender neutral, but on the page, "blonds" flaunts its masculine lack of an *e* with relish. Earlier drafts of Vidal's script underlined Sebastian's queerness a bit more blatantly, positioning him as a Wildean aesthete with an appreciation of male beauty and an undercurrent of violence. In Sebastian's old studio, Vidal describes "a copy of Michelangelo's David . . . a Greek male torso, armless, headless, sexless," "a 12th century tapestry of St. Sebastian bristling with arrows and sanctity," and "silver point studies of male anatomy."

Yet as with Brandon and Phillip, Sebastian's homosexuality will be evident to anyone who's actually looking. Vidal remembered an encounter with a police officer who had pulled him over for speeding, and, a few months after the film's release, recognized him. Bringing up *Suddenly, Last Summer*, the cop asked, "Was that guy a faggot?" "I think he was, yeah," Vidal responded. According to Vidal, "The policeman was exultant—because he had figured this out and his wife hadn't."

The nagging meaning and purpose of Sebastian's homosexuality has remained a matter of discussion for decades, especially puzzling and acute for an eternally embattled gay culture that understandably craves images of positivity. In *The Celluloid Closet*, Vito Russo called it a "psychosexual freak show" that essentially reifies the idea of the gay man as evil, writing that Sebastian "comes at us in sections, scaring us a little at a time, like a movie monster too horrible to be shown all at once." Whether one finds value in framing *Suddenly, Last Summer* as an example of classic Hollywood homophobia, Williams's own fraught relationship to his sexuality—or, more to the point, to the public definition of that sexuality— complicates matters. Unapologetic in his sexual preferences for men and unabashedly rejecting his mother's Puritanism and his Christian upbringing, Williams dove into gay sexual pursuit as soon as he left home. He first found revelation and refuge in Provincetown, Massachusetts, in the summer of 1940, finding lovers and friends, and normalizing and enjoying an erotic appreciation of the male form.

A year later, after the poet Oliver Evans made a self-loathing, Swiftian remark about the sadness and perversion of being gay ("We ought to be exterminated for the good of society"), Williams wrote in his diary: "To feel some humiliation and a great deal of sorrow at times is inevitable. But feeling guilty is foolish. I am a deeper and warmer and kinder man for my deviation. More conscious of need in others, and what power I have to express the human heart must be in large part due to this circumstance." His later romances with men were known to and accepted by heterosexual collaborators such as Kazan, and from the 1940s to the early 1960s, at the height of his fame, when gay liberation was but a fantasy rarely taken seriously, Williams regularly integrated his lovers into his professional circles, including long-time partner Frank Merlo, with whom he shared a life for fourteen years before Merlo's death from lung cancer at age forty-one.

Yet as relatively "out and proud" as that brief description of Williams may sound, his lack of interest in politicizing his own gayness for positivity or posterity in post-Stonewall America further challenges (or, for some, condemns) knotty queer plays like *Suddenly Last Summer* or *Cat on a Hot Tin Roof,* which bear traces of gay shame while palpating the beating heart of closeted life in the midtwentieth century. In 1971, after the gay liberation movement had begun to make national news, Williams wrote his first direct depiction of a homosexual character in his play *Small Craft Warnings,* yet this hardly opened the floodgates for Williams as a chronicler of gay life. As his biographer John Lahr wrote, "Williams was no poster boy for the strident absolutes of the emerging gay liberationists; and despite his increasing interest in progressive politics, he was also avowedly 'not a person dedicated primarily to bettering social conditions.'" That same year, Williams would even get into a public argument with the political magazine *Gay Sunshine,* which published an open letter accusing him of turning his back on the gay community by not being more outspoken and political. *Gay Sunshine* would also publish a negative review of his newly published (and sexually explicit) *Memoirs,* taking him to task for not more clearly defining himself as a gay man. He responded, "Is there such a thing as precise sexual identity in life? I've never encountered it in sixty-five years of living and getting about widely. Nearly every person I've known has either two or three sexual natures, that of the male, the female, and that of the androgynic, which is far from being a derogatory classification to my way of feeling and thinking. Now, a confession: I contain all three."

Williams's position may have seemed vague and evasive in the politically urgent 1970s, when defining oneself within binary terms was strategic and beneficial to an emergent cause. Times and fashions change, of course, and Williams's response may come across as either prescient or simply reasonable to future generations. His work was never expedient, but reflective of the ruptures and irreconcilable contradictions we hold. The legacy of Williams's gay characters is not one of erasure or shame; rather, his work located an essence of shared American trauma, which allows the curious a peek into the American closet. One could not hold up Sebastian Venable or *Cat on a Hot Tin Roof*'s Brick or the tragic memory of *A Streetcar Named Desire*'s Allan Gray as exemplars of liberalizing social change, but their existence speaks volumes about Williams's wrestling with his gay identity—an ongoing personal drama that lurked, unspoken but emotionally accessible, beneath the surface. For moviegoers, used to sanitized images, coded words, and clear moral messages, adaptations of Williams's plays provided a new keyhole through which to survey an unseen internal landscape, an undiscovered country of the recognizable: frustration, unbelonging, melancholy, distemper.

The unparalleled derangement of *Suddenly, Last Summer* was too extreme to herald a trend in movies, yet the plain fact of its admittance to screens in the first place, and audiences' receptiveness to its violations, points toward a sea change. According to Arthur Knight in the *Saturday Review* upon the film's release, "Its reception at the box office unquestionably will have an important bearing on the future of 'adult' films in this country." As the respectably disreputable *Suddenly, Last Summer* shocked and captivated viewers in the last December of the 1950s, Hollywood took note. The industry was bobbing in choppy waters, loosely tied to a rickety dock of adjustable morality. Under such evolving standards, Hollywood was primed to reconsider its methods of the Code, now regularly contested. The stage was thus set for the big-screen return of a story that had been part of Hollywood censorship lore for the past twenty-five years. But this time, its makers promised, *The Children's Hour* would be done "right."

8

Down and Dirtier

On the evening of April 9, 1962, the Academy Awards were given out at the Santa Monica Civic Auditorium, honoring the cinematic achievements of 1961. Bob Hope, emceeing the ceremony for the thirteenth time since 1940, had long perfected the deployment of the sourpuss one-liner that both celebrated and gently ribbed the gold-greedy establishment.

Regaling the anxious crowd with his opening monologue, Hope offered up jokes about his own Oscar loser-dom, the persistence of international co-productions, ballooning Hollywood budgets (Joseph Mankiewicz's future fiasco *Cleopatra* was in perilous production), and eternal Oscar grump George C. Scott—nominated that night and, per Hope, "sitting with his back to the set." Among such customary cracks, Hope included: "This past year, motion pictures got more and more mature. Today children can go into a theater and see things they used to get their faces slapped for asking about. The new pictures really are adult. Whoever thought Tennessee Williams would be afraid to go? You know, we may be getting *too* adult. One picture got the seal of approval and the director said, 'Where have we *failed?*'"

Hope's wisecrack was met with appreciative laughter. You can feel the sea change in the room. Here were all of Hollywood's major players, chortling together and treating the once coveted Production Code seal as though it were as valuable as fish wrap. What had taken place within mainstream American cinema in 1961 to make that joke such a slam dunk for this insider crowd?

While over the last few years, the film landscape had been dotted with the occasional envelope pusher, now they were everywhere you looked. While the industry was still reeling from the etiquette-slashing of Hitchcock's *Psycho*, the unavoidable 1960 hit that redefined what could be represented on-screen in terms of violence and perversity, 1961's standard breakers were among the year's most prestigious films. Stanley Kramer's star-studded *Judgment at Nuremberg*, nominated for eleven Oscars that night (including for Judy Garland, harrowing as a hausfrau on the witness stand), was the first American film to engage at length with the Holocaust, sixteen years after the end of World War II, and it was teeming with previously untouchable subject matter, including discussions of forced sexual sterilization and unblinking documentary footage of nudity and death taken after the liberation of Europe's concentration camps. Boundaries were also tested in Elia Kazan's *Splendor in the Grass*, starring Natalie Wood and Warren Beatty and with a script by the playwright William Inge—the controversial adult drama abounded with frank dialogue about teenage desire in its depiction of the detrimental effects of American sexual repression, and naturally it was branded as prurient in some quarters.

The continued influx of popular, comparatively gritty international cinema also ensured healthy numbers of curious viewers for entertainments that never had to conform to American standards of propriety. These included *La Dolce Vita*, Federico Fellini's free-spirited, libidinous portrait of a hedonistic tabloid journalist (Marcello Mastroianni), which grossed an impressive $6 million in the United States, and Vittorio De Sica's wartime drama *La Ciociara* (released as *Two Women*), which features the horrific rape of a mother (Sophia Loren) and her twelve-year-old daughter—Loren would win the Best Actress Oscar that night, in spite of subtitles.

For distribution gatekeepers, homosexuality was still a bridge too far, even for imports, as evidenced by the reception for Basil Dearden's *Victim*. This groundbreaking British film starred matinee idol Dirk Bogarde in the unprecedented sympathetic leading role of a married, closeted barrister blackmailed for being gay. (Bogarde's own homosexuality was not yet known to the general population.) A direct response to the 1957 Wolfenden Report, which publicly advocated for the decriminalization of homosexual acts in England, *Victim* showed without equivocation that gay men were the unfair targets of both a repressive government and the criminals who used its laws of intolerance to their advantage. Engrossing, talky, and entirely nonsexual in nature, the film nevertheless caused a stir with the British Board of Film Censors, who marked it with its dreaded X rating, normally reserved for far less respectable products; nevertheless, the film's controversy aroused enough interest to make it a modest hit in August 1961. The same couldn't be said of its U.S. release the following February, when it was denied a seal of approval after Dearden and producer Michael Relph refused to meet the PCA's demands, which included removing the word "homosexuality." As a result, a well-regarded, accessible movie designed to confer dignity on the marginalized was released only in out-of-the-way art houses. (Part of a wave of realist British dramas making their way across the Atlantic, Tony Richardson's irreverent yet sensitive *A Taste of Honey*, which featured Murray Melvin in the highly likable role of the heroine's gay best friend, would be released in the United States to positive notices in April 1962.)

The treatment of *Victim* in this country is of particular interest considering the major shifts that had been inked into the Code only months earlier, in the fall of 1961. The latest thrust in the ongoing battle of wills between studios and censors began in a May 10, 1961, letter from Arthur Krim, president of United Artists, to MPAA president Eric Johnston:

> I have called to your attention recently the fact that we were contemplating several pictures in which references to homosexuality are made. These pictures are: *The Best Man*, to be produced and directed by Frank Capra, *Advise and Consent*, to be produced and directed by Otto Preminger, and *Infamous* (remake of *The Children's Hour*), to be produced by The Mirisch Brothers, and directed by William Wyler.
>
> The first of these to go into production will be *Infamous* and Willy Wyler intends to start this picture within the next six to eight weeks. The screenplay was submitted to Geoff Shurlock and he wrote back that he could not approve it under the present regulation of the Code . . .

Krim's letter to Johnston is remarkable in its appeal for films that hadn't even been made yet, as well as for its palpable confidence that these three films featuring overtly homosexual themes would indeed get produced. Yet the letter is most historically noteworthy for instigating a conversation that would result in the first major alteration to the Code's forbidding of "sex perversion or any inference to it."

Advise and Consent, directed by eternal Code foe Otto Preminger, and *The Best Man*, adapted from a play by *Suddenly, Last Summer* screenwriter Gore Vidal, are films in which homosexuality is an accusation of former indiscretion leveled at a political figure as a means of discreditation. Krim reassured Johnston, "In no one of the three pictures will there be any acts or suggestions of acts of homosexuality itself." But insisting that any potentially offending queerness is "confined to charges of homosexuality in the past," he wasn't being entirely aboveboard with regards to *The Children's Hour*. After all, many had known about Martha Dobie's climactic admittance of "guilt" for decades now.

Revolutions sometimes happen not because of altruism, and here Krim is less a crusading liberalizer than a canny businessman. Krim didn't want to tear down or overhaul the existing superstructure, but rather work within the system. "We are most anxious to distribute these pictures with a Code seal," he concludes, "and I am hopeful that you will initiate the steps necessary for consideration of an amendment to the Code which will permit this."

Johnston was exhausted from hearing the expected appeals for films featuring "unacceptable" subject matter for the greater part of a decade. Geoffrey Shurlock at the PCA likewise knew his organization was increasingly playing a losing game; if Hollywood didn't make a gesture toward change, it would seem out of touch, an existential threat for an industry reliant on mass appeal. Shurlock would request the alterations himself, and work with the MPAA to make them happen. Though Krim had been thinking only of his own studio's exciting new properties, his pleading led to results in the industry as a whole. It would come to pass five months later. A headline in the *New York Times* on October 4 read CODE AMENDED TO ALLOW FILMS TO DEAL WITH HOMOSEXUALITY. Eugene Archer's article would cite *The Children's Hour*, *Advise and Consent*, and *The Best Man*, all in pre- or postproduction, as the prime movers of this change, as well as the specter of Stanley Kubrick's unthinkable forthcoming adaptation of Nabokov's scandalous *Lolita*.

The wording of the Code alteration would be predictably vague, and, as ever, subject to the interpretation of those enforcing it. "Sex aberrations" may now have been on the table, but only "provided any references are treated with care, discretion, and restraint." This new rule would seem tailor-made for *The Children's Hour*, as Lillian Hellman's play contained no outwardly sexual moments—or even any sexual innuendo aside from diabolical tot Mary Tilford's smirking lies. Yet each era has its own definition of what words like "care, discretion, and restraint" mean. For

1961 viewers, a more faithful adaptation of Hellman's play might be seen as either shockingly adult or appropriately respectful; viewers half a century later might see it as either embarrassingly corseted or, in its tragic denouement, emotionally hysterical. It would soon be clear that the new rules would allow for a new logic: one no longer based on sly workarounds. When something is forbidden, it becomes desired; when something is accepted with caveat, it becomes entrenched.

For Hellman's nearly thirty-year-old play to be framed as a herald for Hollywood reform in matters of homosexuality is more than a touch ironic. Hellman's anticonservatism had for decades been strictly within the purview of socialist political activism, international leftist causes, and freedom of speech; sexual identity was nowhere near the top of her list, even after the Lavender Scare of the early 1950s had equated queerness with Communism. If *The Children's Hour* were, per Hellman, a drawing room drama whose homosexuality was merely incidental, what would the tale of Martha and Karen mean to new generations of viewers in the increasingly liberal atmosphere of early sixties America—if anything at all?

. . .

These Three may have been a twenty-five-year-old relic by the time *The Children's Hour* was adapted to the screen for a second time, but Hellman's source play hadn't lost its reputation for controversy in the intervening years. Even before Hellman had pointedly staged her 1952 revival at the height of the House Un-American Activities Committee's witch hunting, she was privy to endless negotiations throughout the forties and fifties with producers who wanted to stage it in England, where it had been banned by royal edict since 1935. In a January 1946 letter to the Globe Theatre impresario Hugh Beaumont, Hellman, after being informed of the continued rejection of the play on appeal, had written, "I am most shocked and disturbed to learn from you that the Lord Chamberlain's office has not as yet approved an English production of *The Children's Hour* . . . certainly there could be nothing more moral than a woman's killing herself over something that she did not do"—a defensive phrasing that indicates Hellman's interest in Martha for her actions rather than her nature.

Because of its official banning, British productions could only appear in venues not licensed for commercial theater, most prominently a 1950 staging by Peter Cotes at the New Boltons Theatre Club starring Joan Miller and Jessica Spencer, and one in 1956 by Graham Evans and starring Clair Austin and Margot Van Der Bergh, which angered Hellman because she wasn't notified in advance of the cast or directors, even though the producers were not contractually obligated to seek her approval. Hellman's lingering preoccupation with seeing *The Children's Hour* staged in London reflected the control she continued to exert over her first play. The obsessive protectiveness she felt for the material is exemplified in a series of correspondences in the late 1940s between Hellman and Landres Chilton of the Greenwich Players, an interracial acting troupe in Baltimore that desired to stage a production of her play with a mixed-race cast. Chilton pleaded with Hellman for the value of the idea, its "purpose to provide meeting ground and outlet for talent of all races and creeds." In a terse response by wire, Hellman wrote, with segregationist overtones betraying a woman of such well-documented leftism, "Sorry must refuse for *Children's Hour* in mixed colored and white cast. Perfectly willing for play to be performed either with entire Negro cast or entire white cast but mixed seems to me to alter the meaning of the play."

Meanwhile, the epic fight to have *The Children's Hour* certified in England trudged on for another decade. It wasn't until November 1958 that the Lord Chamberlain finally relented, agreeing to license plays dealing with homosexuality "which are sincere and serious." Nevertheless, it would be years before the official London West End staging was given the go-ahead—at which time another *Children's Hour* was currently going into production, this time, once again, for the screen. William Wyler's second cinematic attempt at filming Hellman's play may have come as a more enticing prospect to Hellman—and indeed the resulting experience of reconceiving and making it may have been more pleasant—had it come at an earlier or later moment in her life and career. Though he had remained her close friend since they worked together under contract for Samuel Goldwyn in the 1930s, Wyler was opening a can of worms by asking Hellman to revisit and reengage with the text of *The Children's Hour* for a new generation of moviegoers at this precise juncture, when neither Hellman's personal nor professional life was on particularly solid ground.

Hellman's fame and success were, in a sense, one with her ideology: it's difficult to separate the art from the artist when discussing Hellman because nothing she made, from *The Children's Hour* to *The Little Foxes* to *Watch on the Rhine* to *The North Star*, could be handily compartmentalized from her political beliefs. After the war, with the country perceptibly repositioning itself to the right, Hellman's star was no longer on the rise. Hellman would recall the 1950s as her lean years, professionally and otherwise. Two decades after her run-ins with the McCarthyite scoundrels, Hellman, who had ascended to that now retired cultural position of literary personality, was still bemoaning how fearfully broke she had been, in a television interview with Dick Cavett. Of course, financial stability is a highly relative matter: even though she had to sell her beloved Hardscrabble Farm to help pay for legal expenses for Dashiell Hammett after his persecution by the U.S. government, by 1955 she had purchased a three-acre waterfront property on Martha's Vineyard, where she began dividing her time with New York.

The funds for the property had been raised from the proceeds of a surprise hit stage adaptation of French playwright Jean Anouilh's Joan of Arc play *L'Alouette*, retitled *The Lark* and starring up-and-coming Method performer Julie Harris. One can imagine why the subject of *The Lark*—opening three years after her own traumatic cross-examination by HUAC—appealed to Hellman, though another major personal trial had come that would prevent her from completely enjoying her latest success. In August 1955, a month before *The Lark* opened, Hammett had a sudden, serious heart attack, the beginning of an intense four-year period of debilitation. Their relationship was historically on-again-off-again, but they had continued to rely on each other for romantic and friendly companionship. A three-story guest house on the property of her Martha's Vineyard home had provided an escape for Hammett from the city. By spring 1958, though, his health had declined so greatly that he threatened to put himself in a Veterans Administration hospital; having none of it, Hellman encouraged him to move into her Upper East Side apartment, where she converted her writing quarters into his private living space. The bedridden Hammett would be dependent on Hellman for the remainder of a life racked by emphysema, a lung tumor, pneumonia, heart disease, and kidney and prostate failure.

Amid all this, Hellman, still seeing no tangible entrée back into the more profitable world of movies, tried to stay busy in the theater. One of her biggest projects turned out to be one of her greatest disappointments: after collaborating with Leonard Bernstein on *The Lark*, for which the composer and conductor had written incidental music, she brought to him the idea of adapting Voltaire's 1759 philosophical picaresque *Candide* for the stage. So enticed, Bernstein instantly pitched the idea back to Hellman of expanding it into an operetta; considering herself generally unfamiliar with the musical form, Hellman was reluctant. Her concerns hardly abated as the project grew unmanageable, gaining and losing illustrious lyricists from James Agee to Dorothy Parker, adding and cutting songs, and leading to heated disagreements among the collaborators. The play, which befuddled critics and audiences when it opened in December 1956, closed after seventy-two performances. Hellman would call it her "most unpleasant experience in the theater," which might be a sincere surprise for the contemporary theater lover accustomed to the now widely admired glories of Bernstein's musical.

A more tenable Broadway comeback was *Toys in the Attic*, opening on February 25, 1960. Though it was a critical and commercial success that ran for 556 performances and won the year's Drama Critics Circle Award, this Southern gothic, replete with gestures toward incest, was unfavorably compared to the concurrent works of Tennessee Williams. The New Orleans–born Hellman certainly knew a thing or two about Southern decadence and dysfunction, yet Hellman's *The Little Foxes* had been most persuasive as a forensic study of greed, hypocrisy, and how capitalist mechanisms breed within familial systems. The unabashed, unforced devotion to socially aberrant sexuality that Williams embodied in this work didn't come as naturally to the playwright, who was still unwilling to admit that her breakthrough first play had anything to do with lesbianism, *really*. Hellman's biographer William Wright wrote, "It appeared that Hellman had rummaged through her own personal 'attic' to find material for a Tennessee Williams play." The eventual 1963 film version would be a disaster, received as a pale imitation of the big-screen Williams dramas that had been captivating moviegoers and winning awards for more than a decade. Hellman's last hit—and her final original play—was thus a pyrrhic victory, remembered by many as someone else's overheated leftovers.

When Hollywood came calling again in 1960, Hellman was fully an industry outsider. At the time, Hellman was pulled like taffy across multiple simultaneous projects: *Toys in the Attic* was running on Broadway, the long-awaited London production of *The Children's Hour* was in the planning stages, and she had accepted a teaching gig at Harvard, all while Hammett was deteriorating. Nevertheless, the request was tempting. Wyler was enthusiastically and explicitly pitching a new movie of *The Children's Hour* as an honest corrective to *These Three*, which may have bowdlerized her 1934 play by expurgating its homosexuality but had also made their careers in Hollywood. Such a rare "second chance" for her play caught Hellman's imagination, as did the possibility of making a triumphant return to the movies after more than a decade of industry excommunication. Of course, nothing is ever so simple, and the exasperations and recriminatory correspondences between Wyler and Hellman give the initial inklings of what would ultimately go wrong with their righteous redo.

. . .

Wyler had just returned from battle. Working in Rome for nearly half a year, the director had finally finished shooting *Ben-Hur*, the action epic that culminated a decade's worth of bloated sword-and-sandal adventures and widescreen Biblical epics like *The Robe* and *The Ten Commandments*. Still known primarily as an actor's director who excelled at character dramas in close quarters, such as Hellman's *The Little Foxes*, *The Best Years of Our Lives* (1946), and *The Heiress* (1949), Wyler had been resistant to the idea of tackling such a massively budgeted endeavor—especially one with a huge amount of pressure connected to it. If *Ben-Hur* turned a considerable profit, it would save MGM, struggling in the years since the exit of Louis B. Mayer and the myriad post-TV industry changes that rocked Hollywood in the 1950s; if it flopped, it could destroy the studio.

Wyler liked a challenge, though, and the more he told himself it "wasn't his kind of movie," the more intrigued he grew. Shot primarily at Rome's massive Cinecittá studios, and starring *The Ten Commandments'* Moses himself, Charlton Heston, *Ben-Hur* was a potential folly in scope and scale, yet Wyler would bring psychological depth to the film and an unprecedented realism to its most complicated sequences, most famously the climactic chariot race, a marvel of stunt work and camera ingenuity. *Ben-Hur* would prove the most visually refined and technically adventurous of the Bible films, with Wyler's direction evincing a clear emotional attachment to Heston's Judah Ben-Hur as a Jewish hero (regardless of his implied conversion to Christianity at the post-Resurrection climax). Wyler even allowed for an injection of meaningful gay subtext by hiring script doctor Gore Vidal, who, unbeknownst only to Heston, gave an erotic charge to Judah's relationship with his childhood friend and eventual enemy, Messala (Stephen Boyd). Indeed, much of *Ben-Hur* has a purposeful gloss of homoeroticism, more tender than campy, and a veneer of naturalism in the performances that sets it apart from most costume pageantry. MGM succeeded in making a major event out of Wyler's film, which stayed at the top of the box office charts for six months and grossed more than double its budget upon initial release. The film would win a record eleven Academy Awards, including a third Best Director Oscar for Wyler.

The Children's Hour was a chance for Wyler to recharge his batteries with a smaller-scale film, while at the same time flaunt his high-level industry clout. Like *Ben-Hur*, this would be a challenge: he would create something "impossible." Wyler always recalled *These Three* with bittersweet regard—however acclaimed and popular it had been at a crucial juncture in his career, it also was undeniably a work of concession. With chinks in the PCA's armor appearing on a regular basis, the time seemed ripe for a revival.

The first person he reached out to was Hellman. Wyler couldn't imagine moving forward without her involvement; he hoped she would not just give her blessing but also agree to adapt and update her play. Their first meeting on the subject, in Rome in early 1960, was genial, with Hellman agreeing to write a new script despite her escalating series of commitments. As with any ambitious film project, however, the gears grind slowly. As the months wore on, Hellman hadn't heard back from Wyler on the film's progression and her enthusiasm level began to wane, distracted by other work and Hammett's condition.

By August, Hellman was informing Wyler by letter that she wouldn't be able to do the script after all. "When I didn't hear from you in May, I took for granted that the *Children's Hour* deal had fallen through. I thus went ahead and accepted the teaching offer from Harvard...It's very sad—I wanted to do the script—but I couldn't guess your plans and I waited to hear from you as long as I could manage." Laying the blame at Wyler's feet for not being more forthcoming, Hellman set the groundwork for what would become an escalating preproduction battle of wills between the old friends. She floated an idea: "Would you consider getting somebody else to do the script and then I could do the final editing and polishing? We could arrange preliminary conferences and work out a detailed story outline, but if this idea seems wrong to you, please don't hesitate to say so because I will understand."

Wyler accepted her offer, optimistically overlooking the fact that Hellman was notoriously uncompromising in her artistic collaborations and that she was especially ardent in safeguarding the integrity and nature of her first play. Hellman dove into what Wyler believed had become a diminished role, something akin to advisor. Throughout the fall, the two considered the best line of attack for updating Hellman's notorious play. Inspired by the concurrent plans for the long-anticipated London stage opening, Hellman initially pitched the idea of changing *The Children's Hour*'s setting from New England to England and making it a late-nineteenth-century period piece, which made a certain amount of sense considering the scandalous

Drumsheugh case from Scotland that served as original inspiration for the story. To play Dr. Cardin, she suggested a little-known British stage actor named Peter O'Toole, who had yet to make his screen breakthrough in *Lawrence of Arabia*. Hellman also recommended the Southern Gothic novelist Flannery O'Connor to write the script, hoping that "the rumor that she is very sick is only a rumor" (the writer would die four years later of complications from lupus at age thirty-nine). Most pertinently, Hellman wrote in an August 9 letter, "I have done a little research and without question very young ladies now know what Lesbianism is, although I hope they don't know the details."

That mix of brazenness and timidity around sexuality would both catalyze and doom the remake. Hellman and Wyler knew that times were changing in terms of public knowledge—if not acceptance—of homosexuality, and they would not have dared embark on this new adaptation otherwise, yet their squeamishness with the "details" remained. Such remarks indicate that Hellman was continuing to tiptoe around the central issue of *The Children's Hour*: lesbianism, both as social stigma and as biological reality. Yet the entire point of remaking the film was, in spirit, to remove the kid gloves. At this stage in the process, they were still nervous that viewers and censors would disapprove of the subject matter, so they were erring on the side of politesse. There was something contradictory about a film on homosexuality intended to cause a sensation—with the working title *Infamous!*—that would also try to not offend or shock.

Hellman's own initial outline for the script took surprising liberties with her original text, showing a sometimes tone-deaf keenness to modernize for an early-sixties audience. The diabolical rumormonger Mary Tilford is here reimagined as a savvy pop culture monster, loving TV, rock 'n' roll, and horror movies. In a jettisoned scenario, her twistedness is established when she escapes from the boarding school to take in a gruesome *Psycho*esque flick, unperturbed as she watches a woman being hacked to pieces in a shower. (The grown man sitting next to Mary covers his eyes; the young girl tells him when he can open them again.) Other details stayed the same. Hellman described the scene in which Mary whispers the illicit specifics of her lie to her grandmother, Mrs. Tilford: "It is possible that Mary could be more explicit about a Lesbian relationship, perhaps producing the scientific book that has been previously mentioned in this outline. But I think the whispering should stay." Hellman's contradictory impulses can be felt in the desire to maintain the down-low hush-hush of Mary's "reveal" to Mrs. Tilford while also gesturing to something more specific and entirely clinical: a medical-style book explaining the psychological and physical reality of same-sex attraction between women. Now that her original narrative trajectory was back in play, Hellman was also considering how best to cinematically represent her tragic ending, supposing different suicide scenarios for Martha.

On December 2, 1960, Hellman and Wyler officially kicked off what each hoped would be a fruitful collaboration when they sat down for a long conversation to go over the original script for *These Three* scene by scene, deciding what had to be drastically rethought about all these women: Martha, Karen, Mary, Mrs. Tilford, Aunt Lily Mortar. The result provides fascinating insight into a director and writer trying to suss out the mysteries of character motivation, how to visualize emotion, how to transition between acts, how to more realistically establish Martha and Karen's financial struggles through set design (Hellman says she "felt very strongly that the set and furniture used in *These Three* was very bad and was a kind of cliché American house; that they would never have been able to afford the kind of things that were in that set"). The matter of psychological backstory came up, as well. Reflective of the era, Wyler asked whether they should give more of a reason *why* Mary manipulates and behaves so monstrously. Hellman refused: "One of the play's virtues is that nobody explained people and everybody took them for granted. Should we get into a lot of psychiatric explanations as to why Mary is what she is, we are in trouble. She is a much more interesting character if we leave her alone."

The avoidance of psychological motivation would have effects on representing the elephant in the room. "I have a feeling that you from the beginning have been a little more anxious than I am to hit on the subject of the lesbianism, and I think you ought to watch it," Hellman said to Wyler. While this telling statement seems to suggest that Wyler's "anxiety" reflected a reticence to dive right into heretofore forbidden themes, Hellman rather believed he was too eager to rush in. She told Wyler not to "hit on the lesbian business too early. My vote would be to go very lightly with it or otherwise you will find that, why wasn't Mrs. Tilford right?" Hellman also objected to a proposed early scene in which Karen falls asleep and Martha touches her hair, and the proposal that Mary walk by and catch Martha in the act. "Don't tell me it is a lesbian picture now because I think it is wrong commercially and artistically to do so. Because it is unsurprising . . . Don't give her anything which takes away from the lie or tells us long before we should know in the picture." In other words, the viewer needs to be eased into the story more *sympathetically*, to be able to identify with characters we assume are safely straight and susceptible to the evils of the rumor mill. For Hellman, Martha's revelation still needed to come as a twist, her suicide more shocking for being revealed so late—too late.

Wyler pushed ahead throughout the winter trying to secure a screenwriter; Peter Shaffer, the future playwright of *Equus* and *Amadeus*, officially turned down the offer on December 13. But Hellman's involvement—emotionally and otherwise—would change forever after January 10, 1961, when Dashiell Hammett's failing body finally gave out at Lenox Hill Hospital. Their relationship had been unconventional but steadfast for nearly thirty years, and Hammett had been not only an intellectual, emotional, and moral support for Hellman throughout the tumultuous decades but also a professional inspiration. After all, Hammett had first suggested to Hellman the story of the trial that had led to *The Children's Hour*, subsequently written under Hammett's encouragement. Hellman, who had been assisting Hammett in his medical care for the last five years—and who would ultimately acquire a large portion of his estate—would find herself distracted from the details of Wyler's remake project throughout January.

Hellman and Wyler biographers have typified the resulting circumstances with a passing mention: that Hellman turned down the offer to write the script because she was too busy and reeling from Hammett's death. A closer reading of the correspondence between the two of them from this period reveals a more complex network of mistaken intentions and miscommunications. According to Hellman, she had changed her mind and agreed to a deeper involvement, claiming to be free until June 1961, as she reminded Wyler in an irate letter sent on February 22. In the meantime, Wyler had forged ahead, sending his and Hellman's screenplay outline to two possible writers, Ernest Lehman and John Michael Hayes, both more typical Hollywood inside men than those Hellman had wanted. Wyler had never worked with either, but their reputations preceded them. Lehman had recently written such witty, thrilling entertainments as Alexander Mackendrick's coldly cynical *Sweet Smell of Success* (1957) and Alfred Hitchcock's scalpel-precise *North by Northwest* (1959). Hayes had also written for Hitchcock, constructing some of his greatest films of the 1950s, including the crystalline metathriller *Rear Window* (1954). When Lehman summarily turned down the job, Wyler quickly offered it to Hayes, nervous about losing him as well—without informing Hellman. Angered for not being more properly consulted, and for being misheard in her revised intentions, Hellman wrote, "I don't ever again want to be in a position where I am begged to do something, agree to do it, and then am twice rejected.

It ends in shaking one's confidence and in making the head reel and neither condition makes for good work," adding, "I wish to be released from any further work on the script. It wouldn't be good for me, for you or the picture."

Hellman ended her letter on a note of devotional friendship: "I hope we can work together all our lives, and maybe learn a little from this useless and upsetting mess. And certainly it has nothing to do with the very pure love affair we have had since the first day I met you." Despite the mutual encomiums littering their letters, the remainder of their preproduction correspondence reveals a rift that hadn't quite healed. Wyler responded in March, "Dear Lillian, in fairness to the picture; to [producer Walter] Mirisch, who has been most generous to both of us; to United Artists, who are putting up well over $2,000,000; and also to myself and the year and a half of work I will have put in, I simply cannot in good conscience release you from the revisions you have agreed to do on the script." He insisted that "no one else would even remotely have been considered had you been able to do the screenplay under somewhat normal conditions," and concluded by promising, "With your help, the picture could be such as to give you a new and justified sense of pride in this old but timeless and wonderful play."

Wyler's reassurances didn't stanch the flow of resentment. A letter from Hellman's agent, Katharine Brown, arrived, claiming that after Wyler asked her to write the script in March 1960, "She was enormously pleased and said she would like to do the script for you," but that she now feels "rejected and unwanted" and that she wishes to be released from further work on the script. In insistent pen, Wyler scribbled on the letter: "No writer has ever been so pursued. I would like to be 'rejected' like that."

Positioning herself as the wronged party, Hellman proved a successful negotiator. She would eventually get the terms she wanted, both a work fee ($50,000) and on-screen credit ("Adaptation by Lillian Hellman"), and stayed on the project. Inevitably, she found Hayes's screenplay draft, delivered as *The Infamous*, lacking. "The plain fact is that it isn't very good," she declared, citing its "strange, flat quality." Adding insult to injury, Hellman's outline for the new adaptation had been thrown out. "Certainly you will understand, all words to the contrary, that the facts, from the very start, point clearly to the conclusion that I am not really wanted," Hellman reminded Wyler. She then agreed to mark up the script with detailed suggestions, leading to months of back-and-forth negotiations on details between director and playwright.

In the meantime, casting had begun, with Wyler keen on bringing back some favorite former collaborators. In April, Audrey Hepburn agreed to play Karen. Hepburn, whom Wyler had directed to an Oscar in her breakthrough comedy *Roman Holiday* (1953), was a reliable box office star who brought financial clout and respectability to all her projects. Hepburn had just concluded filming what would become her signature role in *Breakfast at Tiffany's* when she signed a contract for *The Children's Hour* guaranteeing $500,000 against 10 percent of the grosses. Following on her heels was sixty-seven-year-old Fay Bainter, as the antagonist Mrs. Tilford; the Best Supporting Actress winner for Wyler's 1938 film *Jezebel*, Bainter was Wyler's second choice after Merle Oberon, *These Three's* Karen, had turned him down. Wyler had wanted to cast both Oberon and Miriam Hopkins, his original accused young women, as the older antagonizers, Mrs. Tilford and Aunt Lily Mortar, to pay sly tribute to the 1936 film. Happily, Hopkins—a crucial link not just to *These Three* but to the more risqué pre-Code cinema where she made her mark—said yes to the part of the meddlesome busybody. Meanwhile, the film's most emotionally perilous role went to Shirley MacLaine, cast as Martha as part of a three-picture deal with the Mirisch Company and coming off her Oscar-nominated leading role in that year's reigning best picture, *The Apartment*. James Garner, best known as TV's western card sharp Maverick, was cast as Dr. Joe Cardin, back to being a third wheel rather than one of "these three."

Final cast selections were the crucial main kid roles. The intensely expressive Veronica Cartwright would play Rosalie, the victim blackmailed by Mary into giving false testimony (the following year, Cartwright would be further terrorized by flocks of gulls and sparrows in Hitchcock's *The Birds*). And in May, after a nationwide search that left Wyler exhausted and skeptical, chipmunk-cheeked cherub Karen Balkin was finally chosen as the troublemaking Mary. The thirteen-year-old from Houston had never appeared on-screen, her most prominent acting experience a Texas stage production of, fittingly, *The Bad Seed*.

As *The Children's Hour* hurtled toward a late summer production, Wyler, Hayes, and Hellman kept plugging away at the script. Arthur Krim's beseeching letter to the MPAA in May notwithstanding, they all planned on moving ahead, even if the film had to be released without a Code seal. Hellman's notes on Hayes's script were helpful and thorough, if tinged with her patented mix of self-righteousness and self-victimization. "Too much is constantly spelled out as if the audience were idiots," she wrote in June. The love scenes between Karen and Joe were too cutesy and didn't reflect the way people talked, she insisted. "Mr. Hayes has a bad ear, and people speak one way in one scene, one way in another." She concluded, "I know you know that my only anxiety now is for you and the picture. I will not be blamed for what went wrong because I didn't do the script."

An important matter remained—one that would have repercussions not only for the movie but arguably for all queer film history. How should Martha's climactic death and its aftermath be treated? Hellman's 1934 play ended with an offstage gunshot, a theatrical gesture deemed unfit for the screen, followed by Karen's merciless upbraiding of Mrs. Tilford after the old woman tries to apologize. Ultimately, the film would alter the order of events, as well as the method of suicide. There was no discussion of *not* ending on Martha's death—the destruction caused by a lie was Hellman's tragic trajectory and, everyone seemed to agree, the point. They discussed various approaches (hanging, jumping from a high window or perhaps the roof); visual representations (a "shadow of hanging feet"? an "open window indicating she has thrown herself out"?); who should find her body (Wyler and Hayes wanted Mrs. Mortar to be the one, while Hellman suggested it should be Karen); and how to provide narrative and emotional closure for the surviving Karen.

Changing the order of events that led to Martha's suicide is hardly incidental or a simple matter of story structure. In the original play, after the two women, having lost their livelihoods and a defamation court case, become social outcasts, and Karen has said her wistful goodbye to Joe, Martha confesses her love for Karen. This is summarily followed by Martha shooting herself, after which Mrs. Tilford arrives at the house to confess that she discovered Mary was lying, an ironic turnabout for its unhelpful lateness. In the new film, Martha is still alive when Mrs. Tilford shows up at the door for her absolution, which, this time, Martha is also able to reject, feebly laughing off the old woman's attempts to clear her conscience before running out of the foyer and up the stairs. Just moments before, Martha has revealed her feelings to Karen in the impassioned monologue that retains the dialogue from the play: "*I have loved you the way they said . . .* I feel so damn sick and dirty I can't stand it anymore." The persistence of these words demonstrates the monstrous power—and stubborn persistence—of Hellman's writing. It's revealing to recall the letter Hellman had received in 1934 from a concerned fan signing herself Mary Frank, who had objected to the scene's specific terminology. Though she kept the letter in her archives, Hellman never revised the phrasing. "I can't rid myself of the impression that the offensive word 'dirty' left. It sounds so physical—as if the girl had not taken a bath for some time," wrote Ms. Frank, adding astutely: "After that, Martha's suicide is an anticlimax. She is already dead."

The new script twists the knife by giving Martha more wrenching dialogue: "I can't stand to have you touch me, I can't stand to have you look at me. It's all *my fault*." In this revised order of events, it is implied that Martha's guilt and disgust over her own sexual aberration are her sole motivations for killing herself rather than their mutual social ruination. Hellman wrote to Wyler, "I think the suicide-after-discovery is a good idea, and could be most dramatic and forceful. But it does have one drawback: a part of Martha's reason for committing suicide has always been her horror over the ruin she brought on Karen. Now, after discovery of Mary's lie, and proof of innocence, Karen's ruin would be less. I think this could be taken care of on basis that nobody's life can be completely restored once damage is done—Karen means just this in final scene in play with Mrs. Tilford—but we ought to consider it carefully."

Such careful consideration, taken for the sake of dramatic expediency, would ultimately lead to what remains a traumatic turning point in queer American cinema. As Vito Russo would write twenty years later in *The Celluloid Closet*, her "self-revelation costs Martha Dobie her life—the first in a long series of suicides of homosexual screen characters." It's horrific for being so tastefully done: Hepburn, with heaving, tear-spattered effort, smashes in Martha's locked bedroom door, and, instead of witnessing Martha's hanging body along with Karen, we are only afforded a glimpse of the dead woman's dangling feet silhouetted off the side of the bed and obscured by an overturned chair. It's an image of hopelessness, primal in its irrevocable destruction and difficult to divorce from the trail of queer representation in its wake. *The Children's Hour*'s cultural pull does not remain merely because of its propagating lasting "tragic lesbian" stereotypes. The film has a complicated, contradictory status for viewers, as described by Patricia White: "It is Martha's self-declaration that makes *The Children's Hour* so persistently interesting to lesbian viewers, her death that makes it so troubling."

Hellman was adamant that Karen should end up alone, rather than in a romantic embrace with Joe, and that the film should conclude with her leaving the town and its small-mindedness behind. She wrote in August 1961, "The one thing about which I have become very certain is that the picture should <u>not</u> end on the suicide unless the suicide can carry a note of Karen's going on with life . . . We must know that Karen will go on, but we must not have the illusion of a happy ending. Going on is not necessarily happiness, and thus I have come to feel that any sign of Joe following Karen is a mistake." More than one of her suggested versions had Karen getting out of Dodge on a train. Though it's unclear where she's heading to in the final version, *The Children's Hour* does end on a note of triumphal wisdom for Karen. Hepburn conveys skillfully that Karen is damaged but, unlike Martha, will persevere. Powerful and persuasive in its portrayal of a woman's indomitability as it may be, this conclusion points toward another persistent narrative stereotype: the sad death of a marginalized person (in this case, an apparent homosexual) contributing to the spiritual growth of someone from the dominant order (a presumed heterosexual). Hepburn walks off alone with her head held high. Her future is boldly uncertain.

. . .

Everyone involved seemed to enter into *The Children's Hour* with the best of intentions. So the overwhelmingly negative, even mocking, critical reaction blindsided the filmmakers. Brendan Gill of *The New Yorker* called the film "thoroughly embarrassing" and wrote, "From the way Mr. Wyler carries on, you might suppose that he had only just learned about the existence of such relationships." Arthur Knight of the *Saturday Review* dubbed it "curiously dated," while in the *Los Angeles Times*, Philip Scheuer wrote, "I had a miserable time at the picture" and quipped, "The Lesbian said about it the better." The *New York Times*'s Bosley Crowther delivered the death blow, damning it as "prim and priggish" and "a cultural antique . . . fidgeting and fuming, like some dotty old doll in bombazine with her mouth sagging open in shocked amazement at the batedly whispered hint that a couple of female schoolteachers could be attached to each other by an 'unnatural' love."

It wasn't just male writers who went after it; Pauline Kael was perhaps the most derogatory, calling it "a portentous, lugubrious dirge" and focusing, oddly, on how Hellman's personal issues around class fogged up her take on homosexuality: "I can't help thinking she wouldn't waste any sympathy on sexual deviation among the rich. Aren't we supposed to feel sorry for these girls because they're so hard-working, and because, after all, they don't do anything—the Lesbianism is all in the mind (I always thought this was why Lesbians needed sympathy—that there isn't much they can do)." Kael's bizarre, discernibly homophobic review would be one of the controversial pieces omitted from *For Keeps*, her bestselling compendium of *New Yorker* reviews published in 1994.

The remarkably widespread feeling from critics was that *The Children's Hour* was making a mountain out of a molehill, and whatever worked about Hellman's barn burner in 1934 no longer applied to this thoroughly modern moment. Part of this was a matter of theatrics: Wyler, long praised as a director of actors and unparalleled at using interior spaces to speak the unspoken between characters, here ceded the floor to histrionics. Meanwhile, many critics singled out little Karen Balkin for particular derision. The stagy tyke's self-evident childish artificiality, it was argued, couldn't fool a single soul into believing her lies.

In a letter to Wyler on December 29, 1961, soon after major city critics had begun filing their reviews, Hellman acknowledged her awareness that criticisms of the film were building around "the feeling that ladies would not take Lesbianism so seriously." She then tried to instruct Wyler in methods for defending the film: "The taking-it-all-too-serious angle, I think, should be in the nature of an attack, and one that has genuine merit: in our modern anxiety to be sympathetic and understanding of homosexuality and, rightly not punish people for it, it is now fashionable to think it kind of cute, or interesting, and our best friends, etc. I don't think you should be afraid of controversy for the picture: we made good use of it in the original production."

Alas, it was not the kind of controversy the studio had wanted. United Artists' hyped-up marketing approach may have turned off critics and audiences by overpromising something scandalous or at least transformative in its heretofore unthinkable representation of such adult themes. The posters played up the story's "forbidden love" angle, an illustration of a teasing, gingerly touch between Hepburn and MacLaine with the ambiguous tagline "Different . . ." hovering beside them. Meanwhile the trailer was predictably provocative, cut like a thriller, and featuring lots of quick shots of appalled faces of gasping terror—including the climactic image of Hepburn furiously breaking open Martha's bedroom door—while never divulging what *it* is that is making everyone so agitated, leaving homosexuality a "dirty" secret. By the time that *it* was revealed, many critics were determined to meet it with an eye roll.

There is a political and professional advantageousness to reviewers certifying themselves as more progressive, wise, and knowledgeable than the filmmakers or characters on-screen. It's a common critical tendency that persists: an assumption on the critic's part that they are more advanced in their thinking than those who created the film. The critical rejection of the film—and its subsequent failure at the box office when it was in wide release by early 1962—looks particularly fascinating in the rearview mirror. The critics, mostly writing their reviews from cosmopolitan enclaves, were not merely positioning themselves in a flattering, elevated stance to the material, they were assuming a cultural shift had taken place that was years away—if not decades, depending on our definition of change. Other than the dubiously reframed Production Code amendment, allowing for "sex perversity" within the boundaries of taste, 1961 did not boast much in the way of progressive thought or politics around homosexuality (though Illinois did remove consensual sodomy from its penal code that year, the first state to do so).

How one feels about *The Children's Hour* will vary based on the viewer's comfort level or need for their art to provide simple answers and closure, but it's unlikely a viewer won't feel *something*. The film courts a certain level of grotesquerie, so it makes sense that its most dramatically extreme elements obscure what is most keenly perceptive. Karen Balkin's pouty, transparent childishness is no match for Bonita Granville's more sophisticated, queerish monster in uniform from *These Three*, but the snub-nosed moppet is sufficiently unpleasant to stand as an arbiter for the kind of rupturing homophobia that's just a primal, social given. Balkin is less sinister or subversive than she is recognizably, childishly infuriating, popping up from behind a bed to scare a schoolmate with boogedy-boo arms or placing something slimy in another girl's hands to shock her during a recital. With Granville's wily, literate Mary Tilford replaced by Balkin's clumsy, whiny brat, one gets the sense of the character as less of an anomaly than a distressingly average manifestation of socially conditioned, mindless bigotry.

Hayes's updated script deviates from Hellman's original in how it tries to hint at Martha's dormant love for Karen, a choice that Hellman had protested, both for ruining the dramatic reveal and for encouraging over-psychoanalysis of her characters. And indeed such moments, performed by MacLaine with thoughtful but overly pregnant pauses, stick out for their clunkiness. Certainly, Hellman would have never written dialogue such as, "I remember how you used to dress in college. First time I ever saw you, running across the quadrangle...your hair flying...I remember thinking: what a pretty girl," sending MacLaine into a brief reverie while drying drinking glasses in the kitchen. And rather than portray Martha's jealousy of Joe as a simmering resentment, Wyler underscores it with unavoidable, dramatic flair, most memorably in the scene in which Karen returns from a date with Joe to find Martha ironing. Karen looks wistfully at a photograph on the wall of the two women wearing graduation caps and clutching diplomas (hearkening back to the opening of *These Three*), which triggers a cut to Martha, who begins flailing in response to Karen's talk of marriage. "I don't understand you. It's been so hard building this place up and now just when we're getting on our feet, you're ready to let it all go to hell!" She drops the iron, the sound of which causes Mary to bolt upright in bed in a nearby room, straight into the camera, her mouth slack-jawed as Alex North's numbing score blasts. One need only compare this sequence to the tender, exquisitely shot parallel scene between Martha and Joe in *These Three*, described in chapter two, in which a shattered milk glass awakens Mary, to absorb the differences in approach between Wyler's two renditions of this story.

The psychological delicacy of Wyler's *These Three* is absent in his *Children's Hour*, which could be attributed in part to industrial and historical conditions. The first film was made at a time of technical experimentation, imbued with the excitement around increasingly sophisticated sound and camera equipment by young artisans eager to prove themselves, including Wyler; cinematographer Gregg Toland, later *Citizen Kane*'s master of mood and visual depth; and soon-to-be-legendary composer Alfred Newman, all in their thirties. The 1961 film is decidedly and palpably a middle-aged movie, with Wyler, now on the cusp of sixty, assisted by the cinematographer Franz F. Planer, an Austrian émigré workhorse in his late sixties; the fiftysomething composer North; and, of course, Hellman, then a cynical seen-it-all fifty-six-year-old. Meanwhile, the film was coming off a decade of feverishly interiorized portraits of barely suppressed psychosexual anguish transplanted from the theater, mostly by Tennessee Williams. This allowed Wyler a dramatic template to work from, which, paired with the play's long history, gives it a sense of being well rehearsed rather than modern and dynamic. It's a film of high professionalism, not autopilot but certainly practiced, its desire to surprise the viewer extending more from its controversial subject matter than its cinematic properties.

It's difficult to deny the newfound, rabid urgency with which the director and the actors administer the basic plot elements of *The Children's Hour*, which speaks to a perceived moral gravity. There's a self-congratulatory level to the production: making socially correct, daring, liberal-minded pictures was increasingly in vogue throughout the latter part of the 1950s, typified by the works of Stanley Kramer, Sidney Lumet, and Otto Preminger. Wyler told *Life* magazine, "*These Three* was an evasion. The present movie is a faithful version of the original stage play." Wyler's need to "do it right this time" after a passage of twenty-five years communicates more about the shifting tides of acceptability and access that define the fickle

American movie industry than anything in the film itself. *The Children's Hour* resurfaced in 1961 because its director was chafing at the bonds of an industry that had for too long limited expression. Future generations have come to accept on-screen images of the past as simply the way things were, but to believe people were naïve rather than part of a heavily policed system is to misunderstand where popular art comes from. The cultural persistence of *The Children's Hour* reminds us that filmmakers worked with, against, and around such limitations.

If *The Children's Hour* had never been remade, *These Three* would remain the only cinematic evidence of Hellman's play. In the movie world at least, Martha, uncorrupted by perverted thoughts, would still be alive. She'd be a shadow on the screen from 1936, a character whose happy ending exists only because a newly enforced set of rules made it so. *These Three* is a more satisfying film to watch today because it doesn't have to end in miserable death. Still, *The Children's Hour* reflected a new phase in American culture's struggle to conceptualize queerness. The former film is a beautiful lie, the latter an ugly truth. Movies often give us what we want—the fantasy, the escape, the satisfying final fade-out. They also give us what its makers think we need—the lesson, the sensation, the reality check. Either way, we keep watching because, whether we crave images of relief or melancholy, life or death, love or loneliness, we hope that maybe we will see, feel, be embraced by something human.

. . .

The Children's Hour is both a revolution and an anticlimax. This is appropriate for the decade of cinema to come. Just as Americans were gearing up to fight seismic social battles to effect real change throughout the sixties, the movies were retreating into themselves. It was an era marked by the division between real-world anxiety and big-screen denial. When one recalls the decade, one thinks of political assassination, the unrelenting escalation of war in Vietnam, the violent and hard-won fight for civil rights, the splintering of American social life into politically defined factions, and the fracturing of families via entrenching ideologies. Through most of the decade, mainstream entertainments were bright and cheerful, widescreen spectacles, musicals, and romances that existed wholly in movie-land. It would take a while for the industry to catch up to the public's growing taste for disillusionment. It wasn't until 1967 that darker-toned, purposefully unsteady films like *Bonnie and*

Clyde, In the Heat of the Night, and *The Graduate* began to supplant escapist spectacles like *It's a Mad, Mad, Mad, Mad World, Mary Poppins,* and *The Sound of Music* in the public imagination, hastening the studios' mad dash to unlearn the lessons of the last thirty-plus years.

Movies were already being called out of touch in 1961, with *The Children's Hour* held up as prime evidence; by the end of the decade, such perceptions were so widespread as to threaten the industry's survival. In November 1968, the Production Code Administration, so long in its death throes, was finally and forever dismantled. Commandeered by a recently appointed president, Jack Valenti, the Motion Picture Association of America introduced a new policy for industry self-regulation, a ratings system that branded films as either G ("General" audiences), M ("Mature" audiences, later to be revised to PG, for Parental Guidance "suggested"), R ("Restricted," no admittance to persons under sixteen unless accompanied by an adult parent or guardian), or X (no admittance to anyone under sixteen). Though changes would be made over the decades, it's a lasting hierarchy ingrained in American moviegoers' consciousness today.

While adult themes were suddenly allowed, even encouraged owing to their increasing popularity, Hollywood's lack of interest in gay characters only deepened. The almighty dollar is worshipped far more in Hollywood than is social righteousness, and after *The Children's Hour* tanked—followed in short order by Arthur Krim's other two gay box office hopefuls, *Advise and Consent* and *The Best Man*—homosexuality was considered box office poison for the rest of the decade. Gay characters began to reappear on screens in a handful of mainstream movies in the late sixties, yet they were hardly sympathetic portrayals. When not criminals themselves, they were usually predestined for loneliness or death. The long shadow of *The Children's Hour* drapes over the endings of Paul Newman's *Rachel, Rachel* (1968), with Estelle Parsons's closeted schoolteacher waving goodbye as the straight best friend she loves leaves town, and Mark Rydell's *The Fox* (1968), in which Sandy Dennis's disruptive lesbian is killed by a falling tree. William Friedkin's *The Boys in the Band* (1970), the highest-profile screen adaptation of a gay-themed play since *The Children's Hour,* was weighted with its own fair share of queer self-loathing as well, based as it was on the experiences of its gay playwright, Mart Crowley, and its evocation of a contemporary queer community. First produced off-Broadway in 1968 yet released in movie theaters less than a year after Stonewall, *The Boys in the*

Band, set during its main character's hellish birthday party, stages a literal pity party, depicting gay men as miserable, backstabbing, catty, and given to lines like "You show me a happy homosexual and I'll show you a gay corpse."

That *The Boys in the Band* remains nearly as divisive as *The Children's Hour* communicates a great deal about the continually unsettled nature of gay representation on-screen. Do we desire realism or escape? And what do these standard definitions mean anyway? Is misery inherently real? Is happiness truly escapist? If we continue to demand images of queer positivity in the contemporary media we consume, how do we negotiate with films from the past that no longer conform to an era in which representation comes with a simple checklist?

The Children's Hour continually averts dismissal. It keeps resurfacing; in 2011, Keira Knightley and Elisabeth Moss played Karen and Martha in a politely reviewed revival in London's West End, and in October 2021, it was announced that an updated version of *The Children's Hour* was being planned as a limited streaming series to be adapted by playwright Bess Wohl (the show has yet to surface at the time of this writing). Its cultural persistence cannot be a mistake or shortsightedness on the part of its makers. *The Children's Hour,* especially in its 1961 film version, has the ability, singular in its moment, to dramatize the effects of the closet and the dormant violence surrounding it. Much is unspoken, but, as Eve Kosofsky Sedgwick has pointed out, the silence of closeted living is, for gay and straight alike, a form of performance, with its own language. Hellman's play is the rare text that engages with these realities, even if it was made by ostensibly straight people with little working knowledge of what those realities *feel* like. Of particular resonance is the frightening scene, rarely cited by critics, in which a deliveryman stares at Martha and Karen with unnerving fascination in their own foyer, circling them like a panther. This comes soon after a moment in which heckling local men park outside their front yard fence, hoping for a glimpse of the infamous perverts.

Such scenes cannot help but remind viewers of the very real, physical social threat experienced by outwardly—or rumored—queer people throughout the twentieth century, which persists despite the eventual passing of the Matthew Shepard and James Byrd Jr. Hate Crimes Prevention Act in 2009, the first statute "allowing federal criminal prosecution of hate crimes motivated by the victim's actual or perceived sexual orientation or gender identity." Because statistics did not exist in 1961 about violence against gay, lesbian, bisexual, or transgender people, we cannot point to specific widespread knowledge of attacks, threats, and killings; the first comprehensive report on violence against American gays and lesbians, conducted by the National Gay Task Force, with funds solicited from the United States Justice Department's research arm, wouldn't be opened until 1983, more than twenty years after the release of *The Children's Hour*.

Yet the film's sequences of intimidation and dehumanization speak to a generalized knowledge of such threat. This crystallizes the emotional pull of *The Children's Hour*, even if one's intellectual response—that it feels "outdated"—tugs in the opposite direction. Hellman might have continually insisted it was "not about lesbianism," but the story's instances of social stigmatizing only encourage our empathy with the women, which makes Hellman's humanism objective and incontestable rather than merely political. Hellman would seem to take it as a matter of course that these two women deserve to be treated equally.

Strangely and tellingly, what seemed preposterous to critics who placed themselves above the 1961 film of *The Children's Hour* was that it dared to imply that the humanity of homosexual people needed defending at all, and that it was dramatically turgid that the women's rumored lesbianism should send anyone into paroxysms of agony or fear. The irony of this view is that the film, like the play, is less interested in lesbianism on a narrative level than as a stand-in for social difference.

What's most gratifying about *The Children's Hour* more than a half century later is the gravity of the storytelling that asserts its unique historical position. This was the first film released after the Production Code alterations, so we should hardly expect anything approaching timeless sensitivity in its representation of a lesbian being yanked out of the closet. Yet *The Children's Hour*, even more than *Tea and Sympathy*, remains acutely compelling for flaunting warring tendencies— progressiveness and conservatism, histrionics and tenderness, black-and-white certainty and gray-zone ambiguity—making it a tough nut to crack even today. Its reputation, as the historical breakthrough that was instantly tagged as retrograde, still reflects these contradictions.

Such incongruities speak to the hidden zones that make all the movies in this book worth reckoning with. So many of these films in one way or another prove the insufficiency of instantaneous critical response. Yet they also were subject to the whims of politics and fashion decades hence, placing them in a historical double bind: distrusted and censored in their time for being too queer, dismissed years later for not being queer in the right ways. Just as much as Sebastian Venable's devouring death or Tom Lee's traumatic coming-of-age, the killing of Martha Dobie in *The Children's Hour* created a rupture that continues to trouble the waters of progressive queer identification. As much as we may want to, we cannot look away from them. Maybe there is too much in them that is familiar. In a society that has for so long branded us as sick and dirty, to deny them is to deny a part of ourselves.

Epilogue: I'm (Not) There

This is not a book of heroes. It's not an inspiring, heart-tugging story about a ragtag team of gallant and gutsy artists who changed the world. The directors, writers, actors, and other craftspeople written about in these chapters just went about their work, creating films that manage to challenge and provoke and tease despite the restrictions put upon them. These films aren't "important" in the ways we think about socially courageous art. Very few of them regularly show up on lists of the enshrined greatest movies ever made. They sit in the corners and crevices of film history, offering illumination, not perfection.

American studio moviemaking has always essentially been a system counterproductive to expressions of individual creativity, which is why films directed by and with distinct personalities—Hitchcock, Kubrick, Spike Lee, Francis and Sofia Coppola—are seized upon and hoarded like precious diamonds. We love hero narratives not just in our movies but behind them. Heroes are totalizing forces who help give structure, godlike consciousness, and power to the world around us, and this often applies to our conceptions of art. This is one reason why the notion of the director as a film's sole author (revealed in technique, style, and meaning) ultimately became less a theory than an ingrained way of watching. It's of interest that critic Andrew Sarris's influential essay "Notes on the Auteur Theory," in which he first adapted and explicated the idea from the *Cahiers du Cinéma* crowd, was published in 1962, just months after *The Children's Hour* was released. As the narrative for this story ended, the movies were evolving, but so were the ways we perceived them.

Whatever incremental changes took place across the twenty-five years of filmmaking covered in these pages occurred not because of individual courage but because the profit-dependent capitalist machine of Hollywood reacts to a fickle and unpredictable marketplace. Movies rarely blaze trails, but as indications of cultural narratives they're unparalleled—and their paths are easy to follow for always being so behind the times. A perfect case in point is Jonathan Demme's *Philadelphia*, the first studio film to reckon with the ongoing, unavoidable national crisis of the AIDS epidemic, released at the shockingly late date of 1993. By the time of its ballyhooed premiere, queer voices had already been heard thanks to the independent film boom of the late eighties and early nineties. Names like Marlon Riggs, Todd Haynes, Cheryl Dunye, and Gus Van Sant would forever change the way we talk about queer cinema and still exemplify the kind of bravery and transgression Hollywood has rarely allowed for.

Nevertheless, the people who made the movies that formed the narrative spine of this book managed to seep essences of their selves into their work despite the impossibility of direct articulation. They were straight like Lillian Hellman or gay like Dorothy Arzner; they were indefatigable industry players like William Wyler or self-made iconoclasts like Richard Brooks; they were driven by liberal righteousness like Dore Schary or publicly apolitical creatures like Vincente Minnelli; they were extroverted like Arthur Laurents or painfully private like Montgomery Clift; they were artists fascinated by sexuality like Alfred Hitchcock or disinclined from engaging with it like George Cukor; they were proudly unrefined like Samuel Goldwyn or deeply literate like Tennessee Williams. Yet through them, one can follow a trajectory of expression across an era of censorship—not from naïveté to enlightenment (history sometimes moves in the opposite direction), but from Hollywood's idea of itself as a separate social microcosm with its own rules to its growing realization that it was part of the greater march of time.

The films discussed in the book are distinct from one another in conception, production, and impact, but they're not anomalous pods. There isn't a single film here written about at length not connected to another via someone who worked on it. The world inhabited by these artists was expansive in vision, although it was a small one, made up of seemingly endless layers and crosshatches. The queer presence these creators helped surface feels a lot more palpable and honest to me when discussed as the product of artisans keeping their heads down to achieve the task at hand. They were a constellation of voices, faces, and invisible behind-the-camera workers who collaborated, wittingly or not, on an era of gay filmmaking that echoes down through the ages—a community working for a common purpose, making small gestures rather than large radical moves. These people can be your heroes if you'd like, but idolatry gets you only so far when you are really trying to understand the processes of a past that got us to the present.

. . .

It's apt that so many of the films discussed in this book offer narratives set within or emerging from parochial environments. These are movies that take place in boarding schools (*These Three, Tea and Sympathy, The Children's Hour*) or vocational art schools (*Dance, Girl, Dance*), or whose characters carry with them bad educations instilled in the university (*Rope*) or the military (*Crossfire*). Even the sanatorium of *Suddenly, Last Summer*—where one is forced to be sane/normal by any means necessary—is a place of failed institutional learning. In all these cases, queerness is the counternarrative, the hidden identity that must be corrected, for the characters but also for the makers behind the scenes trying to get past the censors. Each functions as a kind of anti-bildungsroman, a reverse education that doesn't lead to enlightenment so much as confusion and disillusionment.

This thematic connection among the films crystallizes their continued resonance in the third decade of America's twenty-first century, when anti-LGBTQ+ censorship and legislation has again begun to affect school curricula. In an unnerving echo of Anita Bryant's Save Our Children political coalition of the 1970s—which contended that the presence of homosexuality, whether through teaching or the sexual identity of the teachers themselves, impinged on the "religious freedom" of upstanding heteros and thus required state bans—a series of recent laws prohibiting the teaching of gay, lesbian, and transgender content to students of various ages proliferated throughout the early years of this decade. The most prominently covered of these was the Florida Parental Rights in Education Act (colloquially, the "Don't Say Gay" law), which Governor Ron DeSantis signed in 2022 and expanded in 2023 so that sexual orientation and gender identity would be verboten subjects all the way through twelfth grade. States from Alabama to Indiana to Louisiana followed suit with their own similarly prohibitive education laws, while Mississippi, Oklahoma, and Texas left their existing homophobic educational laws untouched. Even outside school settings, the mania over gay and transgender Americans' perceived effect on children has reached a fever pitch in recent years as right-wing-fueled "grooming" conspiracies have broken out of Reddit message boards and contaminated the mainstream. The age-old branding of queer people as dangerous to youth is ever popular.

The Children's Hour remains Hollywood's most direct and notorious reflection on the irrational, very American fear that queers will infect our most vulnerable, that their "sick and dirty" perversions, once unleashed, are contagious. In Hellman's story, parents immediately whisk their children out of school upon hearing the rumor that their kids' instructors are lesbians, leaving the school an empty husk surrounded by dead autumn leaves. *The Children's Hour*'s depiction of homophobia reflected Hellman's inherent disdain for bigotry, conformity, and groupthink, and the 1961 adaptation retains its essential core of humanity, which would be missing from so many dramas in the years to come that were now allowed to depict the pathetic lives of queer people. Once the film was released, movies repeatedly evoked the fears Hellman critiqued, portraying gay people as hated minorities for dramatic expedience. The repulsion that *The Children's Hour* exposes quickly became the given, the underlying standard, in cinematic storytelling.

In an audio interview recorded in 1988, two years before he would die of complications from AIDS, Vito Russo spoke to the gay historian Eric Marcus. When asked if he could recall the first time he saw a homosexual character portrayed in a movie, Russo replies without hesitation, "Yeah, *Advise and Consent* in 1962. I was in high school. I was horrified. Don Murray had slit his throat. I mean, he had to commit suicide at the end only because he's *accused* of being gay . . . I remember being tremendously impressed and warned by this movie, that these kinds of people kill themselves."

Otto Preminger's exposé of Washington, D.C., politics, in which Murray played a Utah senator blackmailed for a same-sex love affair during World War II, was one of the three films that Arthur Krim had used as leverage when he wrote to the MPAA's Eric Johnston to request an exception to the Code, along with *The Children's Hour*, resulting in the October 1961 amendment. The grandstanding moral righteousness of business-minded figures like Krim, Preminger, and Wyler would lead to films that sought to humanize gay people the only way they seemed to know how: by casting them as sad, desperate, suicidal outcasts. The films were "different," per

The Children's Hour's poster tagline, but they were hardly radical. Nevertheless, Russo was radicalized.

The twinge of humiliation and anger Russo felt from *Advise and Consent* at such a young age eventually became the spark that led to *The Celluloid Closet*. Much of the book's ire was targeted at the films that came out in the years directly before and after Stonewall, films that indicated the inability of Hollywood to grapple with the moment as it's happening. In addition to being a relentless activist, Russo was a tireless archivist, rummaging through old 35mm and 16mm reels of films from around the world at the Museum of Modern Art's film department for signs of gay life. These images of Russo have been buzzing in my head throughout the writing of this book, as everything he did made everything I do, and everything any gay film scholar does, possible. (If you're looking for a hero in this book after all, Russo is the closest thing to it.)

Russo was desperate for images of positivity. As a result, many of the films in this book have been tagged in subsequent decades as malicious—sick and dirty, not in the way Martha Dobie or Joseph Breen meant, but as diseased emissions from a society plagued by the sickness of homophobia, and responsible for instilling the kind of shame that kept generations in the closet. Today, our needs are more complicated. After decades of post–*Celluloid Closet* course correction, with proper Pride-stamped entertainments available on every streaming service, even our gayest entertainments can feel hopelessly sanitized, and our cravings for perfect representation are subsiding. We prefer our entertainments to offer a full spectrum of humanistic images, which include queer people in all our psychological complexity—the positive, the negative, the loving, the cruel, the fraught, the kind and the demonic, the standard and the unrecognizable, the normal and the unusual. It's a knotty moment, but we should be thrilled to be able to even wrestle with these ideas out in the open.

When the hit *Love, Simon*, the first mainstream American teen comedy featuring a gay male protagonist, was released at the wildly late date of 2018, I had conflicted responses. On the one hand, it was enormously poignant to imagine how meaningful it would have been for me to have such a major multiplex offering come out in the 1990s, when I was a teenager, telling me it was okay to *be* me. On the other hand, it felt like the cinematic equivalent of antibacterial wipes, a spit-shined, upper-middle-class product for the "This Is Me!" era, only possible once its studio felt it was safe enough to make. Surely there is meaning in setting a gay-themed film in the contested educational space of the American high school. Yet the film's opening voiceover narration, also used in the trailer, provides a clue to its address: "My friends and I do everything friends do . . . I'm just like *you* . . . My life is totally normal . . . except for one huge-ass secret." Who is the *you* in this equation? And what is normal? The film is clearly intended to remind straight audiences how reassuringly average a gay kid can be. The hygienic pleasures and pitfalls of *Love, Simon* couldn't be further from "sick and dirty" thoughts. Which is, in a way, heartening, yet one cannot be blamed for craving some of those complicating factors that make characters feel a little more complete.

To my eyes, Cheryl Dunye's independently financed *The Watermelon Woman*, released in 1996, speaks most brilliantly and effectively to how subversive, daring ideas can be smuggled into essentially generic packages in the postclassical movie era. The movie centers on a Black lesbian amateur filmmaker, Cheryl (portrayed by the director herself), who works a day job at a video store. Borrowing a tape of a cornball racist movie from the 1930s called *Plantation Memories*, she discovers a forgotten Black actress named Fae Richards, aka the Watermelon Woman, as erotically appealing to her as she is historically fascinating ("girlfriend has it going on"). She vows to learn more about Richards, sparking a personal archival research project. (I'm convinced Russo, who didn't have the luxury of videotape access when he began his own movie sleuthing, would have adored this film.) Further research uncovers tantalizing hidden details, including Richards's rumored lesbian identity and a long-term sexual relationship with a female director clearly modeled on Dorothy Arzner.

The Watermelon Woman was another of the many queer-themed movies of the 1990s, like Marlon Riggs's *Tongues Untied* and Todd Haynes's *Poison*, targeted by conservative politicians for producing overtly gay sexual content with some production funds from the National Endowment for the Arts. (The Michigan Republican congressman Pete Hoekstra, decades later a Trump appointee to a U.S. ambassadorship, called the film "pornographic" and unsuccessfully tried to defund the NEA.) I single it out here because Dunye's delightful film is such a winning continuation and corrective to our country's history of movie marginalization. Every aspect of the film would be inconceivable in Hollywood during the years covered in this book: the sexual and gender identity of the filmmaker and star, the romantic interests of the character she plays, the frankness of its erotic scenes, the notion of a personal cinematic archival project, the explicit inquiries around race and queer-ness, the existence of videotapes! Yet it's also a dialogue with the past, connecting contemporary gay life and moviemaking with a lineage that clarifies the meaning and power of queer existence itself.

So many touchstones of late-twentieth- and early-twenty-first-century queer cinema, like Dunye's film, exist in conversation with a cinematic past in which we were made invisible. There's also Todd Haynes's *Far from Heaven* (2002), which reconceives Douglas Sirk's 1955 Technicolor melodrama *All That Heaven Allows* by surfacing the era's gay undercurrents; Ira Sachs's *Love Is Strange* (2014), which reimagines Leo McCarey's devastating *Make Way for Tomorrow* (1937), a tale of an elderly couple's mistreatment by their offspring, as a portrait of an aging gay couple increasingly untethered from the world around them; Jane Schoenbrun's *I Saw the TV Glow* (2024), which uses a horror framework to explode notions of queer iden-tification and trans belonging, questioning how the entertainment we watch at a young age becomes part of us—burrows deep, deep down inside—whether it ever represented us at all. We make room for fictions that never made room for us.

The feeling this creates in us is akin to a psychic split, a quivering of belonging and unbelonging at once. During the reign of the Code, there may have officially been no such thing as gays and lesbians on-screen, but many of us knew, felt in our blood, that this was more *our* world than anyone's. Even if for nearly a century they consistently betrayed us by feigning ignorance of us, we went back over and over, even made ourselves up in their image. To some, this may sound like delusion, or being stuck in an abusive relationship. I'd rather think of it as a form of silent communion, not unlike Sedgwick's positing of "closetedness" as a language all its own. Queerness persists in our cinema past because the term is more than identity-based; it's political. Schoenbrun told me, "If you view queerness as some kind of solidarity with radical forms of existence, you could make a pretty wide-ranging argument for the queerness in any movie or any piece of art that's being subversive in the mainstream." Queer people's connection to classical Hollywood movies is pleasingly contradictory: we are there because we are *not* there. There cannot be overt homophobia on screens where homosexuals don't exist (the conundrum of *These Three*), so it's easy to get pleasantly lost in them.

Queer cinematic history is counterintuitive: it's most fascinating for what you don't see. In a sense, all queer American movies from the era of the Production Code operate on the same principles as the musical, toggling between the "real" world as presented and the fantasy one beneath the surface. As D. A. Miller wrote about the nascent queer child's emotional response to the musical, "The boy sought not the 'integration' of drama and music on the thematic surface, but a so much deeper formal discontinuity between the two." Each of the films discussed offers such formal discontinuities: the film on the surface and the unspoken one beneath, the one that's a little gayer because of what we suspect, or know, or read into it. We as viewers produce gay meaning, and that's active, empowering, and thrilling—it feeds off our imaginations. Most queer movies today, not fettered by restrictions, capture the spirit but not the imagination. Of course, we wouldn't have it any other way; no one wants to move backward. But what do we do when the dreaming has come to an end?

. . .

I discovered an array of precious ephemera during my research of this book, from queer fans' letters to Lillian Hellman in the 1930s, to the tortured but loving back-and-forth correspondences between Hellman and William Wyler in wrestling *The Children's Hour* to the screen again in the 1960s, to the heartrending notes of emotional support Dorothy Arzner received from friends after losing her beloved Marion Morgan in the 1970s. Yet nothing proved quite as revelatory as those class-room screenings of such films as *Dance, Girl, Dance, Rope, Tea and Sympathy*, and *The Children's Hour*. My students' emotional responses to them proved for me, finally and beyond a shadow of a doubt, that these films hold enormous resonance—and that film history as it's often discussed is far too attached to simple dichoto-mies, both in terms of quality (a movie is good or bad) and morality (a movie is good or bad *for* you). In our culture, if a movie hasn't been officially deemed a "classic" then it's "minor." Decades of complex, expressive, difficult, and often extraordinary work can thus get lost in the folds of time.

I think *Tea and Sympathy* and *The Children's Hour* still resound because they do something that goes beyond trend or fashion or aesthetic evaluation: they evoke the *feeling* of difference, the craving for acceptance by a society that has no interest in you. Even the outcast demons of *Rope* and *Suddenly, Last Summer* are appealing, because we also know what it feels like to be deemed an aberration.

How does one measure oneself if not against what came before? It's hard to conceive of a modern interpretation of queerness without placing it in opposition to our troubled, tragic legacies. Movies from the past constitute a kind of haunting, and we voluntarily invite in the ghosts. Queers like me can't let go of the miserable death of Martha Dobie or the tortured ambiguity of Tom Lee or the phantom evil of Sebastian Venable or the murderous delight of Brandon and Phillip or even the sublime emotional purgation of Judy Garland, because the work of self-identification is a constant negotiation with our history of images. These films, these phantoms, persist because they speak to the unsettled parts of ourselves that don't fit into acceptable standards of contemporary queerness, the parts we hush away, the parts that creep into our thoughts at night when we draw the shades and close our eyes after a full, tiring day of being so sure and pure and proud and righteous.

I came out of my own closet in my early twenties, only a few years into the twenty-first century. Thanks to contemporary movies, I had long been used to thinking of gay people as pathetic, disgusting, or villainous. This feeling would be compounded by the fact that I had come of sexual age during the AIDS crisis. Growing up with constant awareness of AIDS meant that sex was on some very tangible, physical level associated not just with "risky behavior" but with death itself. And for closeted young gay men, these associative feelings of self-loathing and fear were so strong that traces of them would survive long after the catharsis of coming out. We were either so demonized or pitied by the mainstream—in news reporting as well as entertainment—that it was difficult for me to conceive of myself as a future individual. I would, I feared, forever be a type—and for someone for whom movies were everything, types were paramount, as essential to the creation of one's social self-definition as genre is in the classifying of VHS boxes.

I recall my own experience not because it was in any way unique; quite the contrary. A fear of sex was part and parcel of the media we consumed at the height of the epidemic, from teen comedies to erotic thrillers, and it was a mindset that had to be broken if people of my generation were to live anything resembling healthy, proud existences. Movies were not only an "escape from reality" but a means of liberating oneself from the shame of the body—the people on-screen were beautiful and confident, they wanted to touch and be touched. The Code was just one method of regulating sex, but as anyone knows, any attempt by a governing body—in politics, parenthood, entertainment—to censor human nature and freedom always ends up fevering the imaginations of those most suppressed. The era of the Production Code may have taken a red pencil to moviemaking, but it left a scarlet smear of eros in its wake: its barely submerged eroticism still makes us lusty.

As someone who's been greedily imbibing cinema since childhood, I only grad-ually came to realize how much of me both wasn't and was in them. The movies that were most enchanting—the ones I watched over and over until they were part of my emotional makeup—were never intended, I thought, to reflect anything about me or my world. Later, I saw that even the most seemingly fanciful of these movie fixa-tions were not reflecting the contours of my experience but creating them. This was true of *Vertigo*, a descent into a sexual obsession I could never (and probably still don't entirely) understand; of *Singin' in the Rain*, an expression of joy so manic and unrestrained that it couldn't be of this earth; of *2001: A Space Odyssey*, a voyage to the outer limits of space and human knowledge. And if these movies became a part of me, an essential ingredient in how I would forever identify myself, then all the movies that mattered would be expressions of my deepest self. If I'm queer, then so are they.

We're jigsaw puzzles of what we watch, hear, learn, love, and hate. It's hard to envision myself—my pride, my fear, my shame—without Martha Dobie some-where upstairs in my mind's attic.

It was only partway through writing this book that I had a sudden flashback to the moment I first encountered *The Children's Hour*. I was probably no older than ten, visiting my grandmother at her apartment at the senior adult community in Newton, Massachusetts, where she lived during my entire childhood. Bustling in and out of the kitchen, preparing lunch for my family, Grandma Bertha had the television tuned to PBS. Stopped in my tracks as I often was by movies on TV, I saw an image of a snotty-looking little girl sitting in the back seat of a town car. Next to her was an old woman wearing a well-maintained expression of imperiousness, which quickly faded when the little girl began whispering in her ear. The woman's face fell, a look of horror overtaking her.

At that moment, my grandmother walked past the television toward the lunch table, likely carrying a basket of challah or a jar of pickles. She briefly stopped, turned to the TV, and pointed at the little girl.

"That one"—she wagged her finger—"she's a troublemaker."

I didn't have time to ask further questions, as Grandma Bertha was already back in the kitchen.

I remember in that moment wanting to know what that little troublemaker was telling this older woman, clearly her grandmother. What could have made her so disgusted and aghast? And what about my own grandmother, a movie devotee since the silent era? She seemed to know so well the plot of this random black-and-white movie, and was so struck by the sight of little Karen Balkin's naughty, pouty face that she felt the need to editorialize about it even while engaged in the important task of preparing food.

Whatever this queer little movie was, its dark secrets had stayed with her, decades later. In her own way, she was haunted by *The Children's Hour*. Was it because the film showed, per Lillian Hellman, "the power of a lie"? Was it because it demonstrated the destructiveness of one bratty kid? My grandmother has long passed, so I cannot ask her, but I am going to guess it was something more jarring and specific and likely inarticulable. *The Children's Hour* stuck in her mind because no other film in her day had ever dared to surface the realities it did.

When I finally saw the movie in its entirety many years later, I would bring my own psychological baggage to the experience. In the closet, I saw myself in Martha, however much I may have denied it. Yet my response was somehow similar to my grandmother's. For both of us, this was a movie that stirred up trouble, insisting on communicating with us down through the years. *The Children's Hour* dredged up something unclean, wrong, a sick and dirty past that was still very much present. Like it or not.

ACKNOWLEDGMENTS

This book culminates nearly a decade of exploring the history and meaning of queer cinema. My fondest regards and deepest thanks to my agent Farley Chase; he doesn't just consistently believe in me—he believes that what I want to write and say will matter to others, and that there is still a place for serious critical and historical film writing. The same can clearly be said for the pair of exacting editors who helped tag team this book to print at Bloomsbury: Ben Hyman, who brought me on, and Callie Garnett, who kept it alive. Their perception and enthusiasm gave me the boosts of confidence I needed throughout. Also, shout-outs to Jillian Ramirez, Laura Phillips, Marie Coolman, Lauren Moseley, Olivia Treynor, Laura Wilson, and the whole Bloomsbury brain trust.

I feel it only appropriate to acknowledge the various editors, colleagues, and fellow travelers who enabled this book's development—whether they know it or not: editor Nicolas Rapold for first indulging my biweekly Queer & Now & Then column for *Film Comment* magazine so many years ago, and to the fine folks at the Criterion Collection for allowing me to delve into these histories in curating, hosting, and writing for my Queersighted series on the Criterion Channel, especially Peter Becker, Kim Hendrickson, Elizabeth Helfgott, Andrew Chan, Aliza Ma, Ashley Clark, and Penelope Bartlett. A special shout-out to Grant Delin for always making me look good—literally.

Thanks to Genevieve Yue at the New School's Eugene Lang College of Liberal Arts for first allowing me to teach on the topic, and to Susan Sandler for making this happen again at NYU's Tisch School of the Arts, my alma mater. As is clear from page one, the give-and-takes I had with students in those classes deeply informed this book and became a catalyst for writing it. So, my gratitude extends to each of those engaged and participatory people, for opening my mind to how a new generation views films that might be otherwise written off.

Huge thank you to my friends and colleagues at Museum of the Moving Image, past and present, who have all been encouraging and helpful, including—but not limited to—Aziz Isham, Carl Goodman, Tomoko Kawamoto, Elaine Bowen, Katie

Kita, Edo Choi, and especially Barbara Miller for her guidance on the history of the Astoria Studios. To the Museum's founding director Rochelle Slovin and her husband Edmund Leites, for their bracing advocacy of my work and friendship. To Michael Barker for his knowledge of and eternal adoration for classical Hollywood cinema (and the queer histories of Edward Dmytryk). And to Eric Hynes, who merits special mention for his unflagging friendship and support throughout my entire writing and editing career.

My acute joy at rummaging through archives—and discovering so many treasures—was made possible by a host of beyond-helpful folks: Genevieve Maxwell, Louise Hilton, Matt Severson, and Ben Del Vecchio at the Margaret Herrick Library at the Academy of Motion Picture Arts & Sciences; Gabriela Sanchez and Amy Armstrong at the Harry Ransom Center at University of Texas, Austin; and Maxwell Zupke at UCLA Library Special Collections. And deepest thanks to the dear ones who housed, fed, and hung out with me during those archive trips: David Connelly and Maxi Witrak; Danielle McCarthy and Brian Boles; Suzanne Scott and Luke Pebler—your gracious hospitality made it all possible. Also, thanks to the meticulous research collection staff at the New York Public Library for the Performing Arts.

Many others have been immeasurably helpful in getting this book to where it ended up. My sincerest thanks and admiration to all of them, but especially Tony Kushner for his invigorating and thrilling conversation; Shonni Enelow for her exquisite feedback; Jenni Olson, Andrea Weiss, and Michael Lumpkin for their invaluable perspectives on the work and life of Vito Russo; and Jane Schoenbrun for our winding discussions on the meaning of queer cinema.

Bushels of thank-yous to Melissa Anderson, Kameron Collins, Caden Mark Gardner, Michael Garofalo, Mark Harris, Dennis Lim, Roberta Mercuri, Adam Nayman, Asha Phelps, Jeff Reichert, Mayukh Sen, Imogen Sara Smith, and Farihah Zaman for various combinations of friendship, assistance, and inspiration.

And finally, above all, there is Chris Wisniewski, who sees everything so clearly. To be married to someone so loving, supportive, and legitimately brilliant is a gift I hope to one day be able to reckon with.

NOTES

INTRODUCTION: TELL US HOW YOU REALLY FEEL

There is a wealth of writing, research, scholarship, and statistics out there on the issue of the ongoing trauma—systemic and residual—experienced by gay, lesbian, bisexual, and transgender Americans, especially youths. The issue remains so prevalent and all-consuming for so many lives that this chapter's insistence on the falseness of a "post-gay" America might seem to some unnecessary or at least overly defensive. Yet for those of us who experienced adolescence in the 1990s and came of adulthood in the early years of the twenty-first century, there had been a genuine feeling in the culture that the bad old days were done and the political gains had produced an end. It hasn't, and the struggle isn't over. My eternal regard for the work of Amin Ghaziani in elucidating the true meaning of a "post-gay" collective identity in the era of queer assimilation; Walt Odets for his enlightening work on persistent gay male trauma; and, on the more theoretical side, Heather Love for her brilliant writing reclaiming the "backwards" feeling inherent in queer life, and, of course, Eve Kosofsky Sedgwick, whose work can, I believe, lay claim to generating these conversations in the first place. All of the above were also crucial in helping me think through my syllabi for the Queerness in American Cinema classes I taught at NYU and The New School, the experiences of which directly led to the conception of *Sick and Dirty*.

Vito Russo's book *The Celluloid Closet* was necessarily crucial, to both work with and occasionally push back against, as was the biographical writing on Russo by Michael Schiavi in *Celluloid Activist*. Yet I couldn't have properly understood the full commitment and emotional effect without the interviews I was able to conduct with those who knew him personally and who also worked in the nascent queer film scene of the 1980s, Michael Lumpkin, Jenni Olson, and Andrea Weiss. A word must go out to the late Robert Sklar, a legend in the film studies field whom I was lucky to have as an undergrad professor at NYU. There's a surfeit of writing on the industrial and cultural history of American cinema, but nothing as stubbornly trenchant as Sklar's *Movie-Made America*, which was a reference and guiding light for this book.

CHAPTER 1: THE ORIGINAL SIN

Lillian Hellman's life and work have been so fully and richly documented and puzzled over by so many biographers and scholars that I was nervous I might not uncover anything not already pored over by previous authors. Luckily, the copious Lillian Hellman archives at the Harry Ransom Center at the University of Texas at Austin offered a hearty number of poignant surprises that shed light not only on Hellman's process but also the cultural realities of the era in which she worked. Hellman's scrapbooks and hoarded mementos were wildly helpful and insightful, and I fear my phone is overburdened with snapshots of articles, letters, and midcentury memos that I will never want to delete. Otherwise, I am indebted to the biographical work of Dorothy Gallagher, Alice Kessler-Harris, Deborah Martinson, Joan Mellen, and William Wright, who helped untangle the details of this complicated and often highly divisive personage. Of course, Hellman's own memoirs, which defined the final decades of her career, were entertaining and instrumental—even if one must take them with the occasionally large grain of salt. Meanwhile, the queer sociocultural moment in which Hellman wrote her 1934 play *The Children's Hour* was made vivid by the work of George Chauncey, whose *Gay New York: Gender, Urban Culture, and the Making of the Gay Male World, 1890–1940* is a rightful milestone.

CHAPTER 2: THE CHILDREN

Lillian Hellman's re-arrival in Los Angeles and William Wyler's concurrent ascendance into the upper ranks of the industry both coincided with the coalescing of Hollywood into its untouchable golden age—which also coincided, for better and worse, with the entrenchment of the Motion Picture Production Code under Joseph Breen's iron grip. With so much ground to cover, this chapter would have been unthinkable without the comprehensive and inspirational touchstone work by Sklar, Neal Gabler (*An Empire of Their Own*), A. Scott Berg (*Goldwyn: A Biography*), and the William Wyler scholarship by Jan Herman, Gabriel Miller, and Axel Madsen.

A leading light here and throughout is the marvelous work by Thomas Doherty (*Hollywood's Censor: Joseph I. Breen & the Production Code Administration*), whose detailed account of the foundation of the Hays Code and the rise of self-regulated censorship in Hollywood should be on the shelf of anyone who cares about how Hollywood worked. Rounding things out are writings by Allan Ellenberger on Miriam Hopkins and Mayukh Sen on Merle Oberon. Any dots, here and elsewhere, were filled in by findings at the Margaret Herrick Library at the Academy of Motion Pictures Arts and Sciences, whose elegantly maintained and wonderfully accessible Production Code Administration files are just one highlight of a vast and thrilling trove.

CHAPTER 3: SUITABLE WOMEN

What we know—or think we know—about Dorothy Arzner is because of the heroic scholarship of Judith Mayne, whose book *Directed by Dorothy Arzner* set the template for decades of study and appreciation of the private Hollywood director. Yet it was a treat to uncover more invaluable photos, clippings, essays, interviews, and letters in the Dorothy Arzner Papers at the UCLA Library Special Collections. Meanwhile, the critical writing on Arzner in the seventies by the likes of Molly Haskell, Claire Johnston, Karyn Kay, and Gerald Peary laid the groundwork for any serious appreciation of the director as auteur. The definition and function of lesbian life in the late nineteenth and early twentieth century, as both political construct and sexual identity, were delineated and interpreted in books by Carroll Smith-Rosenberg (*Disorderly Conduct: Gender in Victorian America*) and Laura Horak (*Girls Will Be Boys: Cross-Dressed Women, Lesbians, and American Cinema, 1908–1934*) and essays by Sherrie Innes and Esther Newton. Even more central for these purposes are the cornerstone books on lesbian cinematic representation by Andrea Weiss (*Vampires and Violets*) and Patricia White (*Uninvited*). Apologies for the persistence of "gaze" in this chapter; I may be guilty, Laura Mulvey is not!

CHAPTER 4: CAPABLE MEN

Interweaving the personal and professional stories of Richard Brooks, Arthur Laurents, Farley Granger, and Alfred Hitchcock would never have been possible without the extant published work on each of these artists. I'm only glad that we have such witty and wildly unfettered autobiographical writing from Laurents and

Granger, whose *Original Story* and *Include Me Out*, respectively, are fine specimens of heedless self-exposure. I wish I could have made room for Granger's sexual encounters with Hellman frenemy Leonard Bernstein. Brooks's *The Brick Foxhole* remains a pugnacious revelation, and does more to explain his psyche than any bio could. For Brooks scholarship, one needs Douglass K. Daniel; for Robert Ryan, there is J. R. Jones. For Hitchcock, there is, alas, so much that it's almost essential to cast it aside. Nevertheless, Patrick McGilligan's hefty and entertaining *Alfred Hitchcock: A Life in Darkness and Light* was enormously helpful in getting it all straight, while Edward White's more recent *The Twelve Lives of Alfred Hitchcock* persuaded me in thinking there are more stories to tell. (And one cannot engage with Hitchcock in any playful way without diving into the interpretive depths of D. A. Miller.) The sometimes contentious facts around Hitchcock's wartime cinematic output and his participation in shaping the concentration camp documentary footage were given due (and unresolved) attention by McGilligan and Ulrike Weckel, with the Imperial War Museums' Toby Haggith and Peter Tanner important voices.

For postwar American masculinity and the post-Kinsey era, I turned to historical reportage and scholarship by Allan Bérubé, Vern Burrough, Chris Cagle, David K. Johnston, Regina Markell Morantz-Sanchez, and others noted in the bibliography, past and present. The Herrick Library's files proved essential for sorting out the do-gooder antics of Dore Schary and company in the production of *Crossfire*, helping set the stage for the coming decade of baby steps toward timid liberal reform. And speaking of what's on the horizon: personal writing by Adrian Scott and Edward Dmytryk helped situate *Crossfire* in the saga of the Hollywood Left, who were about to be cannon fodder for the opportunistic ascendant Right.

CHAPTER 5: MUSICAL INTERLUDE

Judy Garland needs no introduction—nor does she need more tragedienne sob stories. We'll leave that to the comprehensively heartbreaking work by Gerald Clarke and Gerold Frank. Richard Dyer's analysis "Judy Garland and Gay Men" is a central text not only in my consideration of Garland but also in how one relates any life to any popular art, and how one's identity can be shaped by cultural forces that might be beyond our control. Even less extricable from my overall critical thinking is D. A. Miller's deeply pleasurable journey into the symbiosis between gay men and musical theater, *Place for Us*, which has helped me burrow even deeper into how my own sexual identity functions as a cultural reality—and also makes me fully appreciate just how much beautiful, mischievous critical language can benefit me by short-circuiting my normal faculties. His book is as pivotal to the understanding of musicals as the cinematic studies on the subject by Rick Altman and Jane Feuer. The case of Cukor was illuminated by McGilligan and Emmanuel Levy's biographies as well as by Boze Hadleigh's fearless interviews in the 1980s, and preservationist Ronald Haver thankfully narrativized his valorous reconstruction of *A Star Is Born* in book form so that future generations like us could understand how something that went so wrong now seems so, so right.

CHAPTER 6: BACK TO SCHOOL

Lillian Hellman's treatment at the hands of the House Un-American Activities Committee and her battles with them form the centerpiece of much of her subsequent life's work—and, as many would claim, her self-mythologizing. We have a strong enough sense of her actions and thoughts, thanks to her accounts in her bestseller *Scoundrel Time*, as well as the sharp-pointed takedowns she published at the time, calling out cowards in the face of HUAC's oppression. Biographers Wright, Gallagher, and Martinson help contextualize all this historical trauma, and further shine a light on *The Children's Hour*'s critique of the abuse of power and the disappointments of American conformity. *Tea and Sympathy* has been less written about in any long-form way, outside of crucial chapters in volumes and biographies on Vincente Minnelli, with special shout-out to David A. Gerstner's essay "The Production and Display of the Closet: Making Minnelli's *Tea and Sympathy*." The Herrick Library files proved a revelation in this case, with their thorough cataloguing of the almost exhilaratingly frustrating back-and-forth between MGM and the Production Code Administration over *Tea and Sympathy*. Meanwhile, Minnelli, cagey and tight-lipped though he may have been, did leave us with an entertaining autobiography, *I Remember It Well*, a book that declines easy engagement with normal codes of masculinity.

CHAPTER 7: AMERICA'S NIGHTMARE

Perhaps even more ink has been spilled and suppositions made about Tennessee Williams than Lillian Hellman, so I am thankful—as have been so many—that John Lahr's *Tennessee Williams: Mad Pilgrimage of the Flesh* exists. Then there are

Williams's priceless *Memoirs*, which allow the reader to luxuriate in the nonlinear rumblings of a mind nearing the end of a desperately great career. Both were inestimable in helping me understand Williams's eternal tethering to his sister Rose, and therefore my comprehension of the gruesome ecstasies of *Suddenly, Last Summer*, whose queerness remains the trickiest to define out of all the films in this book. Nevertheless, its unsettled nature doesn't stop Williams from being such a fundamental figure in the creation of a modern cinema quietly letting queerness seep in, especially as a post-Breen PCA was loosening up to an alarming degree, as evidenced by Herrick's files. Barton R. Palmer and William Robert Bray's *Hollywood's Tennessee: The Williams Films and Postwar America* is prime evidence of Williams's centrality to this period of moviemaking. Thrilling autobiographical accounts of the period by Elia Kazan and Gore Vidal help color in some of Williams's lines, as do details gleaned from the starry lives of Montgomery Clift, Elizabeth Taylor, Katharine Hepburn, and Joe Mankiewicz. But all you really need is Tennessee.

CHAPTER 8: DOWN AND DIRTIER

How thoughtful of bosom buddies Lillian Hellman and William Wyler to embark on a resentful battle royale on their last project together. It was certainly a charming discovery for me as I scoured through reams of personal letters and legal memos kept at both the Harry Ransom Center and the Herrick Library regarding the making of 1961 version of *The Children's Hour*, their at-odds relationship providing both evidence of what went wrong with the eventual movie and a gripping climax for this book. Piecing the correspondences together chronologically was at times a challenge, coming as they did from two separate archives, yet there's nothing like cleanly dated, typed letters of grievance from the midcentury to assuage any and all doubts about intent. If only, after all that, *The Children's Hour* had proven a success for its beleaguered duo. Interviews and biographies about Shirley MacLaine and Audrey Hepburn provided only bare-bones information about a film that wasn't much loved in their day. Its time is still to come.

BIBLIOGRAPHY

BOOKS

Adler, Thomas P. *Robert Anderson*. Purdue University. Twayne Publishers. G. K. Hall. Boston. 1978.

Altman, Rick. *The American Film Musical*. Indiana University Press. Bloomington. 1987.

Anderson, Robert. *Tea and Sympathy*. Random House (first edition). New York. 1953.

Auiler, Dan. *Hitchcock's Notebooks*. Spike Books. New York. 1999.

Bach, Stephen. *Marlene Dietrich: Life and Legend*. University of Minnesota Press. Minneapolis and London. 1992.

Balio, Tino. *The American Film Industry*. University of Wisconsin Press. Madison. 1976/1985.

Balio, Tino, ed. *Grand Design: Hollywood as a Modern Business Enterprise, 1930–1939*. University of California Press. 1993.

Barnes, Djuna. *Nightwood*. Harcourt, Brace. New York. 1937.

Barrios, Richard. *Screened Out: Playing Gay in Hollywood from Edison to Stonewall*. Routledge. New York and London. 2003.

Benshoff, Harry, and Sean Griffin. *Queer Images: A History of Gay and Lesbian Film in America*. Rowman & Littlefield Publishers. Oxford. 2006.

Berg, A. Scott. *Goldwyn: A Biography*. Alfred A. Knopf. New York. 1989.

Bérubé, Allan. "Marching to a Different Drummer: Lesbian and Gay GIs in World War II." In *My Desire for History: Essays in Gay, Community, and Labor History*. Eds. John D'Emilio and Estelle B. Freedman. University of North Carolina Press. Chapel Hill. 2011.

Blount, Jackie M. "School Workers." In *LGBTQ Issues in Education: Advancing a Research Agenda*. Ed. George L. Wimberly. American Educational Research Association. 2015.

Bosworth, Patricia. *Montgomery Clift: A Biography*. Harcourt Brace Jovanovich. New York and London. 1978.

Brooks, Richard. *The Brick Foxhole*. Harper and Brothers Publishers. New York and London. 1945.

Bryer, Jackson R. *Conversations with Lillian Hellman*. University Press of Mississippi. Jackson and London. 1986.

Butler, Isaac. *The Method: How the Twentieth Century Learned to Act*. Bloomsbury Publishing. 2022.

Cagle, Chris. "Rough Trade: Sexual Taxonomy in Postwar America." In *RePresenting Bisexualities: Subjects and Cultures of Fluid Desire*. Eds. Donald E. Hall and Maria Pramaggiore. NYU Press. New York. 1996.

Casillo, Charles. *Elizabeth and Monty: The Untold Story of Their Intimate Friendship*. Kensington Books. New York. 2021.

Chauncey, George. *Gay New York: Gender, Urban Culture, and the Making of the Gay Male World, 1890–1940*. Basic Books. Perseus Books Group. 1994.

Clarke, Gerald. *Get Happy: The Life of Judy Garland*. Delta. 2001.

Cohen, Paula Marantz. *Alfred Hitchcock: The Legacy of Victorianism*. University Press of Kentucky. 1995.

Connelly, Mark, Jo Fox, Stefan Goebel, and Ulf Schmidt, eds. *Propaganda and Conflict: War, Media, and Shaping the Twentieth Century*. Bloomsbury Academic. 2019.

D'Emilio, John. *Making Trouble: Essays on Gay History, Politics, and the University*. Routledge. New York & London. 1992.

Daniel, Douglass K. *Tough as Nails: The Life and Films of Richard Brooks*. University of Wisconsin Press. Madison. 2011.

Dauth, Brian, ed. *Joseph L. Mankiewicz Interviews*. University Press of Mississippi. 2008.

Dick, Bernard F. *Hellman in Hollywood*. Associated University Presses. 1982.

Dmytryk, Edward. *Odd Man Out: A Memoir of the Hollywood Ten*. Southern Illinois University Press. 1996.

Doherty, Thomas. *Hollywood's Censor: Joseph I. Breen & the Production Code Administration*. Columbia University Press. 2007.

———. *Pre-Code Hollywood: Sex, Immorality, and Insurrection in American Cinema, 1930–1934*. Columbia University Press. New York. 1999.

Doty, Alexander. *Making Things Perfectly Queer*. University of Minnesota Press. Minneapolis and London. 1993.

Dyer, Richard. *Heavenly Bodies: Film Stars and Society*. Routledge. London and New York. 1986.

———. *Now You See It: Studies on Lesbian and Gay Film*. With Julianne Pidduck. Routledge. London and New York. 1990.

Edwards, Anne. *A Remarkable Woman: A Biography of Katharine Hepburn*. William Morrow. New York. 1985.

Ellenberger, Allan R. *Miriam Hopkins: Life and Films of a Hollywood Rebel*. University Press of Kentucky. Lexington. 2018.

Enelow, Shonni. *Method Acting and Its Discontents*. Northwestern University Press. Evanston. 2015.

Euripides. *The Bacchae of Euripides*. A new translation with a critical essay by Donald Sutherland. University of Nebraska Press. 1968.

Feuer, Jane. *The Hollywood Musical* (second edition). Indiana University Press. Bloomington and Indianapolis. 1993.

Fishgall, Gary. *Pieces of Time: The Life of James Stewart*. Lisa Drew Book/Scribner. New York. 1997.

Forman, Henry James. *Our Movie Made Children*. MacMillan. New York. 1985.

Frank, Gerold. *Judy*. Harper & Row. New York. 1975.

Freedland, Michael. *Shirley MacLaine*. Salem House. 1986.

Gabler, Neal. *An Empire of Their Own*. Anchor Books. Random House. 1988.

Gallagher, Dorothy. *Lillian Hellman: An Imperious Life*. Yale University Press. New Haven. 2014.

Garber, Linda. *Identity Poetics: Race, Class, and the Lesbian-Feminist Roots of Queer Theory*. Columbia University Press. New York. 2001.

Gardner, Caden Mark, and Willow Catelyn Maclay. *Corpses, Fools and Monsters: The History and Future of Transness in Cinema*. Repeater Books. 2024.

Gates, Racquel J. *Double Negative: The Black Image & Popular Culture*. Duke University Press. 2018.

Gerstner, David A. "The Production and Display of the Closet: Making Minnelli's *Tea and Sympathy*." In *Vincente Minnelli: The Art of Entertainment*. Ed. Joe McElhaney. 275–294. Wayne State University Press.

Ghaziani, Amin. *There Goes the Gayborhood?* Princeton University Press. New York. 2014.

Gitlin, Martin. *Audrey Hepburn: A Biography*. Greenwood Publishing Group. Westport. 2009.

Gottlieb, Sidney, ed. *Alfred Hitchcock Interviews*. University Press of Mississippi. 2023.

Granger, Farley (with Robert Calhoun). *Include Me Out*. St. Martin's Griffin. New York. 2007.

Griffin, Mark. *A Hundred or More Hidden Things: The Life and Films of Vincente Minnelli*. Da Capo Press. 2010.

Hadleigh, Boze. *Conversations with My Elders*. St. Martin's Press. New York. 1986.

Hall, Radclyffe. *The Well of Loneliness*. Sun Dial Press. Garden City, NY. 1928.

Hamilton, Ian. *Writers in Hollywood: 1915–1951*. Harper & Row. 1990.

Hamilton, Patrick. *Rope*. Samuel French. New York and London. 1929.

Harris, Mark. *Pictures at a Revolution*. Penguin Press. New York. 2008.

Harvey, Stephen. *Directed by Vincente Minnelli*. HarperCollins. New York. 1990.

Haver, Ronald. *A Star Is Born: The Making of the 1954 Movie and Its 1983 Restoration*. Alfred A. Knopf. New York. 1988.

Hellman, Lillian. *Four Plays by Lillian Hellman*. Modern Library. New York. 1942.

———. *Pentimento*. Little, Brown. Boston. 1973.

———. *Scoundrel Time*. Little, Brown. Boston. 1976.

———. *An Unfinished Woman*. Little, Brown. Boston. 1969.

———. *Six Plays by Lillian Hellman*. Vintage Books. New York. 1979.

Herman, Jan. *A Talent for Trouble: The Life of Hollywood's Most Acclaimed Director, William Wyler*. G. P. Putnam's Sons. New York. 1995.

Higdon, Hal. *Leopold and Loeb: The Crime of the Century*. University of Illinois Press. Champaign, IL. Originally published by G. P. Putnam's Sons. 1975/2023.

Higham, Charles. *Lucy: The Life of Lucille Ball*. St. Martin's Press. New York. 1987.

Higham, Charles and Ron Moseley. *Princess Merle: The Romantic Life of Merle Oberon*. Coward-McCann. New York. 1983.

Hirshman, Linda. *Victory: The Triumphant Gay Revolution*. HarperCollins. 2012.

Horak, Laura. *Girls Will Be Boys: Cross-Dressed Women, Lesbians, and American Cinema, 1908–1934*. Rutgers University Press. 2016.

Inglis, Ruth A. "The Production Code: Self-Regulation in Action." In *The American Film Industry*. Ed. Tino Balio. 377–400. University of Wisconsin Press. Madison. 1976/1985.

Johnson, David K. "America's Cold War Empire: Exporting the Lavender Scare." In *Global Homophobia: States, Movements, and the Politics of Oppression*. Eds. Meredith L. Weiss and Michael J. Bosia. University of Illinois Press. 2013.

Johnston, Claire. "Women's Cinema as Counter Cinema." *Feminist Film Theory: A Reader*. Ed. Sue Thornham. Edinburgh University Press. 1999.

Jones, J. R. *The Lives of Robert Ryan*. Wesleyan University Press. Middletown. 2014.

Kael, Pauline. *I Lost It at the Movies*. Little, Brown. Boston. 1965.

Kalem, Ted. "Tennessee Williams: 'The Agent of the Odd.'" *Time*. March 9, 1962.

Kanfer, Stefan. *Ball of Fire: The Tumultuous Life and Comic Art of Lucille Ball*. Alfred A. Knopf. New York. 2003.

Kazan, Elia. *Elia Kazan: A Life*. Alfred A. Knopf. New York. 1988.

Kessler-Harris, Alice. *A Difficult Woman: The Challenging Life and Times of Lillian Hellman*. Bloomsbury Press. New York. 2012.

Koresky, Michael, ed. *From Silent Films to Streaming: 100 Years of History at Kaufman Astoria Studios*. Museum of the Moving Image. New York. 2023.

Lahr, John. *Tennessee Williams: Mad Pilgrimage of the Flesh*. W. W. Norton and Company. New York and London. 2014.

Langdon, Jennifer. *Caught in the Crossfire: Adrian Scott and the Politics of Americanism in 1940s Hollywood*. Columbia University Press. New York. 2009.

Lasky, Jesse. *Whatever Happened to Hollywood?* Funk & Wagnalls. New York. 1973.

Laurents, Arthur. *Original Story: A Memoir of Broadway and Hollywood*. Applause Books. New York and London. 2000.

Leaming, Barbara. *Katharine Hepburn*. Crown. New York. 1995.

Levy, Emmanuel. *George Cukor: Master of Elegance*. William Morrow. New York. 1994.

Leyda, Jay, ed. *Filmmakers Speak*. Da Capo Press. 1984.

Love, Heather. *Feeling Backward*. Harvard University Press. 2007.

Madsen, Axel. *William Wyler*. Thomas Y. Crowell. New York. 1973.

Mann, William J. *Behind the Screen: How Gays and Lesbians Shaped Hollywood 1910–1969*. Viking. 2002.

Martinson, Deborah. *Lillian Hellman: A Life with Foxes and Scoundrels*. Counterpoint. Berkeley. 2005.

Mayne, Judith. *Directed by Dorothy Arzner*. Indiana University Press. Bloomington. 1995.

McGilligan, Patrick. *Alfred Hitchcock: A Life in Darkness and Light*. ReganBooks. 2003.
———. *A Double Life: George Cukor*. St. Martin's Press. 1991.

Mellen, Joan. *Hellman and Hammett: The Legendary Passion of Lillian Hellman and Dashiell Hammett*. HarperCollins. New York. 1996.

Miller, D. A. *Hidden Hitchcock*. University of Chicago Press. 2016.
———. *Place for Us*. Harvard University Press. Cambridge and London. 1998.

Miller, Gabriel. *William Wyler: The Life and Films of Hollywood's Most Celebrated Director*. University Press of Kentucky. Lexington. 2013.

Minnelli, Vincente. *I Remember It Well*. Angus & Robertson. UK. 1975.

Mordden, Ethan. *The American Theatre*. Oxford University Press. New York. 1981.

Odets, Walt. *Out of the Shadows: Reimagining Gay Men's Lives*. Picador. New York. 2019.

Palmer, R. Barton, and William Robert Bray. *Hollywood's Tennessee: The Williams Films and Postwar America*. University of Texas Press. Austin. 2009.

Paris, Barry. *Audrey Hepburn*. Berkley Books. New York. 1996.

Potter, Susan. *Queer Timing: The Emergence of Lesbian Sexuality in Early Cinema*. University of Illinois Press. 2019.

Powell, Ryan. *Coming Together: The Cinematic Elaboration of Gay Male Life, 1945–1979*. University of Chicago Press. 2019.

Revault d'Allonnes, Judith. "Garden Conversations with Todd Haynes: From Childhood to Superstar: The Karen Carpenter Story." In *Todd Haynes: Rapturous Process*. Ed. Michael Koresky. 221–246. Museum of the Moving Image. New York. 2023.

Rich, B. Ruby. *New Queer Cinema: The Director's Cut*. Duke University Press. 2013.

Rich, Jennifer A. "(W)right in the Faultlines: The Problematic Identity of William Wyler's 'The Children's Hour.' In *The Queer Sixties*. Ed. Patricia Juliana Smith. 187–200. Routledge. New York and London. 1999.

Riva, Maria. *Marlene Dietrich: The Life*. Pegasus Books. New York. 1992.

Roughead, William. *Bad Companions*. Duffield & Green. New York. 1931. First edition: W. Green & Son. 1930.

Russo, Vito. *The Celluloid Closet*. Harper & Row. New York. 1981/1987.

Schiavi, Michael. *Celluloid Activist: The Life and Times of Vito Russo*. University of Wisconsin Press. Madison. 2011.

Sedgwick, Eve Kosofsky. *Epistemology of the Closet*. University of California Press. 1990, 2008.

Sen, Mayukh. *Love, Queenie: Merle Oberon, Hollywood's First South Asian Star*. W. W. Norton. New York and London. 2025.

Sklar, Richard. *Movie-Made America: A Cultural History of American Movies*. Vintage Books. Random House. 1975.

Smith, Patricia Juliana. *The Queer Sixties*. Routledge. New York and London. 1999.

Smith-Rosenberg, Carroll. *Disorderly Conduct: Gender in Victorian America*. Alfred A. Knopf. New York. 1985.

Soren, David. *Art, Popular Culture and the Classical Ideal in the 1930s: Two Classic Films* (includes the unfinished autobiography of Dorothy Arzner). Midnight Marquee Press. Baltimore. 2010.

Spoto, Donald. *Enchantment: The Life of Audrey Hepburn*. Harmony. 2006.

———. *The Kindness of Strangers: The Life of Tennessee Williams*. Little, Brown. Boston. 1985.

Stern, Sydney Ladensohn. *The Brothers Mankiewicz: Hope, Heartbreak, and Hollywood Classics*. University Press of Mississippi. 2019.

Studlar, Gaylyn. "Marlene Dietrich and the Erotics of Code-Bound Hollywood." In *Dietrich Icon*. Ed. Gerd Gemünden and Mary R. Desjardins. 211–238. Duke University Press. Durham and London. 2007.

Suarez, Juan. *Bike Boys, Drag Queens, and Superstars: Avant-Garde, Mass Culture, and Gay Identities in the 1960s Underground Cinema*. Indiana University Press. Bloomington. 1996.

Truffaut, François. *Hitchcock*. Simon & Schuster. New York. 1967. Revised 1985.

Vidal, Gore. *Palimpsest*. Penguin Books. 1995.

Walker, Michael. *Hitchcock's Motifs*. Amsterdam University Press. 2005.

Weckel, Ulrike. "People Who Once Were Human Beings Like You and Me: Why Allied Atrocity Films of Liberated Nazi Concentration Camps in 1944–46 Maximized the Horror and Universalized the Victims." In *Humanitarianism and Media: 1900 to the Present*. Ed. Johannes Paulmann. Berghahn Books. 2018.

Weiss, Andrea. *Vampires and Violets: Lesbians in Film*. Penguin Books. New York. 1992.

White, Edward. *The Twelve Lives of Alfred Hitchcock*. W. W. Norton. New York and London. 2021.

White, Patricia. *Uninvited*. Indiana University Press. Bloomington and Indianapolis. 1999.

Williams, Tennessee. *Memoirs*. University of the South. 1972, 1975.

———. *Suddenly, Last Summer*. Signet Books. 1958.

Wright, William. *Lillian Hellman*. Simon and Schuster. New York. 1986.

ARTICLES

Anderson, Robert. "Theatre; The Playwright; Some Reflections on the Unknown." *New York Herald Tribune*. August 5, 1956. Section IV. 3.

Archer, Eugene. "Code Amended to Allow Films to Deal with Homosexuality." *New York Times*. October 4, 1961.

Associated Press. "'Children's Hour' Banned in Boston." *New York Times*. December 15, 1935.

Associated Press. "Divorce for Judy Garland. Husband Made Her Ill When He Left Her Alone, She Says." *New York Times*. March 23, 1951.

Atkinson, Brooks. "At the Theatre." Review of *The Children's Hour* revival. *New York Times*. December 19. 1952.

———. "Theatre: 2 by Williams." Review of *Suddenly Last Summer*. *New York Times*. January 8, 1958.

———. "Lillian Hellman's First Drama Has Lost None of Its Power or Pertinence." *New York Times*. December 28. 1952.

Barry, Iris. *Daily Mail*. July 13, 1927.

Beebe, Lucius. "An Adult Hour Is Miss Hellman's Next Effort." *New York Herald Tribune*. December 13, 1936. Sec 7, 2. Reprinted in *Conversations with Lillian Hellman*. Ed. Jackson R. Bryer. University Press of Mississippi. Jackson and London. 1986.

Bengry, Justin. "Films and Filming: The Making of a Queer Marketplace in Predecriminalisation Britain." *British Queer History: New Approaches and Perspectives*. Ed. Brian Lewis. Manchester University Press. Manchester. 2013.

Blow, Charles M. "Yes, We're in an L.G.B.T.Q. State of Emergency." *New York Times*. June 7, 2023.

Brady, Thomas F. "Hollywood Tackles the Facts of Life; Several Films Being Made About Racial Issues." *New York Times*. March 16, 1947.

Brown, John Mason. "Two on the Aisle." *New York Post*. November 21, 1934.

Bullough, Vern. "Alfred Kinsey and the Kinsey Report: Historical Overview and Lasting Contributions." *The Journal of Sex Research*. Vol. 35, No. 2 (May 1988).

Bullough, Vern and Bonnie Bullough. "Lesbianism in the 1920s and 1930s: A Newfound Study." *Signs*. Vol. 2, No. 4 (Summer 1977).

Chapman, John. "The Right People." *Chicago Tribune*. December 22, 1934.

Chuba, Kirsten. "Francis Coppola Helps Paramount Dedicate Building to Pioneer Director Dorothy Arzner." *Variety*. March 1, 2018.

Churchill, David S. "The Queer Histories of a Crime: Representations and Narratives of Leopold and Loeb." *Journal of the History of Sexuality*. Vol. 18, No. 2 (May 2009).

Clarke, Mollie. "'Queer' history: A history of Queer." The National Archives Blog. February 9, 2021. https://blog.nationalarchives.gov.uk/queer-history-a-history-of -queer.

Collins, K. Austin. "The Signifyin' Works of Marlon Riggs: Positive Images." Criterion Collection. June 22, 2021.

Colman, David. "A Night Out with James Collard." *New York Times*. July 19, 1998.

Cousins, Russell. "Sanitizing Zola: Dorothy Arzner's Problematic 'Nana.'" *Literature/ Film Quarterly*. Vol. 23, No. 3 (1995).

Creelman, Eileen. "Picture Plays and Players: Lillian Hellman, Author of 'The Children's Hour,' Writes a Movie." *New York Sun*. July 7, 1935.

Crowther, Bosley. "The Screen: New 'Children's Hour.'" *New York Times*. March 15, 1962.

———. "'Crossfire' Study on Tolerance, Starring Robert Young and Robert Ryan, Opens at Rivoli." *New York Times*. July 23, 1947.

——. "Loosening the Code: Understanding 'Tea and Sympathy'." *New York Times.* October 7, 1956.

——. "'Rope,' an Exercise in Suspense Directed by Alfred Hitchcock, Is New Bill at the Globe." *New York Times.* August 27, 1948.

——. "Screen: 'Tea and Sympathy' Arrives." *New York Times.* September 28, 1956.

Fearing, Franklin. "Warriors Return: Normal or Neurotic?" *Hollywood Quarterly.* Vol. 1, No. 1 (October 1945).

Fine, Gary Alan. "Scandal, Social Conditions, and the Creation of Public Attention: Fatty Arbuckle and the 'Problem of Hollywood.'" *Social Problems.* Vol 44, No. 3 (August 1997). Oxford University Press.

Flatley, Guy. "At the Movies." Includes interview with Dorothy Arzner. *New York Times.* August 20, 1976.

Friedman, Lester D. and James M. Welsh. "A Very Narrow Path: The Politics of Edward Dmytryk." *Literature/Film Quarterly.* Vol. 12, No. 4 (1984).

Gaines, Jane. "Dorothy Arzner's Trousers." *Jump Cut: A Review of Contemporary Media.* No. 37 (July 1992).

Gardner, Fred. "An Interview with Lillian Hellman." Transcript of audio cassette, from Jeffrey Norton. Guilford, CT. 1968. Reprinted in *Conversations with Lillian Hellman.* Ed. Jackson R. Bryer. University Press of Mississippi. Jackson and London. 1986.

Ghaziani, Amin. "Post-Gay Collective Identity Construction." *Social Problems.* Vol. 58, No. 1 (February 2011).

Ghorayashi, Azeen, and Roni Caryn Rabin. "Teen Girls Report Record Levels of Sadness, C.D.C Finds." *New York Times.* February 13, 2023.

Gilroy, Harry. "The Bigger the Lie." *New York Times.* December 14, 1952.

Grant, Jack D. "*Crossfire* Dramatic Smash Indicting Anti-Semitism." *Hollywood Reporter.* June 25, 1947.

Greene, Mabel. "Miss Hellman Off to Coast. Successful Play Hasn't Made Her Blase." *New York Sun.* December 12, 1934.

Harrington, Curtis. "Personal Chronicle: The Making of an Experimental Film." *Hollywood Quarterly.* Vol. 4, No. 1 (Autumn 1949).

Haskell, Molly. "Wild Girls: Dorothy Arzner Started Out as a Typist at Paramount—and Ended Up a Trailblazing Director." *Guardian.* January 8, 2004.

——. "Women in Pairs." *Village Voice.* April 28, 1973.

Herman, Jan. "Interview with Shirley MacLaine." *Los Angeles Times.* March 19, 1991.

Hift, Fred. "Code Works, Schary Says." *Motion Picture Herald.* September 24, 1949.

Hobson, Janell. "Viewing in the Dark: Toward a Black Feminist Approach to Film." *Women's Studies Quarterly*. Vol. 30, No. 1/2 (Spring/Summer 2002).

Hoffman, Irving. "Interview with Robert Ryan." *Hollywood Reporter*. February 18, 1948.

Innes, Sherrie A. "Who's Afraid of Stephen Gordon? The Lesbian in the United States Popular Imagination of the 1920s." *NWSA Journal*. Vol. 4, No. 3 (Autumn 1992).

Jewel, Richard. "RKO Film Grosses: 1931–1951." *Historical Journal of Film, Radio, and Television*. Vol. 14. No. 1 (1994).

Kael, Pauline. "'The Innocents' and What Passes for Experience." *Film Quarterly*. Vol. 15, No. 4 (Summer 1962).

Kahan, Benjamin. "The Walk-in Closet: Situational Homosexuality and Homosexual Panic in Hellman's 'The Children's Hour.'" *Criticism*. Vol. 55, No. 2 (Spring 2013).

Kasman, Daniel. "German Concentration Camps Factual Survey: An Interview with Toby Haggith of Imperial War Museums." *Cineaste*. Vol. 40, No. 3 (2015).

Kay, Karyn, and Gerald Peary. "Dorothy Arzner's 'Dance, Girl, Dance.'" *Velvet Light Trap*. No. 10 (Fall 1973).

———. "Interview with Dorothy Arzner." *Cinema*. 1974. Reprinted in *The Work of Dorothy Arzner: Towards a Feminist Cinema*. Ed. Claire Johnston. British Film Institute. London. 1975.

Kazan, Elia. "Pressure Problem: Director Discusses Cuts Compelled in 'A Streetcar Named Desire.'" *New York Times*. October 21, 1951.

Kingsley, Grace. "Lasky Names Woman Director—Former Script Girl Is Cinderella of Megaphones." *Los Angeles Daily Times*. December 11, 1926.

Kirchick, James. "The Struggle for Gay Rights Is Over." *Atlantic*. June 28, 2019.

Koresky, Michael. "All I Desire: Rummaging Through the Barely Closeted History of the Notorious British Magazine *Films and Filming*." *Film Comment*. March-April 2019.

Leff, Leonard J., and Jerold L. Simmons. "The Narrative Scheme of 'Crossfire.'" *Literature/Film Quarterly*. Vol. 12, No. 3 (1984).

Lord, M. G. "Why Hollywood Owes a Debt of Gratitude to Gore Vidal (Appreciation)." *Hollywood Reporter*. August 9, 2012.

Maltin, Leonard. "Francis Ford Coppola Salutes His Teacher, Dorothy Arzner." Leonardmaltin.com. March 2, 2018.

Mercer, Benjamin. "The Final-Hour Preservation of *Dance, Girl, Dance* in Nitrate." Criterion Collection Current. August 10, 2020.

Meyer, Dan. "Bess Wohl Is Adapting Lillian Hellman's *The Children's Hour* for TV." *Playbill* online. October 12, 2021.

Miller, D. A. "Anal Rope." *Representations*. No. 32 (Autumn 1990).

————. "Visual Pleasure in 1959." *October*. Vol. 81 (Summer 1997).

Mitchell, John D. "Applied Psychoanalysis in the Drama." *American Imago*. Vol. 14, No. 3 (Fall 1957).

Mitgang, Herbert. "Robert Anderson: The Drama of Being a Dramatist." *New York Times*. June 12, 1988.

Morantz, Regina Markell. "The Scientist as Sex Crusader: Alfred C. Kinsey and American Culture." *American Quarterly*. Vol. 29, No. 5 (Winter 1977).

Morgan, Kim. "*Design for Living*: It Takes Three." The Criterion Collection. December 6, 2011.

Mulvey, Laura. "Visual Pleasure and Narrative Cinema." *Screen*. Volume 16, Issue 3 (Autumn 1975). Reprinted in *Film Theory and Criticism*. Ed. Leo Braudy and Marshall Cohen. Oxford University Press. Oxford and London. 1999.

Murphy, Mary. "Film Director Dorothy Arzner: Tribute to an Unsung Pioneer." *Los Angeles Times*. January 24, 1975.

Nash, Margaret A., and Jennifer A. R. Silverman. "An Indelible Mark: Gay Purges in Higher Education in the 1940s." *History of Education Quarterly*. Vol. 55, No. 4 (November 2015).

Newton, Esther. "The Mythic Mannish Lesbian: Radclyffe Hall and the New Woman." *Signs*. Vol. 9, No. 4 (Summer 1984).

Noriega, Chon. "'SOMETHING'S MISSING HERE!': Homosexuality and Film Reviews During the Production Code Era, 1934–1962." *Cinema Journal*. Vol. 30, No. 1 (Autumn 1990).

Nugent, Frank. "Heralding the Arrival of 'These Three,' at the Rivoli. *New York Times*. March 19, 1936.

O'Brien, Geoffrey. "*The Story of Temple Drake:* Notorious." Criterion Collection. December 3, 2019.

Othman, Frederick C. "Movie Player Eyes Art of Strip Tease." *Hollywood Citizen-News*. March 23, 1940.

Peak, Mayne Ober. "Only Woman Movie Director." *Boston Globe*. December 2, 1938.

Pryor, Thomas M. "MGM Solves Its 'Tea and Sympathy' Script Problem." *New York Times*. September 25, 1955.

Rensberger, Boyce. "AIDS Cases in 1985 Exceed Total of All Previous Years." *Washington Post*. January 16, 1986.

Roe, Amy. "Fighting Censorship of 'The Children's Hour' Set the Stage for the ACLU." ACLU Washington website blog. September 4, 2014. https://www.aclu-wa.org /blog/fighting-censorship-children-s-hour-set-stage-aclu.

Sarris, Andrew. "Notes on the Auteur Theory in 1962." *Film Culture*. Winter 1962–63. Reprinted in *Film Theory and Criticism*. Ed. Leo Braudy and Marshall Cohen. Oxford University Press. Oxford and London. 1999.

Scheuer, Philip K. "'Children's Hour' Woeful Film Saga." *Los Angeles Times*. December 20, 1961.

——. "Suddenly, Last Summer" review. *Los Angeles Times*. December 20, 1959.

Schulman, Michael. "Fatty Arbuckle and the Birth of the Celebrity Scandal." *New Yorker*. October 4, 2021.

Scott, Adrian. "Some of My Worst Friends." *Screen Writer*. October 1947.

Siegel, Janice. "Tennessee Williams' 'Suddenly Last Summer' and Euripides' 'Bacchae.'" *International Journal of the Classic Tradition*. Vol. 11, No. 4 (Spring 2005).

Terrall, Ben. "Book vs. Film: 'The Brick Foxhole' vs. 'Crossfire.'" *Noir City Magazine*. No. 30.

Thomson, David. "Ryan and Shaw." *Film Comment*. Vol. 30, No. 1 (January-February 1994).

Time magazine review of *Crossfire*. "Cinema: New Picture." August 4, 1947.

Time magazine review of *Sylvia Scarlet*. "Cinema: The New Pictures." January 13, 1936.

Time magazine review of *The Children's Hour*. "The Theatre: New Plays in Manhattan." December 3, 1934.

Tinkcom, Matthew. "Working Like a Homosexual: Camp Visual Codes and the Labor of Gay Subjects in the MGM Freed Unit." *Cinema Journal*. Vol. 35, No. 2 (Winter 1996).

Vicinus, Martha. "'They Wonder to Which Sex I Belong': The Historical Roots of the Modern Lesbian Identity." *Feminist Studies*. Vol. 18, No. 3 (Autumn 1992).

Watts Jr., Richard. "Sight and Sound: Forbidden Bypaths." *Herald Tribune*. December 16, 1934.

Weaver, William R. *Rope* review. *Motion Picture Daily*. August 26, 1948.

Wertheim, Albert. "The McCarthy Era and the American Theatre." *Theatre Journal*. Vol. 34, No. 2 (May 1982).

Whyte, Max. "The Uses and Abuses of Nietzsche in the Third Reich: Alfred Baeumler's 'Heroic Realism.'" *Journal of Contemporary History*. Vol. 43, No. 2 (April 2008).

Wilcox, Grace. "The Meaning of Glamour." *Screen & Radio Weekly*. May 19, 1935.

Williams, Tennessee. "Five Fiery Ladies: Tennessee Williams Tells of Heroines in His Dramas." *Life*. February 3, 1961.

——. "Williams' Well of Violence." *New York Times*. March 8, 1959.

Winsten, Archer. "Interview with Joseph L. Mankiewicz." *New York Post*. December 28, 1959.

Wood, Bret. "Foreign Correspondence: The Rediscovered War Films of Alfred Hitchcock." *Film Comment*. Vol. 29, No. 4 (July-August 1993).

CLIPS

Universal Newsreel: "Jos. Breen Says No One Man to Rule the Movies. Hollywood, Cal." September 19, 1934. (Available online from CriticalPast, a historic footage archive.)

AUDIO

Making Gay History podcast. Season 7, Episode 5: "Revisiting the Archive: Vito Russo." 1988 interview with Vito Russo by Eric Marcus. April 18, 2020.

McCabe, Allyson. "Some Advice from Filmmaker Cheryl Dunye: 'Keep Putting Yourself out Where You Belong.'" NPR. July 8, 2023.

GLOSSARY OF FILMS

Advise and Consent (Otto Preminger, 1962)

All About Eve (Joseph L. Mankiewicz, 1950)

All That Heaven Allows (Douglas Sirk, 1955)

An American in Paris (Vincente Minnelli, 1951)

Anatomy of a Murder (Otto Preminger, 1959)

Aventure Malgache (Alfred Hitchcock, 1944)

Baby Doll (Elia Kazan, 1956)

The Bad and the Beautiful (Vincente Minnelli, 1952)

Ben-Hur (William Wyler, 1959)

The Best Man (Franklin J. Schaffner, 1964)

The Best Years of Our Lives (William Wyler, 1946)

The Bicycle Thief (Vittorio De Sica, 1947)

Bon Voyage (Alfred Hitchcock, 1944)

The Boys in the Band (William Friedkin, 1969)

The Bride Wore Red (Dorothy Arzner, 1937)

Brokeback Mountain (Ang Lee, 2005)

Cabaret (Bob Fosse, 1972)

Cabin in the Sky (Vincente Minnelli, 1943)

Calamity Jane (David Butler, 1953)

Carol (Todd Haynes, 2015)

Cat on a Hot Tin Roof (Richard Brooks, 1958)

Cat People (Jacques Tourneur, 1942)

Cavalcade (Frank Lloyd, 1933)

The Celluloid Closet (Rob Epstein and Jeffrey Friedman, 1995)

The Children's Hour (William Wyler, 1961)

A Chorus Line (Richard Attenborough, 1985)

Christmas U.S.A. (Gregory J. Markopoulos, 1949)

Christopher Strong (Dorothy Arzner, 1933)

La Ciociara (*Two Women*, U.S.) (Vittorio De Sica, 1947)

The Cobweb (Vincente Minnelli, 1955)

The Color Purple (Steven Spielberg, 1985)

The Corn Is Green (Irving Rapper, 1945)

Crossfire (Edward Dmytryk, 1947)

Dance, Girl, Dance (Dorothy Arzner, 1940)

The Dark Angel (Sidney Franklin, 1935)

Dead End (William Wyler, 1937)

Design for Living (Ernst Lubitsch, 1933)

Detour (Edgar G. Ulmer, 1945)

La Dolce Vita (Federico Fellini, 1960)

Dorothy Arzner: Longing for Women (Katja Raganelli, 1983)

Double Indemnity (Billy Wilder, 1944)

Dr. Jekyll and Mr. Hyde (Rouben Mamoulian, 1931)

Far from Heaven (Todd Haynes, 2002)

Fireworks (Kenneth Anger, 1947)

For Me and My Gal (Busby Berkeley, 1942)

The Fox (Mark Rydell, 1967)

Fragment of Seeking (Curtis Harrington, 1946)

Gaslight (George Cukor, 1944)

Gentleman's Agreement (Elia Kazan, 1947)

German Concentration Camps Factual Survey / Memory of the Camps (Sidney Bernstein, 2014)

Gigi (Vincente Minnelli, 1958)

Gilda (Charles Vidor, 1946)

The Glass Menagerie (Irving Rapper, 1950)

The Harvey Girls (George Sidney, 1946)

The Heiress (William Wyler, 1949)

I Saw the TV Glow (Jane Schoenbrun, 2014)

It's Always Fair Weather (Stanley Donen/Gene Kelly, 1955)

Judgment at Nuremberg (Stanley Kramer, 1961)

Julia (Fred Zinnemann, 1977)

Laura (Otto Preminger, 1944)

The Little Foxes (William Wyler, 1941)

Love Is Strange (Ira Sachs, 2014)

Love, Simon (Greg Berlanti, 2018)

Mädchen in Uniform (Leontine Sagan, 1931)

The Magnificent Ambersons (Orson Welles, 1942)

The Maltese Falcon (John Huston, 1941)

The Man with the Golden Arm (Otto Preminger, 1955)

Meet Me in St. Louis (Vincente Minnelli, 1944)

Men of the Lightship (David MacDonald, 1940)

Merrily We Go to Hell (Dorothy Arzner, 1932)

The Merry Widow (Ernst Lubitsch, 1934)

Milk (Gus Van Sant, 2008)

The Moon Is Blue (Otto Preminger, 1953)

Morocco (Joseph von Sternberg, 1930)

New York, New York (Martin Scorsese, 1977)

The North Star (Lewis Milestone, 1943)

Notorious (Alfred Hitchcock, 1946)

On the Town (Stanley Donen/Gene Kelly, 1949)

Out of the Past (Jacques Tourneur, 1947)

A Painful Reminder: Evidence for All Mankind (Brian Blake, 1985)

The Pirate (Vincente Minnelli, 1948)

Poison (Todd Haynes, 1991)

Portrait of Jennie (William Dieterle, 1948)

The Postman Always Rings Twice (Tay Garnett, 1946)

Psycho (Alfred Hitchcock, 1960)

The Purple Heart (Lewis Milestone, 1944)

Queen Christina (Rouben Mamoulian, 1933)

Rebecca (Alfred Hitchcock, 1940)

Red River (Howard Hawks, 1948)

The Robe (Henry Koster, 1953)

Rope (Alfred Hitchcock, 1948)

Salomé (Alla Nazimova, 1922)

Scarlet Street (Fritz Lang, 1945)

The Seventh Victim (Mark Robson, 1943)

The Sign of the Cross (Cecil B. DeMille, 1932)

Singin' in the Rain (Stanley Donen/Gene Kelly, 1952)

Some Came Running (Vincente Minnelli, 1958)

Some Like It Hot (Billy Wilder, 1959)

Splendor in the Grass (Elia Kazan, 1961)

Stage Door (Gregory La Cava, 1937)

A Star Is Born (William Wellman, 1937)

A Star Is Born (George Cukor, 1954)

A Star Is Born (Frank Pierson, 1976)

A Star Is Born (Bradley Cooper, 2018)

The Story of Temple Drake (Stephen Roberts, 1933)

The Strange One (Jack Garfein, 1957)

Strangers on a Train (Alfred Hitchcock, 1943)

A Streetcar Named Desire (Elia Kazan, 1951)

Suddenly, Last Summer (Joseph L. Mankiewicz, 1959)

Summer Stock (Charles Walters, 1950)

Sunset Boulevard (Billy Wilder, 1950)

Sweet Charity (Bob Fosse, 1969)

Sylvia Scarlett (George Cukor, 1935)

Target for Tonight (Harry Watt, 1941)

A Taste of Honey (Tony Richardson, 1961)

Tea and Sympathy (Vincente Minnelli, 1956)

The Ten Commandments (Cecil B. DeMille, 1956)

These Three (William Wyler, 1936)

Tongues Untied (Marlon Riggs, 1989)

Toys in the Attic (George Roy Hill, 1963)

2001: A Space Odyssey (Stanley Kubrick, 1968)

Transamerica (Duncan Tucker, 2005)

The Uninvited (Lewis Allen, 1944)

Vertigo (Alfred Hitchcock, 1958)

Victim (Basil Dearden, 1961)

Walk on the Wild Side (Edward Dmytryk, 1962)

Warlock (Edward Dmytryk, 1959)

Watch on the Rhine (Herman Shumlin, 1943)

The Watermelon Woman (Cheryl Dunye, 1996)

The Wizard of Oz (Victor Fleming, 1939)

TELEVISION

1962 Academy Awards ceremony. April 9, 1962. Available on the official YouTube channel of the Academy of Motion Picture Arts and Sciences.

Buffy the Vampire Slayer. (1997–2003, created by Joss Whedon)

The Dick Cavett Show. Interview with Lillian Hellman. 1973, Episode 41.

Sneak Previews with Siskel & Ebert, Season 5, Episode 29: "Changing Attitudes Toward Homosexuality." 1982.

INDEX

A NOTE ON THE AUTHOR

MICHAEL KORESKY is Editorial Director at New York's Museum of the Moving Image and a member of the National Society of Film Critics. Previously he held editorial positions at Film at Lincoln Center and the Criterion Collection, where he continues to host and curate the Criterion Channel series Queersighted. He has taught at NYU and The New School; cofounded MoMI's online film criticism publication *Reverse Shot*; and has written for *Film Comment, Sight & Sound,* the *Village Voice, Film Quarterly,* and other publications. He is the author of *Films of Endearment* and a monograph on the British director Terence Davies.